P9-EMP-541

WOMAN

Also by Natalie Angier

The Beauty of the Beastly:
New Views of the Nature of Life

Natural Obsessions:
Striving to Unlock the Deepest Secrets of the Cancer Cell

WOMAN
AN INTIMATE GEOGRAPHY

NATALIE ANGIER

A *Virago* Book

Published by Virago Press 1999
by special arrangement with Houghton Mifflin Company

First published in the United States by
Houghton Mifflin Company, New York

Copyright © 1999 by Natalie Angier

The moral right of the author has been asserted

All rights reserved.
No part of this publication may be reproduced, stored in a retrieval system, or
transmitted in any form or by any means, without the prior permission in writing of the publisher, nor be otherwise circulated in any form of binding or
cover other than that in which it is published and without a similar condition
including this condition being imposed on the subsequent purchaser.

A CIP catalogue record for this book is available from the British Library

ISBN 1 86049 685 7

Printed and bound in Great Britain by
Clays Ltd, St Ives plc

Virago
A Division of
Little, Brown and Company (UK)
Brettenham House
Lancaster Place
London WC2E 7EN

FOR KATHERINE IDA

1

UNSCRAMBLING THE EGG

IT BEGINS WITH ONE PERFECT SOLAR CELL

PUT A FEW ADULTS in a room with a sweet-tempered infant, and you may as well leave a tub of butter sitting out in the midday sun. Within moments of crowding around the crib, their grown-up bones begin to soften and their spines to bend. Their eyes mist over with cataracts of pleasure. They misplace intellect and discover new vocal ranges — countertenor, soprano, piglet. And when they happen on the baby's hands, prepare for a variant on the ancient Ode to the Fingernail. Nothing so focuses adult adoration as a newborn's fingernail, its lovely condensed precocity. See the tiny cuticle below, the white eyebrow of keratin on top, the curved buff of the nail body, the irresistible business-like quality of the whole: it looks like it really works! We love the infant fingernail for its capacity to flatter, its miniature yet faithful recreation of our own form. More than in the thigh or the eye or even the springy nautilus shell of the ear, in the baby's nail sits the homunculus, the adult in preview. And so, we are reminded, the future is assured.

Myself, I prefer eggs.

At some point midway through my pregnancy, when I knew I was carrying a daughter, I began to think of myself as standing in a room with two facing mirrors, so that looking into one mirror you see the other mirror reflecting it, and you, off into something approaching an infinity of images. At twenty weeks' gestation, my girl held within her nine-ounce, banana-sized body, in a position spatially equivalent to where she floated in me, the tangled grapevines of my genomic future. Halfway through her fetal tenure, she already had all the eggs she would ever have, packed into ovaries no bigger than the letters *ova* you just passed. My daughter's eggs are silver points of potential energy, the light at the beginning of the tunnel, a near-life experience. Boys don't make sperm — their proud "seed" — until they reach puberty. But my daughter's sex cells, *our* seed, are already settled upon prenatally, the chromosomes sorted, the potsherds of her parents' histories packed into their little phospholipid baggies.

The image of the nested Russian dolls is used too often. I see it everywhere, particularly in descriptions of scientific mysteries (you open one mystery, you encounter another). But if there were ever an appropriate time to dust off the simile, it's here, to describe the nested nature of the matriline. Consider, if you will, the ovoid shape of the doll and the compelling unpredictability and fluidity of dynasty. Open the ovoid mother and find the ovoid girl; open the child and the next egg grins up its invitation to crack it. You can never tell a priori how many iterations await you; you hope they continue forever. My daughter, my matryoshka.

I said a moment ago that my daughter had all her eggs in mid-fetushood. In fact she was goosed up way beyond capacity, a fatly subsidized poultry farm. She had all her eggs and many more, and she will lose the great majority of those glittering germ cells before she begins to menstruate. At twenty weeks' gestation, the peak of a female's oogonial load, the fetus holds 6 to 7 million eggs. In the next twenty weeks of wombing, 4 million of those eggs will die, and by puberty all but 400,000 will have taken to the wing, without a squabble, without a peep.

The attrition continues, though at a more sedate pace, throughout a woman's youth and early middle age. At most, 450 of her eggs will be solicited for ovulation, and far fewer than that if she spends a lot of time being pregnant and thus not ovulating. Yet by menopause, few if any eggs remain in the ovaries. The rest have vanished. The body has reclaimed them.

This is a basic principle of living organisms. Life is profligate; life is a spendthrift; life can persist only by living beyond its means. You make things in extravagant abundance, and then you shave back, throw away, kill off the excess. Through extensive cell death the brain is molded, transformed from a teeming pudding of primitive, overpopulous neurons into an organized structure of convolutions and connections, recognizable lobes and nuclei; by the time the human brain has finished developing, in infancy, 90 percent of its original cell number has died, leaving the privileged few to sustain the hard work of dwelling on mortality. This is also how limbs are built. At some point in embryo-genesis, the fingers and toes must be relieved of their interdigital web-bing, or we would emerge from our amniotic aquarium with flippers and fins. And this too is how the future is laid down.

The millions of eggs that we women begin with are cleanly destroyed through an innate cell program called apoptosis. The eggs do not simply die — they commit suicide. Their membranes ruffle up like petticoats whipped by the wind and they explode, releasing their yolky hearts into the bloodstream, thence to be cleaned up by scavenger cells that do that sort of thing. By graciously if melodramatically getting out of the way, the sacrificial eggs leave their sisters plenty of hatching room. I love the word *apoptosis,* the onomatopoeia of it: *a-POP-tosis.* The eggs pop apart like poked soap bubbles, a brief flash of taut, refracted light and then, ka-*ping!* And while my girl grew toward completion inside me, her fresh little eggs popped by the tens of thousands each day. By the time she is born, I thought, her eggs will be the rarest cells in her body.

Scientists have made much of apoptosis in the past few years. They have sought to link every disease known to granting agencies, whether cancer, Alzheimer's, or AIDS, to a breakdown in the body's ability to control when pieces of itself must die. Just as a pregnant woman sees nothing but a sea of swollen bellies all around her, so scientists see apoptosis gone awry in every ill person or sickly white mouse they examine, and they promise grand paybacks in cures and amelioratives if they ever master apoptosis. For our purposes, let us think not of disease or dysfunction; let us instead praise the dying hordes, and lubricate their departure with tears of gratitude. Yes, it's wasteful, yes, it seems stupid to make so much and then immediately destroy nearly all of it, but would nature get anywhere if she were stingy? Would we expect to see her flagrant diversity, her blowsy sequins and feather boas, if she weren't simply and reliably *too much?* Think of it this way: without the unchosen, there can be no choosing. Unless we break eggs, there can be no soufflé. The eggs that survive the streamlining process could well be the tastiest ones in the nest.

And so, from an eggy perspective, we may not be such random, sorry creatures after all, such products of contingency or freak odds as many of us glumly decided during our days of adolescent sky-punching (Why me, oh Lord? How did that outrageous accident happen?). The chances of any of us being, rather than not being, may not be so outrageous, considering how much was winnowed out before we ever arrived at the possibility of being. I used to wonder why life works as well as it does, why humans and other animals generally emerge from incubation in such beautiful condition — why there aren't more developmental horrors. We all know about the high rate of spontaneous miscarriages during the first trimester of pregnancy, and we have all heard that the majority of those miscarriages are blessed expulsions, eliminating embryos with chromosomes too distorted for being. Yet long before that point, when imperfect egg has met bad sperm, came the vast sweeps of the apoptotic broom, the vigorous judgment of no, no, no. Not you, not you, and most definitely not you. Through cell suicide, we at last get to yes — a rare word, but beautiful in its rarity.

We are all yeses. We are worthy enough, we passed inspection, we survived the great fetal oocyte extinctions. In that sense, at least — call it a mechanospiritual sense — we are meant to be. We are good eggs, every one of us.

If you have never had trouble with your eggs, if you have never had to worry about your fecundity, you probably haven't given your eggs much thought, or dwelled on their dimensions, the particular power that egg cells enclose. You think of eggs, you think food: poached, scrambled, or forbidden. Or maybe you were lucky enough as a child to find in your back yard a nest with two or three robin's eggs inside, each looking so tender and pale that you held your breath before venturing to touch one. I was unhappily familiar in my girlhood with another sort of animal egg, that of a cockroach; usually I found the empty egg case after its cargo had safely departed, a sight as disturbing as that of a spent shotgun shell and more evidence of the insect's supremacy.

The symbolic impact of the egg in many cultures is as an oval. The egg of the world, thick toward the bottom to ground us, thinner at the apex as though pointing toward the heavens. In medieval paintings and cathedral tympana, Christus Regnans sits in a heavenly ovoid: he who gave birth to the world was born unto the world to secure it from death. At Easter we paint eggs to celebrate rebirth, resurrection; in the egg is life, as life is cradled in the cupped, ovoid palms of the hands. The Hindu gods Ganesha and Shiva Nataraja sit or dance in egg-shaped, flame-tipped backdrops. In painting her vulval flowers, the petals opening onto other petals like abstract pastel matryoshkas, Georgia O'Keeffe evoked as well the image of the egg, as though female genitalia recapitulate female procreative powers.

The egg of a chicken or other bird is a triumph in packaging. A female bird makes the bulk of the egg inside her reproductive tract long before mating with a male. She supplies the egg with all the nutrients the chick embryo will require to reach pecking independence. The reason that an egg yolk is so rich in cholesterol, and thus that people see it as gastronomically risqué, is that a growing fetus needs ample cholesterol to build the membranes of the cells of which the body, any body, is constructed. The bird gives the egg protein, sugars, hormones, growth factors. Only after the cupboards are fully stocked will the egg be fertilized by sperm, sealed with a few calciferous layers of eggshell, and finally laid. Bird eggs are usually oval, in part for aerodynamic reasons: the shape makes their odyssey down the cloaca, the bird's equivalent of a birth canal, that much smoother.

We gals have been called chicks, and in Britain we've been birds, but if our eggs are any indication, the comparison is daft. A woman's egg, like that of any other mammal, has nothing avian about it. There is no shell, of course, and there really is no yolk, although the aqueous body of the egg, the cytoplasm, would feel a bit yolky to the touch if it were big enough to stick your finger in. But a human egg has no food with which to feed an embryo. And though one springs to fullness upon ovulation each month, it most certainly is not the pit-faced, frigid moon.

I have another suggestion. Let's reject the notion that men have exclusive rights to the sun. Must Helios, Apollo, Ra, Mithras, and the other golden boys take up every seat in the solar chariot that lights each day and coaxes forth all life? This is a miscarriage of mythology, for a woman's egg resembles nothing so much as the sun at its most electrically alive: the perfect orb, speaking in tongues of fire.

Dr. Maria Bustillo is a short, barrel-bodied woman in her mid-forties who frequently smiles small, private smiles, as though life dependably amuses her. She is a Cuban American. Her features are round but not pudgy, and she wears her dark hair neither short nor long. As an infertility expert, Bustillo is a modern Demeter, a harvester and deft manipulator of human eggs, a magician in a minor key. She helps some couples who are desperate for parenthood get pregnant, and to them she is a goddess. But others she cannot help. For those others, it is no metaphor to say they flush many thousands of dollars down the toilet with each cycle of IVF or GIFT or other prayers by alphabet.* That is the reality of infertility treatment today, as we have read and heard and read again: it is very expensive, and it often fails. Nevertheless, Bustillo smiles her small amused smiles and does not coddle gloom. She manages to seem simultaneously brisk and easygoing. Her staff loves working with her; her patients appreciate her candor and her refusal to condescend. I liked her instantly and almost without qualification. Only once did she say something that reminded me, oh, yes, she is a surgeon, a wisecracking cowgirl in scrubs. As she washed her hands before performing a vaginal procedure, she repeated a smirking remark that she'd heard from one of her instructors years earlier. "He told me, 'Washing your hands before doing vaginal surgery is like taking a shower before taking a crap,'" Bustillo said. The vagina is quite dirty, she continued, so there is nothing you could introduce into it with your hands that would be worse than what's already there. (This bit of orificial wisdom, by the way, is an old husbands' tale, a load of crap, as we will discuss in Chapter 4. The vagina is not dirty at all. Really, is it too much for us who mount the gynecologist's unholy stirrups to ask, "Physician, clean thyself"?)

I am visiting Bustillo at the Mount Sinai School of Medicine in New York to look at eggs. I have seen the eggs of many species, but I have never seen the eggs of my own kind, except in pictures. Seeing a human egg is not easy. It is the largest cell in the body, but it is nonetheless very small, a tenth of a millimeter across. If you could poke a hole in a piece of paper with a baby's hair, you'd get something the size of an egg. Moreover, an egg isn't *meant* to be seen. The human egg, like any

---

*IVF means in vitro ("in glass") fertilization, as opposed to in vivo ("in body"), the old-fashioned way. GIFT, or gamete intrafallopian transfer, is a variant on IVF in which eggs and sperm are injected into a woman's fallopian tube, with the hope that they will find each other and create a zygote.

mammalian egg, is built for darkness, for spinning stories in visceral privacy — and you can thank that trait, in part, for your smart, fat, amply convoluted brain. An internally conceived and gestated fetus is a protected fetus, and a protected fetus is a fetus freed to loll about long enough to bloom a giant brain. So we lend new meaning to the term *egghead:* from the cloistered egg is born the bulging frontal lobe.

How different is the status of the sperm. A sperm cell may be tinier than an egg, measuring only a small fraction of the volume, so it is not exactly a form of billboard art either. Nevertheless, because it is designed to be externalized, publicly consumed, sperm lends itself to easy technovoyeurism. One of the first things Anton van Leeuwenhoek did after inventing a prototype of the microscope three hundred years ago was to smear a sample of human ejaculate onto a glass slide and slip it under his magic lens. And men, I will set aside my zygotic bias here to say that your sperm are indeed magnificent when magnified, vigorous, slaphappy, whip-tailed tears, darting, whirling, waggling, heading nowhere and everywhere at once, living proof of our primordial flagellar past. For mesmerizing adventures in microscopy, a dribble of semen will far outperform the more scholastically familiar drop of pond scum.

A woman's body may taketh eggs away by apoptosis, but it giveth not without a fight. How then to see an egg? One way is to find an egg donor: a woman who is part saint, part lunatic, part romantic, part mercenary, and all parts about to be put under the anesthesia that Bustillo calls the "milk of amnesia," so she will not feel her body crying bloody hell on the battlefield.

Beth Derochea pats her belly and booms, "Bloated! I'm full of hormones! I tell my husband, Stay away!" She is twenty-eight but looks a good five years younger. She is an administrative assistant at a publishing company who hopes to work her way up to an editing position. Her hair is long, dark, parted on the side, casual, and her smile is slightly gappy and toothy. "I hope nobody inherits my teeth!" she says. "Anything but that — I've got really weak teeth." Derochea is a woman of gleeful, elaborated extroversion; even being in a flimsy hospital gown doesn't make her act shy or tentative. She bounces; she laughs; she gestures. "She's so good!" a nurse in the room exclaims. "I'm so broke," Derochea says. "I'm a little ashamed to admit it, but I'm in debt." That's one of the reasons she's here, at Mount Sinai, to donate eggs, her pelvis tender, her ovaries swollen to the size of walnuts when normally they would be almonds, tubing about to be slipped into her nostrils to bathe her in milky amnesia.

If somebody were to design a line of fertility fetishes, Beth Derochea could be the model. Clips of her hair or fingernails could be incorporated into the amulets as saints' parts are encased in reliquaries. This is her third time at playing egg donor. She gave eggs twice during graduate school, and each time she yielded up a bumper crop of twenty-nine or so. Now she is back, in part for the fee of $2,500. But only in part. There are other reasons that she doesn't mind, even enjoys, donating eggs. She and her husband don't yet have children of their own, but she told me she likes playing mama. She mothers her friends; she urges them to dress warmly in the winter and to eat their fruits and vegetables. She likes changing diapers on other people's babies and rocking the infants to sleep. She likes the idea of her seed seeding other people's joy. She doesn't feel proprietary about her gametes. A fan of science fiction of the eggheaded variety, she tells me about something that Robert A. Heinlein once wrote. "'Your genes don't belong to you,' he said. 'They belong to all humanity.' I really believe that. My eggs, my genes, they're not even something that's me, they're something I'm sharing. It's like donating blood."

By this generous, almost communistic imagery, we are all aswim in the same great gene pool, or fishers from the river of human perpetuity. If my line comes up empty, perhaps you will share your catch with me. For such reasons of heart and rightness, Derochea said she would donate eggs even if she weren't paid. "I might not have done it three times, but I definitely would have done it at least once," she says.

Her sentiment is rare. In many European countries, where it is illegal to pay a woman for donating eggs, almost nobody does it. Bustillo said that when she attended a conference on bioethics recently, the audience of doctors, scientists, lawmakers, and professional ponderers was asked, just out of curiosity, whether anybody there would donate eggs. "Nobody raised her hand," Bustillo said. "Though two people later said they'd consider doing it for a relative or good friend." Derochea is not donating eggs for relatives or friends. She never meets the couples who receive her eggs, she will never see any progeny that might come of them, and she doesn't care. She doesn't moon over sequelae, she doesn't fantasize about her mystery children. "I've managed to disengage myself from any sense of investment," she says, as calm as a Renaissance madonna.

I say to Bustillo that it's a good thing the best egg donors — women at the peak of their fertility, in their early thirties or younger — are at a point in life when they are likeliest to need the cash. An egg donor earns every dime of her blood money. Three weeks before I met her, Derochea had begun injecting herself with Lupron, a synthetic version of gonadotropin-releasing hormone, a potent chemical bred in the brain that begins the entire cycle of egg-dropping. For a week she injected herself nightly in the thigh with a narrow needle of the type diabetics use. No big deal, she said. Barely noticeable. Uh-huh, I said, thinking, Oh, sure, sure, anybody could do it, anybody except me, who's always thought the worst thing about heroin addiction is not the way it ruins your life or may give you AIDS but that you have to inject *yourself* with a *needle*.

After the Lupron came the hard stuff. She had to switch to a double-barreled shot of Pergonal and Metrodin, a mix of ovulatory hormones designed to spur the ovaries into a state of hyperactivity. (Pergonal, incidentally, is isolated from the urine of postmenopausal women, whose bodies have become so accustomed to the menstrual cycle that they generate ovulatory hormones in extremely high concentrations because of a lack of feedback from the ovaries.) Preparing this sweet brew demanded concentration, to assure that as she pulled the fluid into the hypodermic syringe, no potentially embolizing bubbles were pulled up with it. She also needed to use a much heavier-gauge needle than she did for the Lupron, which means a bigger and more painful shot. This time Derochea had to aim for the rear part of her hip, every night for about two weeks. Not terrible, not an ordeal, but something she admitted she wouldn't want to do each month. Toward the end of this non-ordeal, to stimulate the final stage of ovulation, Derochea gave herself a single shot of human chorionic gonadotropin, again through an ominously large hypodermic.

All the while, between nightly inoculations, she had to return repeatedly to the hospital for sonograms, to check on the expansion of her ovaries. She thickened with excess fluid and jested about her snappishness. When I talked to her, she was more than ready to give up her grams of flesh. Her two ovaries were like overstuffed sacks of oranges, each orange an egg ripened with unnatural haste by three weeks of hormone treatments. In a normal cycle, only one egg would be pushing its way from its ovarian pocket. But at the moment Derochea was an Olympic cycler, and two or three years' worth of oocytic offerings had been condensed into a single month. There's no evidence that she has lost those years — that her childbearing potential has in any way been compromised or truncated. We are, after all, overbudgeted with eggs, and think of what management does at the end of the fiscal period to budgets that don't get used: ka-*ping!* So the medical Demeters of the world simply cannibalize what otherwise would apoptose into the void.

In any event, fertility fetishism runs in Derochea's family: all of her siblings have already reproduced repeatedly. "Having babies is just something we do," she says. Derochea also doesn't worry about the risk of ovarian cancer, which some experts have proposed is heightened by the use of fertility drugs. The data on this question remain inconclusive, and in any case are more associated with the drug Clomid than with any of the follicular stimulants that Derochea has received. "If my family had a history of ovarian cancer, I'd be more concerned about it," she says. "But at this point, I'm not worried. Maybe that's stupid, but I'm not worried."

She lies down on the operating table. They pump her first with oxygen, then with anesthesia. They ask her if she's sleepy yet. "Mrrph!" she mumbles. A moment later she's as limp as a Dali clock. The surgical assistants stick her legs in stirrups and douse her genitals with iodine, which looks like menstrual blood as it dribbles along the inner folds of her thighs and onto the table. Bustillo barrels into the room, washes her hands, and jokes about crap and vaginas — but no matter, she scrubs. She sits down at the end of the table, at the gynecologist's stirrup-side post, ready for one of the easier breaches of the body's barrier. Her assistants wheel a portable ultrasound machine over to the table and hand her the ultrasound probe, an instrument shaped like a dildo. She slips a stretchy latex casing over the probe — "the condom!" she says — and threads a needle through the device that will suck the readied eggs from their pockets.

Bustillo inserts the wand into Derochea's vagina and up into one of the two fornices, the culs-de-sac of the vaginal canal that pouch up around either side of the cervix. The needle pierces the fornix wall, moves across the pelvic peritoneum — the oily membrane that surrounds most of the abdominal viscera — and finally perforates the ovary. Bustillo does the entire extraction procedure by watching the ultrasound screen, where the image of the ovary looms in black and white, made visible by bouncing high-frequency sound waves. Coming in on the top lefthand side of the screen is the needle. The ovary looks like a giant beehive honeycombed with dark bloated egg pockets, or follicles, each measuring two millimeters across. These are all the follicles that were matured by Derochea's diligent nocturnal injections. The sonogram screen is full of them. Manipulating the needle-headed probe with her eyes fixed on the sonogram, Bustillo punctures every dark honeycomb and sucks all the fluid out of the follicle. The fluid travels down the tube of the probe and into a catchment beaker. You can't see the egg suspended in that fluid, but it's there. Immediately after the fluid has been extracted from the follicle, the pocket collapses in on itself and disappears from the screen. A few moments later it slightly distends again, this time with blood.

Prick! Prick! Prick! Bustillo pierces and vacuums out every follicle so quickly that the honeycomb seems alive with accordian motion: pockets fall in, reengorge with blood. Prick! Prick! Prick! It hurts vicariously to watch; I want to cross my legs in discomfort except that I'm standing up. One of the surgical assistants tells me that sometimes the women who have this procedure done demand that it be performed without anesthesia. They regret their choice. At some point they start screaming.

When the left ovary is picked clean of ripe eggs, Bustillo moves the probe over to the other vaginal fornix and repeats the maneuver on the right ovary. The entire bilateral pricking and sucking takes ten minutes or so. "Okay, that's it," Bustillo says as she withdraws the probe. A stream of blood flows from Derochea's vagina, like a fire set by a departing army. The nurses clean her up and start calling her name and shaking her arm to wake her. Beth! Beth! You're done, we're done, we've plucked you clean. Your genes are now floating in the communal pool in which another woman soon will immerse herself, seeking baptism with baby.

Back in the lab, Carol-Ann Cook, an embryologist, separates and counts the day's plunder: twenty-nine eggs, the same number harvested from Beth Derochea twice before. This woman's vineyards are fruitful! Cook prepares the eggs, these grapes of Beth, for fertilization with the sperm of another woman's husband, a woman who lacks viable eggs of her own.

The use of donor eggs for in vitro fertilization is one of the few promising things that have happened to the technique since its introduction in the 1970s. Most women who attempt IVF are nearing the end of their patience and fecundity. They are in their late thirties, early forties. For reasons that remain entirely opaque, the eggs of an "older" woman — and it annoys me to use that term for anybody under eighty, let alone *my peers* — have lost some of their plasticity and robustness. They don't ripen as readily, they don't fertilize as well, and once fertilized, they don't implant in the womb as firmly as the eggs of a younger woman do. Older women usually start by trying IVF with their own eggs. They are partial to their particular genomes, their molecular ancestry, and why not? There's little difference between a baby and a book, and it's usually best to write about what you know. So they go through what Beth Derochea went through, weeks of preparatory hormonal injections. At the other end, though, they give forth not dozens of eggs but perhaps three or four, and some of those may be barely breathing. The fertility gods do their best. They join the healthiest-looking eggs and a partner's sperm in a petri dish to form embryos. After two days or so, they deliver the embryos back to the woman by squirting the clusters of cells, afloat in liquid, through a thin tube inserted into the vagina, across the cervix, and into the uterus. No big deal: blink and you miss it. Alas, for the women too it's a case of blink and you lose it. In the vast majority of patients, the technique fails. The chance of an older woman giving birth to a baby conceived from her eggs through IVF is maybe 12 to 18 percent. If you heard that these were your odds of surviving cancer, you'd feel very, very depressed.

An older woman may try IVF once or twice, even a third time, but if by then she hasn't conceived with her own harvest of DNA, she probably never will. At that point a doctor may recommend donor eggs, combining the seeds of a younger woman with the sperm of the older woman's husband (or lover or male donor) and then implanting the resulting embryo in said senior's uterus. Using donor eggs can make a woman of forty act like a twenty-five-year-old, reproductively speaking. Who knows why? But it works, oh girl does it work, so well that suddenly you're no longer in the teens of probability but instead have about a 40 percent chance of giving birth in a single cycle of in vitro maneuvers. That number starts to sound like a real baby bawling. If the wine is young enough, it seems, the bottle and its label be damned.

And so the egg rules the roost. It, not the womb, sets the terms of tomorrow. Carol-Ann Cook takes one of Derochea's eggs and puts it under a high-powered microscope, which transmits the image to a video monitor. "This is a beautiful egg," Bustillo says. "All her eggs are beautiful," Cook adds. They are eggs from a healthy young woman. They have no choice but to shine.

To think of the egg, think of the heavens, and of weather. The body of the egg is the sun; it is as round and as magisterial as the sun. It is the only spherical cell in the body. Other cells may be shaped like cinched-in boxes or drops of ink or doughnuts that don't quite form a hole in the middle, but the egg is a geometer's dream. The form makes sense: a sphere is among the most stable shapes in nature. If you want to protect your most sacred heirlooms — your genes — bury them in spherical treasure chests. Like pearls, eggs last for decades and they're hard to crush, and when they're solicited for fertilization, they travel jauntily down the fallopian tube.

Carol-Ann Cook points out the details of the egg. Surrounding the great globe that glows silver-white on the screen is a smear of what looks like whipped cream, or the fluffy white clouds found in every child's sketch of a sky. This is in fact called the cumulus, for its resemblance to a cloud. The cumulus is a matting of sticky extracellular material that serves to bind the egg to the next celestial feature, the corona radiata. Like the corona of the sun, the corona of the egg is a luminous halo that extends out a considerable distance from the central orb. It is a crown fit for a queen, its spikes and phalanges emphasizing the unerring sphericity of the egg. The corona radiata is a dense network of interlocking cells called nurse cells, because they nurse and protect the egg, and it may also act as a kind of flight path or platform for sperm, steering the rather bumbling little flagellates toward the outer coat of the egg. That thick, extracellular coat is the famed zona pellucida — the translucent zone — the closest thing a mammalian egg has to a shell. The zona pellucida is a thick matrix of sugar and protein that is as cunning as a magnetic field. It invites sperm to explore its contours, but then it repels what doesn't suit it. It decides who is friend and who is alien. The zona pellucida can be considered the mother lode of biodiversity, the place where speciation in nature often begins, for it takes only a minor change in the structure of its sugars to make incompatible what before was connubial. The genes of a chimpanzee, for example, are more than 99 percent identical to ours, and it is possible that if the DNA of a chimpanzee sperm cell were injected directly into the heart of a human egg, the artificial hybridization would produce a viable, if ethically repulsive, embryo. But under the natural constraints of sexual reproduction, a chimpanzee sperm could not breach the forbidding zona pellucida of a human egg.

The zona also thwarts the entry of more than one sperm of its own kind. Before fertilization, its sugars are open and genial and seeking similar sugars on the head of a sperm. Once the zona has attached to the head of a sperm, it imbibes the sperm, and then it stiffens, almost literally. Its sugars turn inward. The egg is sated; it wants no more DNA. Any sperm that remain at its threshold soon will die. Still, the zona's task is not through. It is thick and strong, an anorak, and it protects the tentative new embryo during the slow descent down the fallopian tube and into the uterus. Only when the embryo is capable of attaching to the uterine wall, a week or so after fertilization, does the zona pellucida burst apart and allow the embryo to join its blood with mother blood.

The corona, cumulus, and zona all are extracellular, auxiliaries to the egg but not the egg. The egg proper is the true sun, the light of life, and I say this without exaggeration. The egg is rare in the body and rare in its power. No other cell has the capacity to create the new, to begin with a complement of genes and build an entire being from it. I said earlier that the mammalian egg is not like a bird's egg, insofar as it lacks the nutrients to sustain embryonic development. A mammalian embryo must tether itself to the mother's circulatory system and be fed through the placenta. But from a genetic perspective, the cytoplasm of a mammalian egg is complete, a self-contained universe. Somewhere in its custardy cytoplasm are factors — proteins, or bits of nucleic acid — that allow a genome to stir itself to purpose, to speak every word its species has ever spoken. These maternal factors have not yet been identified, but their skills have been showcased in sensational ways. When Scottish scientists announced in 1997 that they had cloned an adult sheep and named her Dolly, the world erupted with babble about human clones and human drones and God deposed. The endless exercises in handwringing resolved very little of the ethical dilemma that surrounds the prospect of human cloning, if dilemma there be. But what the sweet ovine face of Dolly demonstrates without equivocation is the wonder of the egg. The egg made the clone. In the experiments, the scientists extracted a cell from the udder of an adult sheep, and they removed the nucleus from the cell, the nucleus being the storehouse of the cell's genes. They wanted those adult genes, and they could have taken them from any organ. Every cell in an animal's body has the same set of genes in it. What distinguishes an udder cell from a pancreatic cell from a skin cell is which of those tens of thousands of genes are active and which are silenced.

The egg is democratic. It gives all genes a voice. And so the scientists harvested a sheep egg cell and enucleated it, taking the egg's genes away and leaving behind only the egg body, the cytoplasm, the nonyolk yolk. In place of the egg nucleus they installed the nucleus of the udder cell, and then they implanted the odd chimera, the manufactured minotaur, into the womb of another sheep. The egg body resurrected the entire adult genome. It wiped the slate clean, washed the milky stains from the dedicated udder cell, and made its old genes new again. Maternal factors in the egg body allowed the genome to recapitulate the mad glory of gestation — to recreate all organs, all tissue types, the sum of sheep.

The egg alone of the body's cells can effect the whole. If you put a liver cell or a pancreatic cell into a uterus, no infant would grow of it. It has the genes to make a new being, but it has not the wit. Small wonder, then, that the egg is such a large cell. It must hold the secrets of genesis. And perhaps the molecular complexity of the egg explains why we can't produce new eggs in adulthood, why we are born with all the eggs we will ever have, when men can sprout new sperm throughout their lives. Scientists often make much of the contrast between egg and sperm, the prolificacy and renewability of the man's gametes compared to the limitations and degradative quality of a woman's eggs. They speak in breathless terms of sperm production. "Every time a man's heart beats, he makes a thousand sperm!" Ralph Brinster burbled to the *Washington Post* in May of 1996. But a woman is born with all the eggs she'll ever have, he continued, and they only senesce from there. Yet the mere ability to replicate is hardly cause for a standing ovation. Bacteria will double their number every twenty minutes. Many cancer cells can divide in a dish for years after their founder tumors have killed the patient. Perhaps eggs are like neurons, which also are not replenished in adulthood: they know too much. Eggs must plan the party. Sperm only need to show up — wearing top hat and tails, of course.

2

THE MOSAIC IMAGINATION

UNDERSTANDING THE "FEMALE" CHROMOSOME

KEITH AND ADELE fought all the time, like a pair of tomcats, like two drunken lumberjacks. Keith would find grist for the arguments in his reading. He read widely and thirstily, and sometimes he would come across a stray fact that fed his theorizing about the natural cosmology of male and female. Males are the seekers, he had decided, the strugglers and the creators; they build all that we see around us, the artifactual world of towering cities and invented divinity, yet they suffer for their brilliance and busyness. Females are the stabilizers, the salve for man's impatient expansionism, the mortar between bricks. Nothing surprising there: it's a familiar dialectic, between the doers and the be-ers, the seethers and the soothers, complexity and simplicity.

Then one day Keith read about chromosomes. He read that humans have twenty-three pairs of chromosomes and that the pairs of chromosomes are the same in men and in women, with the exception of pair number 23 — the sex chromosomes. In that case, women have two X chromosomes and men have one X and one Y. Moreover, a woman's two X chromosomes look pretty much like all her other chromosomes. Chromosomes resemble Xs. Not when they're inside the cells of the body, at which point they're so squashed and snarled together they resemble nothing so much as a hair knot. But when they're taken out of the cell and combed apart for viewing under a microscope by a geneticist or a lab technician who is checking a fetus's chromosomes as part of amniocentesis, they look like fat and floppy Xs. So women have twenty-three pairs, or forty-six, of these X-shaped structures, while men have forty-five Xs and that one eccentric, the Y chromosome. The Y physically resembles the letter it was named for, being stubby and tripartite and quite distinct in shape from all the other chromosomes in the cell.

It struck Keith that even on a microscopic level, even as inscribed in the genetic clay from which human beings are constructed, men demonstrate their edge over women. Women have as their sex chromosomes two Xs: monotony. The story we've heard before. Men have an X and a Y: diversity. Genetic innovation and an escape from primal tedium. The Y as synecdoche for creativity — for genius. And so he said to Adele, The chromosomes prove the case for male superiority. You have two Xs and hence are dull, while I have an X and a Y and am accordingly interesting.

Neither Adele nor Keith knew much about genetics, but Adele knew enough to recognize mental manure when she smelled it. She dismissed his theory with a sneer. He grew angry at her refusal to submit to his logic. The argument escalated, as their arguments always did. Keith wasn't talking about all men, of course, but about himself. He was insisting that his needs and insights took precedence over Adele's, and that she acknowledge as much. She refused to surrender.

Of the many arguments that my parents had in the theater of our apartment before the reluctant audience of their children, this is the only one whose substance I remember. The clash of the century, Y versus X. I remember it in part because it seemed so oddly theoretical, and because it was the first time I heard an argument put forth for all-around, across-the-board male dominance. I took it personally. My feelings were hurt. It was one thing for my father to attack my mother — that I was accustomed to. But there he was, describing all females, including me, as chromosomal bores.

The chromosome case remains very much open, a source of irritation and debate. In some ways, sex is fundamentally determined by the sex chromosomes. If you're female, you're assumed to have a pair of Xs tucked into just about every cell of your body, along with a set of those twenty-two other pairs of chromosomes. If you're a male, you know of your Y and you just might be proud of it, as your molecular phallus, and for the koanic wordplay of it: Y? Why? Why? Y! The sex chromosomes tell a technician — and you the parent, if you choose to know — whether the fetus under scrutiny in an amniocentesis screen is a girl or a boy.

So in one sense the demarcation between X and Y is clear, clean, an inarguable separation between femaleness and maleness. And my father was right about the predictability and monochromaticity of the female chromosomal complement. Not only will you find two X chromosomes in every body cell of a woman, from the cells that line the fallopian tubes to the cells in the liver and brain, but break open an egg cell and look within the nucleus, and you'll find one X chromosome in each (again with the other twenty-two chromosomes). It is indeed the sperm cell that can add diversity to an embryo, and that determines the embryo's sex by delivering either another X, to create a female, or a Y chromosome, to make a male. X marks the egg. An egg never has a Y chromosome within it. An ejaculate of sperm is bisexual, offering a more or less equal number of female and male whip-tailed sperm, but eggs are inherently female. So in thinking again about the mirrors into infinity, the link between mother and daughter, the nesting of eggs within woman within eggs, we can go a step further and see the continuity of the chromosomes. No maleness tints any part of us gals, no, not a molar drop or quantum.*

But of course it is not that simple. We are not that simple, appealing though the idea of a molecularly untainted matriline may be. Let us consider the nature of the sex chromosomes, the X counterpoised against the Y. To begin with, the X is bigger, much, much bigger, both in sheer size and in density of information. The X chromosome is in fact one of the largest of the twenty-three chromosomes that humans cart around, and is about six times larger than the Y, which is among the tiniest of the lot (and it would be the smallest of all if it didn't have some nonfunctional stuffing added to it just to keep it stable). Gentlemen, I'm afraid it's true: size does make a difference.

In addition, many more genes are strung along the female chromosome than along its counterpart, and it is as a shoetree for genes that a chromosome takes on its meaning. Nobody knows exactly how many genes sit on either the X or the Y chromosome; nobody yet knows how many genes, in total, a human being has. Estimates range from 68,000

---

*This system of sex determination by the male gamete is a mammalian phenomenon. Among birds, the opposite method holds true: the female has two different sex chromosomes, an X and a W, and it is her egg, not her mate's sperm, that determines the sex of the chick.

to 100,000. What is incontestable, though, is the vastly higher gene richness of the X than of the Y. The male chromosome is a depauperated little stump, home to perhaps two dozen, three dozen genes, and that's the range scientists come up with when they're feeling generous. On the X, we will find thousands of genes, anywhere from 3,500 to 6,000.

What does this mean to us women? Are we the mother load of genes, so to speak? After all, if we have two Xs, and each X holds about 5,000 genes, whereas a man has but one X with 5,000 genes and a Y with its 30 genes, then you don't even need a calculator to figure that we should have about 4,970 more genes than a man. So why on Gaia are men bodily bigger than we are? The answer is among the neat twists of genetics: all those extra genes are just sitting around doing nothing, and that's just the way we want them. In fact, if they were all doing something, we'd be dead. Here is what I love about a female's X chromosomes: they are unpredictable. They do surprising things. They do not act like any of the other chromosomes in the body. As we shall see, to the extent that chromosomes can be said to have manners, the X chromosomes behave with great courtesy.

Esmeralda, Rosa, and Maria live in Zacadecas, Mexico, a village of 10,000 people that, though obscure to Americans north of the border, is big enough to be a center for the smaller and more obscure towns around it. Many people in Zacadecas earn their living picking chilis and packing them up for export. Esmeralda and Rosa are sisters, both in their teens, and Maria, two years old, is their niece.* They share an extremely rare condition, so rare that their extended family may be the only people in the world to carry it. Called generalized congenital hypertrichosis, the syndrome is an atavism, a throwback to our ancient mammalian state, when we were happily covered in homegrown fur and had no need of sweatshops and Calvin Klein's soft-core porn. The term *hypertrichosis* explains all, *trichosis* meaning hair growth, and *hyper* meaning exactly what it says.

Atavisms result when a normally dormant gene from our prehistoric roots is for some reason reactivated. Atavisms remind us, in the most

---

*The names are pseudonyms.

palpable and surreal manner possible, of our bonds with other species. They tell us that evolution, like the pueblo builders of the Southwest, does not obliterate what came before but builds on top of and around it. Atavisms are not uncommon. Some people possess an extra nipple or two beyond the usual pair, a souvenir of the ridge of mammary tissue that extends from the top of the shoulder down to the hips and that in most mammals terminates in multiple teats. Babies on occasion are born with small tails or with webbing between their fingers, as though they are reluctant to leave the forest or the seas.

In the case of congenital hypertrichosis, a gene that fosters the generous growth of hair across the face and body has been rekindled. Nothing else happens out of the ordinary, no skeletal deformities or mental retardation or any of the other sorrows that often accompany a genetic change. The people with the condition, this large and locally renowned family living on the border of Zacadecas, simply grow a kind of pelt. They make you wonder why human beings ever shed their fur in the first place, a puzzle that evolutionary biologists have yet to crack. And despite your nobler sentiments, they also make you think of werewolves. In fact, historians of myth have suggested that conditions like hypertrichosis — other types of excess hirsutism exist beyond this rare mutation — gave rise to the legend of the werewolf.

Another element of the werewolf story resonates with the case of Esmeralda, Rosa, and Maria. As you may recall, the werewolf crosses over to his bristly alter ego on a night of a full moon only gradually. At ten P.M., the first anomalous whiskers begin clouding the sides of his face. At eleven, the hair has crept down his forehead and across his cheeks. By midnight, the coverage has become complete, and he is free to explore his nocturnal appetites. The girls of Zacadecas are like points on the werewolf's clock. Esmeralda, who at seventeen is the eldest, is barely ten o'clock. You can see patches of dark downy hair at the edges of her chin and cheeks and around the ear area, almost as though she were standing in the shadows beneath the brutal sun of summer. It's enough to mark her as a member of her rare tribe, but not enough to inhibit her verve or keep her from dating a handsome selection of boys.

Maria, the toddler, stands at the eleven o'clock mark. Her cheeks, her chin, and the top of her forehead are streaked with dark, fine, slightly wavy hair, which will darken and thicken with age. She looks as though she has bangs growing up from her eyebrows toward the scalp. Her eyes are dark and bright and full of joy. She has not yet learned to feel shame.

Rosa, fifteen years old, nearly qualifies as the werewolf at midnight. Much of her face — the cheeks, chin, forehead, nose — is covered by hair; there is far more hair than skin to be seen. She is in fact hairier than a chimpanzee or a gorilla, both of which lack hair around the cheeks, nose, and eyes. Luis Figuera, of the University of Guadalajara, who is studying hypertrichosis, told me that when he first met Rosa he was startled by her appearance, but that after talking with her for a while he stopped noticing it. Eventually, he felt confident enough to ask her if he could touch her face, and she agreed. "It was like stroking the head of a baby," he said. "It was like petting a cat." Rosa's facial hair is thicker than that of any other female in her family. It is almost as dense as that of some of her male relatives, in whom the congenital condition finds its fullest expression. Two of the men earn their living in circus sideshows, where they are displayed as "dog men" or "people of the forest." Others shave their entire face, twice a day. Neither Rosa nor her older sister shaves; they are afraid that shaving will make the hair grow back coarser and darker. Instead, Rosa keeps herself largely hidden from the world. When she's not in school or at the marketplace, she stays indoors. She prefers to keep the shutters closed. She is gentle and shy and doesn't expect to have much of a social or love life.

People commonly dream about being caught naked in public, and they wake up embarrassed. I imagine Rosa dreaming of losing her hair, every last dark muffling lock on her body. In her dreams she is neither ashamed nor afraid, but instead feels free, able to float above the flesh of earth and fate, her upturned face as smooth as a stone.

The spectrum of hair growth seen on the girls of Zacadecas illustrates an outstanding feature of female heritage. My father thought the male had the edge in variation, the chromosomal complexity. To the contrary. It is the woman who is the greater mosaic, a patchwork of her past. Every person has two copies of each of the twenty-three chromosomes, one from mother, one from father. For twenty-two sets of those chromosomes, both versions operate. They make us who we are, an idiosyncratic porridge of our parents — his Roman nose, her rotten teeth, the worst and best of their mediocrities and charms.

For us women, something different from the rest of our genetic legacy happens to our sex chromosomes. The two X chromosomes come together in the formation of the embryo, and as with all the chromosomes, copies of each are apportioned to each cell of the growing baby. But then, during our embryonic unfolding, each cell makes its own decision: do we want Mom, or do we prefer Father? Will we keep the maternal X chromosome active, or the paternal? Once the decision is made — and usually it is made randomly — the cell shuts down the other X, snaps it off chemically. It is a dramatic event, the shutting down of thousands and thousands of genes aligned along the entire length of a chromosome. It is like one of the great New York City blackouts, when thousands of brilliantly lit buildings suddenly blinked off. Click! cries a liver cell. There goes mother love! But then a brain cell makes up its mind, and the maternal chromosome is kept alive while the father X is nullified. Not every gene is shut off on the so-called inactivated X; a few stay lit, to match the handful of genes found on the male's dwarf of a Y chromosome. Nevertheless, thousands of genes are dispensed with in a given cell, and they are either thousands from the mother or thousands from the father.

So we can understand why the hirsute girls demonstrated such outstanding discrepancies in appearance. The gene behind congenital hypertrichosis, the atavism that once helped lend us a mammalian mantle, is located on the X chromosome. In most of us, the gene doesn't operate. The shaggy look does not suit human aesthetics, it doesn't do much to attract a mate, and so the gene has fallen fallow. But in the family with hypertrichosis, the gene has risen from its coma. It works. It makes a kind of fur. Each of the girls has inherited one copy of the fully awakened gene, Esmeralda and Rosa from their mother, niece Maria from her father. And each child is a mosaic of X chromosomes with the trait and X chromosomes without. Esmeralda's face is thus largely the face of her father, he of the unaffected X. Just by chance, the vast majority of the follicle cells on her cheeks, forehead, nose, and chin switched off the maternal X chromosome, allowing the unaffected paternal chromosome to dominate her appearance and thus keep the mark of the werewolf at bay. Her sister's face took nearly the opposite path, the cells switching off the paternal chromosome and putting the woolly maternal X to work. Maria ended up with six of one, half a dozen of the other. All was chance, all was a crapshoot. The switching pattern of the chromosomes could as easily have gone the other way for the sisters; and indeed, if they themselves have daughters, the child of the merry popular one could prove to have cheeks that feel to the touch like the face of a cat.

The world may not make it out so easily, but we are all of us gals strange little quilts, patches of father-tone in some of our tissues, shades of mother in the others. We are more motley by far than our brothers. A son, in fact, may rightfully be thought of as a mama's boy: he has her X chromosome alive in every cell of his body. He has no choice — it's the only X he's got, and every cell needs it. Thus he has more of his mother's genes operating in his body than he does of his father's, thousands more. Yes, the Y chromosome is there, and that is solely a father-to-son transaction; but remember that the Y is genetically impoverished compared to the X. If you do the calculations, your brother works out to be about 6 percent more related to your mother than to your father, and he is 3 percent more related to your mother than you are, because half your cells, on average, have the mother chromosome turned off, while all of his remain turned on. These are not inconsequential figures. In a way, I'm sorry to mention them. They disrupt the image of the matriline, of our female connectedness to the ancestral parade of mother, grandmother, great-grandmother, the blessed founding matriarch. (On an interesting side note, male identical twins are more identical than female twins, again as a result of X inactivation. Male twins share the totality of their maternal X chromosomes, as well as having all the other chromosomes in common, but female twins have a diverging patchwork of maternal and paternal X chromosomes operating in different parts of their bodies.)

Men, perhaps, will be hardly more delighted at the thought of their maternal vinculum. Don't men want so badly to *individuate,* to pull away from the omnipotent female who dominated their world for the first fragile years of their lives? And then to find out that she is more a part of them than they thought! I know my father would not be pleased. He felt smothered by his mother, in all the classic ways. People would tell him, You should read D. H. Lawrence — you'll identify with the story of him and his mother! And my father would say, Why should I read about it? I lived it, and that was bad enough.

In lieu of another link to the matriline I offer this enchanting thought: we have, with our female quilts, with the mosaicism of our chromosomes, a potential for considerable brain complexity. Admittedly, the claim requires a leap of faith and fancy, but let's try it anyway. To begin with, think of the X chromosome as the Smart Chromosome. I suggest this not out of simple chauvinism — although I am a female chauvinist sow — but because a preponderance of genes situated on the X chromosome seem to be involved in the blooming of the brain. Studies suggest that mutations in the X chromosome are a frequent cause of mental retardation, a more frequent cause than mutations in any of the other twenty-two chromosomes. The corollary of all that retardation is brilliant: if so many things can go wrong with our favorite chromosome to result in mental deficiency, that means it holds an awful lot of important targets — genes necessary for the construction of intelligence. When one or more of those genes fail, brain development falters, and when all hum in harmony, genius is born.

Now take this notion of the Smart Chromosome a step further and imagine your brain as a chessboard built of mother squares and father squares. In the mother squares, the maternal X and all its brain genes are active; in the father squares, the pater X rules. You have pieces of your parents scattered throughout that hardworking three-pound organ — you are of two minds about it. No wonder you're confused. No wonder nobody can figure you out. No wonder you're so damned clever.

A woman's mosaic brain complicates the work of our modern mind-readers, neurologists and psychiatrists. Women are known to have highly variable expression of some types of epilepsy, for example, possibly because of the patchwork nature of the chromosomes that control their brain cells. Genes that dictate the output of essential brain signaling chemicals — those neurotransmitters that allow brain cells to talk to one another — also sit on the X chromosome. The result is that a woman's mind is truly a syncopated pulse of mother and father voices, each speaking through whichever X chromosome, maternal or paternal, happens to be active in a given brain cell. Thus, the course of a woman's mental illness, be it schizophrenia or manic-depression, often is more unpredictable and labile than that of a man. Could brain mosaicism also explain why multiple personality disorder (assuming we give it the benefit of the doubt as a genuine psychiatric disorder) so often seems to strike women? Could sufferers indeed be afflicted with internal clashing commandos, mother-speak and father-speak, cacophonous enough to spin off other fragmentary characters? As Teresa Binstock, of the University of Colorado, pointed out to me, nobody can answer such questions yet, because the idea of brain mosaicism is so new "that most neurologists, neuroanatomists, and cognitive neuropsychologists have not yet thought about it."

Until they do, let us all, scientists and nonscientists alike, do some musing for ourselves. Let us toy with the idea that, say, the legendary female intuition has some physical justification — that with our brain mosaicism, we have comparatively more gray-doh to pinch into shape, a greater diversity of chemical opinions, as it were, which operate subconsciously and which we can synthesize into an accurate insight. This is not a notion I plan to live or die by. I have no evidence to back it up. It's nothing more than a . . . hunch. And because in my family it was my father who thought of himself as the intuitive one, my mother who came across as the more rational, mathematically inclined member of the pair, I will give credit, or blame, for the idea to the mystical X that I secured from him.

To X out is to negate, to nullify. To sign one's name with an X is to confess to illiteracy. Yet we must take pride in our X chromosomes. They are large, as chromosomes go. They are thick necklaces of genes. They define femaleness, or rather they can define femaleness.

Jane Carden is a woman of medium-short height (five foot four), medium age (late thirties), and large style. She projects a dome of charisma all around her. I notice her from across the room: she glows. In part it's her great skin, the sort of skin that appears in Dove commercials but that no soap or cream can slather up for you. Later she tells me that she's never had a blemish in her life, that she is in fact incapable of breaking out. Instead of pores, it seems, she has freckles. She wears a white and brown cotton sweater that extends down to her hips, a rope-chain necklace, and big plastic-framed glasses that make her look at once owlish and girlish. Her hair is brown and very thick — guaranteed thick for life, she says. Just as she is immune to acne, so she is protected against alopecia areata, or male-pattern baldness, a condition that, despite its name, regularly patterns itself across female scalps.

Another reason for Jane's radiance is her live-wire intelligence. She starts talking excitedly as soon as we meet. She's a gifted yakker, the sort who speaks in tumbling, racing sentences that remain articulate despite the speed with which she forces them out. She is a tax lawyer in California. Jane Carden isn't her real name; it's the pen name she uses when she writes about her story on the Internet or in newsletters. She made it up as an anagram of Jeanne d'Arc, a heroine of hers. We sit down for lunch, and she orders toast but then doesn't eat much of it. She's too busy talking. We talked at length that day, and many times subsequently. The only times she slowed down during our conversations were when she started to weep.

Jane of Arc was born in New York City to middle-class Jewish parents, her mother a medical secretary in a hospital, her father an accountant for the city housing authority. They already had two sons quite a bit older than Jane. They considered themselves liberal and open-minded, the sort who assumed, if a son brought a girlfriend home for a weekend, the two would sleep together. Jane was a smart girl, an excellent student who loved school from the first day of kindergarten, and was outgoing and popular. She was neither an athlete nor a tomboy, in the sense of wishing to be and acting as though she were a boy, although she noticed, as so many of us girls did, that boys had an arbitrarily better deal in the world. "I remember my first-grade teacher saying, 'The beauty of America is that any little boy could grow up to be president,'" Jane recalls. "That upset me, because *I* wanted to be president." Later, in seventh grade, when another teacher said, "Girls have no business being lawyers — there are too many strong words used in the courtroom," Jane decided, Well, that clinches it; I'm going to be a lawyer.

In most ways, Jane liked being a girl. She dressed up in her mother's clothes and high heels and reddened her mouth with lipstick whenever she got the chance. She joined the Campfire Girls. She was happily high-pitched and subject to the usual sense of exuberant entitlement and manifest destiny. She was, in short, normal — except that she had a big scar running across her pubic region. "When I inquired about it as a child, I was told I had some sort of hernia operation," she says. Hernia operation: just the sort of thing that sounds forbidding and confusing enough to keep the kid from asking anything else.

But on turning eleven, just as she was about to enter the magic time when girls start dwelling on one topic — menstruation — the story was changed. "I was told that I had twisted ovaries at birth and that they were removed to prevent them from becoming cancerous," she says. "I was told at the same time that I'd have to commence hormone replacement therapy, take estrogen. I was told that I would never have menstrual cycles, that I would never have children." Jane distractedly smears jam over a cold piece of toast, takes a nibble, and puts the toast down again. "One of the problems with being told you had twisted ovaries is that it fixates you on cancer. You get so flipped out that you're dying of cancer that you can't even sort out anything else about what the hell is going on. I was absolutely convinced that my end was near."

Well, not quite convinced. Part of her also recognized the story for what it was: bad fiction. "It didn't make sense, it didn't add up," she says. "But I was too paralyzed with fear to be able to talk about it with my family." Her father told her he was proud of her for not crying about her condition. That was that. From that moment on, there would be no more discussion of Jane's "twisted ovaries" or what this clunky phrase really meant. Certainly there would be no discussion of Jane's feelings or fears. "Sometimes my mother made cryptic allusions to the sub-ject, like suggesting that I should think about marrying an older man, because an older man either wouldn't want children or would have children by a prior marriage, so he'd find it acceptable." "It" being Jane's infertility. "Infertility. That's all that counted, my infertility. Once, during a fight I had with my brother, who's now a psychologist, he screamed at me that I'd grow up to be an old, bitter, childless woman."

She was getting a bit bitter, not about her life or her infertility but toward her family, for their attitude about her condition, their apparent indifference stained dimly with hostility. She knew something was seri-ously unusual about her case when she was taken as a young teenager to an endocrinologist. The doctor wouldn't explain anything more to her than her parents had, but he clearly found her condition so remarkable that he invited groups of medical residents to examine her while she lay in stirrups, and he never failed to invite outside observers to attend each time she came for a visit. If her twisted ovaries were long gone, what in hell were they looking at up there?

Still, she didn't turn sullen or introverted. She went off to college, spending one year at the all-female Wellesley and three years at the mostly female Vassar. It was the late 1970s, and she embraced feminism. She thrived, academically and socially. She graduated from Vassar at the top of her class. She made throngs of friends. The only thing she didn't do was lose her virginity. She felt too ashamed of everything below her umbilicus. She didn't want to think, in any intimate sense, about her missing organs, her amenorrhea, the vagina that had been such a source of fascination to so many medical students, and she didn't want a lover thinking about any of it either.

But she didn't stop dwelling intellectually on her disorder. After graduating from college, she went to law school in Florida. It was during her first year there, while poking around in the medical library, that she found the story of herself. She saw pictures — the kind where the patients' bodies are shown but the faces are Xed out — and she read descriptions, and she knew the truth immediately and absolutely. She had what was then called testicular feminization and is now more commonly known as androgen insensitivity syndrome, or AIS. This is a fairly rare condition, affecting about one in 20,000 births. But in its rarity it has something to teach all of us, about how to think about the genetics of sex, and about the correspondence between our chromosomes — the readout from a fetal chromosome screen that will tell you, Ta da!, your baby is a girl or a boy — and our brains and our bodies.

People with AIS do not exist to instruct a benighted world, and some resent being regarded as genetic anomalies that clarify genetic commonness, being the ones in the doctor's steel stirrups, being the ones whose faces are blotted out in textbooks but whose bodies are naked and available for public scrutiny. Nevertheless, we all need help in learning the obvious, which Jane Carden embodies and which we'll discuss here and in the next chapter: that women are made, not born; that women are born, not made; and that both statements are true in their profound and limited fashion.

If Jane's mother had had amniocentesis while pregnant with Jane, and if she wanted to know the sex of the baby, she would have been told, It's a boy — another son in a son-heavy family. And then, when the baby was born, the mother would have been told, Disregard the previous announcement, it's a girl. Jane has the external genitals of a girl: outer labia, clitoris, and vagina. She has no inner labia, though, and her vagina is short, extending to only about a third the length of a normal vagina. It ends abruptly in a kind of membrane, rather than leading to a cervix that serves as the gatehouse to the womb. She has no uterus or fallopian tubes. She used to have testes in her abdominal cavity, but they herniated noticeably downward into her pelvis and so were removed ten days after her birth. The excised testes were her "twisted ovaries."

Here is what happened to Jane. She has a Y chromosome, in which are embedded a few dozen genes, most of them of as yet undeciphered function. But one gene on the forked-tongue chromosome is quite renowned for initiating the male narrative. It is called SRY, for sex-determining region on the Y chromosome. It used to be called TDF, for testes-determining factor, but genes, like syndromes, often go through periodic, inexplicable rehabilitations in which they get new names. In any event, SRY does something rather dramatic when it switches on during the eighth week or so of pregnancy: it starts building testes in a male fetus's abdominal cavity. Much later in fetal life, those magical little sacs of maleness drop down to the outside of the body, into the scrotum, and later still they paradoxically become pendulous symbols for bravery and strength — He's got balls! — despite their reputation as the most vulnerable region on a man's body.

In the fetus, the testes bud quickly and begin excreting androgens, hormones such as testosterone. Androgens in turn sculpt the primordial genital buds into a penis and scrotum. But it's not enough to make a male; at the same time, the fetus's female program must be stifled. To that end, the testes also secrete a hormone called müllerian inhibiting factor, which makes fetal structures that might otherwise develop into a uterus and fallopian tubes wither away.

In Jane's case, much of this action unfolded according to standard operating procedure. Her Y chromosome performed as expected, and SRY switched on. She grew little internal testes. The testes worked. They secreted androgens. They secreted müllerian inhibiting factor. The inhibiting factor prompted the dissolution of Jane's primordial womb and tubes. But then something happened, or rather didn't happen. As it turns out, the Y needs the X to complete the creation of Adamically correct genitals. The quintessential female chromosome holds on its grand expanse a surprisingly large piece in the puzzle of man-making. Of its 5,000 genes, one is the gene that allows the body to respond to androgens. It's not enough to manufacture androgens; the various tissues of the body must be capable of sensing the hormones and reacting accordingly. That requires the contribution of an androgen receptor protein. The tissues of the fetus's immature genital bud must be dotted with androgen receptor proteins if the bud is to respond to androgens and form a penis. And that protein is encoded in the androgen receptor gene, on the X chromosome.

Isn't it romantic? The androgen receptor gene could have been located anywhere in the genome, on any of the twenty-three chromosomes — on chromosome three, say, or number sixteen. But no, it's on *our* chromosome, the big fat boring X chromosome. Sheer coincidence, perhaps — although scientists can't say that for sure* — but still worth a fleeting "hah!" We make females, we make males; if you don't see what you want in the window, ask for it inside.

Jane Carden had inherited on her X chromosome a mutated, nonworking version of the androgen receptor gene. As a result of the mutation, her body could not respond to the androgens her testes were releasing in considerable abundance, which meant she couldn't grow a penis or a scrotum. Her body was, and is, androgen insensitive, hence the name of her syndrome.

And so, being androgen-deaf, Jane's body took the course that a mammalian fetus will in the absence of androgens: it chose to go girl. The little knob of her external genitalia became outer labia, clitoris, and a short blind tunnel. The transformation was not complete — no inner labia, and the skin of her vaginal folds is oddly pale, not the usual mauve tone, as Jane puts it, of other white women's genitals. Still, she is a woman, as much of a woman as I or any menstruating, childbearing female I've ever met. With her breasts and rounded hips and comparatively slender neck (to me, one of the biggest giveaways of the female body), she can't help but strike the world as a woman. Most important, she has never doubted her female identity, even as she stood in the

---

*Very little is understood about large-scale gene organization — that is, why genes are distributed across the twenty-three chromosomes the way they are. Most of the placement appears to be a matter of chance and convenience, but some genes may be where they are because of how they are designed to perform during development, their accessibility to essential control elements, and the like.

medical library, stunned, desperate, reading about her Y chromosome and the testes she had once possessed.

There are quirky elements to androgen insensitivity syndrome. The absence of acne and male-pattern baldness: androgens are behind pimples and most cases of thinning hair, in men and women alike. They also stimulate the growth of body hair in both sexes. Jane has no underarm hair and nothing but a downy mist of light baby hair over her pubic region, again for lack of responsiveness to androgens. Some people with the syndrome look like *mama mia* women, the sort who become actresses and models. Jane had her testes taken out soon after birth and needed to take estrogen replacement therapy at adolescence to fill out her female form (and to protect her bones, which are dependent on estrogen). But some women with AIS are not diagnosed until well into adolescence. Their testes didn't herniate in infancy and nobody had reason to question their chromosomal status. When such girls reach puberty, the testes begin releasing substantial amounts of hormones, mostly androgens but estrogen as well. The hormones travel through the bloodstream to sites like the breast area, where the estrogen acts directly on the tissue. In addition, some of the androgens are converted enzymatically to estrogen. The breasts begin to grow, and grow, and grow, to larger proportions in fact than in most women, for it is a woman's capacity to respond to androgens that is part of what holds her breast growth in check. (High levels of androgens likewise keep a teenage boy's chest flat. The gynecomastia, or breast growth, seen in some older men is probably the result of declining testosterone levels; freed of the counteractivity of androgens, the men's circulating estrogen succeeds in prompting a modest growth of the bosom.) AIS women also often grow fairly tall, though why they do is not clear — perhaps another testicular hormone or gene on the Y chromosome promotes a manly height. Eventually, by age sixteen or so, after the AIS girls have developed adult bodies without starting to menstruate, they end up at a doctor's office, at which point their condition is diagnosed.

Good skin, great head hair, full breasts, tall stature. And naturally nude armpits and scant leg hair — and a strapping immune system, Jane insists, because testosterone can suppress immune cells. A number of models and actresses have androgen insensitivity syndrome. Wallis Simpson, the spirited divorcée for whom King Edward abdicated his throne, may well have been an AIS woman. Some historians have said that Joan of Arc had the condition, but most have disputed the theory; nonetheless, Jane Carden took her name as a nom de plume.

The physical specifics of AIS women provide a delicious counterweight to the arguments put forth by some evolutionary psychologists, who claim that a woman's sexual appeal lies in her possession of traits that tell a man, I am fertile and will make you many babies. They have shining skin and thick hair — the signs of health and youth; and youth, youth, youth, we are told, is the measure of a woman's market value. And those generous breasts are supposed to be the emblem of an estrogenic woman, a reliably fecund cycler. Oh, yes, to each body part on a pinup girl a Darwinian tag can be fastened. But these AIS superwomen, these amply endowed icons of fantasy and autoerotic spasm, just aren't Honest Signalers, as the evolutionary jargon puts it. They are, in fact, Cheaters, luring men into the foaming waters of carnality without even the vaguest possibility of conception. What a delight, what a subversion of expectation. The healthiest and most womanly of women are in fact a rendition of Amazon queens, self-possessed and self-defined, women whose bodies have an enviable integrity and a fleshy, non-replicative beauty that razzes Charles Darwin. The buck, the stud, the bull, stops here.

However much women with AIS identify themselves as women, they still feel set apart. Most keep their condition secret from all but a few close friends. Interestingly, many of them say the thing they regret most is not their inability to have children but the lack of menstruation, the event they see as a monthly voucher of femaleness. When other girls talk about their periods, girls with diagnosed AIS keep quiet and emotionally shrink away, as though, like the title character in the movie *Carrie*, they're worried that the "normal" girls will start pelting them with tampons and sanitary napkins.

Jane spent fifteen years feeling like an untouchable freak, having diagnosed herself by textbook but having no clue how to locate another soul with her condition. "All I wanted was to meet someone else with AIS. It was my life's dream," she says. "I walked around like an adopted child who looks into the eyes of every person and thinks, are you my parent? I'd hear about somebody who couldn't have children, or some other variable like that, and I'd wonder, could she be like me?

"I asked my own physician, I asked everyone I could if they knew other people. I called a doctor in Dallas who's probably the foremost researcher in the United States on AIS. Everyone kept saying no. They would act like I was out of my mind for asking, and they not so subtly suggested, who the hell would want to talk about it? Who would want to admit it? My own doctor told me that she had two patients with AIS, one a woman in her forties who was so prominent in the community that she would never want her identity revealed. And the other was an eighteen- or nineteen-year-old girl who my doctor insisted was just doing so well that she really had no need to have contact with anyone. That sounded like bullshit. I *knew* it was bullshit, because that supposedly well-adjusted eighteen- or nineteen-year-old was *me*."

Finally Jane again found her answers in a library. While looking through an issue of the *British Medical Journal* two years ago or so, she read a letter written by a mother of a seven-year-old girl with the syndrome. The family lived in England, and the woman said they were in the process of forming a support group for AIS girls and women and their relatives. She included her phone number at the end of the letter, but Jane could hardly make it out because the page she was reading was already stained with her tears. Jane cries freely as she talks about the day she found the letter. She doesn't bother daubing her eyes with her napkin. "I can never describe for you what that felt like," she says. "I will never be able to describe that." She photocopied the page. She drove home and practiced. She practiced trying to speak in a normal voice, without sobbing and choking. She practiced saying, "I have AIS," which she had never said to anybody but a doctor before. Still, when she called the woman, she broke down on introducing herself. Several weeks later she flew to England for the support group's first meeting. "I will never have a success in my life parallel to having found the support group and other people with AIS," she says. "Without a doubt, that's the greatest success in my life."

At the group meetings, the women talk about practical issues, such as how to find Lucite vaginal dilators that stretch the short canal into something big enough to accommodate a penis. They avoid euphemism. They talk about themselves as having a birth defect. They talk about scrutinizing their bodies in the mirror, searching for any lingering evidence of maleness. They talk about myths: the myth that links testos-

terone to libido, for example, in both men and women. If the myth were
true, then these women should have no sex drive; they can't, after all,
respond to the testosterone their bodies produce. Some sex researchers
have said as much about AIS patients — that they're frigid, uninterested, dead in bed. The women themselves come close to spitting in rage
at that sort of talk. Whether or not they manage to inflate their vaginas
sufficiently to have intercourse, their erotic nature remains intact. They
fantasize about sex. They are orgasmic. They lust when there is somebody worth lusting after.

Another myth they defy is the one that promotes testosterone as the
"hormone of aggression." If that platitude held, AIS women should be
milder and more violet in their shrinking than the average woman. But
the opposite is true: the women are, in their way, Joans of Arc of the
temperament. One woman says she deliberately plays at being demure
so that nobody will catch on to her condition. Jane claims she has balls
when she needs them; the surgeons haven't excised them from her
character. "I'm just like my mother, an aggressive, obnoxious human
being," she said to me. "I'm the daughter my mother created. I'm the
woman I was meant to be."

3

DEFAULT LINE

IS THE FEMALE BODY A PASSIVE CONSTRUCT?

ONE OF THE FIRST THINGS I noticed as I began shopping during pregnancy for baby ballast is that three decades after the birth of the current feminist movement, there is still no escaping the binary coding by color. Whether you're looking at clothes for newborns, for six-month-olds, or for that relatively recent store category, preemies, everything is either pink or blue. Maybe it's because the promiscuous use of sonograms and prenatal tests means that most people know the sex of their baby ahead of time, so there's little need to hedge your purchase even when buying a gift for a prenate. Whatever the reason, the emphasis on sartorial sex distinctions seems stronger than ever before. Just try finding an item of infant clothing that isn't trimmed or beribboned or beanimaled in either pink or blue, and you'll realize how limited your fashion options are. Oh, here it is, the lone ungendered baby outfit: a yellow T-shirt with a picture of a duck on it.

I also realized, as I floated distractedly through the aisles of the baby megamarts, that I didn't much care. For all my crustiness and deeply held feminism, the pink-and-blue breakdown didn't irritate me as much as I expected it would. One reason for my indifference was that the adorableness factor took over. All baby clothes are adorable, whoever they're meant for (and in the end, of course, they're meant for the parents). All remind you of how vulnerable an infant is, how wholly incompetent and in need of adult largess. You don't look at blue clothes and think "strong" or pink clothes and think "fragile." You look at everything in these micromatized dimensions and think, "How precious! How ridiculous! What was evolution thinking of?"

I also consoled myself with the knowledge that the association of pink with girls and blue with boys is fairly recent. In the early part of the nineteenth century, the color codes were less absolute than they are today, but if anything, pink was likelier to be put on boys and blue on girls than the reverse. So though we may at this point be convinced that one color is inherently feminine and the other masculine, the conviction clearly is nonsense. (If you want to spend a few minutes on pleasant mental thumb-twiddling, you can make up plausible fables to justify either interpretation, to wit, that blue, in lying on the high-energy end of the electromagnetic spectrum, is a more appropriate color for those high-energy boys, or, alternatively, that blue, being a color of cool objects such as ice and water, better suits the supposedly sedate nature of girls.) The arbitrariness of the distinction gives me comfort and lets me think, Eh, let's not get too frazzled over this one. When it comes to girls' clothing, I'm less opposed to pink than I am to dresses, for the simple reason that I hated dresses and skirts as a child. I hated the way they impeded my mobility and playground power, and I hated the fear I had while wearing them that with one stiff breeze I would be exposed to the world, with no choice afterward but to slip quietly into a permanent vegetative state.

Yet if there's one thing about the pink-blue dichotomy that annoys me, it's the unidirectional manner in which we sometimes let it slide. It's fine to dress a girl in blue, but think about pink on a boy. Think hard about subjecting your son to girl clothes. Think about dressing him in a pink T-shirt, and even you, my most rad-chic mother, will hesitate and, in compromise, reach instead for the yellow shirt with the duck on it. None of this is surprising or limited to babies, of course. A woman can wear stovepipe trousers or blue jeans or a farmer's bib or tails and a top hat and so what — she's just exercising her options as a consumer; but if a man puts on a skirt he'd better be ready to pick up a bagpipe and blow. We've known this for years, but it's still a nuisance to know it. "I guarantee that even if you were given a case of free diapers and they happened to be pink, you would use them for gift wrapping before you would put them on your firstborn *son*," Vicki Iovine writes in her very amusing book, *The Girlfriends' Guide to Pregnancy.* "It's an illness, I know, and we could all keep our therapists busy for weeks over this issue of gender stereotypes, but it's the truth." When I first read that line, I thought in irritation, She wouldn't say that about using a box of free *blue* diapers for your firstborn *daughter;* yet I knew that for all her flippant shoulder-shrugging, Iovine was right. You don't dress your first or second or twelfth-born son in pink diapers, unless you are a mother in a Hollywood horror movie who will soon be revealed as having Medea-sized intentions.

So what exactly are we afraid of when we fear polluting a boy with pink? Are we worried that we might turn him gay? The evidence strongly suggests that sexual orientation has little or nothing to do with one's upbringing, and in any event gay sons love their mothers, so what's the problem there? Is it the usual misogyny, the association of masculine with "fully human" and "quality controlled," and feminine with "circa human," the "chipped goods on the remainder table"? In part, yes, we're still very much a misogynist culture, and therefore the boys' stuff is good enough for girls — it may even, when used judiciously on daughters, reflect a certain parental panache — but never, ever vice versa. Girl goods are too silly, too icky, and, let's not mince our words, too inferior for a boy.

This thought is familiar. It's disheartening. And since we're not about to change the pattern anytime soon, it's distinctly unhelpful. So in my ongoing campaign to sweeten brackish waters and to give a female-friendly twist to an old truism, let me suggest the following: our willingness to clothe females in male garb but not the opposite, and the concomitant acceptance of the tomboyish girl and distaste for the sissy-ish boy, indicate, albeit on an unconscious level, an awareness of who is the real primogenitor, the legitimate First Sex, and therefore which is ultimately the freer sex. Simone de Beauvoir may have been right about a lot of sociocultural inequities, but from a biological perspective women are not the runners-up; women are the original article. We are Chapter 1, lead paragraph, descendants of the true founding citizen of Eden, whom we may cheerfully think of as Lilith, Adam's first wife. Lilith is not mentioned in the canonical Old Testament, and in the sources where she does make an appearance — for example, the sixteenth-century *Alphabet of Ben Sira* — she is predictably described as having been created *after* Adam, designed for his companionship and erotic pleasure. In these accounts, the couple took to quarreling when Adam announced that he was partial to the missionary position. He liked it not so much for the way it felt as for the political point it made. "You are fit to be below me and I above you," he said to Lilith. His companion refused to acknowledge her subordinate status. "Why should I lie beneath you?" she demanded. "We are both equal because we both come from the earth." Lilith's act of rebellion cut short her tenure in the Garden and assured that all her children would be cursed by God ever after (then again, her more pliant replacement hardly fared much better). But in my unkosher retelling of the story, Lilith was outraged at Adam's pronouncements for their imperialist trash. She knew, even if he did not, bloody hell, *she* was there first.

By saying that Lilith preceded Adam, that she, not he, was the one with the rib to spare, I'm not being gratuitously contrarian. In a basic biological sense, the female is the physical prototype for an effective living being. As we saw with Jane Carden, fetuses are pretty much primed to become female unless the female program is disrupted by gestational exposure to androgens. If not instructed otherwise, the primordial genital buds develop into a vulva and at least a partial vagina. (The brain may also assume a female configuration, but this far fuzzier issue we will discuss later.) By the conventional reckoning of embryology, females are said to be the "default" or "neutral" sex, males the "organized" or "activated" sex. That is, a fetus will grow into a girl in the absence of a surge in fetal hormones, with no need for the impact of estrogen, the hormone we normally think of as the female hormone. Estrogen may be indispensable for building breasts and hips later in life, and for orchestrating the monthly menstrual cycle, but it doesn't seem to have much of a role in mapping out girlness to begin with. The male body plan, in contrast, is wrought when the little testes begin secreting testosterone, müllerian inhibiting factor, and other hormones. The hormones organize — or, more precisely, reorganize — the primordial tissue into a masculine format.

But the term *default sex* has such a passive ring to it, suggesting that girls just happen, that making them is as easy as unrolling a carpet downhill; you don't even have to kick it to get it going. A number of women in biology have objected to the terminology and the reasoning behind it. Anne Fausto-Sterling, of Brown University, has complained that the notion of female as default is an intellectual vestige of the male domination of developmental biology. The reason that nobody has found any of the chemical signals that activate the female blueprint, she argues, is that nobody has looked for them. From a man's perspective, the mechanism behind the growth of fallopian tubes simply can't hold the fascination of the recipe for a penis. Just because hormones don't appear to be responsible for female sex determination doesn't mean that *nothing* is responsible; other signaling systems exist and participate in fetal growth, though they're harder to find and study than a sharp and unmistakable burst of androgens.

What we can do is reformulate the principle of female first into something less simplistic and inert than the ho-hum default mode. David Crews, of the University of Texas, proposes a lovely system for discussing the sex determination of an animal: the female is the ancestral sex while the male is the derived sex. The female form came first, and eventually it gave rise to the male variant. Athena was said to have sprung from the skull of Zeus. Perhaps we might better imagine Apollo springing from the head of Hera.

What the notion of female as ancestral sex means, when stretched to its most interesting dimensions, is that males are more like females than females are like males. Males, after all, are derived from females; they have no choice but to hold in common those features — those girlish features, those pink pajamas! — that were modified in the making of them. But females have no such reliance on the male prototype to invent a sense of self. Self was there to begin with; we defined self. We don't need Adam's rib, we didn't use Adam's rib; our bones calcified and our pelvises hardened entirely without male assistance.

Crews arrived at his thesis through a couple of lines of reasoning. To begin with, he studies sex determination in reptiles rather than in mammals, so he sees a different system at work, from which he can extract novel principles to counter the conventional wisdom held by the warm-bloods. He has observed that the sex of a crocodile or a turtle is not dictated by an X or a Y chromosome, the SRY gene or the testes it can build. Instead, a baby reptile is sexualized by environmental elements, particularly the air or water temperature surrounding the egg while the creature is developing. All embryos begin with bisexual potential, and then, depending on whether it is mild or cold outside, they grow either ovaries or testes. (Generally, a colder temperature yields males, a warmer one yields females, and an intermediate temperature will give rise to a brood of 50 percent males and 50 percent females.)

Importantly, neither sex is a "default" sex. A crocodile can't become a female just by not becoming a male. The pre-she must receive some kind of stimulus, pegged to temperature, that in turn sets off a physiological chain of events to build ovaries. So too to construct testes: the young reptile requires signals from the outside world to set the masculine protocol in motion. In other words, the business of sexualizing a reptile is active and multistep whatever the final outcome will be.

Reptiles are very different from mammals; nevertheless, the details of their sex determination program tempt us to question assumptions about the neutrality of the female. There may be much that we're overlooking in the embryonic establishment of sex. For example, a male fetus's testes release müllerian inhibiting factor to destroy the primitive ducts that otherwise would flower into the fallopian tubes, uterus, and vagina. Yet in addition to her müllerian ducts, a female embryo possesses until the ninth week of gestation what are called the wolffian ducts, structures that have the potential to become the seminal vesicle, the epididymides, and other elements of male anatomy. In the female, most of the wolffian ductal structures dissolve away during development, but has anybody ever found a wolffian inhibiting factor, a WIF? No. Supposedly no such factor exists. Supposedly the wolffian ducts disappear in the *absence* of a signal from the testes to persist and flourish. This is part of the female-as-default model. The wolffian ducts will self-destruct unless they're given a reason to live. This hypothesis is possible, but it is hardly plausible. We've seen with the development of eggs and brains that nature, Shiva-child that she is, creates abundance only to destroy the bulk of it. But does destruction just happen, or must it be initiated? If death is an active process — and the new creed of apoptosis claims it is — well, then, it needs activation. Somewhere there must be a wolffian inhibiting factor: not a hormone, not something easily isolated like a hormone, but a signal. A subtle set of teeth that eliminates one aspiration and gives the female principle the run of the shop, to shape the body temple so that Lilith might lie as she likes.

In fact, in 1993 scientists presented preliminary evidence that they had found an active ovarian initiator, that the construction of ovaries wasn't merely a question of a passive unfolding. They had identified a genetic signal that could aggressively override testosterone's actions and turn primordial fetal genitals into the female format — in this case, not because a signal was missing or because the tissue couldn't respond to androgens, as happens in androgen insensitivity syndrome, but because this factor, whatever it is, had become hyperactive and pushed the androgens out of the way. Eau d'Amazon! But none of this work has been replicated yet, nor explored in any detail, so whether we have found the long-sought girl growth factor, nobody can say.

Assuming, then, that it takes work to generate either a male or a female form and that there are active ovarian initiators out there able to do for gals what testosterone does for our brothers, why does Crews give ancestral primacy to the female while consigning the male to the status of the derivative? In this, his training as a herpetologist colors his worldview. Among mammals, sexual reproduction is obligatory. If a mammal is to have offspring, it must mate with a member of the opposite sex. There is no such thing as a parthenogenetic mammal in nature, a female who can spin out her own clones. But some lizards — and fish, and a few other types of vertebrates — breed through self-replication, almost always producing daughters only, no sons. Parthenogenesis is not a terribly common strategy, but it occurs. In fact, it tends to appear and disappear over evolutionary time. A species that once was a sexually reproducing one, requiring the existence of males and females, will for any number of reasons lose the male and turn parthenogenetic. In other cases, a parthenogenetic species will discover the benefits of having a fellow around — specifically, because sexual reproduction gives rise to enhanced genetic diversity and thus to children with sufficiently varied traits to withstand changing times. Desiring change, the formerly hymeneal females, the cold-blooded madonnas, retreat to the Garden of Eden and start bickering over who is to take on the role of the male and get to be on top. In either evolutionary scenario, males come and males go, but the female remains. There is no species where there is no female. The female, the great Mother, is never lost.

(You may wonder whether it's fair to call a parthenogenetic animal a female rather than a neuter, or even, just for the jazz of it, a male. The short answer is, of course it's fair. It's even accurate. A parthenogenetic lizard produces and lays eggs from which infant lizards eventually emerge, and a female animal, in her purest sense, is the animal with the eggs.)

"Males evolved only after the evolution of self-replicating (=female) organisms," Crews writes. "Males have been gained and lost, but females have remained. The male pattern is derived and imposed upon the ancestral female pattern."

My father was not an unregenerate defender of male privilege. He saw the sense of the goddesshead and the unnatural quality of the unrelievedly patriarchal structure of the Judeo-Christian-Islamic axis. We were in the Metropolitan Museum together once, and we passed by a painting depicting the Father, the Son, and the Holy Spirit. I don't remember the artist or the century or the country of provenance. In fact, I remember little about the work except my extreme dislike of it. The three Omnipotences were painted as identical triplets, a troika of brown-bearded men in long robes. My father, the angry lapsed Christian, sneered at the painting. The Holy Trinity, the supposed creators of life on earth — and not a female among them, he grumbled. The least the artist could have done, my father said, is to portray the Holy Spirit ambiguously enough that you might mistake it for a woman. We walked away from the painting, the sneer now a shared experience.

Twenty years or so later, I wonder: could the artist have been unconsciously projecting an innate understanding that the male is derived from the ancestral female, as the Roman temple is derived from the Greek basilica? Just as the Romans outflaunted their antecedents down to every detail — in the grandeur of the engineering, the elaboration of the architectural orders — so the male ups the ante and outbarks the female, becoming stylistic hypertrophy, all flourish and brawn. Crews says that in conceptualizing the ancestral female and the derivative male, "the intriguing possibility emerges that males may be more like females than females are like males." If he is right, then it makes crude sense, in a monotheistic culture that insists on abandoning the pantheon and choosing one god to reign symbolically over a two-sexed species, for the god to be male; for the male incorporates the female, is like the female — in a sense, begins as an imitation of the female — but the female cannot say the same. The female does not incorporate the male, did not originally need the male. Who knows? She may not in the future need him again.

On his side, the male needs the female, as he needs the basal parts of himself. He cannot escape her, and so he coopts her greatest power, her generative capabilities. But being male and of a Roman cut, he goes her one better. Remember that a parthenogenetic female can give birth only to daughters. A male god, though, is reinvented as a super-parthenogen, able without assistance to create sons and daughters alike. Imagining, incorrectly but understandably, that he can thenceforth go it alone, he takes it upon himself to be the one god, a fabulist creature whose like can't be found in nature.

Deities have their problems and delusions, we humans have ours. If among gods males are likelier to encroach on female prerogatives than the reverse, among humans women feel more comfortable coopting the male than men do behaving in a manner that may be seen as womanish — or, worse, womanly. Freud suggested that men had to individuate by wrenching themselves free of the world of women — mothers, grandmothers, aunts, nursemaids — the monotonously, claustrophobically feminine habitat in which they spent their infancy and youth. Women threaten because women rule for so long. If men are to find autonomy, they must denounce femininity. Women do not need to pull themselves away to achieve womanhood; they do not need to reject the mother who cared for them and defined them.

Forget Freud. It could well be that men must pull away not from the external world of women but from the internal female template. Maybe men feel driven to emphasize their distinctiveness over their derivation, to escape the ancestral female as though escaping a dynastic hex, the femuncula within. We women therefore may have, at our core, an easier time with fluid sexuality. We can afford to play around with clothes and personas and attitudes, to be as ballsy as we want to be; still we will be women. Men's brief and much-derided foray into the land of sensitivity and Alan Alda suggests that men cannot say the same; to the contrary, their edges blur and their convictions become hesitant if they toy with androgyny too long. Jane Carden said that for this reason, the freedom of role plasticity, she was glad to have been born woman — glad, we might say, that her ancestral female template was not overlaid with male appurtenances.

"I wouldn't want to have been born without AIS," she said. "It was the only way for me to go through this lifetime as a woman. Female experiences are richer, I think, and we have a more complete emotional life. The range of personalities that men can exhibit is much narrower. I have the luxury of being extremely demure, what people associate with being very feminine one day, and being very aggressive and macho the next day. Both are tolerated in women, at least at this point in history. The analogues in men — well, we're just not there yet."

When Crews says that the male pattern is derived from and imposed on the ancestral female pattern, he is talking about many things: the pattern of hormone release and activity, the pattern of brain structures, the pattern of behaviors, and of course the pattern of the reproductive systems. It is our genitals that we think of as the clearest difference between male and female; it is our genitals that most fascinate us and inculcate notions of gender in us as children (along, of course, with our divergent styles of using the toilet). The reproductive system is supposedly what most clearly distinguishes a man from a woman.

Except that when you take a close look, you'll see that we're remarkably the same. If you look at a woman in stirrups, for example, you'll see that the plumpness of her labia and the way they fall slightly into the folds of her thighs are reminiscent of a man's scrotum. The ancients knew as much. Hippocrates, Galen, and other early anatomists and body philosophers knew as much. They were not saints. They were not gynophiles. In *Making Sex: Body and Gender from the Greeks to Freud,* Thomas Laqueur describes the ideas of Galen as "phallocentric," taking the male pattern as primary and describing the female from that reference point. The Greek doctors also made errors in their understanding of anatomy. Nevertheless, they were on to something. They thought that the human body was basically unisexual and that the two sexes were inside-out versions of each other. The ancients emphasized the homology between female and male organs.

"In the one-sex model, dominant in anatomical thinking for two thousand years, woman was understood as man inverted: the uterus was the female scrotum, the ovaries were testicles, the vulva was a foreskin, and the vagina was a penis," Laqueur writes. "Women were essentially men in whom a lack of vital heat — of perfection — had resulted in the retention, inside, of structures that in the male were visible without." Galen even used the same words to describe male and female structures, calling the ovaries *orcheis,* the Greek word for testes. (Orchid flowers also were named after testicles, because the water bulb at the base of the plant looks like a little wrinkled scrotum. So when Georgia O'Keeffe used the orchid to represent female genitals, she incidentally committed a minor act of conjoinment of maleness with femaleness.) Sexual parallelism was gospel; a fourth-century bishop said he realized that women had the same equipment as he, except "theirs are inside the body and not outside it."

Nor was it only the genitals that were assumed to be homologous; so too were the body's excretions. Semen was man's version of menstrual blood; milk and tears were as one. The ancients also saw no difference between men's and women's capacity for sexual pleasure and the necessity of mutual orgasm for conception. Galen proclaimed that a woman could not get pregnant unless she had an orgasm, and his view prevailed until the eighteenth century. This is a sweet thought, one of my favorite glaring errors of history, and a roundabout acknowledgment of the importance of the female climax to life as we know it. Unfortunately, the insistence that an expectant woman was a postorgasmic woman spelled tragedy for a number of our foresisters. Women who became pregnant after rape, for example, were accused of licentiousness and adultery, since their swollen bellies were evidence of their acquiescence and their pleasure, and they were routinely put to death. In more recent times, women have been advised that when rape is inevitable, they should just "lie back and enjoy it," and they also have been blamed in any number of ways for their predicament — why did you dress that way, why did you invite him back to your apartment, why did you go for a walk in the park after dark?

Galen was wrong about a number of things. The vulva is not a foreskin, though it may be treated as such in countries that practice female genital mutilation; and neither women nor men need to reach orgasm for a woman to conceive (men secrete sperm in their pre-ejaculates, and I knew a woman who became pregnant without having intercourse, when a smear of pre-ejaculate deposited on her thigh during a thrashabout of heavy petting migrated insidiously upward). But about the unisexual quality of the body he was prescient. The female may be the ancestral form, yet in our current bodies we develop bipotentially; the clay can be shaped either way. We are hermaphrodites, legatees of the son of Hermes and Aphrodite, who merged his body with that of the nymph of the Salmacis fountain. Male and female fetuses look identical until the ninth week of gestation, and our adult organs are analogous structures, male to female. Inside its apricot-sized body, the antesexual two-month-old fetus has a pair of immature seedpods, the primordial gonads, which become testes in males, ovaries in females. It has a set of wolffian and müllerian ducts, one of which will be chosen depending on whether the fetus is to develop a seminal duct system or fallopian tubes. Externally, each begins with an undifferentiated genital ridge, a bump of tissue above a small membrane-shielded slit. Starting in the third month, the nub of flesh either grows gracefully into a clitoris or grows more emphatically into the head of a penis. In girls, the membrane around the primordial slit dissolves, and the slit opens to form the vaginal lips, which will surround the vagina and the urethra, from which urine flows. In boys, androgens prompt the slit to fuse and push forward to generate the shaft of the penis.

As symbols go, the phallus is a yawn. Tubes that point and shoot, and there you have it. The obelisk pierces the heavens, the gun ejaculates bullets, the cigar puffs like a peacock, the hot rod screams, the hot dog is eaten. A phallus doesn't give you much to play with, metaphorically, and it doesn't lend itself to multiple interpretations. A hose is a hose is a hose.

But the vagina, now there's a Rorschach with legs. You can make of it practically anything you want, need, or dread. A vagina in its most simple-minded rendering is an opening, an absence of form, an inert receptacle. It is a four- to five-inch-long tunnel that extends at a forty-five-degree angle from the labia to the doughnut-shaped cervix. It is a pause between the declarative sentence of the outside world and the mutterings of the viscera. Built of skin, muscle, and fibrous tissue, it is the most obliging of passageways, one that will stretch to accommodate travelers of any conceivable dimension, whether they are coming (penises, speculums) or going (infants). I'm sure I'm not the only woman who dreamed during pregnancy that she was about to give birth to a baby whale, in my case an endangered blue whale. Oh, the human vagina in its role as birth canal can stretch, all right, and it must distend in proportion to the rest of us far more than the pelvis of a mother whale. You've heard, or experienced firsthand, how the cervix must dilate to ten centimeters, or four inches, before the laboring woman is given sanction to push. It must become as wide as the vagina is long.

But those ten centimeters, O grunting, flailing lady, are not the width of the baby's head. No, the average seven-pound baby has a head five inches across, and some fat-headed infants have skulls nearly six inches wide. While the baby's head does compress into something the shape of a keel as it rams and glides its way to the light — thank Ishtar for the sutures, fontanel, and ductile plates of the newborn's skull — nonetheless you can count on your vagina's stretching during delivery to proportions unimagined when you had trouble negotiating your first tampon insertion. So the vagina is a balloon, a turtleneck sweater, a model for the universe itself, which, after all, is expanding in all directions even as we sit here and weep.

Yet mouths are expandable clefts too, and who would think of the mouth as a passive receptacle? So it is that the vagina is sometimes thought of as a toothed organ, by analogy with the mouth: a hungry, sucking, masticating, devouring orifice, capable of depleting a man's resources fatally if he gives in to its allure too often. Or the vagina is the moist, soothing, kissing mouth; the word *labia* means lips, of course, and human ethologists such as Desmond Morris have proposed that women wear lipstick to emphasize the resemblance between upper and lower labia, to recapitulate the lines of the hidden genitals on the poster of the face.

Nor is the vagina limited to metaphors of opening. It can be thought of as a closed system, hands pressed together in prayer, the Big Crunch rather than the expanding universe of the Big Bang. Most of the time, a woman's vagina is not a tube or a hole; instead, the walls drape inward and firmly touch each other. The vagina thus can switch states between protected and exposed, introverted and inviting. And so it gives rise to the imagery of flowering, of bursting open: lotuses, lilies, leaves, split pecans, split avocados, the wings of a damselfly. The artist Judy Chicago took the notion of the blooming, procreative vagina and fairly hoisted it up a flagpole in one of her most famous works, *The Dinner Party,* in which such feminist heroines of history and mythology as Mary Wollstonecraft, Kali, and Sappho are seated at a table, preparing to eat from dinner plates shaped like female genitals. Some criticized Chicago's work for its piousness and vulgarity (a neat trick, combining the two), while others attacked it as "reinforcing womb-centered, biologically deterministic ways of thinking," as Jane Ussher recounts in *The Psychol-*

ogy of the Female Body. Whatever the abstract artistic worthiness of *The Dinner Party* may be, Chicago had an excellent germ of an idea: a woman's genitals are a force of nature, and they do have a life, or lives, of their own. I'm not talking about their role in procreation; I refer instead to a very different sort of imagery, that of the niche, the habitat, the ecosystem. The vagina is its own ecosystem, a land of unsung symbiosis and tart vigor. Sure, the traditional concept of the vagina is "It's a swamp down there!" but "tidal pool" would be more accurate: aqueous, stable, yet in perpetual flux.

Beginning on the border of the vaginal environment, we come to a small mountain, the mons pubis, also called the mons veneris, which means "mountain of Venus," the Love Mount. But let's not get carried away with woozy romance; *veneris* also gives rise to the term *venereal disease.* The mons veneris is made mons by a thick pad of fatty tissue that cushions the pubic symphysis, the slightly movable joint between your left and right pubic bones. The joint, which is relatively delicate and easily bruised by a bad jolt on a bicycle, is further cushioned at adolescence when the carpet of pubic hair grows in (assuming that you have requisite responsiveness to androgens). The pubic hair serves other purposes as well. It traps and concentrates pelvic odors, which can be quite attractive to a mate if they are the odors of health, as I will discuss below. Moreover, the pubic hair is a useful visual cue for us primates, who are, after all, a visually oriented species. The hair showcases the genital area and allows it to stand out from the less significant landscape around it. If women wear lipstick as a subconscious way of evoking their pudenda in public, perhaps they are only following in men's footsteps. By growing a beard, a man turns his face into an echo of his crotch; and the capacity to grow a beard very likely predates the use of cosmetics by a few hundred thousand years.

Extending down from the mons veneris are two long folds of skin, the labia majora, or major lips. The outer sides of the labia are covered with pubic hair, while the inner sides have no follicles but are well supplied with oil and sweat glands. Beneath the skin of the labia majora is a crisscross of connective tissue and fat. The fat of the labia, like that of the breasts and hips — but unlike that of the mons veneris — is sensitive to estrogen, the hormone of sexual maturity. Thus the labia swell when adolescence sends a surge of estrogen through the body and retreat when the hormone subsides at menopause. Under the fat is erectile tissue, which is a spongy mesh that engorges with blood during sexual arousal. Because the labia absorb blood so readily, they also become incessantly engorged during pregnancy, when the volume of circulating blood doubles (at the same time, they can turn a coppery maroon color like the punkiest vampire shade of lipstick on the market).

The erotic and mythic taxonomy of our genitals continues. Inside the labia majora are the nymphae, named for the Greek maidens of the fountain, whose libidos were reputedly so robust that they gave birth to the concept of nymphomania.* The more pedestrian name for nymphae is labia minora, or little lips, the exquisite inner origami of flesh that enfolds the vagina and nearby urethral opening. The inner labia have no hair, but the sebaceous, or oil, glands within them can be felt through the thin skin as tiny bumps, like a subcutaneous scattering of grain. The nymphae are among the most variable part of female genitals, differing considerably in size from woman to woman and even between one labium and its partner. Like the labia majora, the labia minora swell with blood during sexual excitement, and to an even more emphatic extent, doubling or trebling their dimensions at peak arousal. Some of our primate relatives have very exaggerated labia minora, which they drag along the ground to dispense pheromones that advertise their ovulatory status. In the spring of 1996, scientists discovered a new species of marmoset in Brazil, whose most outstanding trait is the female's inner labia. Each flap of skin hangs down visibly, fusing at the bottom into a sort of genital garland.

The marmoset's labia sound remarkably like the notorious Hottentot Apron, the absurdly pronounced inner labia that naturalists from Carolus Linnaeus on insisted were a defining feature (or deformity) of the women of South Africa. The best-known Hottentot woman was the so-called Hottentot Venus, who was taken to England and France in the

---

*As Ethel Sloane points out in her excellent *Biology of Women*, "Everyone knows that a nymphomaniac is a woman with an excessive sex drive. Why is it that hardly anyone knows the same condition in males is satyriasis?" Is it because in women excessive lust is considered a disease worthy of a name tag, while in men the same drive is considered mandatory?

nineteenth century and given the name Sarah Bartmann. In Europe she was paraded in front of curious spectators as a kind of circus animal — though a clothed one — and later she was made to strip naked in front of teams of zoologists and physiologists. After her death, her genitals were dissected and preserved in a jar of formalin. Georges Cuvier, the French anatomist who performed the autopsy, declared in his memoirs that his investigations "left no doubt about the nature of her apron." But as the historian Londa Schiebinger comments in *Nature's Body,* the prurient obsession that Western men of science had with Hottentot genitals had less to do with the reality of hypertrophied labia (never proved and rightfully doubted) than with the desire to place African women in a phylogenetic category closer to orangutan than to human.

Whatever the size of the labia, inner and outer, they sweat. The entire vulval area sweats, with the same insistence as the armpits. If you've ever worked out in a bodysuit, you've probably noticed after a good sweaty session that you have three fetching triangles staining your clothes, one under each arm and a third at the crotch. You probably have felt embarrassed and exposed, the Hottentot Venus in Lycra, or maybe you're worried that others will think you've peed in your pants. Don't be ashamed; be grateful. You need to wick away all that internal body heat if you're going to stay in the running, and frankly, a woman's armpits aren't as efficient as a man's at sweating. Be glad that the female crotch at least is more so.

The vulval area also secretes sebum, a blend of oils, waxes, fats, cholesterol, and cellular debris. The sebum serves as waterproofing, helping to repel with the efficiency of a duck's back the urine, menstrual blood, and pathogenic bacteria that might otherwise settle into the crevices of the mons veneris. The sebum gives the pelvis a sleek and slippery feel, as though everything, including the pubic hairs, had been dipped in a melted candle. Stationed at the outskirts of the genital habitat, the sebum acts as the first line of defense, the Great Wall of Vagina, to thwart disease organisms that seek to colonize the rich world within.

In my career as a science writer, I've encountered all sorts of noble zealots and missionaries, biologists who perform an important if queer sort of spin control. They sing the beauties of nature's rejected and despised. They speak with Demosthenean eloquence and a mother's love of spiders, flies, scorpions, roaches, vipers, sharks, bats, worms, rats. In each case, they are determined to reform the public image of their pet leper and to make us salute what before we might happily have squashed.

None has quite the task of Sharon Hillier, a gynecologist at Magee-Women's Hospital in Pittsburgh. She is out to buff the image of the vagina. I found her while looking for somebody who could tell me why the vagina has the odor it does. I was thinking human pheromones; I was thinking oil of musk and essence of civet — small, silly, trendy things that lock us into the Darwinosphere and glib theories of mate attraction. Then I saw in a conference program the title of a talk she was giving: "The Ecosystem of the Healthy Vagina." I knew I'd found a woman who thought about the big picture, in an area most of us would rather not think about at all.

Hillier knows that people generally think of the vagina as dirty, in every sense of the term. The word *vagina* sounds both dirtier and more clinical than its counterpart, *penis*, while a curse like *cunt* has a much more violent sting to it than *prick* or *dick*, either of which would sound at home on primetime television. As we've seen, American doctors jestingly compare the vagina to the anus. "In Nairobi, the word for vaginal discharges translates as *dirt*," Hillier told me. "Almost all of the women there try to dry the vagina, because a moist, well-lubricated vagina is thought to be disgusting.

"But really, anywhere you go, the story is the same," she said. "Women are taught that their vaginas are dirty. In fact, a normal healthy vagina is the cleanest space in the body. It's much cleaner than the mouth, and much, much cleaner than the rectum." She sighed. "The negative training starts early. My five-year-old daughter came home from school the other day and said, 'Mommy, the vagina is full of germs.'" Part of the brainwashing involves a lot of big fish stories. The vagina is said to have a fishy odor, a source of great merriment to male comedians. "You've heard the jokes," Hillier said. "My favorite is the one about the blind man who passes by the fish store and says, 'Good morning, ladies.'" Ha-ha. I complained once to a male friend about a line in a movie when a gay male character, in the middle of a discussion about fellatio, turned to a woman and said, "Sorry, hon, I don't eat fish."

Fish! I cried. It's not fishy! My friend replied, "Well, you've got to admit it's closer to tuna than to, say, roast beef." Yes, all analogies to meat must be reserved for a different sort of organ. In any event, men may well think of a vagina as smelling fishy, for as it happens, sperm is one of the ingredients that can make a good thing go bad.

The crux of the vaginal ecosystem, said Hillier, is symbiosis, a mutually advantageous and ongoing barter between macroenvironment and microorganism. Yes, the vagina is full of germs, in the sense of bacteria; it swims with life forms, and you hope it stays that way. But there are germs and germs. When conditions are healthy, the germs, or rather bacteria, in the vagina do a body good. They are lactobacilli, the same bacteria found in yogurt. "A healthy vagina is as clean and pure as a carton of yogurt," said Hillier. (Why do I suspect that we're not likely to see Dannon picking up on this slogan anytime soon?) And so the smell: "A normal vagina should have a slightly sweet, slightly pungent odor. It should have the lactic acid smell of yogurt." The contract is simple. We provide lactobacilli with food and shelter — the comfort of the vaginal walls, the moisture, the proteins, the sugars of our tissue. They maintain a stable population and keep competing bacteria out. Merely by living and metabolizing, they generate lactic acid and hydrogen peroxide, which are disinfectants that prevent colonization by less benign microbes. The robust vagina is an acidic vagina, with a pH of 3.8 to 4.5. That's somewhat more acidic than black coffee (with a pH of 5) but less piquant than a lemon (pH 2). In fact, the idea of pairing wine and women isn't a bad one, as the acidity of the vagina in health is just about that of a glass of red wine. This is the vagina that sings; this is the vagina with bouquet, with legs.

Nor is ordinary vaginal discharge anything to be mortified about. It is made up of the same things found in blood serum, the clear, thin, sticky liquid that remains behind when the solid components of blood, like clotting factors, are separated away. Vaginal discharge consists of water, albumin — the most abundant protein in the body — a few stray white blood cells, and mucin, the oily substance that gives the vagina and cervix their slippery sheen. Discharge is not dirt, certainly, and it is not a toxic waste product of the body in the sense of urine and feces. No, no, no. It is the same substance as what's inside the vagina, neither better nor worse, pulled down because we're bipedal and gravity exists, and because on occasion the cup runneth over. It is the lubricant beneath the illusion of carapace, reminding us that physiologically we are all aquatic organisms.

But, gals, there's no denying it: sometimes we stink, and we know it. Not like strawberry yogurt or a good Cabernet but like, alas, albacore. Or even skunk. How does this happen? If you haven't bathed for a week, I'll let you figure it out for yourself. But sometimes it's not a question of hygiene; it's a medical issue, a condition called bacterial vaginosis. For a number of reasons, the balance of flora within the vagina is upset, and the lactobacilli start to founder. In their stead, other organisms prolifer-ate, particularly anaerobic bacteria, which thrive in the absence of oxy-gen. These microbes secrete a host of compounds, each fouler than the last. Here is where the unflattering comparison to seafood comes in. Distressingly, the microbes make trimethylamine, which is the same substance that gives day-old fish its fishy odor. They make putrescine, a compound found in putrifying meat. They make cadaverine, and I need not tell you from whence that chemical was named. The amount and combination of these rank byproducts depends on the severity of the vaginosis.

In other words, if you're having a problem with unspeakable "femi-nine odor," that syndrome so coyly referred to in all the ads for douches and feminine deodorants, you could have an infection, often a low-grade, chronic one, with no symptoms beyond the odiferous. Some of the causes of such infections are known. Among the biggest is . . . douching. In an effort to get fresh 'n' clean and to look like the dewy, virginal women pictured on the packages of Massengill, women can make themselves dirtier than ever. Douching kills off the beneficial lactobacilli and paves the way for infestation by anaerobes and their trails of cadaverine. So while I rarely dispense medical advice, this one is easy: don't douche, ever, period, end of squirt bottle.

Vaginosis can also arise in the wake of other infections, such as pelvic inflammatory disease. Moreover, some women are born with an unfor-tunate predisposition toward imbalances of vaginal flora, just as some women are susceptible to acne. Even the generally desirable lactobacilli differ in their potency, with certain strains more able than others to generate hydrogen peroxide and thus more efficiently fend off contend-ing microorganisms. Some women have "lucky lactos," said Hillier, and some have so-so lactobacilli. The so-sos are more susceptible to vaginosis, as well as to infection with yeast, another type of microbe that thrives in highly anaerobic conditions.

To rectify any imbalance, you can try eating a lot of yogurt to derive the benefit of lactobacilli in yogurt culture, but very few ingested bacteria are likely to find their way to your genitalia, and any postprandial improvements in the pelvic ecosystem will probably be transitory. Chronic cases of vaginosis can be treated with antibiotics, the course of action usually suggested for pregnant women, in whom the infection raises the risk of a premature delivery. Better than antibiotics, which are indiscriminate when taken systemically, will be a type of suppository now under development, which can provide the lucky lactos exactly where they are needed.

Another cause of vaginosis is sleeping around with men who don't use condoms. Even a single shot of semen will temporarily disturb the ecosystem of the vagina. Sperm can't swim in the biting climate of a healthy vagina, so they're buffered in a solution of acid's biochemical yang, alkaline. Semen is highly alkaline, with a pH of 8. It is more alkaline than any other body fluid, including blood, sweat, spit, and tears. For several hours after intercourse, the overall pH of the vagina rises, momentarily giving unsavory bacteria the edge. Usually the change is fleeting and the woman's body has no trouble readjusting the pH thermostat back to status quo. The restoration is particularly easy when the sperm looks familiar — that is, when it belongs to the woman's regular partner. But in a woman who is exposed to the semen of multiple partners, the homeostatic mechanism sometimes falters, for reasons that remain unclear and probably have to do with an immunological reaction to all that strange sperm.

Thus, even though a woman with catholic tastes in sex may be exposed to no more semen overall than a woman who sleeps regularly with a husband, her vagina is at greater risk of becoming chronically alkaline. She loses her wine-and-yogurt tartness. So maybe it was not mere misogyny that prompted the authors of the *Kama Sutra* to describe licentious women as smelling like fish.

Are you a masochist? Do you like to look for patterns in life, morals to the story? You can think of this as another case of divine justice. If you sleep around a lot, your vagina becomes more alkaline. It becomes fishy, yes, but worse than that, an alkaline vagina is less able to defend itself against pathogens, including agents of venereal disease. Women with bacterial vaginosis are more susceptible to gonorrhea, syphilis, and AIDS. At the same time, if you sleep around a lot, you'll be exposed to a greater load of such venereal microbes. In sum, just when you need an acidic vagina the most, yours is turning alkaline. Is this not an argument for monogamy, or abstinence? Doesn't this suggest that Somebody is watching, keeping track of the notches on your lipstick case?

To me, the association is not fraught with moral or ironic underpinnings, but rather merely confirms what is ancient, prehominid news. Sex is dangerous. It always has been, for every species that engages in it. Courting and copulating animals are exposed animals, subject to greater risk of predation than animals who are chastely asleep in their burrow; not only do mating animals usually perform their rituals out in the open, but their attention is so focused on the particulars of fornication that they fail to notice the glint of a gaping jaw or the flap of a raptor's wings. Pregnancy, disease, threat of death by stoning — yes, sex has always been chancy. Momentum is chancy, and sex is nothing if not momentous. Let us not forget that. Let us not be so intimidated by overwork or familiarity or trimethylamines that we forget the exquisite momentum of sexual hunger.

The vagina is both path and journey, tunnel and traveler. Seeing beyond it requires invasion, which is why most women have only the vaguest sense of what their interior design is like, the appearance of the long-exalted, often-overrated womb and its tributaries. Again O'Keeffe has given us a visual translation of the uterus, fallopian tubes, and ovaries, evoking them through the cattle's skull and horns stripped bare on the desert floor, again a reverie of life-in-death. I think instead of water and coral reefs, where the rosy fingers of sea pens and feather anemones brush hungrily from side to side, enlivened as though with wills of their own.

4

THE WELL-TEMPERED CLAVIER

ON THE EVOLUTION OF THE CLITORIS

AT SOME POINT when I was an infant, a friend of my mother's asked her to babysit for her little girl, whom I'll call Susan. My mother already had an older daughter as well as my newborn self, so she thought she was pretty well versed in the appearance of a female baby's genitals. Thus she was taken aback, while changing Susan's diaper, to see the girl's clitoris protruding from between the rounded mounds of her labia. It didn't quite look like a penis — my mother had a son and knew what to expect on that score — but it wasn't strictly girlish either. It looked like the tip of a nose or a pinkie, and when my mother wiped it with a cloth, it stiffened slightly, to my mother's embarrassed amusement. My mother didn't care for the look of Susan's prominent, inflatable clitoris. She thought of her own daughters and how much she preferred their genitals, neatly packed and contained as they were, the clitoris subsumed by the chubby vulva and any tactile sensitivity it may have obscured from view.

It is an assumption universally held that men know more or less where they stand relative to other men when it comes to the dimensions of their genitals. As teenagers, they may compare organs directly. As mature adults, they may resort to a variation of their breast-appraisal mechanism, a southward flickering of the eyes while standing at a public urinal or sauntering through the men's locker room, where the rule of thumb seems to be that towels should be draped over the shoulder, not around the waist. (For the record, the average penis is about 4 inches long when flaccid, 5.7 inches when erect. That's a bit bigger than the gorilla's 3-inch erection, but then there's the blue whale, the world's largest mammal, who has, yes, a 10-foot pole).

Women may think they know the clitoris pretty well. They count it as an old friend. They may even believe there is a goddess out there somewhere named Klitoris, Our Lady of Perpetual Ecstasy. They never bought Freud's idea of penis envy: who would want a shotgun when you can have a semiautomatic? But ask most women how big their clitoris is, or how big the average clitoris is, or whether there are any differences at all from one woman to the next, and they probably won't know where to begin or what units to talk about. Inches, centimeters, millimeters, parking meters? Men worry that penis size matters to women, and women vigorously assure them that it doesn't. But does clitoral size matter to a woman? The girl I called Sue is now about my age. Assuming that she kept her enlarged clitoris — and she may not have, as I'll discuss — is she a superorgasmic adult, stimulated by the slightest rub, mistress of her pleasure no matter how inept her partner? Or does mass again not matter, and is there something else about the clitoris that gives it its kick?

The clitoris is usually spoken of as the homologue of the penis, and embryonically that's true: it arises from the same region of the fetal genital ridge as the shaft of the penis. But the comparison is not wholly accurate. A woman doesn't pee or ejaculate through her clitoris, of course. No urethra runs through it. She does nothing practical at all with her clitoris. The clitoris is simply a bundle of nerves: 8,000 nerve fibers, to be precise. That's a higher concentration of nerve fibers than is found anywhere else on the body, including the fingertips, lips, and tongue, and it is twice the number in the penis. In a sense, then, a woman's little brain is bigger than a man's. All this, and to no greater end than to subserve a woman's pleasure. In the clitoris alone we see a sexual organ so pure of purpose that it needn't moonlight as a secretory or excretory device. For this reason, maybe it's best that the clitoris normally is hidden within the vulval cleft: it is, in its way, a private joke, a divine secret, a Pandora's box packed not with sorrow but with laughter.

The clitoris is a good package, and so it is small, and best thought of metrically. Its fetal growth is complete by the twenty-seventh week of gestation, at which point it looks like what it will look like on the girl once she's born. Like the classic Greek column, the clitoris is a cylindrical structure with three sections — base, shaft, and crown. But it is an archaeologist's column, for the lower two sections of it are largely subterranean, hidden beneath the skin of the vulva. The part that is most easily visible when you spread open the vulva is the glans of the clitoris, the equivalent of the column's capital. The glans sits proudly, maybe a bit smugly, beneath its A-lined roof, a hood formed by the junction of the inner labia. *Glans* is an annoying word, similar enough to *gland* to make you wonder if there is something glandular — that is, secretory — about this magic button. There isn't. *Glans* means "a small, round mass or body" or "tissue that can swell and harden," both of which apply to the glans clitoris. If you looked closely, you'd see that the glans clitoris resembles the glans, or head, of the penis, with the same deco bulbousness bordering on heart-shaped, though because it has no opening it does not stare back with a Cyclopean eye, as the penis does. The clitoral glans surmounts the shaft, or body, of the clitoris, which is partly visible and then extends under the muscle tissue of the vulva, up toward the joint where the plates of the pubic bone meet, the pubic symphysis. The shaft is surrounded by a capsule of fibroelastic tissue, a kind of latex jacket that you might slip into to go for a skin-dive. It is the meat of the clitoris, the tube that you feel dancing under flesh if you take an onanistic moment and rub the meadow of the mons. The shaft is attached to twin crura, or roots, which arc subcutaneously like the two halves of a wishbone out toward the thighs and obliquely toward the vagina. The crura anchor the clitoris to the pubic symphysis. Glans, shaft, crura: a tripartite Greek column whose order changes depending on mood, from the stately Doric of a working day through the volute, unwinding Ionic and cresting in the extravagant, midsummer foliage of Corinthian, when leaves and flowers are as fat as fists and life is drunk on its gorgeous, fleeting infinity.

Considering its largely veiled configuration, the clitoris is hard to measure — it is, in fact, more easily felt than seen — but doctors have done their calipered best to be systematic about it and to offer up "normative values." Mostly they are concerned with the head and body of the clitoris, as these are the components that give the organ its heft, and hence its perceptibility to anybody inspecting it. The average infant clitoris, when measured from the base of the shaft to the top of the glans, is about 4 or 5 millimeters, the height of a pencil eraser. Grow, and your clitoris grows with you, to an average adult length from base to glans of 16 millimeters, the diameter of a dime. About a third of that span is the glans, two thirds the shaft. Despite published standards, the clitoris, like any other body part, rejoices in deviance. Masters and Johnson noted that some women have a long thin shaft surmounted by a petite glans, others a fat glans on a short thick shaft, and so on through any number of variations and combinations. After reaching maturity, the clitoris stays pretty much the same into old age. It can get bigger during pregnancy, possibly as a result of mechanical and vascular changes, and often it stays enlarged forever after. But the nice thing about the clitoris is that it is not particularly responsive to estrogen and thus does not care whether you are taking birth control pills or estrogen replacement therapy. It will not atrophy after menopause, the way the vagina can. It will always be there for you.

The clitoral glans is the wick of Eros, the site where the 8,000 nerve fibers are threshed together into a proper little brain. For many women, the glans is so sensitive that touching it directly is almost painful, and they prefer circuitous stimulation of the shaft or the entire mons. The shaft has relatively few nerves, but it is threaded through with thousands of blood vessels, allowing it to swell during arousal and push the head ever higher. Further facilitating the great clitoral expansion are two bundles of erectile tissue wrapped in muscle called the bulbs of the vestibule, which help impel blood headward. Thus insanguinated, the passionate clitoris inflates to twice the size of the clitoris supine.

Yet, again, let us not think of the clitoris as a literal counterpart to the penis. An aroused clitoris is swollen and springy, but it does not become rigid like a prepenetrant penis. We know that. Anybody with an intact sensory cortex and the right opportunities can affirm that an erect clitoris does not feel quite as stiff as a hard-on. What's surprising is that the reason for the difference only lately has come to light. In 1996, a team of Italian scientists exploring the microarchitecture of the clitoral shaft reported that, textbooks be damned, the clitoris does not have a venous plexus. In men, this tight-knit group of veins serves as the major conduit through which blood leaves the organ. During arousal, muscles in the shaft of the penis temporarily compress the venous plexus, with the result that blood flows in but then cannot depart, and lo, it is risen.

The clitoris does not seem to have a distinct, compressible plexus; the vascularization of the organ is more diffuse. On sexual kindling, arterial flow into the clitoris increases, but the venous outflow is not clamped shut, so the organ does not become a rigid little pole. Why should it? It has no need to go spelunking or intromitting. And it may be that the comparatively subtle nature of its blood trafficking allows the clitoris to distend and relax with ease and speed, giving rise to a woman's blessed gift, the multiple orgasm.

During the feminist movement of the 1970s, activists may not have burned their bras, as the cliché has it (the phrase *bra-burner* was a sloppy conflation of the burning of draft cards, which did occur during antiwar protests, and a demonstration against the Miss America competition, when a group of feminists threw their brassieres into a trash can in a symbolic rejection of constructed femininity). They did, however, hoist a metaphorical flag to the clitoris. They spoke like explorers who had stumbled on a lost land, the Garden of Eden, perhaps, as Lilith had known it. Even the 1990s edition of *Our Bodies, Ourselves* proclaims that "until the mid-1960s, most women didn't know how crucial the clitoris was." Such ignorance was blamed on Freud, who came up with the theory that a clitoral orgasm is an "infantile" orgasm, a vaginal one a "mature" orgasm, and that only by shifting her focus from her vestigial phallus to her unmistakably feminine vagina would a woman find psychosexual fulfillment.

Yet while indignation over this theory may have been justified, the clitoris did not always suffer from neglect, nor are women who live in the last gasp of the twentieth century the first to exult in it. To the contrary, Freud's proposal was an anomaly, a blot on history's understanding of female sexuality. For thousands of years, experts and amateurs alike recognized the centrality of the clitoris to a woman's pleasure and climactic faculty. The origins of the word *clitoris* are unclear. It is found in all modern European languages and comes from the Greek, but how the Greeks got it is subject to dispute. No matter. Nearly all proposed roots carry libidinous connotations. One second-century source suggests the word is a derivation of the verb *kleitoriazein*, meaning to titillate lasciviously, to seek pleasure. Some etymologists have proposed that *clitoris* stems from the Greek word for key, as in the key to female sexuality, while others link it to the root that means "to be inclined" and that also gave rise to the word *proclivity*. (In non-European languages, the word for clitoris may refer to its appearance rather than its function. For example, in Chinese, the ideogram combines *yin*, for female, and *tee*, for stem, as the stem of an eggplant resembles a clitoris.)

"Authorities in French, German and English during Freud's time, and stretching back to the early seventeenth century, were unanimous in holding that female sexual pleasure originated in the structures of the vulva generally and in the clitoris specifically," Thomas Laqueur says. "No alternative sites were proposed." In tones that united prurience and primness, early anatomists referred to the clitoris as an "obscene organ of brute pleasure" or "an instrument of venery." In 1612, Jacques Duval wrote of the clitoris: "In French it is called temptation, the spur to sensual pleasure, the female rod and the scorner of men; and women who will admit their lewdness call it their *gaude mihi* [great joy]." Duval did not explain why he construed of the female rod as a "scorner of men." Was it because he thought a woman's capacity to feel sensual pleasure was threatening to the larger social and sexual order? Or was he saying what we gals want to hear: that he, and presumably other men, are jealous of the *gaude mihi's* monomania? "All our late discoveries in anatomy," Geoffrey de Mandeville concluded in 1724, "can find no other use for the clitoris but to whet the female desire by its frequent erections."

With the exception of the great eighteenth-century taxonomist Carolus Linnaeus, who inexplicably argued that human females alone had a clitoris, most of the early anatomists and naturalists correctly recognized that other female mammals also possess the venerable instrument. How venerable a particular example might be judged was subject to delicious embellishment. The Dutch naturalist Johann Blumenbach wrote that the clitoris of a beached baleen whale he examined in 1791 measured fifty-two feet long — quite an accomplishment when you consider that the total body length of an adult baleen whale averages only forty to fifty feet.

Blumenbach's appraisal skills may be open to question, but of the superior clitoral dimensions found on a number of nonhuman primates there is no doubt. Queen among the clitoral nobility is the bonobo, sometimes called the pygmy chimpanzee. The bonobo is a close cousin of the common chimpanzee, and the two species together are our closest living relatives. The bonobo is a sexual Olympian. Males, females, old, callow, no matter — it's sex, grope, hump, genito-genital rub-a-dub-dubbing, all the day long. Most of this sex has nothing to do with reproduction. It serves as the code of ethics by which bonobos survive group living. It is their therapy, their social lubricant and postquarrel salve, a way of expressing feelings, and it is often quick to the point of perfunctory. In a species in which sexuality is so important, and in which females engage in frequent homosexual as well as hetero-sexual and pangenerational trysts, it is no surprise that the clitoris assumes considerable stature. As a young adolescent, a female bonobo is maybe half the weight of a human teenager, but her clitoris is three times bigger than the human equivalent, and visible enough to waggle unmistakably as she walks. Only later, when the bonobo matures and her entire labial area swells, does it become difficult to descry the organ. But the clitoris is still there, and is drafted into service by its owner several times an hour.

Female spider monkeys and lemurs also have exceptionally large clitorises. The spotted hyena of Africa has a clitoris so large that it looks exactly like the male hyena's penis. The organ is nothing like the typical mammalian clitoris but is a vagina and clitoris in one elongated pack-age. A female hyena has intercourse through this phallic projection. She gives birth through her clitoris, and if that thought makes you want to wince, go ahead and wince, because she sure does. Unlike the bonobo, the spotted hyena does not use her prodigious clitoris for quotidian sensuality, her interest in sex being confined to periods of estrus. Instead, the organ appears to be enlarged incidentally, as a result of the female's having been exposed prenatally to large concentrations of testosterone, which masculinizes the external genitals. (The hormo-nal status of the spotted hyena is of interest to us for reasons apart from genital anatomy, as I discuss at length in the chapter on female aggression.)

The bizarre clitorivagina works well enough for the hyena, which is one of the most abundant of the big carnivores in Africa, but it is not appealing enough for evolution to have tried it more than once. As a rule, the clitoris of a female mammal is a thing apart, with no through traffic in either direction. And for many species, the clitoris probably works — that is, has orgasmic capacity. I say "probably" because while you may think it's easy to know if an animal has climaxed or not, solid proof is hard to come by. Researchers have watched primates copulate and have seen the female forming the same enraptured O with her mouth, the same shark-style lifting of the eyes toward the back of the head, that the male displays while he ejaculates. But does the female experience the spasming and muscle contractions that we of the sexual cognoscenti consider a requisite sign of orgasm? Scientists have gone the experimental distance for only a handful of species, inserting a transmitter into the vagina and then measuring uterine activity while the female engages in a few romps (of a homosexual nature, so as not to disturb the equipment). For every monkey tested, the needle of the EEG did its little jig, indicating neuromuscular vibrato, at just the moment when the monkeys were telling the story of O.

Early anatomists and other interested parties may have appreciated the significance of the clitoris, but that doesn't mean the organ has been the subject of exhaustive research, then or now. Nancy Friday has complained about the silence in which the clitoris is cloaked and the fact that girls aren't taught the details of their sexual anatomy in the same way that boys are, which results, she says, in girls' being subjected to a "mental clitoridectomy." Matriphobe that she is, Friday blames mothers and their thin-lipped repressive ways for performing the psychosurgery, but the scientific and medical literature is hardly more garrulous on the subject of the clitoris. A search of Medline, the world's largest medical computer database, pulled up only sixty or so references to *clitoris* over a five-year span (compared to thirty times that number for the term *penis*). Only two academic volumes are devoted to the clitoris, one called *The Clitoris,* the other *The Classic Clitoris,* and both are decades old. Even gynecology textbooks give the clitoris short shrift, a mere page or two. Some of the professional disregard may be attributed to the fact that medicine focuses on illness and the clitoris, thankfully, is not a common site of disease. But at least in this country, the inattentiveness also reflects ordinary prudishness and the difficulty of winning a federal grant to study the morphology of small Greek keys. The clitoris obviously needs more Italian researchers.

In one aspect only has the clitoris piqued contemporary scientific interest, and that is the question of whether we are supposed to have it in the first place. Maybe you've pondered along these lines yourself. Maybe you've idly rolled the old sexual chestnuts around in your mind and wondered why it is that women are the ones with the organ dedicated exclusively to sexual pleasure, when men are the ones who are supposed to be dedicated exclusively to sexual pleasure. Men are portrayed as wanting to go at it all the time, women as preferring a good cuddle; yet a man feels preposterously peacockish if he climaxes three or four times in a night, compared to the fifty or hundred orgasms that a sexually athletic woman can have in an hour or two. Maybe you thought it was some sort of cosmic joke, in the same category of sexual dissonance as the fact that a man is at his libidinous peak before he is quite a man, by age eighteen or twenty, while a woman doesn't reach full flower until her thirties or even forties (about the time, a female comedian once put it, that her husband is discovering he has a favorite chair). Or maybe you've thought the clitoris is a kind of accident, barely there, more Ariel than anatomical. The clitoris is small, after all, and hardly distinct from the surrounding folds and crevasses of the vulva. For women who are anorgasmic, who cannot climax no matter how they thrash and struggle, the clitoris may seem the most overhyped and misleading knob of flesh this side of Pinocchio's nose. Sure, it works for some, but for others it is notoriously undependable. Marilyn Monroe, the most elaborated sexual icon of the twentieth century and surely the source of autoeruptive glee for thousands of fans, confessed to a friend that despite her three husbands and a parade of lovers, she had never had an orgasm. Could even Immanuel Kant, said to have died a virgin, be considered such a sorry sexual naif?

As it happens, evolutionary thinkers are engaged in a vigorous debate over the point, or pointlessness, of the clitoris and its bosom buddy, the female orgasm. They are asking whether the capacity for orgasm does a woman any good and thus can be counted an adaptation that has been selected over the wash of time, or whether it is, to borrow a phrase from Stephen Jay Gould, a glorious accident. The debate is good clean dirty cortical fun, so much more amusing than being abjured, as we were in the 1970s, to get a mirror and inspect our genitals for ourselves. It gives the clitoris a jaunty new consequence; a brush with Darwinism can do that. But it is also an unnerving debate. Some researchers have argued, in print, that the female climax may be so unnecessary as to be on its way out. One unlucky lurch of the evolutionary wheel, and those fibers may fire no more. But let's not get ahead of the game. Let us take a look at the clitoral balance sheet with a dispassionate eye and consider the theories behind its provenance. You can then decide independently whether you can relax in confidence of the organ's enduring purpose or whether it's time to break out the offerings to the goddess Klitoris and her earthly ecclesiastic, Bonobo-à-go-go.

There are three basic verities to bear in mind about the clitoris and female climax. First, let's admit it up front: the female orgasm is dispensable. A male ordinarily must reach orgasm if he is to reproduce, whereas a female can conceive perfectly well without feeling a thing, and even, in the case of rape, while feeling fear and revulsion. Second, the female orgasm is capricious, its reliability and frequency varying greatly from woman to woman. Third, there's the matter of genital homology — the fact that clitoris and penis develop from the same genital ridge of the fetus.

We are not done with bundles of three. The physiological verities in turn suggest three possible evolutionary categories into which our star organ might fit, three overarching explanations for why the clitoris is there and does what it does (or sometimes fails to do). And though I hate being anthropocentric, the scenarios below apply specifically to women rather than to mammalian clitorises generally. To wit:

1. *The clitoris is a vestigial penis.* A girl has one because the body is inherently bisexual, poised as a fetus to grow either male or female sex organs. In the event she had been designated a male, she would have needed a functioning, ejaculating, innervated penis. Instead she received a penile remnant, a small nubbin of sensory tissue with the same underlying neuronal architecture as that found in a genuine phallus. The clitoris, then, is like nipples on a man, an atavism, the faint signature of what might have been but no longer really needs to be.

By this scenario, the clitoris and female climax do not rank as adaptations. The ejaculatory penis, a.k.a. the DNA delivery van, is the adaptation, the point of it all, while the clitoris is the booby prize.

Which doesn't mean that we can't make the best of happenstance. Stephen Jay Gould, one of the more prominent proponents of the vestigial penis theory, considers the female climax to be a prime example of a spandrel in Saint Mark's Cathedral, his famous metaphor for a body part or trait that looks like an adaptation but is really the byproduct of something else. When you first see the lavishly ornamented spandrels in the Venetian basilica, you might think that they have an independent purpose, that the master builder said, I want spandrels there, there, and there. But it turns out that you can't build an arch or a dome without incidentally making a triangular bit of wall — the spandrel. The spandrel is not the goal; it's a means to the goal, the goal being the construction of an arch. Yet once the spandrel is in place, you can go ahead and gild it. Make it gorgeous. Enjoy sex all you want, or can. And if it sometimes seems that it's rough work scaling the peaks of ecstasy, hey, it could be worse. Have you ever seen a lactating man?

2. *The clitoris is a vestigial clitoris.* The previous scenario posits that the clitoris is not now and has never been an adaptation; it's a residual penis. Another argument has it that the clitoris may not be of obvious utility today, but that in the past it was an adaptation — it shone with the light of a whole damned byzantine dome. In this parable, our ancestral sisters behaved rather as the bonobo does, using sex as the universal key — to curry friendships, to placate tempers, to solicit meat or favor from any number of partners, and to disguise issues of paternity. The clitoris gave females incentive to experiment, to shop around, to play the erotic entrepreneur. Such a notion could explain why women are slow to burn: their sexuality is geared toward serial encounters with multiple hair-trigger males. Well, that one didn't quite do it; I'd better go out, cruise the brush, and finish what I started.

Sarah Blaffer Hrdy, one of my favorite evolutionary biologists, is an adherent of the once-upon-a-time theory. In her view, the organ's fitful behavior, its demand for sustained and perhaps collective attention to perform at its optimum, is evidence of its transitional status from adaptive to nonadaptive. If female climax were a core feature of monogamy and pair bonding, the old saw has it, if it were designed to encourage intimacy between loving partners, then the human clitoris would be far more efficient than it is, Hrdy has said. It would be readily responsive to the motions of copulation alone, and it would rest easy once the man was through. Instead, only a minority of women are capable of orgasm strictly from wham-bam intercourse; most need a bit of prior groundwork. And then there's the asymmetry between a man's ejaculatory limits and a woman's trick birthday candle, the one that keeps popping back no matter how hard you blow. All of which suggests that women once were promiscuous, appetitive, roving diplomats, as many female primates are. They caroused with as many consorts as was practical, and took on the risks that come with multiple matings to quench what Hrdy sees as the far more dire and pervasive threat of infanticide — the tendency of males to kill babies they think are not their own. Well might our ancestresses have shuffled their Latin and cried, Vidi, veni, vici!

In today's world it is hardly adaptive for a woman to flit about like a Barbary macaque, and in some cultures such wanton behavior is punishable by death. As a result, the clitoris may no longer be considered a woman's best appendage. Indeed, Hrdy and others propose that because its personal and reproductive benefits no longer apply, the organ has been shrinking slowly over the millennia, retreating ever further behind Venusian blinds. If such trends continue . . . well, I'm not going to spell it out. I'm just going to stand here and scream.

3. *The clitoris is the music of Johann Sebastian Bach.* I have listened to the music of Bach and thought, Without this there would be nothing. I have listened and thought, It was inevitable. Evolution has no goal, with the possible exception of giving the world the Second and Fifth Brandenburg Concertos, the Goldberg Variations, and the Well-Tempered Clavier. The dinosaurs died so that Bach may live.

In other words, the clitoris is an adaptation. It is essential, or at least strongly recommended. It is also versatile, generous, demanding, profound, easy, and enduring. It is a chameleon, capable of changing its meaning to suit prevailing circumstances. Like Bach's music, it can always be reinterpreted and updated. So perhaps we should start exploring this thesis with a simple question: would the planet now hold six billion people if women did not seek sex? And can you expect them to play a fugue if their organ has no pipes?

Proponents of the idea that the clitoris has merit and motive — that it is an adaptation and has been selected — start by turning certain assumptions on their head. We said earlier that, generally speaking, a man must reach orgasm if he is to reproduce, so it seems clear that male orgasm is a product of evolution's hand. But Meredith Small, a primatologist who can always be depended on to question biology's bromides, has pointed out that male orgasm is not really necessary for insemination. The penis begins releasing viable sperm well before it ejaculates, and those gun-jumpers can thrash their way toward an egg just fine, which is why coitus interruptus is such a poor form of birth control.

Moreover, who is to say that the experience of orgasm was a prerequisite when the details of male physiology were being selected? As the archaeologist Timothy Taylor has noted, a male theoretically could inseminate a female through a system like urination, a kind of hypodermic injection, no ecstasy required. Chances are that male insects, with their relatively simple nervous systems, operate in just such a no-nonsense manner, releasing a spermatic package as anhedonically as a female later dispenses eggs. If the orgasmic experience evolved in "higher" males for reasons other than mechanical necessity, if we decouple the logic behind male pleasure from the details of gamete conveyance, then we lose a big part of the argument that the female climax is an atavistic echo of something indispensible to men. All pleasure, by this rendering, becomes hypothetically optional. Yet pleasure does not appear to be beside the point. Indeed, nearly all of us are born with the capacity to seize or be seized by it. And nothing defines an adaptation so well as universality.

If we agree that the clitoris and female climax are adaptive, then we can delve into the particulars of their performance. Let us assume that the clitoris exists to give us pleasure, and that pleasure provides the spur to seek sex — that without the promise of great reward we'd be content to stay home and catch up on our flossing. Then we must revisit the matter of disappointment, the frequency with which the clitoris fails us. Why do we have to work much harder for our finale than men do? The clitoris is an idiot savant: it can be so brilliant, and so stupid. Or is it a Cassandra, telling us something that we ignore to our grief?

In my view, all the intricacies we've been mulling — the apparent fickleness and mulishness of the clitoris, its asynchronicity with male responsiveness, and the variability of its performance from one woman to the next — can be explained by making a simple assumption: that the clitoris is designed to encourage its bearer to take control of her sexuality. Yes, this idea sounds like a rank political tract, and body tissue has no party affiliation. But it can vote with its behavior, working best when you treat it right, faltering when it's abused or misunderstood. In truth, the clitoris operates at peak performance when a woman feels athunder with life and strength, when she is bellowing on top, figuratively if not literally. The clitoris hates being scared or bullied. Some women who have been raped report that their vaginas became lubricated even as they feared for their lives — and a good thing too, for the lubrication prevented them from being ripped apart — but women almost never have orgasms during a rape, male fantasies notwithstanding. The clitoris will not be hurried or pushed. A woman who worries that she is taking too long for her partner will take that much longer. A woman who stops watching the pot sends a message to the clitoris — I'm here! — and within moments the pot boils over.

The clitoris loves power, and it strives to reinforce the sensation of playing commando. The anthropologist Helen Fisher has found that women who are easily and multiply orgasmic have one trait in common: they take responsibility for their pleasure. They don't depend on the skillfulness or mind-reading abilities of their lovers to get what they want. They know which positions and angles work best for them, and they negotiate said postures verbally or kinesthetically. Moreover, the positions that offer many women the greatest satisfaction are those that give them some control over the sexual choreography: on top, for example, or side by side. A movie that shows a woman reaching frenzied crescendo while being hoisted up and slammed against a wall in classic *Last Tango in Paris* fashion is not a movie directed by a woman.

In addition, most women get better with time and experience. The 1950s Kinsey report on sexuality found that 36 percent of women in their twenties were anorgasmic, while for those in their thirties or older the number dropped to 15 percent. Several studies done since then have found a greater capacity for orgasm among all women, yet still the older women as a group remain more orgasmic than their younger counterparts. Of course, part of the explanation could be that the older women are having sex with older men, who are defter and less precipitous than young men and who have enough self-control to sustain a session for as long as it takes their partners to climax. However, older lesbians are more easily roused to orgasm than young lesbians, suggesting that we are not talking about the deficiencies of callow Quick-Draw McGraws. Instead, the power of knowing yourself, a power cultivated over the years, translates into greater collaboration from below.

The clitoris not only applauds when a woman flaunts her mastery; it will give a standing ovation. In the multiple orgasm, we see the finest evidence that our lady Klitoris helps those who help themselves. It may take many minutes to reach the first summit, but once there the lusty mountaineer finds wings awaiting her. She does not need to scramble back to the ground before scaling the next peak, but can glide like a raptor on currents of joy.

The intimate connection between a woman's psychic humor and her clitoral power means that the clitoris must be wired up to the brain — the big brain — before it can sing. The brain must learn to ride its little rod the way it must learn to balance its body on a bicycle. And once learned, the skill will not be forgotten. Some women learn how to climax in childhood, while others do not make the connection until adulthood. It is not an engineering problem, though. You can't figure it out with the neocortex alone, the new brain, that thickly ruffled top layer of fish-gray tissue that cogitates, hesitates, and second-guesses every impulse. Instead you must tap into a more ancient neural locus, the hypothalamus, which sits on the floor of your brain a few inches behind your eyeballs and reigns over appetite: for food, salt, power, sex. Sometimes wiring the clitoris to the hypothalamus demands a rerouting, a circumvention of the neocortex. The neocortex is clever and imperious, and it can be too controlling to grant its owner honest control. The control I'm speaking of is a whole-brain operation, a delicate negotiation between neo and primal, intellect and desire. And so if a woman's neocortex is stentorian, it must be muffled just long enough for the hypothalamus and the clitoris to seal their partnership. Alcohol might accomplish the task, if it weren't such a global depressant of the nervous system. More effective are drugs that distract the intellect without dampening the body's network of impulse relays. Most of these drugs are illegal. Quaaludes were said to be extraordinary aphrodisiacs, but Quaaludes no longer exist. They were too good, which meant too dangerous, and so had to be eliminated. But marijuana is still with us, and marijuana can be a sexual mentor and a sublime electrician, bringing the lights of Broadway to women who have spent years in frigid darkness. All the women in my immediate family learned how to climax by smoking grass — my mother when she was over thirty and already the mother of four. Yet I have never seen anorgasmia on the list of indications for the medical use of marijuana. Instead we are told that some women don't need to have orgasms to have a satisfying sex life, an argument as convincing as the insistence that some homeless people like living outdoors.

We should not be surprised that the clitoris loves power, or that its nature is complex. For women, sex has always been risky. We can become pregnant, we can contract disease, we can forfeit our lucky lactose. At the same time, we are primates. We use sex for many reasons beyond reproduction. We may not be bonobos, but neither are we seasonally breeding sheep. In the face of vulnerability, we need effective defenses. The clitoris is our magic cape. It tells us that joy is a serious business and that we must not take our light, our sexual brilliance, lightly. The clitoris integrates information from diverse sources, conscious and unconscious, from the cerebral cortex, the hypothalamus, the peripheral nervous system, and it responds accordingly. If you are frightened, it becomes numb. If you are uninterested or disgusted, it remains mute. If you are thrilled and strong, it is a taut little baton, leading the way, cajoling here, quickening there, andante, allegro, crescendo, refrain.

Some experts have argued that natural selection has given women a lower sex drive than men, and that such inhibition makes sense: we shouldn't be out there screwing around and taking the chance of being impregnated by a genetic second-rater. The theory is rank nonsense. Sex is too important on too many social and emotional counts for us to be indifferent about it. Women display abundant evidence of a robust sex drive. They respond physiologically to sexual stimuli as rapidly as men do. Show a woman a pornographic film, and her vagina swells with blood as rapidly as the penis of a male observer does. Yet there is no doubt that a woman's sex drive is an involved instrument. It is tied to mentation, mood, past experience, the Furies. At the eye of the storm is the clitoris. It knows more than the vagina does, and is a more reliable counselor than the vagina — remember that a woman may lubricate during rape, but she will almost never climax. Surely it is more logical for a female to have a sophisticated sex drive than to have either a simple-minded or a stifled drive. If a woman retains control over her sexuality, if she feels powerful in her sexual decisions and has sex with whom she wants when she wants to, her odds of a reasonable outcome are good. She is likely to have sex with men she finds attractive, men with whom she feels comfortable for any number of reasons, and thus to further her personal, political, and genetic designs.

The clitoris is flexible. It can adapt to different habitats, different cultural norms. Among our ancestors, who adhered to the comparatively promiscuous schedule that is the primate norm, the clitoris might well have fostered restless experimentation, as Hrdy said. Yet unlike Hrdy, I believe that the clitoris can accommodate the contemporary strictures of monogamy as well — that it will nourish the bonds of love and marriage when such bonds are useful to a woman's interests. In this country, which exalts marriage to extravagant heights, married women are quite orgasmic. According to the University of Chicago's 1994 *Sex in America* survey, three quarters of wedded women say they always or usually reach climax during sex, compared to fewer than two thirds of single women. Of all the subgroups queried, married, conservative Christian women were the likeliest to say that they came every single time they copulated. And why not? For our God-fearing sisters, marriage is a sacrament, which means that every bounce on the matrimonial mattress is a holy and ennobling event. Right makes might, and with power comes the glory, and so it is that foes of the sexual revolution can emerge as orgasmic empresses.

There is another body of evidence suggesting that the clitoris trades in the currency of power. Recent work from the British researchers Robin Baker and Mark A. Bellis suggests that orgasm offers women a recondite way to control male sperm, either by imbibing it or by repelling it. They propose that the timing of a woman's orgasm relative to a man's ejaculation influences whether or not his semen has a shot at fertilizing her eggs. If a woman climaxes shortly after her partner ejaculates, her cervix, the gateway to the uterus, will do a spectacular thing. As it pulses rhythmically, the cervix reaches down like a fish's mouth and sucks in the semen deposited at its doorstep. This has been shown on video. A microcamera was attached to a man's penis and the deep events of intercourse were recorded: the milky ejaculate streaming forth like woozy pennants, followed by the cervix dipping into the proferred gene pool and with viscous, fluttering motions appearing to paddle the semen up into the uterus. Now whether the cervical palpitations truly enhance the chance that the semen will reach an egg is not known. Baker and Bellis have preliminary evidence suggesting that when a woman climaxes anywhere from several seconds to forty minutes after her partner, her chances of being impregnated are slightly higher than if she doesn't climax or if the orgasm occurs before or after this rather widely gaping window of opportunity.

The scientists' data are open to quarrel, but their general argument is compelling — that female orgasm is the ultimate expression of female choice. If a woman's sexual responsiveness is tied to her sense of power, of having freely chosen this partner at this moment, then her cervix might very well go the next step, taking up what the woman demonstrates through her rapture is the chosen seed. Baker and Bellis promote the concept of sperm competition: that just as males compete with one another by locking horns or swords, so their sperm compete in the vaginal tract for access to the egg. Female orgasm is thus a woman's way of controlling the terms of the underground debate. Small wonder, they say, that men often are obsessed with their sexual prowess, their ability to turn women on — and that even when a man cares very little for his partner's emotional well-being, he nonetheless wants to satisfy her sexually. The fate of his sperm, it seems, may depend on his erotic skills. Hypothetically, natural selection has favored those males who abide by the axiom "We aim to please."

By the flip token, small wonder that many women say they have faked an orgasm at one time or another. How better to persuade a disappointing partner to get it over with and *go away* than to pretend to give him what he's been waiting for — proof that your cervix is at his service?

The Baker and Bellis scenario makes the assumption that our ancestors in whom various traits and drives took root were highly polygamous, and that the semen of any given male was likely to brush up against the output of other pretenders to paternity. But even now, they claim, the sperm wars continue beneath our mantle of monogamy. Married women have affairs (no!), and when they do, Baker and Bellis say, their chances of conceiving an "illegitimate" child turn out to be higher than might be expected from a simple accounting of ratio of sex acts with spouse to sex acts with lover. The scientists attribute the excessive extramarital fecundity to the comparatively greater orgasmic pleasure that a woman has with her lover (why else would she bother with adultery, if she weren't having a good time of it?). Again, some of the data with which the scientists buttress their arguments — including paternity statistics gathered in Liverpool, an international seaport that may or may not be representative of communities everywhere — are open to dispute. Nevertheless, it is amusing that the new information at least partly supports an ancient belief, first promulgated by Galen in the second century A.D. and prevailing for the next twelve hundred years or so, that a woman must reach orgasm if she is to conceive. That absolute stricture is false, of course, but if female orgasm subtly enhances fecundity, there are practical implications to consider. For example, a couple struggling to conceive should not become so grimly task-oriented that the woman's climax is neglected as a discretionary frill. No, better to be sure that there's enough grim pleasure around for two.

Throughout this chapter, I've been using the terms *clitoris* and *female orgasm* and *female sexuality* almost interchangeably, and in my view they are all rightly joined at the hip. The clitoris is at the core of female sexuality, and we must reject any attempts, Freudian or otherwise, to downgrade it. Yet the clitoris overspills its anatomical borders and transcends its anatomy. Other pathways feed into it and are fed by it. The 15,000 pudendal nerve fibers that service the entire pelvis interact with the nerve bundles of the clitoris. That's why the anus is an erogenous zone. Nerves are like wolves or birds: if one starts crying, there goes the neighborhood. In some women, the skin around the urinary opening is exceptionally sensitive, and because this periurethral tissue is pushed and pulled quite vigorously during coitus, such hypersensitivity could result in a comparatively easy stroll to orgasm through the thrustings of intercourse alone. Other women say they can climax best with the application of pressure deep within the vagina, which led the gynecologist Ernst Grafenberg and his partisans to propose the existence of a Grafenberg, or G, spot, a sort of second, internalized clitoris. The G spot is said to be a two-inch cushion of highly erogenous tissue located on the front wall of the vagina, right where the vagina wraps around the urethra, the tube that carries urine from the bladder. Some have said that the G spot is embedded in the so-called Skene's glands, which generate mucus to help lubricate the urethral tract. Others have said that the gee-whiz spot is actually the sphincter muscle, which keeps the urethra clamped shut until you're read to void. Still others question the existence of a discrete G spot altogether. Let's not bother inventing novel erogenous loci, they say, when the existing infrastructure will do.

The roots of the clitoris run deep, after all, and very likely can be tickled through posterior agitation. In other words, the G spot may be nothing more than the back end of the clitoris.

Anatomy is not epiphany. When scientists have tried to quantify the discrete components of orgasm, they've had very little luck. In one study, for example, researchers at the University of Sheffield recruited twenty-eight adult women to measure the duration, intensity, and vaginal blood flow associated with climax. A small heated oxygen electrode was inserted into each woman's vagina and held in place on the vaginal wall by suction. The woman was then asked to masturbate to orgasm, to indicate when the orgasm began and when it ended, and to grade its intensity on a scale from one (pitiful) to five (transcendent). Throughout the session, the electrode gauged vaginal blood flow, indicating how congested the vaginal tissues became. The average orgasm, as indicated by the woman's signing of "start" and "all done," turned out to be surprisingly prolonged, lasting an average of twenty seconds — much longer than the twelve seconds, on average, the women guessed in retrospect. Yet there was no correlation between length and strength; the intensity rating a woman assigned to her orgasm had nothing to do with how long it lasted. Neither did relative blood flow correlate with perceived pleasure.

The clitoris is complex. It is never just a clitoris. Like blood flow, its proportions probably bear no relation to its potential. Yes, a female bonobo has an immense clitoris, but her endowment might have more to do with assuring a petitioner easy access than with signifying in any way that she is more orgasmic than her human counterparts. Nobody has studied whether women with large clitorises are hyperorgasmic. But another sort of "experiment" has been done that is relevant to the question of whether function follows form. Children with unusually large clitorises have had their protrusions surgically reduced — whittled back, towed in, or amputated altogether. They have been clitoridectomized. This is not an operation that we normally associate with high-minded Western medicine, but clitoridectomies are fairly common. In this country, about two thousand babies a year undergo some form of "adjustment" to reconfigure a clitoris deemed abnormally prominent. There are no official guidelines for what constitutes "clitorimegaly," but anything projecting beyond the mollifying lips of the vulva is a candidate for a clitoridectomy. When a baby is born with equivocal genitals, surgery was, and is, the norm. We may tolerate sexual ambiguity in rock stars, but not in infants. Susan, the girl whose diaper my mother changed, very likely ended up in the hands of a pediatric plastic surgeon early in her childhood, never again to embarrass a peeping mom. Sometimes the young patient will undergo other surgery as well, to open up a fused vagina, repair a defective urethra, or remove imperfectly formed gonadal tissue. Though some of the surgery may be necessary for the child's health, in the case of clitoral reduction we're talking aesthetics. A big clitoris doesn't hurt anybody, certainly not the baby. But it looks funny, boyish, obscene, and parents are advised to fix it while the child is young enough to escape any putative psychological trauma that might accompany uncertainty about her sex. And so we may ask, what happens to girls whose clitorises are surgically micrometized or cauterized? Do they lose sexual sensation? Can a woman have an orgasm if she doesn't have a clitoris?

The clitoris is complex. Pandora's box is a hope chest and a box of rain, and results from the ongoing, ad hoc exploration of clitoral aptitude, brought about by the insistence on surgery for clitorimegaly, are mixed. Consider the following two cases.

Cheryl Chase is a computer analyst in her early forties. She wears wire-frame glasses, keeps her hair short, and often puts on dangling earrings and bright mulberry lipstick. She is quietly attractive and ferociously bright, fluent in Japanese. She is also angry. She thinks she will die angry. Cheryl has two X chromosomes, the conventional female complement, and today she looks very much the woman. But for unknown reasons she was born with hermaphroditic gonads that were part ovary and part testes, and a clitoris so big that at first the doctors told her parents, It's a boy. A year or so later, doctors at another hospital realized, Wait a minute, this child has a normal vagina, uterus, and fallopian tubes: it's a girl. They told her parents, The other doctors were wrong. You have a daughter, not a son. You'll have to rename her, move to a new town, and start over again. But first give us permission to fix her genitals. Immediately. Permission granted. "They removed my clitoris on the spot," Cheryl says, with the soft voice of somebody who's talking through clenched teeth. "They cut at the division of the crura, where the nerves enter the clitoral shaft. I have a small amount of crural tissue around the pelvic opening, but no innervation. Therefore, no feeling." A lesbian, she is sexually active, but she has never had an orgasm. She has tried everything. She has written to doctors and begged for their help, to find whatever nerve fibers might remain in her residual tissue to be rallied, resurrected. Most have ignored her pleas. Do I look like some sort of surgical Dr. Ruth? they say. She consulted surgeons who perform transsexual operations, changing males into females or females into males, and who attempt to preserve sexual responsiveness in the transformation. They told her, Forget it, they took away every-thing we would use. "I would have preferred to grow up in a place with no medicine," Cheryl says, "rather than to have had happen to me what did happen."

Martha Coventry is an editor and writer in her mid-forties and the mother of two children. She is thin, lanky, and has a cap of dark, springy curls. Martha is the sort of person you like having around because she makes you feel likable. Martha also was born with a beefy clitoris, the result of her mother's taking high doses of progesterone during preg-nancy to prevent miscarriage. As an infant, her clitoris measured 1.5 centimeters, three times the average. Not an emergency case of megaly, but her parents decided that she shouldn't attend school with such a conspicuous knob and risk the verbal savagery of her peers. And so, at the age of six, she was shorn. "They snipped it off at the base," said Martha. "If you saw me now, you'd know something was missing." If the body is gone, the spirit yet lives. "I have emotional scars, but I'm not bitter," said Martha. "The reason is simple. I still have clitoral sensation. I'm orgasmic."

Cheryl and Martha are activists seeking to prevent the subjection of other babies born with intersexed genitals to cosmetic surgery, as they were. They and their fellow agitators have lobbied Congress to pass a law prohibiting clitoridectomies on patients too young to consent to the procedure — or to cry, You want to do what, where?! Such legislation has yet to be passed, but Cheryl Chase and her peers gradually are persuading pediatricians that Hippocrates' familiar advice, First, do no harm, applies to them and theirs, for nobody knows how a given clitoris will respond when you start whacking away at it. Even a big clitoris on an infant is a small target, and with all the nerves and blood vessels bundled up in it, it is easily harmed. There are no long-term follow-up studies of children who have been clitoridectomized, to see how they fare sexually. All we have are anecdotes. Martha and Cheryl each had her clitoris cut off at the base, yet one sings and the other doesn't. Nobody knows why. Some surgeons claim that their clitoral reduction techniques now are far superior to the crude hacksmanship of the past, but they have no proof. Nor do they have proof that life with a large clitoris presents an insuperable psychospiritual challenge to either a child or her parents.

What is it about the clitoris, our orchid style, our semi-clandestine Corinthian column, that makes it so vulnerable to the hatchet? Like an artist, the clitoris has won its greatest fame only upon its death — its murder. The intersexual activists in this country truss their grievances by equating their stories with the far more publicized custom of ritual genital amputation practiced in Africa. The unarguably vile practice goes by various names, including female genital mutilation, or FGM; African genital cutting; and female circumcision — although as many have pointed out, it is more akin to penile amputation than to male circumcision and should not be given the courtesy of comparison. The tradition dates back at least two thousand years, and it has never been much of a secret, but the general impression until recently was (a) that it was fairly uncommon, confined mostly to small remote villages, and (b) that it was on its way out. Neither has proved to be true. At least one hundred million women living in twenty-eight countries have had their genitals cut, and two million girls are added to the ranks of the lacerated each year. In some countries, including Ethiopia, Somalia, Djibouti, Sierra Leone, Sudan, and Egypt, the prevalence rate approaches 100 percent. Some girls and young women have fled their native homes, vulva intact, and sought asylum abroad, but putatively enlightened nations such as the United States have been slow to sympathize, or to acknowledge that the threat of genital carnage counts as persecution. Now we in America have a self-congratulatory bill banning African genital cutting in this country, though the bill doesn't prevent the medically approved cutting of any clitorimegalic Susans who may be born; nor does it come with the necessary teeth of economic sanctions against nations where girls are sheared en masse.

In learning about genital vandalism, we have heard about the gradations of the procedure. The "mildest" form is a straightforward clitoridectomy that removes part or all of the organ. Intermediate dismemberment eliminates the inner labia along with the clitoris. Infibulation, the grisliest horror show of all, chops away clitoris and inner labia, and then incises the outer labia to create raw surfaces that can be stitched together to cover the urethra and vagina, leaving just enough of an opening for the passage of urine and menstrual blood. Eventually, when the infibulated girl marries and must accommodate her husband's penis, the stitches are removed and the scarred skin of the outer labia is pushed apart.

However limited or extensive the cutting, it is done without anesthesia, under unsterile conditions, and the tool used is whatever crude blade the local low priestess of mutilation — it is often a woman — has deemed the most appropriate instrument for the ritual. It is usually performed on a young girl of seven or eight, who may anticipate the ceremony with a certain excitement, thinking at last she will be counted a woman, but who ends up screaming in pain and must be held down by several adult women as she flails to escape, unless she is fortunate enough to pass out from the shock and pain and loss of blood. Sometimes the girl hemorrhages to death immediately, or dies soon afterward of sepsis, tetanus, or gangrene. If she survives, she may suffer chronic pelvic pain from wounds that do not heal, or infections from urine and blood that cannot flow cleanly. Cysts often form along the line of the scar, some growing as big as grapefruits and making the woman feel ashamed, fearful that her genitals are returning in monstrous form or that she is dying of cancer. When an infibulated woman gives birth, she is like a poor, mewling hyena on first parturition, her infant having no choice but to tear its way to the light.

According to its proponents, genital cutting serves several purposes. It supposedly tames a woman, abridging her innate wantonness and discouraging her from any thoughts of cuckoldry. Less familiar to westerners is the cosmetic objective of the pruning, the desire to accentuate the visual discrepancy between female and male. Eliminating the clitoris, the woman's penis-equivalent, is a start; losing the labia, which can resemble a scrotum, takes the polarity to an extreme. No protrusion, no pouches, no confusion. As photographs of infibulated women show, the operation can produce a smooth pelvic profile that is superfeminine by some infantile mental module of femininity. In fact, it looks like it belongs on everybody's favorite feminine fetish, the smooth-groined doll named Barbie.

Many have written of genital mutilation, and many have denounced it. Even those who are sensitive to cultural traditions see genital cutting as a tradition worth destroying. I feel enfeebled here, unable to add a constructive word or insight, depressed by the persistence of a repulsive "rite," and made small, as we all are, by capitulation through inertia. Genital cutting is an extreme abuse of human rights. Like slavery and apartheid, it is unacceptable. How can we stop it? By talking about it with angry, unbitten tongues. By never forgetting about it, and by not letting the issue slide back into obscurity now that we have learned of its pervasiveness and tenacity. Some recommend that efforts to end the practice respect the underlying belief systems of those who cut and have been cut. The nonprofit organization Population Council has argued that it is no good barking about a woman's right to sexual integrity to an audience that values sexual modesty. Instead, the council recommends we should emphasize the risks of genital cutting to a woman's most cherished asset: her fertility. Fine. Let's be sensitive, not self-righteous. Emphasize reproductive health over a carnal entitlement program, responsibility over narcissism. Say what you will — just put down that knife.

I'm all for pragmatism, but the clitoris is idealistic, utopian, and in the end it's hard to kill a good fantasy. Which may offer us a paradoxical argument against cutting a girl's genitals: the operation doesn't always work. Destroying the clitoris in body may or may not destroy it in spirit. Like Martha Coventry, some African women who have been clitoridectomized, even infibulated, describe themselves as erotic beings who enjoy sex and experience orgasm — very fierce orgasms, they add. Their phantom clitorises, it seems, are like the ghost of Hamlet's father: persistent, present, incorrigible. These women may have been subjected to grave medical risks during their ceremonial evisceration, but ultimately they were not tamed or chastened. So why put a girl's life (or fecundity) in danger, when there's no guarantee that her lust will die? And if a woman remains orgasmic and yet does not — surprise! — walk the path of a Barbary macaque, perhaps we can see here proof that the clitoris has no power over a woman, none at all, beyond what she will receive and what she will give it in return.

5

SUCKERS AND HORNS

THE PRODIGAL UTERUS

HOPE PHILLIPS HAS the sort of job that the brain loves but the pampered body hates. She is a project manager for the World Bank, and she is on the road for months at a stretch, traveling to places where there are no roads. Instead, there are bodily threats: parasites of extravagant variety and design; mosquitoes that hum in malarial choirs; two-fisted heat; the combined effluvia of local sewage and imported toxic waste; and a blood supply that should never again see the inside of anyone's veins. She has traveled throughout South America and Asia, but lately most of her work has been in southern Africa. And it was in Africa that she began to wonder if she could afford the luxury of her body's increasingly fitful behavior.

Phillips is a slender woman in her mid-forties with smooth skin, fine bones, and a precise, thoughtful manner. She is American but was raised in Taiwan, where her father, a physician, studied cholera, and there is the faintest hint in her locution of the Chinese she grew up speaking. I visited her in her home in Arlington, Virginia, a boxy, almost prim little house inspirited with rugs and furniture and carvings scavenged during her forays abroad. I drank coffee and nibbled on Milano cookies; she drank tea, ate nothing, and talked about her medical problems and the solution she had settled on.

For the past several years, Hope had been bleeding in what she considered an extracurricular fashion. "About five days a month, apart from my period, I'd start bleeding at nine o'clock in the evening," she said. "It would come out in a gush." She let her torso and arms fall forward slightly to emphasize *gush*. At first she didn't make a big deal of it, but eventually she decided, Oh, yes, I'd better consult a doctor. An ultrasound scan revealed the likely cause of her excessive bleeding: a fibroid, a benign tumor that grows in the muscle tissue, or myometrium, that makes up the middle layer of the uterus. The professional term for fibroid is leiomyoma, or simply myoma, to reflect the tumor's muscular origin, but fibroids are as common as freckles and deserve their common name. At least a quarter of women over thirty have fibroids, and the true figure may be closer to half. In most cases, fibroids are asymptomatic and despite their designation as tumors should just be left alone. But if they grow too big or are located in a bad spot, they can cause cramps, bleeding, constipation, and other unpleasantnesses.

Unfortunately for Hope, her fibroid was of a so-called submucous variety. Rather than remaining in the myometrium, it projected up into the endometrium, the layer of mucus membrane that carpets the inside of the uterus. The growth was not painful, but every time she menstruated and shed the endometrial lining, the blood vessels of the richly vascularized fibroid were exposed. Hence, the excessive bleeding that persisted beyond her period. Her doctor suggested that a dilation and curettage, or D & C, might help stem the red tide. In a D & C, the cervix is widened, or dilated, to allow doctors to insert surgical instruments into the uterus to perform a curettage — to scrape off the endometrium beyond what is normally shed in menstruation.

In Hope's case, the old dusting-and-cleaning procedure didn't help and in fact seemed to make things worse. "It got to the point where there were only ten days a month when I wasn't bleeding or spotting," she said. Her condition was inconvenient when she traveled, but she was a trouper, and she mastered the art of biased packing. Forget the change of shoes. When preparing for a three-month trip, she jammed more tampons and napkins into her suitcase than most women need in a year.

But the bleeding soon bled beyond mere cargo management. During one trip to Zimbabwe, she bled like Saint Sebastian. She worried that she would hemorrhage to the point where she'd need a transfusion, not something one wants to do on the continent where a retrovirus first leaped from monkey to human and in so migrating invented AIDS. Eventually she had another D & C in the United States. Several days later she became seriously ill. Her temperature soared to 102 degrees. She had to cancel a planned trip back to Africa. The doctors said her fibroid had grown so large that they could no longer see her uterus on ultrasound. Eventually she found herself in the office of Dr. Nicolette Horbach, of George Washington University Medical School, talking about removing the only part of the body that is unique to women, the one organ that doesn't have an anatomical equivalent in the male: the uterus.

As we've discussed, Galen and all who followed him for nearly the next two thousand years conceived of the female body as a sock taken off in a hurry — that is, as a male's body turned inside out. The vagina was an inverted penis, the labia a foreskin equivalent, the uterus an internal scrotum, and the ovaries a woman's testicles. Galen was no fool, and he was on the right track in observing the principle of genital equivalency. The adult genitals *are* homologous, though not entirely as Galen reckoned. Yes, the ovaries do correspond to the testes, but the female analogue of the penis is the clitoris, not the vagina, and the labia are the structural counterpart to the scrotum rather than the foreskin. Both sexes have responsive breast tissue as well, and a man's bosom is capable, under certain hormonal conditions, of swelling to brassiere-ready proportions, a condition known as gynecomastia (which means "female-like breasts").

But when we come to the uterus, anatomical homology breaks down. During the development of a male fetus, müllerian inhibiting factor eliminates the proto-womb when the structure is no bigger than a caraway seed, leaving nothing for the fetus's fidgety androgens to reinterpret. MIF also sweeps away the incipient fallopian tubes, but the second set of primordial pipes is retained and retrained into seminal ducts. The uterus alone offers a clear case of presence versus absence, to have or have not.

And what a weight the monosexual organ has borne. It has borne the weight of humanity, of course. Every one of the six billion people who are alive today, and the billions more who have already died, were coaxed into being through uterine tolerance for an implanted conceptus and uterine generosity in sharing a blood supply with the colonizing fetus. The uterus has borne the freight of extraordinary medical myths. Hippocrates believed that the organ wandered untethered through a woman's body, giving rise to any number of physical, mental, and moral failings; the word *hysteria*, after all, comes from the Greek *hystera*, for womb. Hippocrates also believed that the human uterus had as many as seven chambers and was lined with "tentacles" or "suckers." His bizarre errors were the result of laws and religious customs that forbade the dissection of the human body and required the great man of oath to extrapolate from the study of other species, which often do have wombs with multiple cavities and hornlike structures.

Hippocrates' blunder persisted until the Renaissance, when Leonardo da Vinci's gorgeous drawing of an opened uterus, revealing the fetus and its umbilical cord within, showed his awareness that the human womb has only one cavity. But in other anatomical drawings he illustrated a different fable of the time, that a "milk vein" extends from the uterus up to the breast, to transform blood from the pregnant uterus into milk for the newborn child. As recently as the nineteenth century, physicians argued that the uterus competes directly with the brain for an adequate blood supply. Thus any effort a woman made to nourish her mind through education or career could come only at the expense of her fertility.

The war of the womb continues to this day. One of our most bellicose and indefatigable of issues, the abortion debate, distills to a question of who owns the uterus, woman or fetus (or a fetal proxy such as the church or state). Moreover, despite the fact that only half the population is endowed with one, the uterus is the site of the two most common surgical procedures performed in the United States. First is the cesarean section, in which the uterus is sliced open for the swift retrieval of an infant (who may or may not need this Green Beret approach to its delivery). Second is a far more severe storming of the uterus, the hysterectomy. And it is a hysterectomy that Horbach suggested to Hope Phillips as a possible solution to her runaway bleeding.

Horbach is an energetic, dark-haired woman who emphasizes her eyes with carefully applied makeup and who takes a pragmatic, even blunt approach to medicine. But blunt does not mean rushed. When she first met with Phillips, the conversation lasted two hours. Phillips described her symptoms, her medical history, and the demands of her job. She also talked about a recent change in her life that made her reluctant to have a hysterectomy. Phillips had been twice married and twice divorced, and in neither marriage had she ever considered becoming pregnant. But lately she had been dating a man with whom, for the first time in her life, she could imagine having children. "It was ironic, as though God were kicking me in the teeth," Phillips told me. Was there something she could do, she asked Horbach, to get rid of the fibroid while preserving her uterus?

Horbach laid out the options. You could take drugs called gonado-tropin-releasing hormone agonists, she said, to temporarily block pro-duction of estrogen, which feeds fibroid growth. But those drugs tend to work only as long as you take them and have masculinizing side effects.

Alternatively, you could have a myomectomy, she said, the surgical removal of the fibroid from the uterus. Horbach turned on the blunt rigor. You're forty-five years old, she said to Phillips. In the best of circumstances, the chances of your becoming pregnant now are minute. Given the large size of your fibroid, its excision would make childbear-ing even less likely. Horbach pointed out that a myomectomy can be very bloody, possibly resulting in the need for a transfusion during the surgery, and can cause postoperative infections and complications. Should any of that occur, she warned, recovery could take longer than the standard four to six weeks required for a hysterectomy.

Horbach also said that Phillips could continue to do nothing and just live with the intemperate bleeding until she reached menopause. Once the body's natural estrogen production drops off, fibroids tend to shrink to inconsequential proportions.

Phillips went home to think. Five more years of chronic blood loss. She couldn't stand the thought, particularly not as the bleeding was getting progressively worse. She also considered the myomectomy op-tion. But Horbach's words sat hard. What sort of little fantasy was she constructing for herself, that she might have major surgery, recover from surgery, get married to a man she had only recently met, and, at age forty-five or forty-six, instantly conceive? Her siblings were doing a fine job of reproducing, she thought. The family tree did not need her personal buds. Phillips was also disturbed by the thought of a lengthy recovery time from a myomectomy. "I've never defined myself by my uterus or my ability to bear children," she said. "But I do define myself by my work."

She talked with family and with friends. She mentioned the possibil-ity of a hysterectomy to the man she was seeing, but his response did not exactly warm her heart. "Oh, yes," he said vaguely. "Some of my mother's friends have had that." Finally she decided to go through with the hysterectomy. Because of the size of her fibroid, the surgery had to be done abdominally rather than vaginally or through a laparoscopic tube, as hysterectomies sometimes are performed. She and Horbach agreed that I could watch the operation. I wanted to see what the internal reproductive organs look like: ovaries, fallopian tubes, cervix, uterus. The introduction to a fibroid — a huge, purple, ropy fibroid — was thrown in for free.

The surgical team that assembles at George Washington University Hospital for the hysterectomy early one March morning is delightfully unusual: three female surgeons (Horbach and two residents) and a male nurse. With the bottom half of her face covered by a surgical mask and her eyes rimmed with dark eyeliner, Horbach looks like Cleopatra. Phillips lies naked on the operating table, already in the land of happy. She is not under general anesthesia. Instead she has been given a tranquilizer to calm her and a spinal epidural to block sensation below the belt, a minimalist approach that is easier to recover from than a total knockout. She snores lightly as the staff prepares her for the operation. Her body looks young and athletic, too young for a surgery that has "middle-aged" and "my mother's friends" scrawled all over it. The prep team sprays her pelvis and abdomen with Betadine. They sponge her pubic hair into a froth. Once she has been scrubbed, she is draped to the neck with blue sheets, with only a triangle of flesh left exposed around her stomach. Her head is behind a curtain. She is a disembodied body, a woman *en croute*.

At Horbach's request, somebody slips a jazz tape into the OR boom box. The surgeons huddle over their pale white playing field. They make a six-inch slice below Phillips's bellybutton, and her skin beams back a bright red greeting. They cauterize the skin to cut off the bleeding. The surgeons then carve through the rectus fascia, the connective tissue beneath the skin that holds everything in place. They cut through Phillips's very thin layer of fat, which looks like the fat that marbles an uncooked chicken. Under the fat are her abdominal muscles, two pink layers of them, which the surgeons do not cut but merely push aside.

"This is textbook anatomy," Horbach says to her residents. "This is as gorgeous as it gets." Usually the women she operates on are a good hundred pounds heavier than Phillips, and slicing through all the flab is a nuisance. How much nicer to work by the best of the books.

Yet there is blood, blood, blood, and they must sop it up and sop it up and cauterize what they can. Finally they are inside the abdominal cavity. Clamps hold apart the layers of Hope. Her viscera look healthy and sprightly. They sparkle. Hope has become a living museum, open to the world. Thus it is a shock to hear her murmuring behind the curtain. After all, she is not unconscious, but merely in a state of calm, coming in and out of a nap; the epidural is what's doing all the numbing. She talks groggily to the anesthesiologist, and he reassures her that things are going fine. Horbach reaches into the cavity and palpates the various parts, the bladder, the kidneys, the gallbladder, the stomach, checking for abnormalities of any kind. Once you're in there, why not cop a few feels? "We occasionally find something more complicated than what we went in for," Horbach explains.

Not in this case, though: it's textbook anatomy. Horbach points out the ovaries to me. They are each about the size of a large strawberry, and they are smoke-colored and bumpy. They look like moist seedpods. On one is a noticeable white cyst, the probable spot of Phillips's last ovulation, when a ripe egg burst through the follicle and left behind a fluid-filled pocket that is still healing. Horbach also indicates the fallopian tubes, or oviducts, which are attached to the uterus. The tubes are exquisite, soft and rosy and slim as pens, tipped like a feather duster with a bell of fronds, called fimbriae. Gabriel Falloppius, the sixteenth-century anatomist after whom the structures were named, thought that the oviducts looked like trumpets and that they served to expel "noxious fumes" from the uterus. To me they look like sea anemones, flowers of flesh, the petals throbbing to the cadence of blood.

This particular hysterectomy will be a relatively conservative one, Horbach says. She is going to leave the oviducts and the ovaries in place. That doesn't always happen. Often surgeons take out the complete reproductive kit at once, uterus, cervix, tubes, and ovaries, snip, snip, snip. They reason that if a woman is near menopause, the system is about to retire anyway, so why leave things possibly to become cancerous later on? Beware the seedpods! Ovarian cancer is deadly, the line goes, and it's usually silent until the disease has progressed beyond redemption. As long as we're performing major surgery, let's make it a little more major, eliminate the risk of ovarian cancer, and put the woman on hormone replacement therapy afterward.

But the prophylaxis argument for ancillary organ removal is a dubious one that has outraged many. Unnecessary ovariectomy is rank castration, they say. What is the point of taking out healthy body parts on the small chance that they'll turn cancerous in the future? You might as well take out one kidney before it goes bum, or the 85 percent of the liver you don't need — or, to return to the principle of genital equivalence, the testicles to prevent testicular cancer. Horbach had told Phillips during their consultation that she was strongly in favor of leaving the ovaries and tubes behind, and Phillips saw no reason to disagree.

Before they start removing the uterus, Horbach uses a wire to ligate off the major blood supply to the organ and thus cut down on bleeding. The surgeons scrutinize their target and soon realize that the operation will be more complicated than expected. The main fibroid is very large, and it has grossly deformed the uterus and cervix. It also has grown a big, parasitic blood supply to keep it nourished. Cancerous tumors do the same thing, inveigling the body to sprout new vessels to sustain them; all tissue, whether healthy or malign, needs blood to survive. The surgeons decide they will perform a partial myomectomy, cutting down on the fibroid in an effort to collapse the uterus and make the hysterectomy possible. They discuss how best to ligate and sever the tangle of fibroid blood vessels to prevent hemorrhaging. They find other, smaller fibroids stippling the uterus and making a mess for them. Horbach asks for an injection of vasopressin to constrict Phillips's blood vessels and further diminish bleeding. The doctors reach into the abdominal cavity practically up to their elbows and work with a concentration so palpable that I hold my breath in sympathy.

Ninety minutes pass. The surgeons are not tired, but I am tired for them. Finally they get to the point where they can start removing parts. The pieces are placed on a metal tray, and the nurse holds each one up for me to see. Phillips's cervix: a shiny, taffy-colored tubular structure that reminds me of the head of a penis. The fibroid: it is so big and purposeful in appearance that I can't believe it wasn't a functioning part of Phillips's anatomy. It looks like a turnip, a tough swirl of purplish tissue that Horbach says reminds her of brain tissue. The body of the uterus: at this point, not exactly photogenic. It is an unremarkable pouch about the size of a child's fist, a timorous adjunct to the fibroid that it sustained for so long.

With the cervix and uterus gone, Phillips's vagina now opens directly into her abdominal cavity, so the surgeons stitch it closed. The vagina may not be as dirty as legend has it, but it is an orifice, and you don't want it to serve as a gateway between the public and the personal. Horbach makes sure there is no "schmootzy tissue" left behind, fibroid remnants that could serve as a source of infection. Finally the doctors irrigate the excavated site with sterile water. Over time, Phillips's other viscera will reposition themselves and fill in the space where her reproductive organs once dwelled. The surgeons are ready to close up. Somebody changes the tape and the tempo. "Jazz is for opening, rock is for closing," Horbach says. The song that drifts out from the stereo is a lilting number called "Woman in Chains," which seems almost too blatantly appropriate. But is Phillips in chains, or is she being freed? The surgeons stitch up the layers they cut, working with firm delicacy. One of the residents does most of the stitching, and she clearly loves what she's doing. Her fingers fly. She looks like she's playing an instrument of sutures, fascia, fat, and skin. When the top layer of skin is sewn shut and the body restored to its preferred state of solitary confinement, Phillips's stomach looks surprisingly tidy, with no sign of the recent assault beyond a thin dark line. "We like to make the sutures as cosmetically good as possible, because that's what patients judge us on," says Horbach. "They never see all the hard work we do inside." See, no, but feel — how could they not?

The womb does not define a woman, philosophically, biologically, or even etymologically. A woman does not need to be born with a uterus to be a woman, nor does she have to keep her uterus to remain a woman. We don't want to fall into the trap of womb-worship, or hope that men suffer from womb envy. Very few of them do, and when they are around pregnant women, none of them do. And yet most of us have grown up with the familiar medical image of the female reproductive tract, the O'Keeffeian ram's head, its face the body of the uterus, its beard the cervix, its horns the fallopian tubes. We see this image and we think of the female pelvis, how fine the fit, triangle within triangle.

Aesthetically, at least, we own the uterus; we feel comfortable about it. For about thirty-eight years of our lives, from age twelve to age fifty, we experience the customary tug and flow of the uterus in the form of menstruation. So what is the uterus, and what is its essential geography? Why is it so temperamental, prone to spawning growths that look like tubers dug up from the garden? Let us be appreciative and precise but not obsequious. The nonpregnant uterus is the size of a small fist; let us see how much punch that fist can pack.

In a sense, evolution adheres to the classic twelve-step program: it takes things one day at a time. It does not strive for perfection; it does not strive at all. There is no progress, no plans, no *scala natura,* or scale of nature, that ranks organisms from lowly to superior, primitive to advanced. A fly is brilliant at flydom, and wouldn't you love on occasion to see as a fly does, in all directions? If mammals strike us as higher and worthier and more compelling than insects, it helps to recall that this bias too is the result of evolution by natural selection. We tend to like that which seems most like us, because resemblance implies genetic relatedness, and we like our genes; they have given us us. The tendency to favor our personal gene pool over foreign waters is called kin selection, and it extends into many areas of our lives. It means that we will more readily help a relative than a stranger, and that we feel greater fellowship with a chimpanzee, or even a lion, than with some alien-looking organism that has an external skeleton, a segmented body plan, and appendages that bend backward. But just because we identify with hairy lactating warm-bloods doesn't mean that the mammalian order is any closer to the goddesshead.

Having said all that, I will now argue that the uterus was and is a magnificent invention, a revolution in physiology. I mentioned earlier that an internally conceived and gestated fetus is a protected fetus, and a protected fetus has the luxury of developing an elaborated central nervous system. The uterus and its attendant placenta mother the offspring as it will never be mothered again, not even by its own mother postpartum. The more mothered the animal is, the more apt it is to dominate its environment. At the moment, we placental mammals, we Eutherians, define the mammalian calling. Marsupial mammals certainly do a reasonable job of nurturing a larvalike fetus in their external pouch. Kangaroos are the deer of Australia, koala the squirrels. Here in the United States, opossums are a suburban staple — or thorn — and they are marsupials. Nevertheless, there are far more species of placental mammals than there are pouched ones, and Eutherians have populated far more habitats on earth. Could a humanlike brain have evolved in a species gestated in a pouch, or for that matter in a shelled egg? Probably not. The uterus in its bony and ligamentous pelvic cage is incomparably secure, and the placenta is incomparably nourishing. The womb may have nothing to do with the intellect of the woman who bears it, but it has everything to do with the brain of the fetus it bears.

A fetus certainly knows how good its life is. It does not leave the womb until forced to do so by the gradual retrenchment of the placenta — the mother's body deciding, Enough, enough, we've done enough, out out damned tot! Sensing an impending drought, the fetus releases a series of biochemical signals that result in its expulsion from the only Eden it will ever know.

The geography of the uterus, then, cannot be disengaged from the organ's role as primal mother, fetal tent and fetal supermarket. Consider the contradictory features the womb must embody. It must be labile yet stable. It must be rich yet affordable. It must be capable of growing in adulthood as no other organ grows. It must communicate with the rest of the body, to discern where it is in the do-si-do between ovulation and menstruation. The uterus is a part of the endocrine system, the mac-ramé of glands, organs, and brain structures that secrete and respond to hormones. It is enmeshed biochemically with the adrenals, the ovaries, the hypothalamus, and the pituitary. At the same time it is a privileged place, a dome apart, where the fetus will not be ejected by the body's xenophobic immune cells.

Structurally, the uterus is not complicated. In an adult woman who is not pregnant, it weighs about two ounces and is roughly three inches long. It has two parts, each making up about half its length: the body, or fundus, in which the fetus develops, and the cervix, which projects down into the vagina and opens slightly for the release of menstrual blood and more gapingly for the birth of a baby. If you look at the cervix from a gynecologist's-eye view, it resembles a glazed doughnut. A doctor who worked in a woman's health clinic once said that doing pelvic exams made her hungry, and she wasn't kidding or being lewd; she just liked doughnuts.

In other ways the uterus is a sandwich, a muscle hero. The cervix and fundus are both composed of three tissue types. The meat in the middle is the thick myometrium, built of three interwrapping sheets of muscle. On the outside of the myometrium is a slick covering, the serous membrane, which is similar in texture and function to the sacs surrounding the heart and lungs. Like those sacs, the uterine serous membrane keeps the organ wet and cushioned.

On the other side of the myometrium is the uterine lining, the endometrium. The body likes to work in threes, and so the endometrium is made of three layers of mucous membrane. Unlike serous membrane, mucous membrane breathes and snorts and secretes. It absorbs water, salts, and other compounds. It releases mucus, a mixture of white blood cells, water, the sticky protein known as mucin, and cast-off tissue cells. Menstruation is in part a mucus discharge. During menstruation, two of the mucous sheaths are shed, thence to be reconstructed when the cycle begins anew. Like one who has reached enlightenment, the third, deepest endometrial layer escapes the wheel of death and rebirth, and it is to this stable foundation that a placenta moors itself if a fetus should be favored with a home.

Hippocrates thought that the womb wandered, and he meant *wandered,* took a transcorporeal journey up to the breastbone, even to the throat, becoming particularly frantic when it wasn't fed on a regular basis with semen. (By Hippocrates' estimation, the uterus of a whore would be far calmer than that of a virgin.) He was wrong, of course, but that does not mean the uterus is an immobile stone. In fact, it is springy and fungible. It is held loosely in its pelvic girdle by six ligaments, flexible bands of fibrous tissue that offer support for the organ and also enclose the blood vessels that nourish it. The position of the uterus shifts in the pelvis depending on whether you're prone or upright, your bladder is full or empty, and other such unremarkable circumstances. If you're sitting down now, not particularly in need of a toilet break, and not pregnant, your uterus is probably tipped slightly forward, its fundus leaning toward a spot an inch or two above your pubis, that hard bone in your crotch. If you were to stand up, again with an empty bladder, and push your shoulders back with military crispness, your uterus would assume a nearly horizontal position, like a pear that's fallen over.

The uterus is at its most physiologically flamboyant when pregnant. An organ that weighs two ounces before pregnancy grows to two pounds by pregnancy's end, a gain that is independent of the weight of the fetus or placenta. Its volume increases a thousandfold. No other organ undergoes such dramatic changes in adulthood unless it is diseased. Yet give it a mere six weeks postpartum, and it has retreated to its fisty proportions. In effecting the changes of pregnancy, the myometrium does most of the heavy lifting. The muscle cells multiply at the beginning of pregnancy and then enlarge, or hypertrophy, in the second trimester, just as muscle cells elsewhere do if you diligently subject them to exercise. In the final trimester, the cells neither divide nor hypertrophy, but the whole uterine wall simply stretches and stretches and stretches, until you feel, mama, as though you might burst. In fact, rupture of the uterus during pregnancy is surprisingly rare. Placental mammals, after all, have been around for 120 million years, enough time to work out the bugs of the distendable womb.

As happens so often in life, the problem of expansion is solved through harmonious apposition. The placid madonna, ha! A uterus in pregnancy is an arm wrestle between two well-matched, muscled dames. One arm starts to teeter, it pushes back upright, the other arm flags, and oomph into verticality again. Consider this: the uterus grows because during pregnancy your body is flooded with estrogen. Four thousand years ago, a woman wanting word of her condition mixed her urine together with barley seed; if the barley grew faster than usual, it signified pregnancy. No one knew it at the time, but the test probably worked because estrogen spurs the growth of many cell types — mammal, insect, grain. It is a potent biotroph, an ancient signal from organismic Babel, as I will discuss in detail later. For now, suffice it to say that estrogen stimulates myometrial cells to divide and enlarge.

There's just one problem with the scheme. The hormone also throws muscle cells into a state of electrical excitation. It makes them twitch. A uterus that twitches too much is a uterus that expels a fetus. Therefore, even as it is urged to expand, the myometrium must be tranquilized. That is the job of progesterone, the so-called hormone of pregnancy; progesterone means pro-gestation. Progesterone inhibits the contractibility of muscle cells. Throughout the whole nine months of baby-baking, the negotiation between estrogen and progesterone is a dynamic one. Small, fleeting contractions pass over the swelling womb like local thunderstorms flickering over the desert. The more advanced the pregnancy, the more insistent these so-called Braxton Hicks contractions become. Mother of goddess, how extraordinary it is! Your belly is swelling, and you think, I will explode, I am a supernova. And then contractions seize you up and you think, No, I will collapse, I am a giant black hole.

The uterus grows. The uterus retreats. It is not unlike the heart, a large, powerful muscle that swells, shrinks, twitches, and bebops. Oscillations and deep rhythms are the source of life, the principle of life; even cells work through pulsatile mechanisms. When radio astronomers first discovered pulsating signals coming from a distant neutron star, they thought they were detecting a message from an alien civilization. What but other living beings could emit such rhythmic signals? Only when the scientists determined that the signals were too regular, too mechanical, for life did they trace their source to the spinning core of the ultradense neutron star. If we respond to music viscerally, it is because our viscera are the original percussionists, and the heart and the uterus are among the most perceptible of our natural pacemakers.

Beyond rhythmicity, the heart and the uterus share another quality, their association with blood. Not all women breed, but nearly all women bleed, or have bled. Jane Carden said that she regretted her inability to menstruate far more than she did her inability to become pregnant. In that way alone did she feel she was missing something extraordinary about the female odyssey. And she was. There is no clearer rite of passage, no surer demarcation between childhood and adulthood, than menarche, the first period. When people talk of the indelibility of a strong memory, they speak of recalling exactly where they were when Kennedy was shot or the *Challenger* space shuttle exploded. But what a woman really remembers is her first period; now there's a memory seared into the brain with the blowtorch of high emotion. With some exceptions, a girl loves getting her first period. She feels as though she has accomplished a great thing, willed her presence into being. Emily Martin interviewed a number of women from different social classes about their thoughts on menstruation, and all gave joyful accounts of menarche. One recalled bursting into song in the bathroom. Another rushed to tell her girlfriends in the school cafeteria that her period had just started, and they responded with a small celebration, buying her ice cream. Those who are too shy to celebrate publicly rejoice internally. In her diary, Anne Frank referred to those early periods of hers — and early ones is all she lived to have — as her "sweet secret." If a girl has cramps, she may even love them at first. They are proof of her body's power, the muscular flexes propelling her toward a destiny that looks, for the moment, as bright and as important as blood.

After the heady triumph of menarche, most of us soon begin thinking of menstruation as a hassle, a mess, an embarrassment. We try to be cavalier, and we try to scold ourselves into pragmatism, yet still we feel uncomfortable paying for a box of tampons or napkins when the sales-clerk is male. There are innumerable myths and taboos surrounding menstruation, some, not surprisingly, attributable to our familiar medicine men, Hippocrates, Aristotle, and Galen (most easily remembered by the acronym HAG). Hippocrates argued that fermentation in the blood precipitated menstruation, because women lacked the male ability to dissipate the impurities in the blood gently and sweetly through sweat; to him, menstrual blood had a "noisome smell." Galen believed that menstrual blood was the residue of blood in food that women, having small and inferior bodies, were unable to digest. Aristotle assumed that menses represented excess blood not incorporated into a fetus.

The notion that menstrual blood is toxic has pervaded human thinking, west to east, up to down. Given the noxious fumes they exude, menstruating women have been said to make meat go bad, wine turn sour, bread dough fall, mirrors darken, and knives become blunt. Menstruating women have been confined to huts, to home, to anywhere but here. Some anthropologists have suggested that hunting societies have been particularly stringent in keeping women quarantined during their monthly flow, in part because of fears that menstrual odor attracts animals. Even today, women are warned not to go camping in grizzly country if they are menstruating, lest a very large ursine nostril pick up the scent. Whether the warning has merit remains unclear. When biologists in North Carolina recently tried to determine the best way to lure a bear, they found menstrual blood to be of almost no use. Some men, bearlike or otherwise, claim that they can smell when a woman is on her period, but no study has ever borne out that charming if rather smug conviction, and this writer has certainly not found it to be true even when cohabiting with said sensitive fellows. Certainly men who continue to hold ritualistic prejudice against menstruation don't rely on their olfactory powers to distinguish the clean from the soiled. It is not unusual for an Orthodox Jewish man, for example, to refuse the ministrations of a female physician, on the chance that the doctor may be menstruating and pollute him more profoundly than the disease from which he suffers.

In fairness, views of menstruation have not been uniformly negative, and the same potent ingredients that menstrual blood supposedly carries have on occasion been considered therapeutic. Moroccans have used menstrual blood in dressings for sores and wounds, while in the West blood has been suggested as a treatment for gout, goiter, worms, and, on the theory of using fire to fight fire, menstrual disorders. The ancient practice of bloodletting, which dominated medicine for hundreds of years, may well have been a mimic of menses, although the fact that women shed blood naturally did not spare them from extraphysiologic drainings whenever they fell ill.

We may be amused or angry at the variations on the theme of the bloody succubus, but how much better are we? We modern women too think of menstrual blood as dirty, much filthier than blood from a cut on the arm; which would you rather put in your mouth? Camille Paglia, that most noisome and antifeminist of self-proclaimed feminists, expressed in her book *Sexual Personae* an attitude toward menstruation that is no more inspired than the HAG's. "Menstrual blood is the stain, the birthmark of original sin, the filth that transcendental religion must wash from man," she writes. "Is this identification merely phobic, merely misogynistic? Or is it possible there is something uncanny about menstrual blood, justifying its attachment to taboo? I . . . argue that it is not menstrual blood per se which disturbs the imagination — unstanchable as that red flood may be — but rather the albumin in the blood, the uterine shreds, placental jellyfish of the female sea. We have an evolutionary revulsion from slime, our site of biologic origins. Every month, it is woman's fate to face the abyss of time and being, the abyss which is herself." Placental jellyfish? Forget the menstrual hut — this woman needs to be confined to an aquarium.

We also have dwelled overmuch on the negatives of menstruation and premenstruation: the headaches, the weepiness, the sore breasts, the pimples. We have turned premenstrual syndrome into a distinct genus in the taxonomy of psychiatry, right up there with panic disorder and obsessive-compulsive behavior. We suspect that women may be slightly less competent right around the time of their periods' onset. And yet the opposite may be true. As Paula Nicholson has pointed out, empirical research suggests that "the premenstrual phase of the cycle is frequently accompanied by heightened activity, intellectual clarity, feelings of well-being, happiness and sexual desire." This is an empire I can vouch for. One of my most beautiful memories of college is of a day when my period was due but hadn't yet arrived. I was sitting in my living room, studying, and I felt an unaccountable surge of joy. I looked up from my book and was dazzled by the air. It was so clear, so purely transparent, that the objects in the room were sharply etched and proud against it, and yet it was as though I could see the air for the first time. It had become visible to me, molecule for molecule. My mind was focused and free of anxiety. I felt for a moment as though I had taken the perfect drug, the one that has yet to be invented; call it Liberitium or Creativil.

My enthusiasm quickly vanished, and I couldn't recapture these sensations in subsequent periods. It was the 1970s, and feminists were trying to create a woman's-eye mythology and, among other things, to give menstruation a good name, but I couldn't help greeting their efforts with a sneer. They were, as I'm sure my daughter will say to me someday, so *twentieth-century*. An instructor in my women's studies class, for example, suggested that we students all trade in our tampons for napkins over the next few months, the better to feel the process of menstruation, to go with the flow, as it were. Phooey, I thought. Women have been wearing tampons for at least three thousand years; the ancient Egyptians wrote about what sound like early tampons, and so did our father of the tentacled uterus, Hippocrates. I didn't take my teacher's advice, then or since. I'd been delighted when my mother let me switch from pads to tampons — when she was assured by some doctor, I think, that tampons are safe for a young girl and her hymen — and I was not about to return to the awkwardness of a cotton football between the legs.

Nonetheless, I believe there should be a woman-centered myth of menstruation, a construct of our shared feminine low-giene — some-

thing on a par with the male pissing ritual, perhaps. Men obviously find
their upstanding approach to urination manly, amusing, and potentially
seditious, or the public urinal scene would not be such a fixture of
film and television. Emily Martin has described menstruation's potential to foment rebellion and solidarity, offering as it does an excuse
for wage-earning women to retreat to the one place where their male
managers cannot follow. "In early twentieth-century documents," she
writes, "there are scattered references to groups of two or three girls
frequently found in the washroom 'fussing over the universe' . . . a girl
sobbing in the washroom over her stolen wages and girls reading union
leaflets posted in the washroom during a difficult struggle to organize a
clothing factory." Let us again retire to the chamber for some universal
fussing and fomenting. Let us overthrow the lore, the idiocy, and the
Paglian prissiness that surround menstruation and found a myth on
reality. How and why do we bleed? Why have we evolved the cycle of
endometrial death and renewal? Surprisingly enough, that question was
not asked until recently, and the quest for an answer is still very much
alive. In exploring origins, we may find new blood.

Menstruation is the way that we first experience the uterus, and if we
are Western women who have small families, we experience the uterus
thusly 450 to 480 times in a lifetime. During the average period, we cast
off a volume of material amounting to about six tablespoonfuls, or
three fluid ounces, half of it blood, the other half the shed endometrial
layers, along with vaginal and cervical secretions. Most of us think of
menstruation as a passive business, decay aided by gravity. The uterine
lining builds up and awaits the sacred blastocyst that would be a baby; if
none appears, the lining disintegrates and falls away like so much mil-
dewed wallpaper. The active process, we imagine, is the anticipatory
phase of the menstrual cycle, a time of anabolism, the plumping up of
the endometrium with tissue and nutrients that occurs in concert with
the ripening of the egg. If nothing happens to keep anabolism alive, if
conception and implantation do not happen and the lining is no longer
needed to feed the baby, then activity ceases, the plug is pulled, and
there goes the ruddy bathwater.

That is not in fact what happens. Recall the lesson that contemporary
biology teaches us: dying is as active as living. Eggs die by undergoing
apoptosis; that is, they commit suicide. So too is menstruation a dy-

namic and directed affair. Margie Profet, an evolutionary biologist now at the University of Washington, has described menstruation as an adaptation: it is a product of design, the designer in this case being that greatest and most unpretentious of deities, evolution by natural selection. "The mechanisms that collectively constitute menstruation appear to manifest adaptive design in [their] precision, economy, efficiency and complexity," she has written. "If menstruation were merely a functionless byproduct of cyclic hormonal flux, there would be no mechanisms specifically designed to cause it."

The first relevant mechanism is a specialized type of artery. Feeding into the two superficial layers of the endometrium, the ones that are disposed of each month, are three spiral arteries, so named because they look like corkscrews. During pregnancy, the spiral arteries serve as important conduits of blood for the placenta. Yet their purpose extends beyond fetal feeding. Several days before a woman's period begins, the tips of the spirals grow longer and more tightly coiled, like a Slinky that's being pulled and twisted at the same time. Circulation to the endometrium grows sluggish — the calm that presages calamity. Twenty-four hours before the onset of bleeding, the spirals constrict sharply. The faucets are twisted off, the blood flow ceases. It is a heart attack of the uterus. Deprived of blood and therefore of oxygen, the endometrial tissue dies. Then, as abruptly as the arteries squeezed shut, they temporarily open again, allowing blood to rush in. The blood pools in pockets beneath the dead endometrium, causing the lining to swell and burst, and the period begins. Their mortal work complete, the spiral arteries constrict once again. (Fibroids disturb the ritual of menstruation because their parasitic blood supply does not conform to the squeeze-relax-squeeze pattern of the spiral arteries.)

A second outstanding feature of menstruation is the quality of the blood. Most blood is poised to clot. Unless you are a hemophiliac, when you cut yourself, the blood flows briefly and then coagulates, for which you can thank your platelets and sticky blood proteins such as fibrin. Menstrual blood does not clot. It may seem goopy at times, and the dead tissue accompanying it may pass out in clots — our slimy medusas! — but the blood proper contains very few platelets and does not form the interlocking coagulatory mesh that characterizes blood released from a wound. The only reason that menstrual blood does not keep flowing is that the spiral arteries constrict in the wake of endometrial death.

Corkscrew arteries and blood like wine: surely we are designed to menstruate. Yet this is not the whole story. Every problem in biology, as the evolutionary thinker Ernst Mayr has pointed out, comes in two parts: the how and the why, the proximate explanation and the ultimate one. There must be an ultimate rationale for menstruation, the reason that this precise and intricate system evolved to begin with. Here we run up against the limits of history. Until recently scientists have been almost exclusively male; men do not menstruate, and so scientists have not delved terribly deeply into the ultimate causes of this strictly female phenomenon. The physiology of menstruation, the how of it, was of sufficient interest to gynecologists to be explored in some detail. Not until the early 1990s, though, did anybody seriously ponder the why of menstruation, when Margie Profet presented in the *Quarterly Review of Biology* a theory too provocative to be ignored.

Profet is a slender and beautiful woman in her late thirties, California velvet on the outside, iron maiden beneath. She has long blond hair and blue eyes, talks in a friendly singsong voice, and wears cute outfits like a black leather skirt with large, decorative zippers and a matching short jacket. She has won a MacArthur fellowship — a "goddamn genius award," as Roy Blount, Jr., described it — but she never bothered to earn a Ph.D., for fear the formal accreditation would tempt her toward the path of professional conformity. Politically she is something like a feminist libertarian, the kind of person who thinks Charles Murray of *The Bell Curve* fame is a good guy, the Food and Drug Administration a threat to American liberty. Intellectually she's a radical, a hell-raiser, which is another way of saying she asks annoying questions that are so obvious, nobody has asked them before.

Like any good evolutionary thinker, Profet framed her question about menstruation in economic terms, as a cost-benefit analysis. Menstruation, she decided, is extraordinarily expensive. Shedding and replenishing endometrial tissue on a monthly basis burns a lot of calories, and for our Pleistocene ancestors, who likely spent most of their brief lives on the rim of malnutrition, every calorie counted. Moreover, when you lose blood, you lose iron, an essential micronutrient and another scarce commodity for our forebears. Finally, menstrual cycling makes women less efficient in reproduction. All that building up and tearing down of the uterine lining limits the time when a woman might conceive. If evolution is so keen on reproduction, why devote this much effort to counterproduction?

A pricey feature demands extravagant justification, and Profet had her candidate. Menstruation, she suggested, is a defense mechanism, an extension of the body's immune system. We bleed to rid the uterus of potentially dangerous pathogens that might have hitched a ride inside on the backs of sperm. Think of it. The uterus is a luxurious city just waiting to be sacked, and sperm are the ideal Trojan horse. Bacteria, viruses, and parasites all can find passage to the womb by playing opportunistic gene jockey, and it so happens that scanning electron micrographs of sperm reveal a cartoonish mob scene, the tadpole cell at the center surrounded by a cluster of microbial hangers-on. If permitted to linger in the uterus indefinitely, the pathogens might run amok, sickening, scarring, or killing us. Our endometrium must die, Profet proposed, so that we might live.

Profet also emphasized that menstruation is not the only sort of uterine bleeding that might act to expel pathogens from the uterus. Women bleed at ovulation, they bleed at conception, and they bleed heavily after giving birth. Bleeding in toto should be thought of as the uterus's solution to the perils of internal fertilization.

The novel formulation of menses as defenses put several confounding features of the process into a sensible light. Why, for example, is the shedding of the endometrium accompanied by a river of blood? The body can discard dead tissue without the use of blood. We replace the lining of the stomach on a regular basis, for example, and blood has nothing to do with it. Profet suggested that we bleed because blood carries the body's immune cells, the T cells, B cells, and macrophages, and the immune cells participate in routing out whatever nasty pathogens have tried to infiltrate the uterus. Why shed the lining rather than resorbing it into the body, as a more logically parsimonious system might do? To avoid the risk of recycling diseased tissue. And why do we bleed so heavily compared to other female mammals, any of which, presumably, are at risk of unintended spermatic donations? We bleed by the pint because we are an amorous species. We do not limit intercourse to a defined season of estrus, and we use sex for many nonreproductive reasons — to bond, to barter, to appease, to distract. Therefore, we must bleed heavily to cleanse ourselves: call it the macrophages of sin. Despite the relative heaviness of the human period, though, Profet also predicted that most if not all mammals undergo some sort of protective uterine bleeding and that scientists would find many more instances of menstruation in the animal kingdom than are currently known, if only they would start looking. Most of the species known to bleed are our sister primates, but bats, cows, shrews, and hedgehogs, among others, have been observed on occasion to shed blood from the vagina.

The response to Profet's radical suggestion was immediate, and, from professional quarters, overwhelmingly negative. Outlandish! squawked the gynecologists. Far from being a protective mechanism, they argued, menstruation is the time of month when women are at greatest risk for bacterial infections such as gonorrhea and chlamydia. That's when the cervical mucus thins, allowing microbes in the vagina easy access to the uterus. And forget about sperm as gift-bearing Greeks. Menstrual debris itself frequently backwashes, serving as an especially efficient means of transmitting pathogens from the upper genital tract to the delicate tissue of the uterine cavity and fallopian tubes. Using menstruation for uterine defense, the critics claimed, is like hiring a wolf to guard your flock of prize cloned sheep.

Others pointed out that routine menstruation is a modern invention. Our Pleistocene ancestors didn't have to worry about losing nutrients and iron with their monthly flow; they were too busy bearing children or lactating to menstruate. Even today, in some underdeveloped countries, women may go several years without menstruating. One anthropologist said he had interviewed a thirty-five-year-old woman in India who not only had never menstruated, she had never heard of the concept. Married at age eleven, she'd conceived her first child before menarche and had been pregnant or nursing, and thus amenorrheic, ever since.

In the end, what really bothered Profet's critics was being caught with their intellectual pants down. They had no counterhypothesis to explain menstruation. Only after the first sputterings of scorn and denial did some scientists have the decency to put the proposition to the test and offer a viable alternative should Profet's theory flunk the exam.

Beverly Strassmann, of the University of Michigan, took up the challenge with spitfire enthusiasm, publishing a lengthy exegesis in the same journal that had presented Profet's theory. Strassmann noted that Profet's hypothesis led to several predictions: first, that the uterus should be more riddled with pathogens prior to menstruation than after it; second, that the timing of menstruation should bear some relation to the timing of a female's greatest risk of pathogenic infiltration; and finally, taking a cross-species comparison, that the heaviness of a primate's period should correspond to the relative promiscuity of the animal — in other words, the more sexually active the species, the heavier the bleeding.

Strassmann concluded that none of these predictions were supported by the evidence. In various studies, specimens of uterine smears taken from women throughout their menstrual cycle showed no significant difference in the bacterial load from one phase to the next; if anything, the concentration of microbes was lowest, rather than highest, right before menstruation. In fact, blood is an excellent growth medium for many types of microbial flora, offering not only protein and sugar but iron, and we all know what the iron in spinach does for Popeye. Researchers have shown that they can expedite the proliferation of *Staphylococcus aureus* in culture by feeding it iron, which is probably why a tampon left in place too long is tempting territory for this agent of toxic shock syndrome.

Strassmann also considered whether the timing of menstruation and other types of uterine bleeding corresponds to times when a female might logically need the laundering; whether, to look at it another way, women don't need protection as much when they're not bleeding — during pregnancy and breastfeeding, for example. Might our ancestors have refrained from sex for at least part of the lengthy gestation and postpartum periods? Evidence from contemporary hunter-gatherer tribes that supposedly mimic humanity's formative years indicates scant effort at abstinence. The Dogon of Mali, for example, have sex throughout the first two trimesters of pregnancy and then resume lovemaking a month after birth. Yet the women don't start menstruating again until an average of twenty months postpartum. And women in all cultures have sex after menopause, but there is no indication that risk of infection rises when cycling ends.

Nor did Strassmann's phylogenetic analysis of other primates bolster the antipathogen hypothesis. She found no connection between a species' heaviness of menstruation and the degree to which it monkeys around, if you will. Some types of baboons, for example, are highly licentious and shed little or no uterine blood; other species of baboon are sexually restrained, breed with just one male, and yet bleed heavily. Gorillas are monogamous and menstruate covertly. Gibbons are monogamous and bleed overtly.

So if not for defense against microbes, what of our bleeding? Why the extravagant, wasteful system of menstruation? Here Strassmann strikes at Profet's core assumption — that menstruation is so costly it demands evolutionary justification. Far from being expensive, Strassmann argues, periods are a steal. Calorie for calorie, the Shiva approach to reproduction, the perpetual death and rebirth of the uterine lining, is cheaper than maintaining the uterus in fertile form would be. Consider the endometrium at its peak, right after ovulation, when it is capable of receiving a blastocyst. It is thick, rich, and metabolically dynamic. It secretes hormones, proteins, fats, sugars, nucleic acids. This plump endometrium is the woman's equivalent of an egg yolk, and it is energetically dear. Strassmann calculated that the uterine lining at its ripest uses seven times more oxygen than it does at its thinnest, after menstruation. The need for more oxygen translates into a need for more calories. In addition, the secretory endometrium revs up the entire body, as the hormones it releases stimulate tissues from brain to bowel. Again, a higher metabolism demands more calories. It makes sense to restrict the luxuriant productivity to a time of month when conception is likely — that is, at ovulation. If no embryo arrives, the lining and its secretions become a burden to sustain, so get rid of the whole bundle. Kill it. We can start over again the next month. Strassmann has estimated that in four months of cycling, a woman saves an amount of energy equal to six days' worth of food over what she would have needed to stoke a perpetually active endometrium. Even in lizards, the oviducts shrivel up when breeding season ends.

The uterus, then, is like a deciduous tree, an oak or a maple, and the endometrium acts like the leaves. When the weather is warm, when sunlight sings, the tree awakes and invests in leaves. The branching pattern of the tree — its trunk, its branches, its twigs — is like the branching of the body's vascularization, parceling out water rather than blood. The homology of the pattern is no coincidence. Holy water, sacred blood, they are one and the same, and branching is the most hydraulically efficient means of pumping the fluid from a central source — the heart, the trunk — out to all extremities. Thus nourished, the leaves bud, unfurl, thicken, and darken. The leaves are photosynthetic factories, transforming sunlight into usable energy. That energy allows the tree to create seeds and nuts, the acorns that are embryonic trees. The leaves are expensive to maintain — the tree must deliver them water, nitrogen, potassium, the nutrients from the soil — but they repay the tree by spinning sunlight into gold. In the same way, the endometrium is metabolically expensive and yet generative as well. It has the potential to nourish an embryo. In both cases, too, the investment is worthwhile only at certain times. For a tree considering foliation, that time is spring and summer, when there is abundant sunlight, water that is not frozen, and soil that is soft enough to be mined for nutrients. Then and only then can a leaf repay its debt with interest. For the uterus, the time corresponds to the moment when there might be something worth nourishing, a ripened egg that has met its match. Interestingly, a leaf dies in fall as the endometrial lining dies at the end of a fallow cycle. The corpuscle at the tip of the twig constricts, shutting off water and killing its dependent leaf.

The putative cost-effectiveness of cyclic endometrial death does not, however, explain the need for menstrual blood. Can't we have retrenchment without seeing red? The blood, in Strassmann's view, is beside the point. It is a byproduct of the loss of a tissue that is by necessity highly vascularized. If you're going to lose that tissue, you're going to have to spill some blood. Those fancy spiral arteries that destroy the endometrium and so start the flow, the ones that Profet thought were evidence of the adaptiveness of menstruation? Those arteries are there for the sake of the placenta, Strassmann says. That is their reason to be — and, come menstruation, not to be. The placenta is a spectacular thing, but it is vampirous. It needs blood, and the spiral arteries give it blood. Each month they spread their coiled fingers through the endometrium; if a placenta forms, they will deliver it blood. When the endometrium dies, it takes with it the vascularization, the tips of the spiral arteries, the fingers of blood. As it happens, the vascular architecture of the uterus in many other mammals is less ornate, and those mammals exhibit little or no menstrual bleeding. The species that have spiral arteries — humans and certain other primates — also shed the most blood. It's a structural thing, Strassmann says, a matter of plumbing rather than defense. We could resorb and recycle the tissue and the blood; that would certainly be a parsimonious approach, a nod to Miser Nature. And we do resorb, to a point. But the human uterus is quite large compared to the human body, and we simply can't take it all back. Nor can other primates with wombs large relative to their body size, and those, as a rule, are our sisters in blood.

What, then, can we conclude about this extraordinary and pedestrian aspect of womanness, the monthly flux, the forty quarts of blood and fluid that we discard in a lifetime of menses? Whom should we believe about why we bleed: Profet, Strassmann, the gynecologists, you perhaps, if you have a theory of your own? In fact, we may not need to choose. If there is one lesson I've learned in observing biology, it is that nothing in a living organism is just one thing. Nature's economy lies above all in making maximum use of what is, a process that we may call pleoaptation, the adaptation of an organ or system to multiple uses. The liver, for example, the largest gland in the body, performs more than five hundred tasks, including processing glucose, protein, fats, and other compounds the body needs, generating the hemoglobin that is the soul of a red blood cell, and detoxifying the poisons we consume when we drink wine or eat those fibrous packets of natural toxins called vegetables. Can we say that the liver is really for one thing and only incidentally for the others? No. Regardless of what problem the prototype liver arose to address — and the organ first appeared, in a primitive form, hundreds of millions of years ago in invertebrates — it has since taken on many other essential roles, and has been selected for just such pan-utility ever since. By the same token, we sweat to keep from overheating, but we also sweat when we are anxious or eat spicy food, to help rid the body of noxious chemicals such as stress hormones and curry. And then there is that pair of modified sweat glands known as breasts, which exude an unusual form of sweat of particular interest to newborns.

Menstruation, then, may be a pleoaptation. It is energy-efficient, and it is protective. We can make of these qualities what we will, so let us celebrate them. One is for the greater good, the other for ourselves. Consider the bleeding, and the theory that it is a byproduct of our hypervascularized uterus. Why all the vessels, those arterial Slinkies? The spiral arteries support a large, Draculean placenta. The placenta must be large and rich to support the growth of the fetal brain. Brain tissue is insatiable. Pound for pound, it is ten times more expensive to maintain than any other tissue of the body. During the last three months of pregnancy, the growth of the fetal brain is so explosive that stoking it demands nearly three quarters of all the energy entering the baby through the umbilical cord. No wonder the cord is so fat, so much like a long sausage, and no wonder the expulsion of the meaty placenta after the birth of the baby is considered an event in itself, worthy of being classified as the third stage of labor (the first being the dilation of the cervix, the second the delivery of the infant). The baby's brain must eat, and it eats blood.

One answer to the question of why we bleed, then, may simply be because we humans are so bloody smart.

Ah, but this articulation alone smacks too much of the martyr's plaint: we bleed so that our sons may think. And our daughters too, but they at least will be paying the species' price with their own deciduas soon enough. Camille Paglia claims that by menstruating, "women [bear] the symbolic burden of man's imperfections, his grounding in nature." We are saying something different: that women shoulder the burden of the human brain, the organ that allows at least the illusion of free will, transcendence, the *escape* from nature's grindstone. Nonetheless, what a bore to have the burden of cultivating human consciousness be so one-sided.

Enter the antipathogen aspect of menses, the ability of bloodshed to purify and rout, the womb as warrior. This is a selfish, active, and erotic explanation for menses, an acknowledgment that we are carnal beings whose sexual activity far exceeds any reproductive needs. In our defensive bleeding, we are not helping our offspring or our mates or the whole damned race; we are helping ourselves.

Let us help others too. When your daughter or niece or younger sister runs to you and crows, "It's here!" take her out for a bowl of ice cream or a piece of chocolate cake, and raise a glass of milk to the new life that begins with blood.

6

MASS HYSTERIA

LOSING THE UTERUS

IF THE ULTIMATE PURPOSE of menstruation remains unclear, well, mystery loves company, and two thousand years after Hippocrates dressed the uterus in suckers and horns, it still resists summation. Metaphorically, it continues to wander, and we must continue to chase it. Only in the past few years, for example, have researchers learned of the endometrium's productive capabilities. Our muscular, upside-down little pears, it seems, are pharmaceutical laboratories of admirable industry, giving the lie to yet another medical paradigm. For years the uterus was viewed as a mere recipient of biochemical information, the target of endocrine activity generated elsewhere in the body. It was not thought to manufacture essential chemicals or signaling molecules on its own. The ovaries told the endometrial lining to thicken, and *mirabile dictu,* it thickened. A fertilized egg told it to give up some of its blood, and blood donor it became. ✲

More recently, though, the uterus has emerged as a maker as well as a taker. Yes, it responds to steroid hormones from the ovaries and other organs, but it also expresses hormones and releases them into the global marketplace of the body. It makes proteins, sugars, and fats, all of which figure in Strassmann's analysis of the metabolic costs of menstruation. It makes prostaglandins, chemicals that exert an array of effects on the body. Most notably, prostaglandins prompt the smooth muscle tissue of the body to contract. Smooth muscle means unstriated muscle. The muscles that attach to your skeleton, like those of the arms, legs, face, and vagina, are striated, built of bundles of tough fibers; striated muscles can be flexed voluntarily. The muscles surrounding your internal organs are smooth. They look smooth to visual and microscopic inspection and also are smooth in the sense of "smooth operator" — they're out of your control. (The heart muscle is an exception to this two-party system; it is a striated muscle that happily beats whether you tell it to or not.) The muscle of your uterus is the epitome of smooth muscle. Unless you are a yogi who can tap into supraconscious states of body and will, you cannot make your uterus contract on command — but prostaglandins can. And the uterine production of prostaglandins is in part an autocrine one, that is, acting on itself and causing the mother organ to compress. The uterus makes prostaglandins to help expel decidua during menstruation, causing the contractions we experience as our old companions menstrual cramps. It makes prostaglandins during labor to help widen the cervix and push out the baby. But the uterine prostaglandins are not so provincial, and they will animate other smooth muscle tissue as well. They very likely affect the walls of your blood vessels, improving vascular tone and perhaps preventing the stiffening of the vessels that can lead to high blood pressure and heart disease.

There is more to the womb's inventory. The organ fabricates drugs that in other contexts would be illegal. It synthesizes and secretes beta-endorphins and dynorphins, two of the body's natural opiates and chemical cousins to morphine and heroin. It makes anandamide, a molecule almost identical to the active ingredient in marijuana. Until recently, these compounds were thought to be the exclusive property of the central nervous system — the brain and spinal cord. After all, we learned about natural opiates and natural marijuana by studying the impact of their plant-borne equivalents on the brain. The brain was thought to make these compounds endogenously because the brain sometimes needed them, perhaps to ease pain, perhaps to facilitate pleasure. Now it seems that the brain is an anodynic also-ran. The uterus produces at least as much opiate material as neural tissue does, and it makes ten times more of the cannabis equivalent than any other organ of the body does. We do not yet know why, though it's easy to spin theories. A pregnant woman will tell you in no uncertain terms of what use a steady stream of natural painkillers might be. If the womb is going to make such a spectacle of itself, the least it can do is to offer a source of comfort as it grows. Perhaps it makes opiates and cannabinoids so that it doesn't hurt too much in distention. Or perhaps the fetus is the intended beneficiary of the womb's pharmacopoeia. It is a tight squeeze in there, after all.

But painkilling is surely not the whole story, if indeed it is part of the story at all. Very likely the uterine opiates and their precursors influence the structure and performance of other body systems, including the blood vessels that permeate the uterus. The anandamides, for their part, seem to be part of the mechanism that controls cross-talk between the endometrium and the embryo that would implant in it. In this scenario, the uterus produces the marijuana-like compound in an optimal dose at just the spot where attachment should take place. The embryo has on its surface receptors for that marijuana-like molecule. When it is several days old and ready to fasten itself to the uterus, it moves toward the designated site of attachment and becomes literally hooked, embryo receptors clasping cannabinoid proteins. Now the embryo can invade the wall of the uterus. Now it can start forming the placenta that will feed it for nine months. The blastocyst is as yet brainless. There is nothing here of psychoactivity; the use of anandamide as a signaling molecule is purely coincidental, a molecular pleoaptation. Yet it is a pretty coincidence. A cannabinoid offers to the embryo in hard currency what it gives the recreational mystic only in fantasy: the path to enlightenment, to eyes that see and a mind to make of those sights what it will.

In truth, we know remarkably little about the purpose of the various opiates, chemicals, hormones, and hormone precursors that the uterus secretes with such vigor. We don't know how important the output is to our overall health and well-being beyond considerations of reproduction, nor do we know whether the various secretory skills continue past menopause. When the endometrium ceases to wax and wane, does the secretory program of the uterus likewise lapse into quiescence? Some experts say yes, some say no, all should probably settle with "don't know." We should be humbled by the fact that scientists discovered the very dramatic concentrations of anandamide in the uterus as recently as the late 1990s. And that humbleness should in turn enhance our vigilance against removing the uterus in all but the most extreme circumstances.

The hysterectomy is one of the most ancient surgeries, the first on record having been performed in Rome around the year A.D. 100 by the

Greek physician Archigenes. Today it is routine, like a root canal or the removal of cataracts. Every year at least 560,000 women in the United States are hysterectomized. That figure is so big it hurts to think about it. What it works out to is that every minute of every hour of every day, a woman has her uterus scooped out, sometimes abdominally, as Hope Phillips's was, sometimes through a tube inserted into the vagina or into a small slit in the stomach. Nor are the figures changing much from one year to the next, despite all the fury that has surrounded the practice for the past two or three decades. The rate did dip in the early eighties, possibly as a result of the rise of an activist women's health movement, but it has stayed pretty constant ever since. Some parts of the country are more hyster-happy than others. The incidence of the surgery is highest in the South and higher in rural areas than in major cities. However the geographical particulars shake out, the United States ranks as a world leader in hysterectomies, surpassing by anywhere from two- to six-fold the rates seen in Europe and the developing world. Only Australia and Japan manage to keep pace with us in womb-shucking.

The reasons, or "indications," for a hysterectomy are many. Only about 10 percent of the surgeries are performed to treat life-threatening illnesses such as cervical or uterine cancer. The rest are for so-called benign conditions, though they may feel malign to the women who suffer them. The commonest prompt is fibroids, Hope's hell; they account for almost 40 percent of all hysterectomies. Other typical reasons include endometriosis, when stray bits of endometrial tissue break away from the inside of the uterus and grow where they shouldn't, like on the outside of the uterus or around the fallopian tubes; unexplained heavy bleeding; unexplained pelvic pain, and the dipping down, or prolapse, of the uterus into the vaginal canal. The forties are dangerous years for the uterus. That's when a woman's menstrual cycles start becoming irregular and often heavier than before, when fibroids can start growing with the avidity of a fetus, and when a woman is old enough to think, To hell with it, I'm done with having or avoiding having children, maybe I don't need this bloody pouch after all. A woman who makes it to menopause with her uterus in situ has a good chance of keeping it till death does its part.

The story of hysterectomies is a huge one; with the numbers we're talking about, it has to be. Many books have been written on the subject, some attacking the so-called hysterectomy industry, others offering practical, gal-heart to gal-heart advice for women who are contemplating the procedure. The issue sets off a brushfire of fury — not quite as much as abortion, perhaps; nobody's calling anybody murderer, or holding up bloody pictures of excavated uteri, but people cry and pronounce and trade spitballs over it all the same. If you look into the issue in detail, you'll probably conclude, as I did, that — surprise — it isn't amenable to glib synopsis. There is no blanket solution, no simple explanation for why such a major operation is so routine. It would be nice to have one sovereign demon to heap blame on, one wicked Dr. Yes who hates women and wants to disembowel them all, but no such monster can be found, not under rock or bog, not in the codices of patriarchy, not wrapped around the caduceus of mainstream medicine.

Part of the explanation for the frequency of hysterectomies lies with the organ itself. As we have noted, the uterus is extraordinarily labile. It expands to comical dimensions during pregnancy. Its lining thickens and thins hundreds of times in a lifetime. As a result, it can end up a garden for aberrant formations — turnipy fibroids, mushroom-stemmed polyps, adhesions, windblown fragments of endometrium. Nobody knows what causes fibroids or why so many women have them. Diet may play a minor role. Our diets are too high in fat, and fat stimulates excess estrogen output, and estrogen helps make fibroids grow. But even lean, healthy vegetarians get fibroids, so fat takes us only so far. Some women are genetically predisposed to them. Fibroids run in families, and black women are more susceptible to them than women of other races are. Maybe estrogen-like chemicals in the environment are partly to blame. Whatever the reasons, the uterus is prone to local disturbances, and that is a fact rather than a conspiracy. Moreover, for a large number of women, menstrual bleeding gets considerably heavier in the forties, either because of the presence of fibroids or because of hormonal fluctuations preceding menopause. The midlife uterus runs off at the mouth, and that too is a fact.

How we respond to disturbances and changes in the body's status quo is another, far more subjective matter. Few women who start to bleed heavily in their forties after twenty-five years of moderate periods are aware that many of their peers are navigating the same floodwaters and that heavy bleeding in the premenopausal years is in fact normal.

Instead the woman thinks, This is disgusting, I'm hemorrhaging, I'll turn anemic, there must be something wrong, help! And she seeks help from a gynecologist and so exposes herself to the medical customs and opinions prevailing in her region. If she lives in a hip, eggheaded city where doctors, because of personal conviction or fear of lawsuits, steer away from heavy-handed procedures, she may be told, Wait it out, eat liver and iron pills, this too shall pass. If she lives in a small midwestern town as yet unruffled by activist winds, she may, in that initial doctor visit, be taking her first step toward total uterine eradication. Doctors are creatures of habit, and hysterectomies are a hoary surgeon's habit. They are simple to perform, and they are the surest cure for excess uterine bleeding. "For the people who do these things, it's a nice, comfortable way of life," says Ivan Strausz, the author of the book *You Don't Need a Hysterectomy* and a New York gynecologist of the scalpels-off persuasion. "The gynecologists are not always intellectually motivated to do the right thing. They go along and do what they've been doing all along."

In truth, any time a woman visits a doctor she risks intervention. Which brings us to the intriguing question of why European women have far fewer hysterectomies than Americans do. The issue has not been studied systematically. Some give it a sociocultural spin, pinning it to divergent attitudes toward aging. For Americans, the designation of our continent as the New World is less a detail of history than a directive in perpetuity, and even baby boomers, for all their numerical clout, have done little to improve the image of the non-new beyond making plastic surgery more socially acceptable. Catherine Deneuve, the great beauty whose face has probably sold more bottles of perfume than that of any other woman in history, said to an interviewer that it was hard getting old in any country, but unbearable in the United States. If a middle-aged woman in America is thought to be washed up and vaguely embarrassing, we can't expect that much respect will be accorded to any of her individual, overripe parts.

Maybe — but there's a more interesting possibility. Nora Coffey, the founder of the organization Hysterectomy Education Resource Services, or HERS, who is among the most zealous opponents of hysterectomies, suggested to me that European women keep their organs by keeping to themselves. Quite simply, they don't visit the doctor as often as we do. They reserve the delightful experience for times of real illness. We Americans patronize the health-care profession even when we're healthy. It's part of our chirpy wellness mindset. Women in particular are habituated to regular doctor visits, through the sacred annual gynecological checkup. We go in for a Pap smear, and we go in for a pelvic palpation: everything still in there? We think of this as wise preventive medicine, but doctors can't help themselves. They look for blemishes and portents. They seek the anomalous. And when they find a deviance from the norm, whatever the norm may be, of course they must tell the patient about it. They may counsel no action for the nonce beyond watchful waiting, but it's too late: the egg of worry has hatched. Now the woman will wonder, Is it getting worse? Could it be the reason that I'm feeling fatigued, crampy, not quite divine?

I can vouch for the insidious power of anomaly revealed. During one of my prenatal sonograms, which were being done to scan my fetus for any deviances she had to offer, I was told, You have fibroids.

The primal fear response set in; all systems seized. Is that a problem? I asked. Are they big? Can they harm the baby? Can they cause a miscarriage?

Oh, no, no, no, the sonographers assured me. There are just two, and they're small, maybe a couple of centimeters long. They're in the wall of the uterus.

Oh, I said. So what am I supposed to do?

Nothing, they replied. We just thought you should know. They may grow during pregnancy, or they may not. They may grow afterward, or they may not.

And if they do?

You may feel them. They may hurt. Or they may not. No need to worry. We just thought you should know.

So now I know I have fibroids. So now whenever I feel a twinge in my lower abdomen, the uh-oh routine growls in my head. They're getting bigger! They're taking over! I think of Hope Phillips's ropy purple fibroid, dwarfing the uterus in which it sprouted. I think of the largest fibroid on record, a mass that weighed 143 pounds when it was removed from a woman in 1888. Not surprisingly, the woman died soon after surgery. My fears are never enough to send me out for a fibroid audit, though. I'm better than a European; I'm the daughter of a Christian

Scientist. Years after my father abandoned the church, he retained its distaste for doctors, and I absorbed his phobia. (I won't promote the Angier philosophy too exuberantly, though. When a suspicious mole first appeared on my father's back, he refused to see a doctor until it had grown to the size of a silver dollar, at which point it was diagnosed as malignant melanoma and removed — but too late. A cancer that is eminently curable in its early stages instead had the chance to spread to my father's brain. He died of the metastasis at the age of fifty-one.)

In fact, it's possible that our sisters overseas do not have it right after all. Dr. Joanna M. Cain, of the Pennsylvania State University Medical School, has suggested that more women in Europe might choose to have a hysterectomy if the option were made available to them. Could it be that Europe's rate of the surgery is too low, rather than that ours is too high? It's easy to denounce hysterectomies, she says, and to bewail their frequency, and to argue that women are being misled by hidebound, greedy surgeons. But is it not an insult to women to assume naiveté and gullibility? If a woman spends years in pain and discomfort, sick and bleeding and consumed with the six inches of body between bellybutton and crotch, says Cain, who is she or anybody else to counsel, Oh, no, you mustn't have a hysterectomy. Under no circumstances should you have a hysterectomy. "We don't validate women's pain enough," Cain says. "We underestimate pain, we belittle it, and we undertreat it."

Women get tired of being harangued. I spoke with many intelligent women who had done their homework. They were assiduous and enlightened medical consumers who read everything they could find on hysterectomies. They knew their options, and most had tried other procedures before settling on a hysterectomy. The one thing they resented was the self-righteousness of the wards of the womb. They complained about being made to feel weak and ashamed for their decision. They argued that anti-hysterectomy fever is another example of reductionism and idolatry, of defining a woman by her high holy uterus. It is rank paternalism, they said, the worse for coming from sororal mouths. If a person had an appendectomy, they said, would she be chastised for failure to respect her appendix?

Many of the women said they felt better than ever after a hysterectomy. They felt lighter, freer — the uterus had kept them in chains, and now at last they could wander. Now they hoped to help keep others from going through the prolonged misery that they suffered. They wanted to remove the stigma of the surgery. Again and again in the course of my reporting I heard variations on the line "The one thing I'm sorry about is that I didn't do it sooner!"

We come back to the matter of choices, wonderful choices. Isn't it grand to live in a world that promotes "choices"? A woman should be allowed to choose a hysterectomy without being made to feel guilty or diminished. That is easy to say and to advocate. At the same time, a choice has meaning only if it is freely and knowingly embraced, with all the risks, benefits, and alternatives honestly arrayed before the chooser. Such a state of enlightenment is difficult for anybody to achieve, and we are talking about the necessity of its being achieved half a million times a year. For example, let's return to the matter of fibroids. Doctors in big, hip cities generally will assure a woman with asymptomatic fibroids that nothing needs to be done, everybody has them, the growths recede with menopause, and so on, all of which is true. But if the woman is passing such large clots of bloody tissue that she is becoming ill, or if she is in terrible pain, then the fibroids must be treated, at which point even the most urbane doctors can give bum advice. A woman who still plans to bear children is counseled to have a myomectomy, the removal of the fibroids alone. But for the woman who is past having or desiring progeny, the myomectomy option is presented in terms so dire it might as well be plastered with a skull and crossbones. The woman is told that a myomectomy is much riskier and bloodier than a hysterectomy, with a higher rate of postsurgical complications and infections. I interviewed dozens of women in their forties and early fifties who sought help for their fibroids and were told hysterectomy, period. When they asked about a myomectomy, their doctors argued against it. But is a myomectomy really as bloody and dangerous as it's portrayed? In many cases, the fibroids that give a woman difficulty can be removed hysteroscopically, through a tube like a periscope that is threaded up the vagina and into the uterus. The doctor inserts a tool into the hysteroscope and then shells out the offending tumors, chipping away at them until only their husks remain. This sort of hysteroscopic myomectomy can be done in an office and does not even count as true surgery, let alone as a bloody horror show. Yet few women hear of the option, one reason being that it requires a skillfulness not all gynecologists command. If your doctor has no experience with hysteroscopic myomectomies, find one who does; the procedure is the best first-line attack against symptomatic fibroids.

Even when the fibroids are inaccessible to hysteroscopic scoop-out, they can be removed abdominally, by opening the uterus, cutting out the fibroids, and sewing the uterus back up again. Now we're talking about major surgery, but if you research the medical literature, you'll find that abdominal myomectomies compare favorably with hysterectomies in factors such as blood loss, postsurgical complications and infections, and healing time. I observed an abdominal myomectomy performed at Bryn Mawr Hospital by Dr. Michael Toaff, who specializes in the procedure, and it was surprisingly clean. The woman sacrificed perhaps twenty or thirty cubic centimeters of blood, no more than she would have for a few routine blood tests. She, as well as many others I talked with who had similar operations, recovered in a couple of weeks and felt exhilarated, liberated, resuscitated from the dead — just the way women say they feel after a hysterectomy.

Ah, but doctors can always retort, You may be fine for now, but remember, *fibroids grow back.* Then what will you do, Lady Womb-Keeper? Have another myomectomy? Or accept the hysterectomy at last? In fact, while it's true that a woman who has fibroids is prone to fibroids, the great majority of the tumors will give no trouble at all, so that even if a new fibroid does appear in the wake of a myomectomy, it will likely be meaningless, the way most fibroids are. Just because one fibroid caused you misery doesn't mean your next one will. Nonetheless, accepted verities are hard to shatter, and the purported dangers and futility of a myomectomy continue to influence physicians' attitudes and thus the advice they give to their patients. Yes, women should have "choices," including a hysterectomy, but it's hard to choose wisely when the best items on the menu have been edited out beforehand.

To assert our choices freely, we need stronger tongues — for ourselves, of course, to proclaim what we must about our bodies and our desires, but also for our doctors, so they can hold those tongues in check rather than say thoughtless, callous things. For better or worse, we often feel meek when we visit doctors. They are like our parents, and they can hurt us too easily. Doctors should never tell patients that they are beyond needing a uterus, that the uterus is "just a sack, whaddya want it for anymore?" Yet they do. All the recent emphasis on bedside manners, and still the clichés and witlessisms fly. One woman described to me the miserable time she had with her gynecologist. She was fifty-eight years old, and her uterus was prolapsing into her vagina. The doctor told her, Have a hysterectomy.

I don't want a hysterectomy, she said. I don't want to go into early menopause. I'm not ready for that. Isn't there some alternative?

Early menopause? the doctor said in disbelief. You're fifty-eight years old. You're *post*menopausal.

Believe it or not, she said, I'm still having my periods.

Oh, I see, he replied. So what do you want for that, a medal?

That man should take out malpractice insurance on his mouth. The woman had her hysterectomy. Now she is having other problems. Instead of a prolapsed uterus, she has a prolapsed bladder. Let's learn at least one thing from her misfortune. If a doctor says something inane, callous, or excessively light during a consultation for gynecological problems, find another doctor. Do not trust him, or her, to give you sound advice. Leave the punchlines to sitcoms and Muhammad Ali.

To make a truly informed choice, we need information. Part of that information cannot yet be had, for as we have seen, the uterus is still terra in need of investigative cognition. Much information exists right now but takes work to gather, metabolize, and personalize. A woman must know the particulars of her sexual and emotional demesne. If her erotic life is important to her, for example, and her orgasms tend to be deep and pulsating, she should try anything before relinquishing her uterus. We have been schooled in the primacy of the clitoris to female sexuality, but it is the contractions of the uterus and cervix that lend a climax its subterranean vibrato. A woman should realize that some consequences of a hysterectomy cannot be predicted, no matter how well she prepares herself. She may have decided on a "conservative" operation that removes the uterus while leaving the ovaries in place. By saving her ovaries, she thinks, her biochemical status will remain stable and she will avoid the threats to heart, bone, and brain that come with an abrupt cessation of ovarian hormones. Unfortunately, there are no guarantees; it turns out that a third of the time the ovaries never recover from the physical trauma of the hysterectomy, and they end up *in vivo* but inert. Moreover, even when the ovaries survive, a heightened risk of high blood pressure and heart disease remains, possibly because the extraction of the uterus eliminates one source of prostaglandins that help protect blood vessels.

The aftermath of a hysterectomy can be terrible or wonderful or banal, and there are plenty of women out there who will testify for each possibility (or shall we say ovarify, given the origins of *testify* in the word *testis*, a reference to the male practice of swearing by something while gripping his most sacred possessions?). Some women say they became depressed and fatigued after a hysterectomy and have never recovered. Some say that their feelings for their children are diminished, as though they lost with the uterus a kind of emotional bas-relief of the babies the organ once carried. There are women who say they feel great and wish they had done it sooner. There are women who say they aren't about to celebrate the surgery, but they didn't have much of a choice and they're doing fine. Beth Tiner, of Los Angeles, started a support group on the Internet called Sans Uteri for women who have had hysterectomies or are considering a hysterectomy. The group doesn't judge. It doesn't have a position for or against. Tiner herself had a hysterectomy at the age of twenty-five to treat endometriosis that had tormented her with pain since she was seventeen. She doesn't regret having had the surgery. She doesn't have the pain anymore. Nonetheless, she anticipates that other problems in her life will arise as a result of having lost her uterus and ovaries at such a young age. Some women teach themselves to become strong and libidinous again after a hysterectomy. In a tart and moving fictionalized account of her hysterectomy called "So You're Going to Have a New Body!" the novelist Lynne Sharon Schwartz describes her attempts to recover after the surgery, an ad-lib program that included dumping her insipid male gynecologist, having a brief affair with an old and reliably dexterous lover, and running ever faster around the Central Park reservoir. A year after the operation, she felt much better, fond of her new body, "accepting its hollowness with, if not equanimity, at least tolerance." Still, she retained the "tenuous sense of waiting," like a woman who has come to the edge of a cliff and lingers there too long. What she was waiting for, she had no idea.

Eighteen months after her hysterectomy, Hope Phillips also is fine — not exhilarated, just fine. She is glad she had the hysterectomy rather than trying a myomectomy for the simple reason that she's terrified of

surgery and was not willing to risk needing more later. The hysterectomy initially left her with stomach muscles so weakened that during a
three-month trip to Africa, she could barely sit up as she jostled along
the dirt roads in a putative all-terrain vehicle, and at one point her back
gave out. Returning home, she started a vigorous exercise program, and
the pain and numbness in her belly gradually disappeared. The loss of
her uterus has not affected her erotic life. Her relationship with the man
she was seeing survived the spinning teacup of gynecological surgery, of
her becoming, for at least a moment in his mind, akin to his mother's
friends. They were married in 1997, and I mean married, holding one
wedding in California and another in Zimbabwe. Hope Phillips once
again feels at home on the road, now that her suitcase carries what it
was meant to — which for her, the practiced wanderer, means almost
nothing at all.

7

CIRCULAR REASONINGS

THE STORY OF THE BREAST

NANCY BURLEY, a professor of evolution and ecology at the University of California in Irvine, plays Halloween with birds. She takes male zebra finches and she accessorizes them. A normal, pre-Burley finch is a beautiful animal, red of beak and orange of cheek, his chest a zebra print of stripes, his underwings polka-dotted in orange, and his eyes surrounded by vertical streaks of black and white, like the eyes of a mime artist. One thing the zebra finch does not have is a crest, as some species of birds do. So Burley will give a male a crest. She will attach a tall white cap of feathers to his head, turning him into Chef Bird-o-Dee. Or she'll give him a tall red Cat-in-the-Hat cap. His bird legs are normally a neutral shade of grayish beige, so she gives him flashy anklets of red, yellow, lavender, or powder blue. And by altering the visual pith of him, his finchness, Burley alters his life. As she has shown in a series of wonderful, amusing, important experiments, female zebra finches have decided opinions about the various accouterments. They love the tall white chef caps, and they will clamor to mate with a male so haberdashed. Zebra finches ordinarily couple up and abide by a system of shared parental care of nestlings, but if a female is paired with a white-hatted male, she gladly works overtime on child care and allows him to laze — though he doesn't laze but spends his free time philandering. Call the benighted wife the bird who mistakes a hat for a mate.

But put a male in a tall red cap, and the females turn up their beaks. No trophy he: you can have him, sister. If a red-capped male manages to obtain a mate, he ends up being so busy taking care of his offspring that he has no time for extramarital affairs, and there are no demands for his moonlighting services anyway.

The opposite holds true for leg bands. Dress a male in white ankle rings and he's of scant appeal. Put him in red and he's a lovebird.

Zebra finches have no good reason for being drawn to white toques and red socks. We cannot look at the results of Burley's costume experiments and say, Ah, yes, the females are using the white crest as an indicator that the male will be a good father, or that his genes are robust and therefore he's a great catch. A zebra finch with a white crest can hardly be said to bear superior finch genes when he's not supposed to have a crest in the first place. Instead, the unexpected findings offer evidence of the so-called sensory exploitation theory of mate choice. By this proposal, the white hat takes advantage of a neurophysiological process in the zebra finch's brain that serves some other, unknown purpose but that is easily coopted and aroused. The hat stimulates an extant neural pathway, and it lures the female, and the female does not know why, but she knows what she likes. We can understand that impulse, the enticement of an object we deem beautiful. "Human beings have an exquisite aesthetic sense that is its own justification," Burley says. "Our ability to appreciate impressionistic painting cannot be called functional. In my mind, that's what we're seeing with the zebra finches. The preferences are aesthetic, not functional. They don't correlate with anything practical."

Nevertheless, the evidence suggests that if a male finch someday were born with a mutation that gives him a touch of a white thatch, the mutation would spread rapidly through finchdom, possibly becoming accentuated over time, until a bird had the toque by nature that Burley loaned by contrivance. No doubt some researchers in that hypothetical future would assume that the finch's white cap had meaning and was an indicator of zebra finch mettle, and they'd speculate about the epistemology of the trait.

A woman's breasts, I argue, are like Burley's white crests. They're pretty, they're flamboyant, they're irresistible. But they are arbitrary, and they signify much less than we think. This is a contrarian view. Evolutionary theorists have proposed many explanations for the existence of the breast, usually according it a symbolic or functional value, as a signal to men of information they need to know about a potential mate. How can we not give the breast its evolutionary due when it is there in our faces, begging for narrative. "Few issues have been the focus for a wider range of speculation based on fewer facts than the evolutionary origin and physiological function of women's breasts," the biologist Caroline Pond has written. The stories about the breast sound real and persuasive, and they may all have a germ of validity, because we ascribe meaning wherever and however we choose; that is one of the perquisites of being human. As the actress Helen Mirren said in the movie *O Lucky Man,* "All religions are equally true."

Still, I will argue that breasts fundamentally are here by accident. They are sensory exploiters. They say little or nothing about a woman's inherent health, quality, or fecundity. They are accouterments. If we go looking for breasts and for ways to enhance and display our breasts, to make them stand out like unnatural, almost farcical Barbie-doll missile heads, then we are doing what breasts have always done, which is appeal to an irrational aesthetic sense that has no function but that begs to be amused. The ideal breasts are, and always have been, stylized breasts. A woman's breasts welcome illusion and the imaginative opportunities of clothing. They can be enhanced or muted, as a woman chooses, and their very substance suggests as much: they are soft and flexible, clay to play with. They are funny things, really, and we should learn to laugh at them, which may be easier to do if we first take them seriously.

The most obvious point to be made about the human breast is that it is unlike any other bosom in the primate order. The breasts of a female ape or monkey swell only when she is lactating, and the change is usually so modest that it can be hard to see beneath her body hair. Once the mother has weaned her offspring, her breasts flatten back. Only in humans do the breasts inflate at puberty, before the first pregnancy occurs or could even be sustained, and only in humans do they remain engorged throughout life. In fact, the swelling of the breasts in pregnant and lactating women occurs quite independently of pubertal breast development, and in a more uniform manner: a small-breasted woman's breasts grow about as much during pregnancy, in absolute terms, as a busty woman's breasts do, which is why the temporary expansion is comparatively more noticeable on a small-breasted woman. For all women, maternal augmentation results from the proliferation and distention of the cells of the ducts and lobules (the dairy equipment), increased blood flow, water retention, and the milk itself. Small-breasted women have the same amount of lactogenic tissue as large-breasted women do — about a teaspoonful per nonlactating breast — and when they lactate, they can make as much milk. Given the functional nature of lactation, it is under selective pressure to follow fairly standardized rules of behavior.

The growth of the aesthetic breast is another thing altogether. Here, it is development of the fatty and connective tissues of the breast that accounts for its mass. As tissues with few cellular responsibilities or functional restrictions, fat and its fibrous netting can follow the whim of fashion and the consequences of sensory exploitation. They can be enlarged, exaggerated, and accentuated without exacting a great cost to their possessors, at least up to a point. In Philip Roth's novel *Sabbath's Theater*, the following exchange occurs between the eponymous dilet-tante of the sewer, Mickey Sabbath, and a small-breasted patient in a mental hospital:

> "Tits. I understand tits. I have been studying tits since I was thir-teen years old. I don't think there's any other organ or body part that evidences so much variation in size as women's tits."
>
> "I *know*," replied Madeline, openly enjoying herself suddenly and beginning to laugh. "And why is that? Why did God allow this enor-mous variation in breast size? Isn't it amazing? There are women with breasts ten times the size of mine. Or even more. True?"
>
> "That is true."
>
> "People have big noses," she said. "I have a small nose. But are there people with noses ten times the size of mine? Four or five, max. I don't know why God did this to women. . . .
>
> "But I don't think size has to do with milk production," said Made-line. "No, that doesn't solve the problem of what this enormous variation is *for*."

As mad Madeline says, the aesthetic breast that is subject to such wide variation in scale is not the mammalian breast gland that ranks as an organ, a necessary piece of anatomy. On the contrary, the aesthetic breast is nonfunctional to the point of being counterfunctional, which is why it strikes us as so beautiful. We are not enticed by the practical. We understand the worthiness of the practical, but we rarely find it beautiful. The large, nonlactating female breast has so much intrinsic, irrational appeal that it almost sabotages itself. We love the hemispheric breast for itself, independent of, and often in spite of, its glandular role. We love it enough that we can be made squeamish by the sight of a breastfeeding woman. It is not the exposure of the breast in public that makes us uncomfortable, for we welcome an extraordinary degree of décolletage and want to walk toward it, to gaze at it. Nor is it the reminder of our animal nature, for we can eat many things in public and put pieces of food in a baby's mouth — or a bottle of breast milk, for that matter — without eliciting a viewer's discomfort at the patent display of bodily need. Instead, it is the convergence of the aesthetic and the functional that disturbs and irritates us. When we find the image of a breastfeeding mother lovely or appealing, we do so by negating the aesthetic breast in our minds and focusing on the bond between mother and infant, on the miraculous properties that we imagine human milk to have, or on thoughts of warmth, comfort, and love recalled from our childhood. The maternal breast soothes us and invites us to rest. The aesthetic breast arouses us, grabs us by the collar or the bodice, and so it is used on billboards and magazine covers and everywhere we turn. The two conceptual breasts appeal to distinct pathways. One is ancient and logical, the love of mama and mammary. (Sarah Blaffer Hrdy has written: "The Latin term for breasts, *mammae*, derives from the plaintive cry 'mama,' spontaneously uttered by young children from widely divergent linguistic groups and often conveying a single, urgent message, 'suckle me.'") The other pathway is much newer, specific to our species, and it is noisier and more gratuitous. Being strictly human, the aesthetic breast puts on airs and calls itself divine.

Because the display of the beckoning breast is aggressive and ubiquitous in the United States, we are said to be unusually, even pathologically, breast-obsessed. In other cultures, including parts of Africa and Asia, breasts are pedestrian. "From my research in China, it's very clear that the breast is much less sexualized there than it is in American culture," Emily Martin, the cultural historian and author of *Flexible Bodies*, said to me. "It's neither hidden nor revealed in any particular way in women's dress or undergarments. In many villages, women sit in the sun with their breasts exposed, and older women will be out washing clothes with their breasts exposed, and it's all completely irrelevant to erotic arousal." Yet if breast obsession varies in intensity from country to country and era to era, it nonetheless is impressively persistent, and it is not limited to men, or to strictly sexual tableaux. "Everybody loves breasts," Anne Hollander, the author of *Seeing Through Clothes*, told me. "Babies love them, men love them, women love them. The whole world knows that breasts are engines of pleasure. They're great treasures of the human race, and you can't get away from them." The first thing that women did in the fourteenth century, when they broke free of the shapeless drapery of the Christian era, was to flaunt their bosoms. Men shortened their outfits and exposed their legs, women lowered the neckline and tightened the bodice. They pushed their breasts together and up. They took the soft and floppy tissue of the breasts and molded it with corsets and whalebones into firm, projecting globes. "As a fashion gimmick, you can never go wrong with breasts," Hollander says. "They may be deemphasized for a short period, as they were in the sixteenth century, when tiny breasts and thick waists were in vogue, and during the flapper era of the 1920s. But breasts always come back, because we love them so much."

What we love is not the breast per se but the fantasy breast, the aesthetic breast of no practical value. At a recent exhibition of Cambodian sculpture spanning the sixth through fifteenth centuries, I noticed that most of the female deities depicted had breasts that might have been designed by modern plastic surgeons: large, round, and firm. Helen of Troy's breasts were said to be of such flawless, curved, suspended substance that goblets could be cast from their form, as Ezra Pound told us in Canto 120: "How to govern is from Kuan Tze/but the cup of white gold in Petera/Helen's breast gave that." In the art of ancient India, Tibet, Crete, and elsewhere, the cups never runneth over, and women are shown with celestial breasts, zero-gravity planet breasts, the sorts of breasts I've almost never seen in years of using health-club locker rooms. On real women, I've seen breasts as varied as faces: breasts shaped like tubes, breasts shaped like tears, breasts that flop down, breasts that point up, breasts that are dominated by thick, dark nipples and areolae, breasts with nipples so small and pale they look airbrushed. We erroneously associate floppy breasts with older breasts, when in fact the drooping of the breast can happen at any age; some women's breasts are low-slung from the start. Thus the high, cantilevered style of the idealized breast must be considered more than just another expression of a taste for youth.

We don't know why there is such a wide variety of breast sizes, or what exactly controls the growth of the breast, particularly the fat tissue that gives the human breast its bulk. As mammary glands, human breasts follow the standard mammalian pattern. A mammary gland is a modified sweat gland, and milk is highly enriched sweat. Prolactin, the hormone responsible for milk production, predates the evolution of mammals, originally serving to maintain salt and water balance in early vertebrates such as fish — in essence, allowing fish to sweat. In monotremes, the platypus and the spiny anteater, which are considered the most primitive of living mammals, the milk simply seeps from the gland onto the nippleless surface of the mother's skin, rather as sweat does, and is licked off by the young.

Breast tissue begins to develop early, by the fourth week of fetal life. It grows along two parallel milk ridges, ancient mammalian structures that extend from the armpits down to the groin. Males and females both have milk ridges, but only in females do they receive enough hormonal stimulation later in life to achieve complete breastiness. If we were rats or pigs, our twin milk strips would develop into a total of eight teats, to meet the demands of large litters. Mammals such as elephants, cows, goats, and primates, which give birth to only one or two offspring at a time, require only two mammary glands, and so the bulk of the milk strip regresses during fetal development. Among four-legged grazing animals, the teats that grow are located at the hindquarters, where the young can suckle beneath the protective awning of a mother's powerful hind legs and rib cage. In at least one primitive primate, the aye-aye, the twin teats also are situated at the rear end of the mother. But among monkeys, apes, and humans, who either hold their young or carry them clinging to their chests (the better to navigate arboreally), the nipples graced with milk are the uppermost two, closest to the armpits.

Our potential breasts do not entirely abandon us, though. The milk ridge reminds us of our lineage subcutaneously: breast tissue is distributed far more extensively than most of us realize, reaching from the collarbone down to the last two ribs and from the breastbone, in the middle of the chest, to the back of the armpit. In some people the milk ridge expresses itself graphically, as extra nipples or entire extra breasts. Recalling her years as a lingerie saleswoman, an essayist in the *New York*

Times Magazine wrote about a customer looking for a bra that would fit her unusual figure. The woman bared her breasts to the essayist, Janifer Dumas. The woman was a modern-day Artemis, the goddess of the hunt, who often is portrayed with multiple breasts. In this case, Artemis had three equal-sized breasts, the standard two on either side of her thorax and the third directly below the left one. Dumas found the perfect item, a "bralette," similar to a sports bra but with a more relaxed fit, no underwire, and a wide elastic band to hug the rib cage. "It occurred to me that this was also the type of bra I sold to women with recent mastectomies," Dumas wrote, "a piece of lingerie designed for comfort, and, as it turned out, able to accommodate more or less."

Primordial breast tissue arises early in embryogenesis, yet the breast is unusual among body parts in that it remains primordial until puberty or later. No other organ, apart from the uterus, changes so dramatically in size, shape, and function as the breast does during puberty, pregnancy, and lactation. It is because the breast must be poised to alter its contours repeatedly throughout adulthood, swelling and shrinking with each new mouth to feed, that it is prone to turning cancerous. The genetic controls that keep cell growth in check elsewhere in the corpus are relaxed in the breast, giving malignancy an easy foothold.

The aesthetic breast develops in advance of the glandular one. Early in adolescence, the brain begins secreting regular bursts of hormones that stimulate the ovaries. The ovaries in turn discharge estrogen, and estrogen encourages the body to lay down fat "depots" in the breast. That adipose tissue is suspended in a gelatinous matrix of connective fibers that extend from the muscle of the chest wall to the underside of the breast skin. Connective tissue can stretch and stretch, to accommodate as much fat as the body inserts between its fibers; the connective tissue's spring gives the breast its bounce. Estrogen is necessary to the aesthetic breast, but it is not sufficient; the hormone alone does not explain the wide variability in breast size. A woman with large breasts does not necessarily have higher estrogen levels than a small-breasted woman. Rather, the tissue of the breast is more or less responsive to estrogen, a sensitivity determined in part by genetic makeup. Among the sensitive, a very small amount of estrogen fosters an impressive bosom. Estrogen-sensitive women who take birth control pills may discover that they need bigger bras, while the estrogen-insensitive can swallow oral contraceptives by the foilful and find their breasts unmoved. Even some children are extremely sensitive to estrogen. Berton Roueche, the great medical writer, recounted the story of a six-year-old boy who began growing breasts. Eventually, the source of the hypertrophy was traced to his vitamin tablets. A single stamping machine had been used to punch out the vitamins and estrogen pills. "Think of the minute amount of estrogen the stamping machine passed on to the vitamin tablets," Roueche wrote. "And what a profound effect it had." The boy's breasts retreated on cessation of the vitamin tablets, and his parents could breathe again.

Conversely, androgens such as testosterone can inhibit breast adiposity. As we saw earlier, women who are genetically insensitive to androgen may grow very large breasts. Men whose gonads fail to produce enough testosterone sometimes suffer from gynecomastia. Without testosterone to keep breast growth in check, the men's small amount of estrogen has the opportunity to lay down selective depots of fat hurriedly, demonstrating once again that the line between maleness and femaleness is thin — as thin as the fetus's bipotential genital ridge, as thin as the milk ridge in all of us. Yet androgens don't entirely explain discrepancies in breast size among women either. Many women with comparatively high testosterone levels, women whose visible mustaches and abundant armpit hair make it clear that they are not insensitive to the androgens coursing through them, nonetheless have full frontal shelves. Thyroid hormones, stress hormones, insulin, growth hormone — all leave their smudgy fingerprints on mammogenesis. In sum, we don't know what makes the aesthetic breast. We don't have the hormonal recipe for the universal Mae West breast. If science fiction television is any indication, though, in the future, the heartbreak of "micromastia" (plastic-surgeon-speak for small breasts) will be surmounted, and if our brains don't get bigger, our breasts surely will. Today, the average nonlactating breast weighs two thirds of a pound and measures about four inches across and two and a half inches from chest wall to nipple tip. The average brassiere size is a 36B, and it has been since the modern bra was invented about ninety years ago. On television shows like *Star Trek*, however, every woman of every race, whether human, Vulcan, Klingon, or Borg, is as bold in bust as in spirit, and no cup less than C will be cast.

Estrogen also helps spur the elaboration of the practical breast, the glandular tissue that presumably will soon secrete its clouded, honied sweat. A series of firm, rubbery ducts and lobes begin threading their way through the fat and ligamentous glue. Each breast usually ends up with between five and nine lobes, where the milk is generated, and each lobe has its independent duct, the conduit that carries the milk to the nipple. The lobes are subdivided into about two dozen lobules, which look like tiny clusters of grapes. The lobes and lobules are distributed fairly evenly throughout the breast, but all the ducts lead to a single destination, the nipple. As the ducts converge on the nipple, curling and bending like snakes or strands of ivy, their diameters widen. The circuitry of lactation follows the hydrodynamic pattern that we recognize from trees, or the veins in a leaf, or the blood vessels in the body. The lobes and lobules are the foliage, the fruits and leaves, while the ducts are the branches, thickening into a braid of trunks. But while in a tree or the body's vasculature the fluid of life is pumped from the widest conduit out to the narrowest vessel or vein, here the milk is generated in each tiny lobular fruit and pulsed to the spacious pipeline below. The ducts perforate the skin of the nipple, and though these portals ordinarily are concealed by the warty folds of the nipple tip, when a woman is nursing her nipple balloons out and looks like a watering can, each ductal hole visible and visibly secreting milk.

The ducts and lobules do not fully mature until pregnancy, when they proliferate, thicken, and differentiate. Granular plugs the consistency of ear wax, which normally keep the ducts sealed up, begin breaking down. The lobules sprout microlobules, the alveoli. The dairy farmers commandeer the breast. They push fat out of the way to make more room for themselves. The breast gains as much as a pound while lactating. The areola, that pigmented bull's-eye surrounding the nipple, also changes markedly in pregnancy. It darkens and seems to creep down the hillock of the breast, like lava spreading slowly from the peak of a volcano. The areola is permeated by another set of modified sweat glands, the little goosebumps called Montgomery's glands, and the bumps multiply in the maternal breast and exude lubricating moisture to make the sensation of suckling bearable. After weaning, the lobules atrophy, the ducts regress, the areola retreats, and the fat reclaims dominion over the breast — more or less. Women who breastfeed their children often complain that their breasts never recover their former bounce and bulk. The fat grows lazy and fails to reinfiltrate the spaces from which it was edged out by the gland. The aesthetic breast is a bon vivant, after all, a party favor. For reliability, look to the ducts and lobules. They'll return when needed, and they're not afraid to work up a sweat.

Breasts weigh a few ounces in fact and a few tons in metaphor. As Marilyn Yalom describes admirably in her cultural study *A History of the Breast,* the breast is a communal kiosk, open to all pronouncements and cranks, and the endorsements of the past are easily papered over with the homilies of today. The withered tits of witches and devils represented the wages of lust. In Minoan statues dating from 1600 B.C., priestesses are shown with bare, commanding breasts and snakes wrapped around each arm. The snakes strain their heads toward the viewer, their extended tongues echoing the erect nipples of the figurine, as though to warn that the powerful bosom they bracket might as soon dispense poison as love. The breast is a bralette, able to accommodate more or less. The multibreasted goddess seen in many cultures projects tremendous strength. So too do the Amazons, those mythical female warriors who lived apart from men, consorting with them once a year solely for the sake of being impregnated, and who reared their daughters but slayed, crippled, or abandoned their sons. The Amazons are most famed for their self-inflicted mastectomies, their willingness to cut off one breast to improve their archery skills and thus to resist conquest by the male hordes surrounding them. For men, Yalom writes, "Amazons are seen as monsters, viragos, unnatural women who have misappropriated the masculine warrior role. The missing breast creates a terrifying asymmetry: one breast is retained to nurture female offspring, the other is removed so as to facilitate violence against men." For women, the Amazon represents an inchoate wish, a nostalgic longing for the future. "The removal of the breast and the acquisition of 'masculine' traits suggests this mythic Amazon's desire to be bisexual, both a nurturing female and an aggressive male, with the nurturance directed exclusively toward other women and the aggression directed exclusively toward men." A softened variant of the Amazon icon occurred in eighteenth-century France, when the figure of Liberty often was shown with one breast clothed, the other bared, her willingness to reveal her breast (or at least her indifference to her temporary state of dishabille) evidence of her commitment to the cause. More recently, women who have had a breast surgically removed for the treatment of cancer have assumed the mantle of the Amazon warrior and proudly, angrily publicized their naked, asymmetrical torsos on magazine covers and in advertisements. Where the breast once was, now there is a diagonal scar, crossing the chest like a bow or a bandolier, alarming, thrilling, and beautiful in its fury.

The breast has been used like a cowbrand, to denote possession. In Rembrandt's famous portrait *The Jewish Bride,* the husband, considerably the elder of the two, is shown with his right hand covering the bride's left breast, claiming her, including her within his gentle, paternal jurisdiction, and her hand reaches up to graze his groping one — though whether as an expression of modesty, concurrence, or hesitation is left gorgeously unclear. In nineteenth-century America, female slaves being put up for auction were photographed barechested, to underscore their status as beasts to be bought. In driving a metaphor home, breasts were beaten, tortured, and mutilated. In the seventeenth century, women accused of witchcraft often had their breasts hacked off before they were burned at the stake. When Anna Pappenheimer, a Bavarian woman who was the daughter of gravediggers and latrine cleaners, was condemned as a witch, her breasts were not merely cut off but stuffed into her mouth and then into the mouths of her two grown sons, a grotesque mockery of Pappenheimer's maternal role.

Early scientists too had to have their say on the breast. In the eighteenth-century, Linnaeus, the ever-colorful Swedish taxonomist, paid the breast a dubious honor by naming an entire class after it: Mammalia, literally "of the breast," a term of Linnaeus's invention. As Londa Schiebinger has described, Linneaus could have chosen from other features that mammals were known at the time to have in common. We could have been classified as Pilosa, the hairy ones, or as Aurecaviga, the hollow-eared ones (a reference to the distinctive three-boned structure of the mammalian middle ear), or as bearers of a four-chambered heart (term uncoined and perhaps uncoinable). But despite the derision of some of Linnaeus's contemporaries, we and our fuzzy, viviparous kin became mammals. It was the Enlightenment, and Linnaeus had a point to make, and so again the breast was called upon to service metaphor. Zoologists accepted that humans were a type of animal, as uncomfortable as the notion was and remains. A taxon was needed that would link humans to other species. Whatever feature Linnaeus chose to highlight as the bond between us and them inevitably would become the synecdoche of our beastliness. All mammals are hairy, but men are hairier than women, so Pilosa wouldn't do. The structure of the ear is too dull to merit immortalization through nomenclature. The breast, however, has romance and resonance, and best of all, it is most highly articulated in women. In the same volume in which Linnaeus introduced the term *Mammalia,* he also gave us our species name, *Homo sapiens,* man of wisdom, the category distinguishing humans from all other species. "Thus, within Linnaean terminology, a female characteristic (the lactating mamma) ties humans to brutes, while a traditionally male characteristic (reason) marks our separateness," Schiebinger writes. Thinkers of the Enlightenment advocated the equality and natural rights of all men, and some women of the time, including Mary Wollstonecraft and Abigail Adams, John's wife, argued that women too should be given their due rights — enfranchisement, for example, or the rights to own property and divorce a brutal spouse. The husbands of the Enlightenment smiled with tolerance and sympathy, but they were not prepared to peep over that political precipice. Through zoology and the taxonomic reinforcement of woman's earthiness, rational men found convenient justification for postponing matters of women's rights until woman's reason, her *sapientia,* was fully established. (Interestingly, though, human milk has often been characterized as the purest and most ethereal of body fluids, the least brutish aspect of a woman, as we will see in the chapter that follows.)

In the nineteenth century, some scientists used the breast as phrenologists have used the skull, to demarcate and rank the various human races. Certain breasts were more equal than others. The European breast was drawn as a hemisphere standing at full attention — meet the smart and civilized breast. The breast of an African woman was portrayed as flabby and pendulous, like the udder of a goat. In abolitionist literature, illustrations of female slaves gave them high, round, sympathetic breasts — the melanized counterparts to the pop-up breasts of the slaves' tightly cinched mistresses.

Linnaeus hog-tied us to other mammals by our possession of teats, but our breasts, we know, are ours alone. Evolutionary thinkers have known it too, and they have given us a wide selection of justifications for the human breast. As Caroline Pond says, there is little evidence to support any of the theories. We don't have a clue when in human evolution breasts first began their rise. Breasts don't fossilize. We don't know if they appeared before we lost our body hair or after, and in any event we don't know when — or why — we lost our body hair. But breasts are such a prominent feature of a woman's body that scientists keep staring at them, looking for clues. They are baffled by breasts, and they should be.

Men don't have breasts, but they like to stake their claim on breasts, to grope their Jewish bride, and to feel they had a hand in inventing them. We must not be surprised if many evolutionary theories assume that breasts arose to talk to men. By far the most famous explanation in this genre comes from Desmond Morris, the British zoologist, who in 1967 wrote a spectacularly successful book, *The Naked Ape,* in which he presented a metaphor nonpareil, of breasts as buttock mimics. You've probably heard this theory in some form. It's hard to escape it. Like the Rolling Stones, it refuses to retire. As originally conceived, the theory rested on a sequence of assumptions, the first being that men and women needed to form a pair bond — better known as marriage — to raise children. The pair bond required the cultivation of sustained intimacy between partners, which meant intercourse was best done face to face rather than in the anonymous doggy-style position presumed to be the copulatory technique of our prehuman ancestors. To that end, the clitoris migrated forward, to give early women the incentive to seek frontal sex. For the gentlemen, the breast arose as an inspiration to modify their technique, offering a recapitulation ventrally of a body part they had so coveted from behind. In subsequent books, Morris has repeated the theory, illustrating it with photos comparing a good set of female buttocks with a good set of cleavaged knockers.

Maybe he's right about breasts looking somewhat like buttocks, but who's to say that rounded buttocks didn't develop to imitate breasts, or that the two developed in tandem for their intrinsic aesthetic appeal? The high, rounded human buttocks are unlike the flat and narrow rump of many other primates. Morris and others argue that the gluteal hemisphericity surely came first, because the evolution of upright posture demanded greater musculature in the rump. The vertical configuration also created an area where energy could be stored as fat without interfering with basic movements, Timothy Taylor writes in *The Prehistory of Sex*. Moreover, upright posture introduced a need for alluringly shaped female buttocks, Taylor says. When a woman stands up, you can't see her vulva. The presentation of the vulva serves as an important sexual signal in many other primate species. If a woman isn't going to be flashing her vagina, she requires some other sexual signal rearguard, and the buttocks thus became accentuated. To ensure that she caught men's attention coming and going, the woman's breasts soon swelled too. Which is fine, except that women find a high, rounded butt on a man as alluring as a man does on a woman, and women notice it on women, and men on men. Beautiful buttocks are a thing to behold, but they need not have assumed their globular contours to provide a home for a large muscle. Instead, the curviness of the human rump on both sexes could well have been selected as another example of sensory exploitation, and of our preference for the curved and generous over the straight and narrow. The breast might not imitate the buttock so much as the two converge on a common theme.

There are other reasons to be skeptical about the development of breasts as an encouragement to pursue frontal sex. Several other primates, including bonobos and orangutans, also copulate face to face, and the females wear no sexual badges on their chests, no clever replicas of their narrow rumps or swollen vulvas. Nevertheless, they are sought after — in the case of bonobos, many times a day. What is *P. paniscus*'s secret, and does she have a catalogue?

Because breasts, when not serving as visual lures, play an essential role in reproduction, many theorists have assumed that they developed to advertise to men some aspect of a woman's fecundity. Breasts certainly proclaim that a female is of reproductive age, but so do many other things — pubic hair, the widening of the pelvic bone, the wafting of hormonally activated body odors. A woman needs a certain percentage of body fat to sustain a pregnancy. Breasts are two parcels of fat. Perhaps they proclaim that a woman is nutritionally well stocked and so can bear and suckle children, a point that a prehistoric man, surveying the options among a number of calorically borderline women, conceivably would want to know. Yet breasts, for all their prominence, represent a small fraction of the body's total fat mass — 4 percent, on average —

and their size generally changes less in proportion to a woman's weight gain or loss than other fat depots of the body, like the adipose of the thighs, buttocks, and upper arms; thus breast fatness is not a great indicator of a woman's health or nutritional status. And as we saw above, breast size has nothing to do with a woman's reproductive or lactational capabilities and so is a poor signal of her maternal worth. Others suggest that breasts evolved to deceive, to confuse a man about a woman's current ovulatory status or whether she is pregnant or not, the better to mask issues of paternity and inhibit the tendency of men to kill infants they know are not their own. Why a man would be attracted to such devious commodities is unclear, unless we assume that he is predisposed for another reason to love the look of a breast.

Women have laid claim to breasts too. Meredith Small recasts the idea of breasts as mobile pantries, but sees them as designed to help women rather than to assure men that they are fertile. "A large breast might be simply a fat storage area for females who evolved under nutritional stress," she writes. "Ancestral humans walked long and far in their search for food, and they needed fat for years of lactation." Again, though, breasts are not the most liquid of fat assets, and they are surprisingly stingy about releasing their energy stores on demand. When a woman is lactating, lipid energy from the hips and thighs is far more readily mobilized than the fat of the breasts, even though the breast fat is much closer to the means of milk production. Helen Fisher proposes that breasts are a woman's pleasure chests, the swollen scaffolding beneath the erotogenic nipples ensuring that the breasts are caressed, sucked, and pressed against for maximum stimulation. Yet not all women have sensitive breasts, nor do they necessarily adore chronic fondling. "I've had a lot of experience in life," says a seventy-five-year-old woman in *Breasts: Women Speak*. "I've come to the conclusion that women get breast cancer because men handle their breasts *too much*." At the same time, many men have very sensitive nipples, and they only wish women were more inclined to take a lick now and then.

If not for the woman, then maybe for the child. Elaine Morgan, an original and brave thinker who continues almost single-handedly to push the aquatic ape theory of human evolution, has submitted several breast lines. She believes that humans spent part of their evolutionary development immersed in water, that we are part pinniped, part ape.

One excuse for breasts, then, might be that they were Mae Wests, as the British soldiers of World War II called their life jackets — flotation devices that infants could cling to as they nursed. More recently, Morgan has suggested that hairlessness, another presumed legacy of our nautical phase, gave birth to the breast. Young monkeys and apes can cling to their mother's chest hair while they suckle, she says. Human infants have nothing to grab. In addition, they're so helpless, they can't lift their heads up to reach the nipple. The nipple has to come to them. Consequently, the nipple of the human breast is situated lower on the chest than the teat of a monkey is, and it is no longer anchored tightly to the ribs, as it is in monkeys. "The skin of the breast around the nipple becomes more loosely-fitting to make it more maneuverable, leaving space beneath the looser skin to be occupied by glandular tissue and fat," Morgan concludes. "Adult males find the resulting species-specific contours sexually stimulating, but the instigator and first beneficiary of the change was the baby." It's the empty-closet theory of the breast: if it's there, it will be stuffed. Apart from the lack of any evidence to support the aquatic ape theory, the putative benefits of the loosened nipple to nursing are not obvious. A woman must hold her baby to her breast, or prop the baby up with pillows, or strap the infant in place with a baby sling (which is how the vast majority of women in the developing world nurse their infants). If a mother were to spend much time hunched over a baby in her lap like Daisy the cow, her nipple dangling in the infant's mouth, she might find it difficult ever to straighten back to bipedalism again.

The aesthetic breast won't lift a finger to help you.

Plato called the psyche a sphere. Carl Jung said that the circle symbolizes the self. The Buddha sat on a lotus of eight radially symmetrical petals. The circular mandala signifies the unity of the conscious and unconscious minds. In the great Gothic cathedrals of Europe, where every window is stained with the tears and hymns of every pilgrim and atheist to behold it, the highest artistry is displayed in the rose windows, the symbolic circles of heaven. The crowning achievement of Filippo Brunelleschi, father of the Renaissance, was the Duomo, which returned to the world the forgotten joy of the dome, the conjoiner of the sacred and the humane. To encircle is to love and to possess, as we acknowledge today with a wedding ring. Shakespeare's theater was constructed around a circular stage, and it was named the Globe.

We live life vertiginously, attending to the round. Who knows why. It may have all started with the face. The first thing that a newborn pays visual attention to is not the breast, which the infant cannot adjust its focus to see from its ringside position, but the mother's face. Human faces are round, much rounder than those of other adult apes. The white of the human eye, which is absent in our simian cousins, serves to emphasize the roundness of the iris. When we smile, our cheeks become round, and the uplifted corners of the mouth and the downturned corners of the eyebrows create an image of a circle within a circle. Only humans universally interpret the smile as a friendly gesture. Among most primates, a smile is a grimace, an expression of threat or fear.

Or it may have all begun with fruit, the mainstay of our foraging years, the brass rings we reached for, the fantasy of abundance. Fruit is round, and so are nuts and tubers and most of the edible parts of plants. Or was it our reverence for light? The sources of all light, the sun and the moon, are round, and the rounder they are, the brighter they shine. They die in each cycle by the degradation of their celestial geometry. As long as we have been human, we have observed the preponderance of the circle and the link between that which is round and that which defines us. The circle illuminates and delimits. We can't escape it. We can't get enough of it.

The breast is the body's most transparent way of paying homage to the circle. Over the centuries, the human breast has been compared to all the round things we know and love — to apples, melons, suns, moons, cherries, faces, eyes, Orient pearls, globes, mandalas, worlds within worlds. Yet to focus exclusively on the breast is to neglect the other ways in which the human body commemorates and resonates with roundness. The buttocks, of course, are round and conspicuous. Our long human necks curve into our shoulders, a parabola of grace when seen from behind. Our muscles too assume a species-specific roundness and prominence. Other animals become extremely, densely muscular without forming the projecting curves seen on human athletes. Many creatures can outrun us, but none have our distinctive calf muscles, which, like the buttocks, are curved on men and women alike. The biceps of the arms can look breastlike. So too can the deltoids, the muscles of the shoulders. Highly developed chest muscles give the impression of cleavaged breasts. The curvaceous sensuality of the muscular male was not lost on the ancient Greeks, nor on Michelangelo, nor on the photographer Bruce Weber, who in his pictures for Calvin Klein underwear gave us a nude male chest as vociferous as the conventional female cleavage shot. Dancers of both sexes, who have radiant, muscular bodies that are as if drawn with spirographs, emphasize and consecrate the curve through movement. To defy the choreographed curve is to renounce, mock, or affront the pretty.

We are attracted to well-defined curves. It has been suggested that humans shed their body hair better to reveal the curviness of female breasts and hips, but why then would we not have had a more targeted hair loss around the areas in question? Instead, the aesthetic benefits of depilation must be viewed globally. The entire body becomes the proscenium, to expose whatever curves we have to offer. Our options are in part determined by our physiology and our hormonal milieu. Women are rich in estrogen, the hormone that controls the maturation and release of the egg each month, and estrogen is adept at laying down fat depots. The primate breast was capable of supporting expansion; it was primed to be curved. Men are moneyed in testosterone, which is necessary to sperm production, and testosterone helps lay down muscle. In neither case do we need our curves. We can be strong and fertile, swift and milky, without them. Still, mysteriously, we have curves and we are drawn to curves, and to those who wave them in our faces. We are drawn to rounded breasts and rounded muscles. We are drawn to prominent cheekbones, those facial breasts, or are they facial buttocks, or minibiceps, or apples, or faces within faces?

Here I must note that the benefits of being considered attractive are not limited to the ability to attract mates. Attractive people attract allies. As an extremely social species, dependent on the group for survival, we can accrue advantages to ourselves and our offspring in a series of harmonics that reinforce and amplify one another. If you have friends, you have defenders, and your children have defenders. Attractiveness is as often used for the purposes of displaying to the members of your own sex as it is to arouse the interest of the opposite sex. Display can be extremely competitive, but it can also be solicitous. Women display for each other, and dress for each other, and are concerned about what other women think of their appearance. We conventionally interpret such preening as competitive, a bit catty, and we assume that the ultimate goal is to show the gals who can win the boys. But female display also can be affiliative, implying the possibility of an alliance. In that sense, women may have "chosen" breasts on each other as much as men chose them on women. And the breast of choice for exhibition and persuasion is not the soft, sloping maternal breast or the virginal rosebud breast, but the strong, prominent breast, the breast that can practically be flexed like a muscle, the breast that stands out in a crowd.

The zebra finch is a natural aesthete, but the bird has its structural and intellectual limitations. It can't fabricate its own hats. If it could, it might become reckless. It might start building crests as high as the hair of Marie Antoinette. Or it might thread the crest with strands of Lycra, to abet its bounce and waggle and to leave no finch's visual cortex unexploited. A crest would be a perfect trait to accentuate. There's not much you can do with a leg band, but a feather cap can be made to crow: Look at me! No, look at *me*.

We have not only taste but the wherewithal to indulge, inflect, and abuse it. Breasts, like crests, lend themselves to manipulation. They are ideal accessories, and we have exploited our sensory exploiters. Breasts are much easier to work with than any other body part. They are soft and compressible. They can be lifted up, squeezed together, thrust forward, padded out, prostheticized. Cinching in the waist is hard, though women have done it, and have fainted and died from the effort; hoisting up the breasts is relatively painless. The fetishization of the breast goes hand in hand with our status as clothinged apes. Not only did necklines plunge in the fourteenth century, the first corsets elevated the breasts to the occasion. More often than not, the ideal breast is an invented breast. Decolletage, the tushy breast, is an artifact of clothing. Naked breasts don't dance cheek to cheek — they turn away from each other. Breasts vary in size and shape to an outlandish degree, but they can be whipped into an impressive conformity, and because we are human and we can't leave anything alone, we have whipped away. We have played on the eye's tendency to follow the round, to be attracted by the hemisphere, and we have inflated and mollycoddled it.

We can take some comfort from the fact that men's curves are under increasing pressure to expand as well. The introduction of the Nautilus machine has ushered in the era of the attainable David, whose chest and arms are breaking out with breasts all over. We can wring our hands raw in priggish despair over the contemporary emphasis on surface and our homogenized appraisal of beauty, but though the technology is new, the obsession is congenital. We've been scolded for our vanity since Narcissus discovered the reflective properties of water. We have been threatened with visions of withered witches' tits if we refuse to mend our ways and stop worrying about our bodies or staring at the moons and melons of others.

To say that all breasts are pretty is like saying that all faces are pretty: it's true but false. Yes, we all have our winsome components, and we are genotypically and anatomically unique and uniqueness has its merit. At the same time, we know beauty when we see it. Beauty is a despot, but so what? Our mistake is in attributing grander meaning to a comely profile than it already has. High cheekbones, a high butt, and a high bosom are nice, but none should be viewed as the sine qua non of womanliness. If breasts had something important to say, they would be much less variable and whimsical than they are. They would be like mere mammary glands, a teaspoon per breast per woman. If breasts could talk, they would probably tell jokes — every light-bulb joke in the book.

8

HOLY WATER

BREAST MILK

THE VIRGIN MARY, mother of Christ, felt no pain in childbirth. She kept her virginity and presumably her hymen throughout life. If she was spared the curse of Eve, she may not have menstruated, or defecated or urinated, for that matter. Her corpse did not decay after death but ascended whole to heaven. She defied anatomy, biochemistry, and the laws of thermodynamics. She had little in common with other women, let alone with the "lower" mammals that women, through Linnaeus, conceptually linked to *Homo sapiens.* Nonetheless, Mary expressed her femaleness and joined her taxon in one unambiguous fashion: she used her mammary glands. She suckled the baby Jesus. The *Maria lactans,* or *Madonna del latte,* is among the most prevalent images in Western art. From the early Renaissance onward, the Virgin often is shown with one breast exposed and the infant Jesus either preparing to suckle or already grazing the tip of the nipple with his lips. The exposed breast is usually an odd-looking object, a sort of billiard ball that seems barely attached to the rest of the chest and may be closer to her clavicle than to the mid–rib cage, where breasts usually reside. Regardless of the technical skill of the artist, the exposed breast was by convention rendered inaccurately. Viewers were meant not to dwell on the carnality of Mary's bosom but to consider the purity and possibilities of the extraordinary nourishment within. How limitless is the power of the breast that suckled the Almighty; it gave life to the one who gives eternal life to all. And just as the mammary gland of an ordinary woman is fortified by its suppliant, generating more milk the more it is suckled, so the breast of Mary was strengthened and sanctified through intimate contact with the holiest of mouths: it secreted *and* absorbed. The Virgin's nipples surely never cracked or blistered.

As a sacred fluid, the milk of the Virgin ranks just below the blood that flowed from Christ's wounds. If there were enough splinters of the True Cross in reliquaries throughout Christendom to construct an entire cathedral, there were enough vials of Mary's milk to feed its congregation, prompting the sixteenth-century Protestant reformer Calvin to wonder cynically "how that milk . . . was collected, so as to be preserved until our time." We can imagine that Mary's breast simply never ran dry, and that it will nourish the world when the world must end. In one fifteenth-century fresco by an anonymous Florentine painter, the Virgin is shown cupping one breast in her hand and pleading with the adult Christ for the salvation of a group of sinners huddled at her feet. The inscription reads, "Dearest son, because of the milk I gave you, have mercy on them."

The Madonna's was not the first *latte* to be exalted, nor the last. The milk of a Greek goddess was said to confer infinite life on those who drank it. When Zeus sought divinity for his son Hercules, born of an adulterous affair with the mortal Alcmene, he sneaked the infant into the bedroom of his sleeping wife, Hera, and put him to her breast for a taste of infinity. A musclehead from the start, Hercules suckled so hard that Hera awoke, and she shook him off in outrage, spurting milk across the skies — hence the Milky Way. Hercules already had swallowed enough, though, to join the ranks of the immortals.

If a woman's menstrual blood is frequently considered polluted, the reputed purity of her breast milk restores her to homeostasis. As Valerie Fildes describes in her classic study, *Breasts, Bottles, and Babies,* the Ebers papyrus of the sixteenth-century B.C. recommended human milk as a treatment for cataracts, burns, eczema, and "expelling noxious excrements in the belly of a man." The wet nurses of ancient Egypt were exalted as no other class of servants was. A royal wet nurse was invited to royal funerals. The children of a royal wet nurse were considered milk kin to the king. Only two characters recognize Odysseus when he returns home in rags after his twenty-year sabbatical: his faithful dog, Argus (who dies happy after seeing his master), and his wet nurse, Eurykleia. Her breasts have long since shriveled, but they retain traces of the purity that once flowed through them, and true purity, like loyalty, does not fade over time. Milk is homeopathic: it holds the memory of every mouth it feeds.

The practical breast is a modified sweat gland, and it is meant to be used, as the pancreas, the liver, and the colon are there to be used. Lactation is a basic biological function. Milk is a body fluid. Yet metaphorically, breastfeeding and breast milk have been and remain in a class by themselves, the class of metaphysiology. They have been accorded a magical status, breathless, declarative, absolute. They have been the source of endless exhortation, celebration, guilt, joy, and pain. We think of breastfeeding as natural and good and lovely, yet throughout history, in a variety of permutations, it has occasioned spleen and hectoring. Nobody has to beseech us to let our heart pump, our neurons fire, or our menstrual blood flow. Breastfeeding is another matter. It may be natural for a woman to nurse her baby, but it is not guaranteed, and so it has been variously mandated by prophets, legislated by politicians, and hoisted onto a sociomedical pedestal that brooks no excuses or complaints. Lactation has not been allowed to be what it is, the business of the body. The mammary gland often has been underrated, which is why in the middle of this century infant formula was thought to be not merely a passable substitute for breast milk, but an improvement on it. Now the gland is overrated. We believe that it can make every baby into Izzy Newton or Jane Austen. Now breast milk is seen as the quintessential female elixir. Through it, we give more than a part of ourselves to our children, we give ourselves purified and improved. Our breast milk is better than we are.

We know ourselves — too well, alas — but we don't know our breast milk. It is mysterious. Scientists continue to analyze it and continue to find unexpected ingredients in it. Is it getting better with time? Is it evolving in advance of us? You might suspect as much if you read comments by breastfeeding advocacy groups. It is "the miracle substance," in the words of Le Ann Deal, the executive director of La Leche League. Even scientists set aside their dustiness and qualifiers when praising mother's milk, calling it "the ultimate biological fluid," "a cocktail of potency," "a truly fascinating fluid," "a human right," "more, so much more, than just food." In believing that breast milk conveys an almost supernatural power to an infant, we echo ancient medical authorities, who posited that a woman's personality, her humors, would mold the character of any infant who supped at her breast. They cited famous examples, such as the emperor Tiberius, a pitiful drunkard, who was said to have been suckled by an alcoholic wet nurse, and the savage Caligula, suckled by a wet nurse who supposedly rubbed blood on her nipples.

Think of your own feelings about breast milk. If you're a woman who has lactated, you've surely tasted your own milk, enough to know that it's sweeter and waterier than cow's milk. But if you saw a full glass of human milk in the refrigerator, would you drink it? The idea is disturbing. It feels almost cannibalistic. We don't know the half of what's in it, or why. Human milk tastes thinner on the tongue than cow's milk, but it is so rich, so pregnant with meaning and attribute, that like a bubbling solution in a mad scientist's beaker, it practically crackles to life — and beyond. If an adult were to drink human milk every day, might that person grow huge, like Alice nibbling from the left side of the mushroom, or become immortal, like Hercules, say, or the vampire Nosferatu?

Let us examine lactation in the clear light of morning. I've talked about the mammary gland as a modified sweat gland, but there is another way to think of it: as a modified placenta. The placenta and the mammary gland have much in common. They are specialists, and they are temporary workers. They are designed to nourish a baby. No other organs are so fleeting, so single-minded, as the placenta-mammary dyad. They exist only for the baby, and if the baby does not call on them, they are retired. They are expensive organs, and they are not maintained unless absolutely necessary. That is why the suckling of the baby is crucial to the productivity of the mammary gland. The mammary gland will not continue making milk unless the mechanical sensation of suckling tells it that lactogenesis is necessary. In evolutionary terms, babies die too often to make automatic milk ejection a sane strategy. It would be terribly wasteful if, after the arrival of a stillborn infant, a woman's body were to generate milk automatically for anything more than a handful of days, at a cost of 600 calories a day. Lactation is a contingent function and a conditioned response, which is why it can be so frustrating to initiate and maintain. The body stands poised to flow, and to stop flowing. In a way, lactation is analogous to blood. Blood must course through your veins nonstop, yet it must be prepared to coagulate if the skin is breached, or else we would bleed to death at the brush of a thornbush. So too must milk be prepared to flow, but it is such a costly fluid, this ultimate cocktail, that the baby must beg for it and suck with the mouth of a divine pretender.

Milk production begins midway through pregnancy. The foliate lobules where milk is made thicken, proliferate, and surround the ducts until you can't see the ducts for the leaves. At the tips of the lobules, the alveolar cells quiver and distend and begin secreting a yellowish fluid of protein and carbohydrates, the colostrum. Some of it may make its way to the nipple and ooze out, but most gets reabsorbed in the ducts; there's no reason for it to go anywhere yet. The alveoli are simply making a dry wet run. Many hormones contribute to the glandular expansion, and to keeping the sequence sensible. Progesterone stimulates the division and maturation of the alveolar cells, but it also prevents them from getting ahead of themselves. If not for the high levels of progesterone (and to a lesser extent estrogen) that characterize pregnancy, the alveolar cells would pay heed to another hormone, prolactin, the breastfeeder's friend. During pregnancy, the pituitary gland, at the base of the brain, begins releasing ever-mounting quantities of prolactin. Prolactin urges the alveolar cells to synthesize milk. Progesterone counsels delay. For as long as gestation lasts, progesterone wins.

After delivery, progesterone and estrogen levels drop precipitously. For some women, the hormone crash leads to temporary depression and stasis, but for their mammary glands the change is bracing. The alveolar cells are freed to take up the circulating prolactin, and they absorb it greedily. At first they make what they are accustomed to making: colostrum, the sticky fluid of protein, carbohydrates, and other ingredients. But no fat — that comes later. Colostrum is yellow because it's rich in carotenoids, the same compounds that give carrots and squash their yellow-orange tint and that are needed to make the A and B vitamins. Colostrum is ten times richer in carotenoids than mature milk will be. If it looks like pus, it also acts like pus: colostrum contains a wealth of white blood cells and antibodies, as pus does, and it helps a newborn, whose immune system has yet to mature, resist the pathogens that will be more than happy to attack it. Colostrum is also rich in the loosened epithelial tissue that had kept the ducts plugged.

The infant suckles colostrum. It wants more than this thin carrot gruel. It suckles and suckles. The yanking and pulling on the nipple somehow is translated into neural idiom, suppressing the brain's production of dopamine. The less dopamine there is, the more the pituitary sends forth prolactin. The alveolar cells become sorcerers and start synthesizing that fascinating fluid milk, virgin white, the blank slate on which all hopes can be written. The cells become engorged with milk. The infant suckles and stimulates the pituitary to secrete another hormone, oxytocin. It is time for the great letdown. On oxytocin's signal, the muscle tissue surrounding the engorged alveoli contracts, forcing the milk out of the cells, down the ducts, out through the nipple, and into the mouth that has worked so hard to persuade the gland that it is here and it is famished.

What is milk? How does a fluid earn its milk stripes? By definition, milk is the product of the mammary gland, just as gastric juice is the product of the stomach and saliva the product of the salivary glands. But milk is chemically far more complex than many body secretions, because its assignment is so complex. The mammary gland accrues the subunits of milk through three avenues. Some components are taken directly from the mother's bloodstream and deployed unaltered. Others are extracted from the blood and then reworked and edited before being incorporated into the milk. Still others are invented in the alveolar cells themselves.

In keeping with its illustrious reputation, milk is often billed as "nature's perfect food," and in this case the ad copy is accurate. It is all that a newborn mammal needs to survive. Never again will an individual's menu be so easily planned as it is early in life. Every species' mammary gland offers a slightly different definition of the perfect food. All milk must give the basics that a neonate needs to survive and grow. Be it piglet, calf, kangaroo, or human, the body needs water, lipids, carbohydrates, and protein, and these are the core components of milk. But how much and what type of each varies from animal to animal. Animals that grow rapidly need milk that is high in amino acids, the constituents of protein. The milk of carnivores such as cats, hyenas, and canids is dense with amino acids. If Romulus and Remus, the founders of Rome, drank the milk of a wolf, as legend has it, they drank meat in solution. Animals that must put on a lot of fat in a short amount of time drink fatty milk. Perhaps the fattest milk in nature is elephant seal milk, which is fatter than butter. An elephant seal pup has but four weeks to suckle, and as it does it expands from its birth weight of seventy-five pounds to a weaning weight of three hundred pounds. For her part, the mother eats nothing the entire time, and so loses six hundred of her fifteen hundred pounds. As one scientist put it, she essentially slices a slab of blubber from herself and slaps it onto her young.

The milk of slow-growing animals has a comparatively low concentration of amino acids. Humans grow slowly, and our milk is among the least proteinaceous mammary product around. Rat's milk has twelve times the concentration of amino acids of human milk. Cow's milk is four times protein-heavier than our milk, which is the main reason that you can't give a baby cow's milk without first processing it into infant formula. A newborn's immature kidneys are not equipped to handle the high protein content of cow's milk. A human infant could handle the milk of a gorilla, chimpanzee, or orangutan, however. The milk of great apes is quite similar to our milk in every aspect that has been examined.

What human (and ape) milk lacks in protein it makes up for in lactose, the principal carbohydrate, or sugar, of milk. Lactose is second only to water as the major constituent of human milk. Our milk has twice as much lactose as cow's milk does. We scold ourselves for our sweet tooth, and we wonder why our children want to eat Ring-Dings, ice cream, and Froot Loops. We should be surprised by none of it. The milk we have evolved tastes as sweet as Kool-Aid. But lactose is not junk food. It is not a simple-minded sugar. It is formed in the alveolar cells through the combination of the simple sugars glucose and galactose, taken from the mother's blood, and it offers the newborn twice the energy content of glucose. Lactose also is important to the absorption of other nutrients in the milk, enabling the infant's gut to maximize its uptake of calcium, fatty acids, and the like. Cow's milk and human milk have roughly the same amount of fat, but the types of fat differ significantly. Human milk has comparatively more essential fatty acids, which are long chains of unsaturated fats that the body can't make on its own but must obtain through the diet — which for a baby means breast milk. Essential fatty acids are involved in the development of the eye, the brain, and the peripheral nervous system. Formula makers are now debating whether to add certain fatty acids to their formulas, particularly docosahexaenoic acid, or DHA. But always there is a question about unexpected outcomes. In one study, infants fed a formula that had been fortified with fish oil, a good source of DHA, showed faster development of visual acuity, but on other measurements of psychomotor performance their progress lagged behind that of infants fed either breast milk or standard formula. Besides, how much fatty acid should be added? A woman who eats a lot of fish will have twenty times the amount of certain long-chain fatty acids in her breast milk as a woman who lives in the Sahara. Do you want to mimic the lipids in the breast milk of a fish eater, or of a vegetarian, or of an omnivorous American?

Apart from differences in some fatty acids and a few other components, human breasts secrete remarkably similar fluid despite wide variability in women's nutritional status. A malnourished woman in a developing country generates surprisingly nutritious milk, while a chubby woman in the Midwest does not have comparatively high-calorie milk. "One of the things about lactation that is an endless source of fascination to those of us who study it," says Peter Reeds, a professor of pediatrics at Baylor College of Medicine, "is the remarkable ability of lactating mammals, humans included, to preserve a narrow range of milk composition in the face of even a disadvantageous diet." If a woman is not eating what she needs to maintain that perfect formula, the mammary gland borrows from her body stores, the 7-Eleven that never closes. At the same time, the woman does not sacrifice quite as much as might be expected, for breast milk has evolved through compromise. The mother gives, but she does not give to the point of risking her future health and fertility. Breast milk is designed to be maximally exploited without maximally exploiting. A nursing woman does not need to lose her teeth or watch her spine shrink so that her baby can get enough calcium; the lactose in the milk ensures that every ion of calcium will be used instead of just peed away, as is much of the calcium that you get from drinking, say, fortified orange juice. The baby digests the proteins in the milk down to the last amino acid, which is why a suckling infant's used diapers hardly smell: there's very little waste matter, very little excreted protein, to lend a stench. A nursing woman does not have to become anemic to give her baby iron. Human milk has very little iron in it, but it has lactoferrin, a protein that allows the iron to be thoroughly absorbed. The same is true of other trace minerals, such as zinc and copper; they're rare in breast milk, but when they're there, the suite of milk proteins and sugars takes them up and guarantees they will not escape. Moreover, human babies in the past probably spent a bit of time rolling around in the dirt and picking up iron and minerals through an infantile form of pica. Babies put everything in their mouths, and they try to lick whatever they can. We see this as an unfortunate and risky little habit, but babies might do it for a reason: to lick up the occasional trace element their cells demand to perform and divide.

Infant formula cannot mimic breast milk, as we've learned, and as every new mother is told by every authority she encounters, and as every can of formula is required by law to warn, in the way that a pack of Marlboros must warn of cigarettes' lethality. Human milk is a solution of more than two hundred constituents, whose manifold roles have yet to be entirely understood. Nothing does just one thing. Milk sugars offer calories, and milk sugars allow other nutrients to be fully metabolized. The sugars of human milk and of infant formula are quantitatively similar but qualitatively different. Lactoferrin permits the scarce iron in milk to be "bioavailable" to the baby, and it also prevents pathogenic bacteria from getting their maws on the metal, which they need to survive. There is no lactoferrin in infant formula. The immune properties of breast milk are legion, and most of them are missing from formula, because the preparation of formula destroys their counterparts in cow's milk. There are B cells, T cells, macrophages, and neutrophils in breast milk, there are antibodies, there is gamma interferon, which stimulates the activity of the immune cells. The fatty acids in milk disrupt the membranes surrounding viruses, while lysozyme does the same to the cell walls of bacteria. Bifidus factor encourages the growth of benign flora in an infant's gut, the better to outcompete insidious strains.

Much research on breast milk over the past ten years has concerned hormones and growth factors. Here is where the human mammary gland is portrayed as a kind of brain, a self-replicating mind, feeding the developing brain of the neonate the proteins that its neurons require to differentiate. The mammary gland synthesizes gonadotropin-releasing hormone, for example, and deposits it in milk. Gonadotropin-releasing hormone is a protein best known as the product of the hypothalamus, located in the midbrain. In adults, it stimulates the gonads and may play a role in sexual behavior. We don't have a clue what, if anything, this hormone might do to a suckling infant, but there it is, swimming in the milk, at a concentration ten times that seen in the mother's bloodstream. Breast milk also has nerve growth factor, and thyroid-stimulating hormone, and factors given vague names like "mammo-trope differentiating peptide." The human newborn is a weak, altricial little creature, a postpartum fetus, and it is possible that some of the factors in mother's milk are "obligate differentiation factors," required to orchestrate the full maturation of the infant's brain and other organs. Infant formula has some of these factors, but again, most of the equiva-lent peptides in cow's milk are destroyed by the processing necessary to make cow's milk digestible. In the absence of these factors, can the infant realize happiness, healthiness, and peak brilliance? We don't know yet. We don't know what these supposed differentiation factors and neuropeptide equivalents are for. It's logical to assume that they're necessary, or at least good for an infant, but logic is not evidence and biology is not always logical.

The more we look at breast milk and the more we find within it, the more we are driven to marvel that anybody can survive, much less thrive, on its wretched artificial substitute. Yet many have. The majority of baby boomers were reared exclusively on infant formula, and they're all around us, and are us, occupying space and every occupation. Today almost 40 percent of infants in this country are still bottle-fed from birth. Among babies in the United States who are breastfed to start, only half still receive breast milk at the age of six months. By a year, only 10 percent of babies still breastfeed. Researchers don't know what to make of it. They wonder if they are asking the wrong questions or neglecting subtle cues, or if it's simply a matter of general ignorance about growth and development, an ignorance reflected in scientists' inability to parse out and pin down all the deficiencies in bottle-fed babies. "As a scientist, I can't help but notice that millions of babies have never seen human milk, and they apparently have not been harmed," said Dr. Reeds. "At the same time, I can't escape the feeling that nature went to enormous lengths to produce a particular food, and that must mean something."

In Third World countries where breast milk may offer the only sterile fluid around, breastfeeding can be imperative to an infant's survival. In the developed world, the advantages of breastfeeding over bottle feeding are less obvious, but they exist. Breastfed infants have fewer infections of the middle ear, gastrointestinal tract, and upper respiratory system than bottle-fed babies do. They suffer less from diarrhea and constipation. When breastfed infants get sick, they recover sooner than those on formula do.

Of the many other benefits that have been ascribed to breastfeeding, though, not all have been proved. Breastfeeding supposedly helps prevent obesity later in childhood, but the evidence is equivocal, and complicated by socioeconomic factors. Breastfeeding is thought to lower the risk of allergies and asthma among children, yet the rates of chronic respiratory diseases have been climbing in recent years right along with an increase in breastfeeding. Some studies have suggested that breastfed children have higher IQs than their bottle-fed cohorts, but other studies that took maternal IQ into account found no connection between breast milk and intelligence. Perhaps the most questionable and philosophically disturbing benefit that has been pinned to breastfeeding is that it improves the emotional bond between mother and infant. Not only is such a bond impossible to quantify, but it pretty much sweeps aside all efforts to engage fathers as full and legitimate participants in child care. If it takes suckling to feel the most intimate and profound love for your baby, then a man with a bottle — even one that holds expressed breast milk — will always be as feeble a substitute for the well-teated mother as formula is for her milk.

Women know they should breastfeed their babies, and many are more than delighted to give it their best shot. But what is their best shot, and what of those who will not? In Scandinavia, it is considered tantamount to child abuse to feed an infant anything except human milk. Scandinavians have milk banks to supply milk when mothers can't or won't. In this country, fears of viral contamination have prevented the institution of a similar network of milk banks. Viruses, like the one that causes AIDS, can be transmitted through milk, and though it's possible to screen milk for the virus as blood is screened, the existence of a reasonable milk facsimile — infant formula — has kept down the demand for human milk that has been put through an expensive series of tests.

Breastfeeding is considered natural, an extension of pregnancy. The mammary gland is an extension of the placenta. All the products found in the placenta reappear in breast milk, including the immune factors, the growth factors, the hormones. Yet pregnancy takes care of itself; lactation doesn't. Pregnancy lasts 240 days. Suckling can last as briefly or as long as you please, or as it pleases others. Various authorities have sought to determine the true, basal human breastfeeding interval, but there is no such animal, and there probably never has been. The Koran advocates that a woman suckle her child for two years, but adds that if the husband and wife wish to wean the infant sooner they may do so, suggesting that many people in the past did so. The World Health Organization and UNICEF recently have recommended that women breastfeed for two years "and beyond," but only among contemporary hunter-gatherers like the !Kung, who nurse an average of 2.8 years per child, do we see much of that "beyond."

Nursing also is a learned behavior, and one that is not always easy to master. Great apes, whose milk is so compositionally similar to ours, must also learn by observing others the proper techniques for suckling their young, but humans are dunces compared to gorillas. We need tutoring from our obstetricians, midwives, and birthing instructors. We need lactation consultants and La Leche League crisis counselors. We have a hard time sitting still, and nursing requires patience and relaxation. Stress hormones can disrupt the flow of milk. Our nipples may crack and bleed from the pull of the infant's mouth, and though the pain is supposed to go away in a few days, for some it lasts much longer. Some women love breastfeeding their babies. They talk of how good it feels, how close to orgasm they come while nursing. They might be away from their baby, but the mere recollection of the sensation of suckling sends a warm rush across their body, and their milk starts to flow — embarrassingly, if they are at work or in a meeting. They fall in love with their suckling infant and think of nothing and nobody else.

Other women never get the knack of joy. The baby cries and rejects the breast. The women keep at it, but they don't find their rhythm. Their milk never feels as though it's flowing. The baby gains weight slowly. Pediatricians are now questioning whether the fast weight gain seen in bottle-fed babies is the appropriate scale by which to measure natural growth patterns, but still, the baby seems perpetually hungry and the mother feels perpetually inadequate. She must go back to work, and she hasn't mastered breastfeeding, or breast pumping, or satisfying her baby or herself. She dislikes breastfeeding and she doesn't want to do it, but she feels guilty, bottomlessly guilty, at the thought of not nursing. She is not allowed to say how she feels. There are neuropeptides in milk, after all, and immune cells, and lactoferrin, and how could a mother ask her child to forgo the perfect food, the better part of herself? Maternal guilt is impossible to assuage. A female primatologist told me she blamed herself for her child's allergies, because she only breastfed the child for six months.

"The act of suckling a child, like a sexual act, may be tense, physically painful, charged with cultural feelings of inadequacy and guilt," wrote Adrienne Rich. "Or, like a sexual act, it can be a physically delicious, elementally soothing experience, filled with a tender sensuality."

Breastfeeding your baby is natural, yet women have long done otherwise, and sometimes it is hard to say whether they chose not to breastfeed or the choice was forced upon them. Wet-nursing is an ancient profession, and among the few open exclusively to women. Wet nurses were so common at certain times of history that they were subject to competition and had to advertise their services. In Renaissance Florence, groups of wet nurses gathered at markets and festivals and sang lacto-jingles: "Always when the baby cries/We feel our milk returning/Acting with energy and speed,/We do our duty." Expectant parents consulted how-to books on the traits to seek in a wet nurse. "The ideal wet nurse should be amiable, cheerful, lively and good-humored, with strong nerves; not fretful, peevish, quarrelsome, sad or timorous, and free from passions and worries," according to one treatise from sixteenth-century England. "Finally, a potential wet nurse must like children." Though for much of history only the wealthy could afford to hire wet nurses, as always the habits of the upper classes trickled down to the lower, and by the seventeenth century half or more of all women were sending their babies to other nipples for nourishment. High-priced wet nurses shipped their own babies off to cheaper wet nurses, to preserve their personal milk supply for professional use. In 1780, according to Marilyn Yalom, as few as 10 percent of all Parisian babies were nursed in their own homes.

Nor was wet-nursing the only alternative to maternal breastfeeding. We think of infant formula as a relatively new invention, another canker of advanced capitalism, but humans have long fed infants on the milk of other mammals, or on liquid gruel and pulverized adult food. Some anthropologists have suggested that dairy animals such as the cow and the goat were originally domesticated to provide milk for babies. The babies may have suckled directly from the animal's teats, or they were fed with weaning cups, or through cow horns, or through nipples fashioned from leather. Clay bottles shaped like breasts have been found at several sites in Europe that date from the late Neolithic era, around 3500 B.C. Many of the infants fed on these substitutes for human milk died, either because they couldn't metabolize the cow's milk or because they contracted infections directly from the animals. According to church and county records of the eighteenth century, babies who were fed cow's milk through a cow's horn in certain parts of Germany and Scandinavia died of diarrhea at a much higher rate than infants in the same area who were breastfed. Nevertheless, the effort to circumvent breastfeeding, to shrug off the mammalian mantle, long predates Nestlé Corp., Ross Laboratories, and the formulas they hawk.

The question is, precisely who wished to avoid the lactational charge? In some cases, the husband demanded that his wife not breastfeed. Suckling ruined a beautiful bosom. A nursing breast was not his breast. He wanted her back to perform her wifely duties, that is, to sleep with him. Neither wives nor wet nurses were supposed to have intercourse while breastfeeding, for it was thought that breast milk was formed in the uterus from menstrual blood; medieval and Renaissance texts show a lacteal duct leading from the uterus to the breasts. Intercourse was thought to cause menstruation, which would then jeopardize or taint the flow of milk to the infant. There may also have been the observation that if a woman didn't breastfeed, she became pregnant again comparatively sooner. Men concerned with progeny and heirs wanted fruitful wives, and the less those wives lactated, the more they multiplied. By this calculation, the use of wet nurses in no way liberated women to possess themselves or pursue their fancies, but rather resulted in their spending that much more time pregnant.

Still, when political and medical tides turned and campaigns were initiated to encourage maternal breastfeeding, women, not men, were the target of the exhortations. In 1694, Mary Astell wrote *A Serious Proposal to the Ladies,* arguing that breastfeeding acted as a check on excessive pride. Women should not "think themselves too *Good* to perform what Nature requires, nor thro' Pride and Delicacy remit the poor little one to the care of a Foster Parent," she said. In the late eighteenth century, Europe was seized by a craze for in-home breast-feeding. Jean Jacques Rousseau attacked women who would not suckle their young as selfish, callous, and — that word again — unnatural. Linnaeus, celebrant of the mammary gland, condemned the practice of wet-nursing and proclaimed that mothers and infants both benefited from maternal suckling. Medical authorities warned of the dangers of entrusting infants to a stranger's breast, which might be feeding many mouths and satisfying none; and in fact, the rate of mortality among infants farmed out to wet nurses was quite high. Such treatises had a righteous, lecturing tone. "Let not husbands be deceived: let them not expect attachment from wives who, in neglecting to suckle their children, rend asunder the strongest ties in nature," wrote William Buchan in his 1769 *Advice to Mothers*. A woman who would not "discharge the duties of a mother" through the literal discharge of her breast "has no right to become a wife." More influential was William Cadogan, whose 1748 *Essay upon Nursing* went through several editions in Europe and America. He urged women to follow the laws of "unerring Nature," and claimed that breastfeeding was troublesome "only for want of proper Method; were it rightly managed, there would be much Pleasure in it, to every Woman that can prevail upon herself to give up a little of the Beauty of her Breast to feed her Offspring." Mothers needed the advice of medical men like himself, he said. "In my Opinion, this Business has been too long fatally left to the Management of Women who cannot be supposed to have proper knowledge to fit them for such a Task." Even Mary Wollstonecraft, in *A Vindication of the Rights of Women*, urged women to breastfeed, claiming that a husband will feel "more delight at seeing his child suckled by its mother, than the most artful wanton tricks could ever raise," the "wanton tricks" being the display of an unused bosom. The importunings of philosophers and physicians were bolstered by the power of the state. In 1793, the French government decreed that if a mother did not breastfeed her child, she would be ineligible for the eighteenth-century equivalent of welfare payments. A year later the German government went further, requiring all healthy women to nurse their young. By the early nineteenth century, motherly succor was a cult, and highborn women bragged of their commitment to breastfeeding.

Still, at least a few women expressed some ambivalence toward the elevation of the maternal mammary gland. In *Belinda*, an 1801 novel by the British writer Maria Edgeworth, a character named Lady Delacour tells her history to Belinda. Her first child was born dead, she said, because "I would not be kept prisoner" during pregnancy, nor would she cease her zealous pursuit of gaiety. A second starved to death in infancy: "It was the fashion in that time for fine mothers to suckle their own children. . . . There was a prodigious point made about the matter; a vast deal of sentiment and sympathy, and compliments and enquiries. But after the novelty was over, I became heartily sick of the business; and at the end of three months my poor child was sick too — I don't much like to think of it — it died."

After the eighteenth century, the practice of wet-nursing never regained popularity, but some of the same themes and counterthemes, the fall and rise of the mammary gland's reputation, have been recapitulated in the twentieth century, with the advent of infant formula. Again medical scientists and well-to-do women have led the way in the do-si-do, first by embracing formula as a scientifically designed product that equals and even surpasses breast milk in nutritiousness and purity, and then in rejecting formula as a pallid and possibly harmful substitute for human milk. In America, the oscillation has been extreme. Before 1930, most women breastfed their babies. By 1972, only 22 percent did, and then for just the first few weeks of life. Formula manufacturers must be held partly responsible for the mass acceptance of their wares. They have pushed their cans and powders relentlessly and often unscrupulously. To this day, they dole out formula samples in maternity wards, even as hospital nurses try to instruct new mothers in the art of breastfeeding.

Yet to say that women have been complete dupes of the formula industry is to assume that women are silly, passive, and gullible and that when allowed to choose freely, they will always choose to breastfeed for months or years. My mother bottle-fed her four children, because she tried breastfeeding but hated it, it was so painful. If she'd had more support and instruction, she says now, she would have tried harder. But my mother-in-law, a retired college dean who also bottle-fed her three children, said she did so because she didn't want to feel like a pair of udders, and she wouldn't do differently today. "Breastfeeding," she said, "was not for me."

Breastfeeding advocates have made spectacular progress, particularly among highly educated women, who now breastfeed their newborns at a rate of about 75 or 80 percent. Many hospitals now offer postpartum nursing instruction. A handful of enlightened companies offer employees facilities where they can breastfeed or pump milk. Breastfeeding has a certain cachet, even sexiness. Former congresswoman Susan Molinari made a show of nursing her infant while carrying out business on the telephone. In 1998, the *New Yorker* ran a Mother's Day cover of a tough, boot-clad, helmeted female construction worker suckling her infant while sitting on a girder high above the city.

This stylishness is decidedly to the good, for infants thrive on breast milk, and any interval of breastfeeding is better than none at all. Still, the tone of some of the La Leche–style literature sounds suspiciously similar to the tracts by Cadogan and Rousseau — judgmental and absolutist. Hiromo Goto, a Japanese Canadian novelist, wrote a short story that appeared in *Ms.* magazine in the fall of 1996, about a mother who dislikes breastfeeding. The character describes the weeks of endless pain and bloody nipples, the engorgement, the pressure from her husband and mother-in-law to keep at it regardless; it will get better, easier, more wonderful. I would do it myself if I could! her husband huffs. In the final phantasmagoric scene, she awakens at three in the morning, slices off her swollen breasts, attaches them to her husband's chest, rolls over, and happily goes back to sleep. *Ms.* readers responded to the story with outrage. They threatened to cancel their subscriptions. "It is hard enough to find social support for breastfeeding, without having it cast in such an extremely negative light in a 'feminist' magazine," one reader said. "While I certainly support the right of any woman to do with her body as she chooses, that decision should be made based upon complete and accurate information," another reader said. "Women do not have many opportunities to learn this womanly art [of suckling] in a culture where breastfeeding is discouraged." In other words, a woman can do as she chooses so long as she makes the right choice — that is, to breastfeed indefinitely, and at any cost.

Can we not forgo the polemics and exercise a little more maternal compassion here? In the real world of the two-career family, most women will breastfeed for the first few weeks or months of their baby's life, and then they will supplement or replace breast milk with formula. Like women throughout history, they will do the best they can under the constraints of work, duty, and desire. They will be generous and selfish, mammals and magicians, and they will flow and stop flowing. Whatever they do, they will feel guilty for not doing enough, and they will wish that they too could drink from the breast of Mary or Hera, thus becoming immortal mothers whose children will never die.

9

A GRAY AND YELLOW BASKET

THE BOUNTEOUS OVARY

THE OVARY IS no beauty. Most internal organs jiggle and glow and are rosy pink. The ovary is dull and gray. Even a healthy ovary looks sickly and drained of blood, as though it had given up hope. It is the size and shape of an unshelled almond, but a lumpy and irregular almond. It is scarred and pitted, for each cycle of ovulation leaves behind a white blemish where an egg follicle has been emptied of its contents. The older the woman, the more scarred her pair of ovaries will be. One might argue that the ovaries are no less visually appealing than the male equivalent, the testicles, but that is hardly high praise; recall that Sylvia Plath in *The Bell Jar* likened testicles to poultry gizzards.

So the ovary isn't pretty. So it is gray and pitted and as lumpy as oatmeal. We would expect nothing less of an organ that works as hard as it does, tending to the disparate but joined needs of the known and the possible. The ovary is a seedpod, the domicile of our fixed portion of eggs, and you are supposed to use some of those eggs, inasmuch as life strives to perpetuate itself. The ovary is gray because it alone among residents of the pelvic cavity is not covered with the pinkish perito- neum, the springy membrane that encloses and protects other organs. The ovary cannot be enclosed because it must give up its belongings so often. It gives up eggs, yes, but it gives more than that. It gives up a kind of pudding, a yellowish tapioca of hormones that feed the reproductive cycle and the bodies we own. The ovary operates as a physiological and allegorical bridge between stasis and sexuality, between anatomy and behavior. Through its periodic hormonal emissions, the ovary makes itself known to us. We have looked at the egg. We turn now to its basket.

As Freud and many others have observed, very young children are more sexual creatures than grade-school children are. A girl of three or four gleefully pokes and prods her body and the bodies of adults. She wants to explore her vagina, her clitoris, her anus, any hole or pole she encounters, and much to the distress of her queasy and hypersensitive parents, she may even ask to touch her father's penis. She is polymorphously perverse, as Freud endearingly put it. If she is going to experience the so-called Electra complex, the female equivalent of the Oedipal complex, when a girl loves her father and wants to vanquish her mother, she may do it during this era of the lewd toddler.

The preschool girl's interest in sex reflects physiology, and the bizarre on-again, off-again dialogue between the gonads and the region of the brain that oversees them. Until girls and boys are three or four, a structure in the hypothalamus called the gonadotropin-releasing hormone pulse generator ticks and tocks and secretes tiny bursts of reproductive hormones. It's like a lighthouse flashing slowly but unerringly in the fog, *blip blip blip;* every ninety minutes or so, out comes another glint of hormones. A girl's ovaries respond to the pulsatile message. They secrete small amounts of ovarian hormones in return. Nothing serious yet, not nearly enough to grow breasts or ovulate, but still the little girl is slightly waggish and slightly erotic. Her body, all bodies, fascinate her.

At the end of toddlerhood, through a mechanism that remains largely mysterious, the pulse generator in the brain shuts down. The clock stops. It ceases to secrete hormone signals. The ovaries too fall silent. They retreat into hibernation. For this reason, as well as through the tutelage of social expectations, the child is likely to turn prudish, to be easily embarrassed by bodily functions, and the thought of touching her father's penis, or any penis, or any part of any boy, may well make her gag. For the next seven years or so, she is an asexual, agonadal creature, blissful and free, the way you are on a journey, when you've left behind one set of cares and have yet to greet the new ones.

The first glimmerings of renewed care and perversity appear at the age of ten, not as a result of gonadal activity but at the behest of another set of organs: the adrenal glands, blood-rich structures that sit atop the kidneys like porkpie hats. Only within the past year or two have researchers discovered the contribution of the adrenals to the first stirrings of adolescence. The adrenals secrete adrenaline, the fire-under-thy-butt hormone, and they also release small doses of sex hormones.

The adrenals mature at around ten years of age, and that is when a child may start fantasizing about sex and forming obsessive crushes on class-mates or pop stars or teachers. The body of a ten-year-old girl may be prepubescent, but her brain is recharged, erotic again. (Do you remember? Oh, I remember. I remember fifth grade, when a boy sitting next to me in class dropped his pencil on the floor. He reached down to retrieve it, and when he sat up again he used my leg as a brace, and though I had no feelings for that boy — he was small and seemed so much younger than ten — still I felt a shock of pleasure run through my body, and I thought to myself, I am going to like sex.) After the adrenals have spoken, there is no turning back, and the pace and the hunger and the noise will only increase. The body will follow the lead of the mind, and it will become sexualized.

At the age of twelve or so, the pulse generator in the hypothalamus is resuscitated, disinhibited. It begins squeezing out packets of hormones again. Just as we don't know what shut it off before kindergarten, we don't know why it starts ticking again. Perhaps cues from the adrenal gland have stimulated it. Or fat may be the culprit. Fat cells release a signaling molecule called leptin, and some experiments have suggested that leptin is the switch that reactivates the brain clock. It is possible that the brain adjudges reproductive readiness by a girl's fat content, and that a girl must attain a certain level of fatness, a certain heft, before she is capable of ovulating. One rule of thumb has long had it that when a girl reaches approximately one hundred pounds, she pubesces, regard-less of her height or even her age. Fat girls menstruate earlier than thin girls or athletic girls. If a quarter of those hundred pounds are fat, then we're looking at twenty-five pounds of fat, which represent an energy reserve of 87,000 calories. The demands of pregnancy are about 80,000 calories. In theory, then, the brain may assess the leptin levels leaking forth from a growing girl's adipose tissue and start its metronome beating again at the hundred-pound mark.

Whatever the trigger, the revived hypothalamus is stronger now by far than it was in its nursery days. And stronger still are the ovaries, the gray sacks of heirloom pearls. They are ready to roll. The adrenals can go only so far. The ovaries know no bounds. They are the primary source of sex hormones that sexualize the body. Before the ovaries are able to serve up a viable egg, they are quite adept at dishing out the sex hormones. The sex hormones cause pubic hair to grow, fat to gather on the breasts and hips, the pelvis to widen, and eventually menstrual blood to flow.

If you are like me and you've been reading for years about the ovulatory cycle, you find it tedious. You've seen the charts of the rise and the fall of hormones, most of them with fusty names that sound like nothing you feel or think about or know of your body. Luteinizing hormone, LH; follicle-stimulating hormone, FSH; the worst of them, mentioned above, gonadotropin-releasing hormone, or GnRH. The cycle is disembodied from the cyclist.

Please, put aside your bigotry. Far from being dull, the cycle is dynamic and athletic. In describing it, I run the risk of sounding like a Victorian anatomist. Those scientists were astounded by the ovarian cycle. Some were simply fascinated by it; others were disgusted by it. All wrote gothically of it, and found in the monthly follicular rupturing and oozing yet another reason to pity the fairer, better, bruised and battered sex. Rudolf Virchow, the father of modern pathology, compared the bursting of the follicle to teething, with the egg forcing its way to the surface of the ovary as a tooth bud pokes through the gums, causing pain and "the liveliest disturbance of nutrition and nerve force." French doctors likened ovulation to the rupture of an acute abscess, while Havelock Ellis saw the monthly release of an egg as a "worm" that "gnaws periodically at the roots of life." In the eyes of the historian Jules Michelet, Thomas Laqueur writes, "woman is a creature 'wounded each month,' who suffers almost constantly from the trauma of ovulation, which in turn is at the center of a physiological and psychological phantasmagoria dominating her life." The ovary may be an almond in size, but for the voyeurs among Victorian physicians, it certainly was no almond of joy.

To me, the swelling of the ovarian follicle and its release is less ghoulish, less an act of carnage, and more in keeping with many acts of reproduction, sexual optimism, and high emotion. The follicle swells like a lobule in the breast swells with milk, or like the tear ducts swell with water and salt, or like the genitals congest during arousal — and then *whoosh*, the tension is released, and the lively fluids overspill their bounds.

Let us take as our starting point the standard day one of the ovulatory cycle (which we generally call the menstrual cycle because we can see the blood but we can't see the egg). Day one is the first day of menstruation, a quiet time for the ovaries. They release no eggs and generate very few, if any, sex hormones. Quiet below means flurry above, in the pulse generator of the hypothalamus. With scant evidence of hormonal output from the ovaries, the pulse quickens. The hypothalamus sends forth its messenger, the brain hormone GnRH, which in turn prods the pituitary gland, right below it. The pituitary expels its own parcel of hormones, and now we return to the young gray ladies, the seedpods. The pituitary signals awaken them. The pods are a collection of follicles, little nests, each enclosing an immature egg, as the honeycomb cells of a beehive enclose bee larvae. Every month, about twenty follicles and their oocytes are hailed by the brain. They start to expand and to ripen. They are like starlets at an audition, their heads stuffed with dreams. Eventually, on day ten or so, a decision is made. One of the contending follicles is chosen for the part. Its egg alone will advance to full fruiting, to the point of ovulation. (On occasion, more than one egg matures in a cycle, which is why we have fraternal twins, triplets, human litters.) Nobody knows how the selection is made. The winning follicle may simply be the one that grew fastest from the start. Or it may have released cues early on as to the genomic acuity of its oocyte and so have been singled out for grooming. However the sifting happens, the other follicles recognize when they have lost, for on the tenth day they cease to swell and start to wither, taking their rejected eggs with them. The chosen follicle persists. The egg within it matures, and its chromosomes are sorted out through meiosis. By the final stages, the follicle is so engorged, so grandiose, that it measures an inch across and half an inch high.

The swelling of the ovarian honeycombs is an exhibitionist act. It attracts attention. The fallopian tubes, those gorgeous pink sea pens, follow the drama with their feather-duster tips. As the follicles grow, the tubes brush over the surface of the ovaries, firmly, insistently, seeking clues — the envelope, please, which follicle will it be? The tubes are extraordinarily flexible. They are like the arms of an octopus, or vacuum cleaner hoses. Although each tube generally attends to the ovary closest to it, one tube can, if necessary, reach across the pelvic cavity to finger the opposite ovary. This happens in a woman with endometriosis, for example, when one of her two tubes is lashed down by a tangle of stray uterine tissue and cannot sample its seedpod. The opposite tube takes up the task of monitoring and snuffling the surface of both ovaries. And when the selected egg is ready, on one ovary or the other, the lone mobile tube will be there to catch it.

The final signal for ovulation, for the liberation of the egg, comes again from the brain, on day twelve or fourteen or thereabouts, with a spurt of luteinizing hormone from the pituitary gland. The hormonal surge persuades the follicle to split open. Sometimes a little blood is released on rupture, the spotting of ovulation that may come with mild cramping, the mittelschmerz. The egg sails out, into the waiting fingers, the fimbriae, of the fallopian tube. The fimbriae are covered with hair-like projections that beat in synchrony and create a current to suck the egg into the tube, the fertility hutch.

(Any woman who has ever used an ovulation predictor kit in an attempt to get pregnant knows of the LH surge, because it is the detection of the surge that tells her, Have sex today, as soon as possible; your egg is ready to pop. Whether the surge is the ideal event to shoot for is open to question, though. A large study of fertility patterns published in 1995 revealed that the day of ovulation is the last possible time for conception to occur, and that most pregnancies are the result of intercourse that took place one, two, up to five days *before* ovulation; sperm is built to endure for days and may need time to reach the egg. The finding was surprising. Fertility experts had thought that you had at least a day and maybe two after the rupturing of the follicle to conceive, but no, the emancipated egg is either too sensitive for this world or a Mussolini for punctuality. In any event, its extrafollicular lifespan is no more than a few hours. Thus, if you wait for the LH peak to have sex, the sperm may well arrive too late. The party is over. The egg has passed out.)

Back at the gray basket, the ruptured follicle lives on. It is not a wound or a ditch. It is a new mother, in a sense, a postpartum mother within a preparous mother. It has given birth to an egg, and now it will seek to nourish the egg. The follicle devotes itself to the production of hormones. The cells lining the pit swell, fill up with cholesterol, and turn soft and yellow, like butter or custard. They form the corpus luteum, which means "yellow body." The corpus luteum generates progesterone in great abundance and estrogens in moderate abundance, and the hormones course into the bloodstream and stimulate the uterus, causing the uterine lining to grow, and they stimulate the breasts, causing some swelling or tenderness. The fattened uterine lining could support the follicle's child, the egg, if the egg is fertilized and destined to survive, and the mammary glands could nurse the fertilized egg once it has grown and crossed over to the other side.

If pregnancy occurs, the corpus luteum will live on throughout gestation. For the first forty-two days its hormones are essential to the fetus's survival, but even after the fetus has built its placenta and the placenta assumes the task of synthesizing the hormones of gestation, the yellow body persists. It is still the dominant follicle, the crowned queen, and it keeps other follicles on the ovaries chastened, immature. One does not want to ovulate during pregnancy, after all.

But the corpus luteum is not just the equity of the possible embryo. For as long as it lasts, it is mother to the woman too. Its fat yellow tissue spills forth hormones, and those hormones impress every organ of her adult body, her bones, her kidneys, her pancreas, her brain. The body takes full advantage of the ovarian feast, as the Native Americans did with a buffalo carcass, putting each splinter of bone and strand of sinew to use in the service of food, shelter, and warmth.

In the absence of pregnancy, the corpus luteum regresses ten days after ovulation. The follicle that once attracted the stroke and suck of a fallopian tube now lures the attention of macrophages, immune system cells that clean up the body's dead and dying. Fibrous tissue forms over the pit. The corpus luteum becomes the corpus albicans, the white body, another scar on the face of experience.

The ovulatory cycle is a matter of physiology, and it occurs more or less on its own. But it is not entirely deaf to the cyclist. We don't want to make the mistake of thinking it is disembodied from the body. To the contrary, the ovaries, lacking the peritoneum and maintaining chronic contact with the brain and body, are quite responsive to us, the environment in which the organs live. The first half of the cycle is the most impressionable time. Women have very different cycle lengths, some as short as three weeks, others as long as forty days, and most of that variability occurs in the days between menstruation and ovulation. After the egg is released, the cycle becomes much more predictable. It lasts two weeks, give or take a couple of days. Before ovulation, the ovary is like an appellate court. It will listen to pleas and hear tales of denial and doubt. It will take the advice of a number of signals — from the brain, surrounding tissues, distal tissues — about what to do, whether to ovulate or vegetate. When you are very sick with the flu, for example, you may fail to ovulate, or take longer to ovulate than when you are well. This delay could be the result of the immune system's conveying a sense of crisis to the ovaries. Recall that under ordinary circumstances, macrophages are attracted to a postovulatory follicle and will help blanch the yellow body into albicans. During illness, your population of macrophages and other immune cells explodes. Some of those excess immune cells may aggregate on the ovary, disrupting the maturation of the follicles and even engulfing one or two in midswell. Alternatively, the immune changes may inhibit ovulation indirectly, by slowing the pulse generator in the brain or the secondary release of secretions from the pituitary. Whatever the details, it is not a bad system. If you're seriously ill, you need to focus on getting well. You can't afford to divert energy to a pregnancy.

Whether stress and anxiety, in the absence of frank illness, can also inhibit ovarian performance remains unclear. Popular wisdom says it does. Friends and relations frequently offer an infertile couple the unsolicited advice to relax. Take it easy, they cluck, and you'll get pregnant in no time. But this is a chicken-and-egg debate. Does stress cause infertility, or does infertility cause stress? Most of the evidence on the subject is anecdotal. We hear stories of infertile women who quit their aggravating, high-pressure jobs and quickly become pregnant, and of couples who spend years trying to conceive, finally decide to adopt, bring the new baby home, and voilà, within weeks they are with child. What we don't hear are the opposite tales, of women under horrible stress in wartime, after a violent rape, who nonetheless become pregnant. Clinical studies of the benefits of stress reduction programs to fertility treatment have yielded mixed results. Some show a significant improvement in conception rates, others show little or no difference. Primatologists seeking to understand why subordinate females in some species of monkeys, like the cotton-top tamarin, fail to ovulate when they are in the presence of the alpha female have been astonished to learn that classic stress hormones have nothing to do with the suppression of fertility. The researchers had theorized that the ruling female kept her inferiors so intimidated that the subordinates' bodies must course with stress hormones such as cortisol, rendering them temporarily sterile. But no, urine samples from the monkeys showed an almost indetectable concentration of stress hormones in the subordinates. In fact, the opposite appeared to be true: when a junior female was removed from the alpha's territory, her cortisol levels soared — resulting in a newfound ability to ovulate.

"Stress" in general is one of those monster topics, a source of abiding stress to those who study it. Nobody agrees on the definition of stress, how to measure it, or how much is too much. If you feel powerless in your life, a very small amount of stress can unhinge you. If you feel in control of your life, your appetite for stress may be large, bottomless. You may get high on stress and try to manufacture a perpetual state of emergency to obtain your crisis fix.

There are other ways, apart from nagging in-laws and looming deadlines, in which the outer world might impinge on the inner world of the ovaries, on the hormonal composition of the maturing follicles, on the bending and twisting and sucking of the feathered oviducts. One of the most famous and tantalizing examples of how external circumstances might influence a woman's private oscillator is the phenomenon known as menstrual synchrony: the possibility that women who live in close quarters convey some as yet mysterious signal to one another — an odorless, volatilized chemical called a pheromone — that ends up harmonizing the timing of women's cycles. The idea was first proposed in 1971 by Martha McClintock, now a biologist at the University of Chicago but then a Harvard graduate student. In a research paper that appeared in the high-profile journal *Nature*, McClintock presented data on the menstrual cycles of several groups of roommates at an all-female college. The women had begun the semester with cycles randomly distributed throughout the month, the way women's cycles are. Over the course of the school year, the cycles of cohabitants gradually converged. After seven months, the dates of onset of menstruation among roommates were 33 percent closer than they had been at the beginning. By contrast, among a control group of women who did not share rooms, there were no signs of menstrual synchrony. McClintock's paper won wide éclat in scientific and lay circles alike. The findings fit with many women's personal observations, the sense that mothers and teenage daughters, sisters, dorm mates, and lesbian lovers had of a mysterious coming together, of the simultaneous raiding of the tampon box, a sisterhood in the blood.

Subsequent studies of menstrual synchrony, however, were not so neat. Some confirmed the original report, others refuted it. According to one recent review of the menstrual synchrony studies published over the past twenty-five years, sixteen have found statistically significant evidence of synchrony and ten have failed to find any statistically meaningful patterns. A few studies have revealed evidence of asynchrony, or antisynchrony: as the months passed, the cohabiting women became *less* harmonized in their periods rather than more, sometimes to the point of diametric opposition. It's as though the women were signaling to each other, We had nothing in common before, so please, let's keep it that way.

McClintock is a woman of verve, rigor, and high, loopy enthusiasm who wears bright scarves over cashmere sweaters and unexpected accessories, like dove-gray socks patterned with black fishes. She explores how the environment influences physiology — how nurture nudges nature. She looks, for example, at the impact of mental attitude on the course of a disease, how the belief that you *can* get well may influence whether you *do* get well. She looks at how social isolation affects health; as a rule, in social animals extended solitude affects health badly, and the questions are why and how can we measure that badness and ferret out its source, the vertex between what looks like whoo-whoo mysticism and the measurable changes in hardcore physiology. Menstrual synchrony is real, McClintock insists, but it is not the whole story. People look at menstrual synchrony and get stuck on a very narrow interpretation of it, she explained to me. They say either women's periods converge in a statistically significant manner when they live together and menstrual synchrony exists, or they don't and it's bunk.

"People focus on menstrual synchrony as the main phenomenon because it's such a compelling idea," she said. "But I can't emphasize strongly enough, it's just the left ear of the elephant. It's just one aspect of the social control of ovulation." In social creatures, she continued, fertility, ovulation, and birth occur in the context of the group. The fallopian tubes may act like little suckers, but we don't conceive or gestate in a vacuum. We are at the mercy of the tribe, and our bodies know it, and they respond accordingly. As the dynamics of the group change, so too do our reactions. To ovulate in step with our female cohorts might behoove us under one circumstance and shackle us under another. McClintock and her colleagues have found that female rats can emit pheromones that suppress fertility in other females and pheromones that enhance it. "Those pheromones can be produced at different phases of the reproductive cycle, and at pregnancy and lactation," McClintock said. "Females send out different signals depending on their state, and the females living with them respond in a variety of ways. In some cases synchrony develops, in other cases it doesn't."

The rat work has yielded a wealth of detail and gives a sense of how nuanced the conversation between ovary and society can be. As a rule, female rats in a group strive to ovulate and conceive within a week or two of one another. They keep in reasonably close gestational step so that when all is done, they can breastfeed together, in a squirming, squealing mass. They're not sweet little communists. They're Norway rats, the kind of surly, toothy scavengers you find in dumpsters and sewers. But it turns out that by pooling pups and breastfeeding duties, each female benefits. She spends less time and energy lactating than she would if she had to attend to her offspring solo, and her pups are comparatively fatter and healthier at weaning. Synchrony, then, is the optimal state. And if a female for some reason miscarries or loses her litter soon after birth, she will do what rats hate to do, which is to hold back before breeding again. She awaits signals from her lactating sister rats. She wants to reset her clock so that it synchronizes once again with theirs.

There is more to the rats' tale of how society shapes biology. If a female for some reason falls out of sync with the group and conceives pups anyway, her sense of her own procreational asynchrony has a profound effect. She ends up giving birth to a litter composed largely of daughters rather than the standard half male, half female brood of the harmonious rat. Here is what happens. The new mother rat is going to be living and breastfeeding around other females, who are on a different bioclock from hers and who are thus likely to have pups that are much older than the newborn litter. Older pups are notorious milk hounds, and no milk is sweeter and more nutritious than the milk of a freshly lactating breast. They will steal much of the new mother's milk, and she can do little to prevent their nips. Therefore, many of her own helpless offspring will die of starvation. If only one or two of her pups are going to make it, it's best that they be females. Among rats (and many other species), daughters are the safe sex, sons the high-risk sex. Daughters are government bonds; sons are junk bonds. A male rat might copulate widely and madly and make scores of babies and make his mother a triumphant, wealthy grandmother, but he might fail completely and inseminate nobody and make nothing of himself or his bloodline. By contrast, it is a very rare female rat who does not breed at all. She can have only so many pups in her lifetime, but she will have some. When times are hard and prospects grim, then, invest in daughters. They will keep the lineage alive. We see here an extraordinary example of the outside elbowing its way into the deepest chambers, into the womb. The pregnant female rat senses her asynchrony, and the status of her social group and of the communal breast, and somehow she translates that sensory information into a bias against male fetuses, resorbing them into her body before they cost her a drachma of possibly fruitless care. Feeling at risk, her body seeks guarantees. It gives her girls.

In 1998, the McClintock team again published a major report in the journal *Nature*, confirming that we have a bit of the rat in us and that our ovaries too are susceptible to the sway of the Weltanschauung of the group. The scientists showed that if they took swabs from the armpits of women at different points in their ovulatory cycle and applied the swabs to the upper lips of other women, the donor secretions could act as pheromones, as odorless chemical signals. The secretions either hastened or prolonged the cycles of many, though not all, of the women exposed to them. Armpit swabs taken from women early in their cycle, in the follicular phase, before ovulation, had the effect of shortening the cycles of the recipient women — that is, the beneficiaries ovulated several days earlier than predicted from prior records of their cycles. If, in contrast, the underarm swabs were taken later in the month, around the time when the donors were ovulating, the pheromones extended the cycles of the women given an upper-lip treatment — the recipients ovulated several days later than predicted from their ordinary cycle span. Pheromone samples taken later still, after the donors had ovulated — during the luteal phase of the cycle, which precedes menstruation — had no impact on the recipients one way or another.

Not all of the women were influenced by the pheromones, but enough of them were to elevate the findings to robust statistical significance and to demonstrate with fair firmness that human pheromones exist. What we see in this carefully controlled experiment is that women can push and women can pull, and they can respond to other women in varying ways, all unconsciously, without knowing why, without the benefit even of olfaction, for the women in the study said they smelled nothing when the swab was applied under their nose, save for the scent of rubbing alcohol used as a prep in the experiment. The results also explain why studies of menstrual synchrony have wandered all over the place, sometimes coming up positive and sometimes negative: because the pheromonal signals can either bring women's cycles together or push them apart, depending on when in the month the signals are produced, studies that just searched for total synchrony missed the equally important asynchronous patterns that emerged.

But what is the good of this social control of ovulation? What is the good of trying to bring other women into concert with you or trying to throw other women out of reproductive joint? We don't know. We can only speculate. We must expand our imaginations, backward, forward, and outward. We must think beyond lunar phases and simple ovulation and menstruation and take into account the months that women spend being pregnant, and the months or years they breastfeed, and the smells and cues they might emit during those protracted states. We must think as well of our emotional and political relationship to our cohabitants and the degree to which we feel camaraderie with them, or competition, or utter disinterest. If we are very comfortable with the women in our intimate domain, then menstrual synchrony might more easily emerge. To feel safe is to feel willing to risk impregnation. It is easier to conceive when ovulation is regular, and one way to entrain the cycle, to stabilize it, is to attend to the resonant frequency of those around you.

If, though, we feel at odds with our den mates, then why expect ovarian collusion, or any sort of stabilizing influence from them at all? Subordinate cotton-top monkeys will not ovulate when they are around the ruling female. The alpha female doesn't hound them. She doesn't beat them or steal food from them. Mostly she ignores them. Yet the smell or sight or aura of her muffles the subordinates' neural oscillator, and they don't ovulate. Might a woman also recoil in the presence of a threatening or irritating female? If that rival is nursing a newborn, might the woman choose to delay her own ovulation a bit — unconsciously choose, of course — so that when she conceives and must meet the demands of pregnancy, she will not face the additional burden of competing for resources against a hostile lactator? The social control of ovulation could be used cooperatively, then, to harmonize cycles, or it could be used defensively, to avoid conflict, or it could be used offensively, to destabilize a competitor's cycle, to attempt to undermine her fertility, if need be.

"Information is the key. It is always the key," says McClintock. "The more information one has, the better. The woman who is able to regulate and optimize her fertility, to ensure that she is fertile at the best possible time in terms of both her physical and her social environment, will be more successful than the woman who hasn't a clue." Pheromones are only one source of information, McClintock says. They are not the sole source, or even necessarily a central source, of information about where you stand and whether it's time to make your move. Pheromones simply add to the mix, and sometimes they're worth attending to and sometimes they're not — and so it was that some of the women in McClintock's study were susceptible to them and some were not.

We are submerged in a sea of sensory advice. Our sexual partners exert influences of their own on our brains and baskets. Women who live with men tend to cycle in a more predictable fashion than women who live alone, and regular cycling augments the chance of conception. A woman might again be responding to pheromones, secreted by the man's armpit, his groin, or the back of his neck, at just the spot where she feels compelled to nuzzle. But why stop at the nose? Your whole body can serve as a busybody. As we saw earlier, a woman is likelier to become pregnant from sex with an adulterous lover than she is from sex with her husband. The data are under dispute and could be explained by something as mundane as the fact that a woman may be unwilling to take birth control to an assignation for fear of discovery. Alternatively, as we have seen, the discrepancy could be the result of orgasm's pulling desired sperm in, as a form of last-ditch female choice. Yet another possibility is that pleasure, like the presence of other females, can have congress with the ovaries and sway the timing of ovulation, perhaps by triggering the LH surge that liberates an egg from its cell. I strongly suspect that climax counts, and that anything capable of causing the uterus to shudder so insistently must impress the neighboring pods and their seeds as well. Maybe a follicle, on feeling the temblor, will quicken its pace of maturation and tell the brain, Hurry up, please, it's time, and the brain will respond with an LH surge, the ovum's hymn of freedom.

Admittedly, I have been seduced by experience, my personal encounter with the fertility spirits. My husband and I had been trying for years to become pregnant. I cycled like a metronome, every twenty-eight days. And for a while our sex became metronomic too, concentrated furiously around midmonth, when I thought I was likeliest to conceive. We tried all the suggested positions. Sometimes I'd have an orgasm during sex; sometimes I consciously refrained. Who knew whether a pulsing cervix would pull in the sperm or spit it out? Best to be catholic in every detail. I would lie afterward immobilized, with buttocks elevated. I used ovulation predictor kits to detect my LH surge. For several months we abided by the thin blue line. Nothing happened, nothing, nothing, nothing.

In November of 1995, my little predictor sticks failed to detect evidence of an LH surge. I was terribly glum about that: an anovulatory cycle, I thought, and there I was, thirty-seven years old, running out of time. But in December I found out that I was pregnant — that I had conceived the month before, when I was certain all lay fallow. I reviewed the sequence of events, and I knew what had happened. Early in my cycle, days before I thought conception was possible, my husband and I had done what we managed so rarely in those times of procreation fixation and had sex for the pure love and pleasure of it. That act, I am sure, that pointless, magic squander, pumped up my cycle as smartly as Jan Ullrich jazzing through the Tour de France. My climax quickened the hatching of an avid egg. It provoked an LH surge, and the surge spurred a follicle, and the egg broke free and dove down a tube, and the sperm from the precipitating event was there to greet it. And everything fell into place so swiftly that by the time I started the usual midmonth screening for an LH surge, I had missed the excitement. I thought I lay fallow, but in truth I already was in clover.

I have no proof of any of this, of course. All I have is my child. A rat's distress will give her daughters. I got mine from joy.

10

GREASING THE WHEELS

A BRIEF HISTORY OF HORMONES

EVERY MORNING I take a little pill that contains thyroxine, a hormone produced by the moth-shaped thyroid gland in the middle of the neck. When I was in my twenties I had Graves' disease, an autoimmune disorder in which the thyroid becomes hyperactive and generates too much thyroxine. I hate going to doctors, and it went undiagnosed for months. I was jittery, anxious, an emotional hacksaw. My heart raced at 120 beats a minute, nearly twice my normal pulse, even when I lay in bed. I had been an athletic woman, but suddenly I lost all my strength and could not walk up a flight of stairs without stopping for a break midway. I ate ravenously and still lost weight, but I looked too sick to elicit compliments on my slimmer figure. My eyes bulged out slightly and lent me the appearance of a tree frog, a symptom that I now recognize in the faces of other Graves' alumnae, like the former first lady Barbara Bush.

I was treated with radioactive iodine, which homed in on the diseased thyroid gland and destroyed much of it. Now I am hypothyroid, making less thyroxine than I need, and so I will have to swallow one of these supplements every day for the rest of my life. It's a dull business. It doesn't change anything about my mood or personality. It doesn't even offer the mild refreshment of other daily rituals, like the brushing of the teeth or the washing of the face.

Yet if I were to stop taking thyroxine, my life would change for the worse. Gradually, over days or weeks, I'd become irritable, depressed, lethargic, and stupid. I'd gain weight, feel cold most of the time, and lose my libido. My heart rate would become slow and irregular, and my blood pressure would rise. Again I'd be sick and at risk of early death; again I'd be crushed by my chemistry.

Thyroxine is not a sexy hormone. It is not what we mean when we talk of being "flooded with hormones" or "high on hormones," as teenagers and lovers are said to be. The hormone family of chemicals is a vast kindred that includes such familiar bio-actors as the sex hormones — the estrogens and the androgens — and the stress hormones, our private hair-trigger sentries that counsel panic whether it's a lion or a landlord snorting at the door. It includes a host of backstage technicians that tell us we need salt, food, or water, and it includes compounds that we don't normally think of as hormones at all, like serotonin, the famed target of Prozac, Zoloft, and the other perimillennial mood brighteners.

Through my years of dependency on hormones, I became curious about their contours, their edges and their limitations. I wondered why something like thyroxine, which could be so brutal and upheaving when generated in excessive or insufficient quantities, was otherwise so unremarkable, so unilluminating. In taking the right amount of thyroxine, I returned to the status quo of myself, the stable instability that I have known since the onset of sentience, but nothing more. The best I could do was to keep the old version operating. Thyroxine, then, was at once global and narrow. No tissue, not even my brain, was spared from an abnormality of its production, yet it was not me, not the flesh of self or of consciousness. What was going on, then? Hormones have effects, they have failings, they have meanings. Hormones are far more important than most of us realize, but not in the ways that most of us think.

Lately there has been a hormone renaissance, a renewed fascination with these chemical messengers and what they can do for us, say about us, solve about us. Part of the interest is rhetorical fashion. It is fashionable now to ascribe such supposedly male traits as the tendency to swagger, posture, interrupt, and belch in public to testosterone. Men in groups are said to "reek of testosterone," to be "poisoned by testosterone," to be "caldrons of testosterone." It sounds cute, it sounds clever, and because yes, men do have a fair amount of testosterone, it sounds accurate as well. Hormone humor does not spare women, though, and so gals on a shopping expedition or sharing a cappuccino become "estrogen sinks" or waft "billows of estrogen." It is also fashionable to talk of love hormones, mommy hormones, and even crime hormones.

We want to explain ourselves to ourselves, and hormones look like a clean and quantifiable way to do so, to distinguish male from female, competitor from cooperator, domesticated from feral. We are incorrigible categorizers.

Popular interest in hormones also reflects a revival of interest among the high priests of organizing principles, scientists. There has been an explosion of hormone research unmatched in ferocity since the first hormones were isolated and synthesized more than seventy years ago. Comforting analogies no longer apply. In the past, hormones were talked of as keys, each designed to fit into a specific receptor — the metaphorical lock — located on different tissues of the body and brain. In so fitting, a hormone would swing wide the door to a defined suite of behaviors and reactions. Now the metaphor has rusted. It turns out that the body offers up multiple locks to the pryings of any given hormone, and sometimes the hormones exert their might without the need for any lock at all. Instead they can ramrod their way through from blood into tissue, or slip in between the cracks, leaving us agog once more at how potent, how exquisite, and how crude these chemical emissaries can be.

Hormones have a music to them, a molecular lyricism that explains why they are potent and ancient: why they work well enough to have merited retention in one form or another through hundreds of millions of years of evolution. Certain hormones are among the things that make us women, and these are the hormones that I will focus on. They are the fashionable hormones: estrogen, progesterone, testosterone, oxytocin, and serotonin. But the hormones are not slaves to fashion. They don't conform to expectations. They hate clichés.

Hormone comes from the Greek *horman,* which means to arouse, to excite, to urge. This is what a hormone does. It excites. It urges, though sometimes what the hormone urges is a sense of calm, a call to rest. By the classic definition, a hormone is a substance secreted by one tissue that travels through blood or another body fluid to another tissue, whereupon the hormone arouses the encountered tissue to a new state of activity. The thyroid gland secretes thyroxine, which stimulates the heart, the muscles, and the intestines. A follicle on the ovary bursts open and releases a draft of progesterone, which cues the endometrium to fatten. The classicists thought that hormones differ from neurotransmitters, the quick-snapping chemicals such as norepinephrine and ace-tylcholine that allow brain cells to communicate; but that distinction has begun to disintegrate as researchers have learned that hormones, like neurotransmitters, can alter the texture and disposition of brain cells, making them more likely to fire. Brain cells talk to one another in a *rat-a-tat-tat* of electrical impulses. And so, while it wouldn't be quite proper to call estrogen a neurotransmitter, it would be proper to call it and the neurotransmitters members of a large chemical family of neuromodulators — brain inflectors. This reclassification is more than a semantic issue. It affects how we think about our thinking and feeling and being. It also brings the body and brain into synchrony rather than continuing the old distinction that said endocrinologists get the chemistry from the neck down, while the neurobiologists claim the domain of the brain.

A hormone is not only complex, it is small, a desirable feature in a molecule that would act as a bio-troubadour, always in voluble transit. This concision is true regardless of whether the nut of the hormone, its structural core, is built of grease, as the sex hormones are, or of meat, as the peptide hormones such as oxytocin and serotonin are.

Let's take a zoom lens to the sex hormones, also called the sex steroid hormones. The word *steroid* lately has been pluralized into idiocy, so that when we think of steroids we think of anabolic steroids, the drugs that bodybuilders and other athletes take, at their peril, in an effort to inflate their strength and bulk. Such drugs are usually a synthetic version of testosterone, and thus they are steroid hormones, but the class of steroid hormones is much more inclusive and more interesting than locker-room dope.

If you've ever looked at a diagram of a steroid molecule, and if your high school chemistry teacher didn't entirely annihilate your capacity to appreciate molecular aesthetics, you surely appreciated the steroid's rigorous beauty. A steroid is built of four rings of carbon atoms, arranged so they touch each other like mosaic tiles. Those rings lend stability to the hormone; they do not dissolve easily and so will not fall apart in your blood or in the thick sea of your brain. Moreover, the steroid rings are amenable to modification. Decorations can be added to their side, each new flounce changing the steroid's meaning and power. Testosterone and estrogen look surprisingly similar, yet they differ enough in their minor appendages to communicate quite distinct messages to a recipient tissue.

Steroids are ancient in nature and play communicative roles in many organisms. Molds secrete steroids. A female mold releases a steroid hormone that will induce a neighboring mold to grow the equivalent of male reproductive organs. Once the solicitee has complied with the request and enmaled himself, he releases another steroid hormone into his surroundings, which induces the female to grow toward him. Come and get it! he cries, and she comes, and she gets it. Plants such as soy and yams have steroid and steroidlike hormones, and in fact a diet rich in these phytoestrogens can help palliate some of the symptoms of menopause. Certain species of aquatic insects synthesize the stress hormone cortisol in such high concentrations that they knock out any fish attempting to eat them. Mexican beetles are like walking birth control pills, generating estrogen and progesterone that some scientists suspect are intended to curb the population of their natural predators. Pigs love steroid hormones; during courtship, a male pig will spit on his sowheart's face and in so doing expose her to a pungent steroid compound that causes her to freeze with rear legs conveniently parted. All of which might help explain the now quaint term *male chauvinist pig* — yessir, a bit of spit and the little woman is yours!

There are hundreds, if not thousands, of varieties of steroid and steroidlike hormones in nature. By definition, a steroid hormone is an elaboration of that ubiquitous and unfairly maligned molecule cholesterol. Cholesterol is a steroid in structure, but it is a no-frills steroid and not in itself a communications vehicle. Only with chemical embellishment does it assume the mercurial role of hormone. All steroid hormones in vertebrates are built of cholesterol. The choice of cholesterol as the foundation for these hormones makes sense, because the body brims with it. Even if you never touch cholesterol-rich food such as eggs, oil, and meat, your liver continues to make cholesterol around the clock, and with reason. Cholesterol is an essential component of the plasma membrane, the fatty, protective coat surrounding every cell. At least half of the average cell's membrane consists of cholesterol, much more than half in neurons. Without cholesterol, your cells would fall apart. Without cholesterol, new cells could not be manufactured. There would be no way of replacing the cells of the skin, gut, and immune system, which die by the millions each day. Cholesterol is the fat of the earth and the fat of the brain.

The steroid hormones, then, are pieces of ourselves, of the skin of our cells. When our cells wish to communicate, they paradoxically turn to the stuff of membranes, the original isolationists. The plasma membrane separates one cell from another, just as a membrane walled off from its environment the mother of us all, the first single-celled organism, some 3.8 billion years ago. The plasma membrane gave birth to selfhood and organismic loneliness. To reconnect, to speak as one cell, one self, to another, there can be no better language than that of the plasma membrane itself.

The word *hormone* wasn't coined until 1905, and the first one wasn't isolated until the 1920s, but people have known about steroid hormones indirectly for millennia, thanks to the external nature of one particular hormone factory, the testicles. Males, including human ones, were the hapless recipients of the first experiments in endocrinology. Game animals were castrated to make their behavior more manageable and their meat tastier. Men were castrated to render them trustworthy. The Old Testament describes the use of eunuchs to guard the consorts of Hebrew kings and princes. Men also were castrated as punishment for sexual crimes or sexual miscalculations. In the twelfth century, Peter Abelard, the great theologian and philosopher, had his testicles excised for having run off with his beloved student, Heloise. Abelard bitterly mourned his stolen manhood and wrote of it in a memoir, *My Great Misfortune.* (For her part, Heloise was sent unscathed to a nunnery, her gonads beyond reach or medieval understanding. Later she rose to prominence as the head of a convent called the Paraclete, founded by her former lover.)

The role of the testicles in cultivating the many changes of puberty also was known for centuries. Boys with promising soprano voices were accordingly gelded before adolescence to prevent their vocal cords from thickening and their pitches from lowering. According to contemporary accounts, the best of the castrati were magnificent to hear, for they combined the sweetness and luster of a woman's timbre with the power afforded by a man's comparatively large lungs. Castration mania reached a peak in the seventeenth and eighteenth centuries, when thousands of parents had their sons orchiectomized in hopes of stardom and wealth; ever and obnoxiously are stage parents among us. But by the nineteenth century, tastes and operatic singing techniques had changed, and the diva soprano supplanted the castrato as the keeper of the angel's registers.

Castration continued in the laboratory, however, as Arnold Adolph Berthold fathered the modern science of endocrinology in the mid-nineteenth century with a series of landmark rooster experiments at the University of Göttingen. He removed the testicles of young male chickens, an operation that if allowed to run its course would give rise to capons. Famed among poultry fanciers for their soft and flavorful flesh, capons lack the plumage, sexual bombast, and tendency to crow exhibited by full-fledged roosters. But Berthold's birds didn't stay neutered for long. He took the excised testicles and implanted them inside the young birds' bellies, and lo, the birds matured into perfectly normal roosters, all crest, comb, and cock-a-doodle-do. Dissecting the animals, he observed that the transplanted gonads had taken root in their new position, doubled in size, and sprouted a blood supply; they were even filled with sperm, as adult testes should be. Because the nerves to the testes had been irreparably damaged in the course of the transplantation, Berthold concluded that the testicles were not exerting their impact on the body by grace of the nervous system. Instead, he correctly surmised, some sort of substance, some *eau vitale,* must be traveling from the gonadal tissue through the bloodstream to other parts of the body, thus transforming cockerel into cock. What that substance might be he had no way of determining.

The male body gave birth to hormone research, but the female body reared it to maturity. In the 1920s, scientists began experimenting with extracts from the urine of pregnant women, seeking interesting compounds. They tested the urine on the genital tracts of rats, and they found that something in the pee had a dramatic effect on the rat uterus and vagina. The endometrial layer of the rat's uterus thickened, while the lining of the vagina became cornified — a nifty, graphic word meaning that the cells lengthened into shapes resembling cobs of corn. Organic chemists sought the source of such transformations and in 1929 isolated the world's first hormone, estrone. Estrone is an estrogen, the family of hormones that we call female hormones, although both sexes — all sexes — have them. There are at least sixty forms of estrogen in the body, any body, but three hold sway: estrone, estradiol, and estriol. They are named for the number of hydroxyl groups (pairs of hydrogen and oxygen atoms) that festoon each hormone's torso. You can teach your baby daughter to count with estrogens. Estr*one* has one hydroxyl group, estra*diol* two, and es*triol* three. Counting hydroxyl groups is a chemist's way of naming names, not a biologist's; the number of hydroxyl groups doesn't predict anything about the molecule's behavior. More doesn't mean better, fewer doesn't mean duller. But the chemists got there first, so they got to play Adam.

Estrone proved to be relatively weak in its ability to prompt vaginal cornification or endometrial thickening, particularly when compared to estradiol, the principal estrogen in premenopausal women. But because estrone is secreted in abundant amounts by the placenta during pregnancy, and because it was a pregnant woman's urine that gave rise to the modern era of endocrinology, estrone was the first to be found. Soon after, chemists were seized by hormone hysteria and in short order had isolated most of the steroid hormones — the androgens, progesterone, the stress hormones of the adrenal gland — and determined their most obvious functions.

Yet their truest love remained their first, the estrogens. Chemists created a pharmacopoeia of synthetic estrogens, yanking off side chains here, tacking on methyl groups there. They designed the notorious estrogen compound diethylstilbestrol, or DES, used to prevent miscarriage from the 1940s through the 1960s but now known to be a cause of cancer and other disorders in the children of mothers who took the drug. They invented birth control pills. They made estrogen pills and estrogen patches for menopause, using either a synthetic version of the hormone or "natural" estrone isolated from the urine of pregnant mares, who piss a lot, the way horses do, particularly when they're with foal.

Estrogens were the first, and they remain, in their way, the finest. They have grown more interesting with time, not less. They are part angel, part anarchist. Estrogens keep us healthy and make us sick. They build our breasts and then corrupt them with tumors. They ripen eggs and nurture new life in the womb, but they also give rise to those ropy purple fibroids that can expand like zucchinis or pumpkins, until we cry aunt and have the uterus abolished.

How difficult it is to keep track of the contradictions. We are told that women in the industrialized world are steeped in too much estrogen, all kinds of estrogen; that what with our excess fat, our perpetual menstrual cycles rarely broken by pregnancy or lactation, our birth control pills, our taste for alcoholic libations, even estrogenic chemicals in our surroundings, we end up being exposed to far more of the hormone than our ancestors ever were, and this abundance is bad and a source of disease. Then we are told that we don't get enough estrogen, that we weren't supposed to live much past menopause, when our ovaries stop serving up significant doses of estrogen. Therefore we need to take estrogen supplements for years and years. We are told that estrogen keeps our hearts strong, our bones sturdy, and our wits sharp: estrogen as a Marvel comics superheroine. Can we therefore discard the old image of estrogen as the hormone that makes women tender, softhearted, practically filleted?

I admire estrogen because it is so obliging of our demands and our capriciousness. It is our scapegoat, our whipping bitch. Over the years it has been demonized, glorified, excommunicated, and resurrected, and just like a woman, it can still take a joke. To appreciate estrogen, we need to begin by separating estrogen the hormone — what we know and what we don't know about its powers and constraints — from estrogen the parable, the imagined ingredient in Wicca's medicine chest, source of lunacy and the malign feminine.

The estrogens are called female hormones, and that is partly inaccurate and partly reasonable. From the age of twelve through fifty, women have three to ten times more estrogen circulating through their bloodstream than men do. In middle age, men and women become closer estrogenic kin, for not only do a woman's levels of the hormone drop, but a man's gradually rise. Keep in mind that regardless of whose hormones are under scrutiny, the concentrations are vanishingly small, measured in laboratory tests in nanograms or picograms — billionths or trillionths of a gram. To obtain one teaspoon of estradiol, we would need to drain the blood of a quarter of a million premenopausal women. By contrast, the blood supply of any one of us contains at least a teaspoon of sugar and several tablespoons of salt. Hormones are peas, and we're all princesses. No matter how many mattresses you put between us and them, hormones still make us squirm.

Roughly speaking, the different estrogens are produced by different tissues of the body, though there's a lot of overlap, redundancy, and the usual unknowns about who does what when and to what end. Estradiol, the principal estrogen of our reproductive years, is the product of the ovaries. It flows out of the cells of the follicles and from the corpus luteum, the yellow matter that forms like a blister on a ruptured follicle. Estradiol is considered the most potent of the three estrogens, at least according to standard assays of estrogen activity — that is, it makes a rat's vagina cornify so clearly it looks like the waving fields of Iowa. Estriol is generated by the placenta and to a lesser extent by the liver. It is the major "pregnancy estrogen," the source of any charming gestational glow you might have — if you aren't green with nausea. As mentioned above, the placenta also synthesizes estrone. So too does adipose tissue. Fat women often are spared overt symptoms of menopause such as hot flashes and covert ones such as thinning bones; even as their ovaries cease the monthly efflux of estradiol, their peripheral tissue compensates by manufacturing estrone. Very muscular women fare well in menopause too, not only because they're fit and their hearts are hardy and their bones are strengthened by years of weight-bearing exercise, but also because muscle makes modest amounts of estrone. For any postmenopausal woman who forgoes patches or conjugated extracts of horse piss, estrone will be the predominant estrogen until departure. Estrone alone for the merry crone.

This is a lesson learned only recently, that the body makes and consumes estrogen *globally*. During the golden age of hormone research, scientists thought that they didn't need to look beyond the gonads: the ovaries made estrogen, the testes made testosterone. Hence the term *sex steroids*. They thought that the gonads made sex steroids to do sexy things, or rather reproductive things — to control ovulation, for example, and thicken the uterine lining. But no, estrogen's role is not limited to good breeding. The body makes estrogen everywhere, and the body eats estrogen everywhere. Bones make estrogen, and bones eat estrogen. The blood vessels make estrogen and devour estrogen. The brain makes estrogen, and it responds to estrogen in ways we are only beginning to understand. The body loves estrogen. It chews it up and then demands more. The half-life of estrogen is brief, maybe thirty to sixty minutes, and then it is broken down, to be recycled or eliminated.

But there's always more, produced and consumed locally or disseminated transcorporeally.

Estrogen is like chocolate. It is strong in very small doses, and it can either excite or soothe, depending on which tissue is doing the devouring. Estrogen stimulates the cells of the breast and the uterus, but it calms the blood vessels and keeps them from getting narrow, stiff, and inflamed. Estrogen is also like chocolate because it is a near-universal symbol for *Eat me*. Rare and mutant is the human who hates chocolate. By the same token, very few parts of the body hate or ignore estrogen. Almost every two-bit organ or tissue wants a bite of it.

Here is what we've learned about the pervasiveness of estrogen. To make estrogen, you need an enzyme called aromatase. With aromatase, a tissue of the body can transform a precursor hormone into estrogen. The precursor may be testosterone — yes, the "male" hormone, which women make in their ovaries, their adrenal glands, and possibly in places like the uterus and the brain. Or the precursor can be another androgen, like androstenedione, a hormone that deserves much deeper scientific understanding than it currently can claim. Who knows but that androstenedione is an amplifier of female aggression and anger? Suffice it to say here that women generate androstenedione in the ovaries and adrenals, and that androstenedione can, through the mediating activity of aromatase, be transmuted into the bittersweet cordial estrogen.

This would all be so much chemistry-set trivia if it weren't for the recent discovery that aromatase is all over the place. The ovaries have aromatase, so the ovaries, which make testosterone, can instantly turn the testosterone into estrogen, and they do, in calendrical spurts, and so women cycle. Other tissues have aromatase too: fat, bones, muscle, blood vessels, brain. The breast has aromatase. Give any of these tissues a bit of precursor hormone, a taste of testosterone, and they'll convert it to estrogen. Not in spurts, not by the menstrual calendar, but sedately, steadily, day after day. Interestingly, aromatase grows more potent with age. Even as most systems of the body slide into decrepitude, aromatase activity picks up its pace, becoming ever more efficient at converting precursors into estrogen. That could explain why older men are more estrogenized than their younger counterparts, and why postmenopausal women don't crumble, don't lie down and die, just because their ovaries no longer give them monthly estradiol highs. Their breasts, bones, blood vessels, are yet creating estrogen. Red wine, redwood, aromatase: how well the years become you.

But it is not enough to make estrogen. The means to understand the hormone must be present too. Estrogen speaks to the body through an estrogen receptor, a protein that recognizes it and surrounds it and then changes shape, as a blanket's shape is changed when someone is lying beneath it. In its altered shape, the receptor activates genetic changes within the cell, turning some genes on, others off. The shifts in gene activity in turn change the state of the cell, and eventually the organ of which the cell is part.

So we know that a given organ is sensitive to estrogen if the cells of that organ contain estrogen receptors. And we are, it seems, outlandishly sensitive to estrogen. As aromatase is everywhere, so too are estrogen receptors. Look in the cells of the liver, bone, skin, blood vessels, bladder, brain. Look anywhere; estrogen receptors are everywhere. The trick nowadays, says Benita Katzenellenbogen, who has studied estrogen biochemistry for twenty-five years, is to find a tissue that *doesn't* have estrogen receptors. Maybe the spleen, she shrugs.

It goes on. The estrogen story is like *Masterpiece Theatre,* highbrow soap. In 1996 scientists realized that we have not just one type of estrogen receptor, as they had thought for decades, but two, each a distinct molecular character but each capable of clasping estrogen and allowing the cell to react to the hormone. The proteins are called estrogen receptor-alpha and estrogen receptor-beta. Some cells of the body are alpha-rich, some beta-rich, some doubly blessed. And within any given cell there may be thousands of copies of each receptor type. Thousands of alpha receptors, thousands of betas. In some cells, tens of thousands. That's why it takes so little hormone to get such a big response: entire armies of receptor proteins stand ready and able to detect whatever tiny amount of estrogen may be floating by.

In different tissues, estrogen receptors do very distinct things — that is, they turn on a different set of genes in the liver than they do in the bone or the breast or the pancreas. For the most part, we don't have a clue which genes are activated by estrogen. But we do know some things. In the liver, for example, the coupling of estrogen and estrogen receptor stimulates the synthesis of blood clotting factors. It thickens the blood. We need good, clot-ready blood to keep us from hemorrhaging during those predictable times of blood loss — during menstruation, of course, but also when the egg bursts from the ovarian follicle, when an embryo burrows into the uterine wall like the chirpy parasite it is, and during childbirth. Because of estrogen's capacity to raise clotting factor synthesis, birth control pills and estrogen replacement therapy can on rare occasions cause clots to appear and travel to undesirable locations, such as the lungs.

The marriage of estrogen and receptor in the liver also stimulates the production of high-density lipoprotein, familiar to many of us as HDL, the so-called good cholesterol that we like to see on our medical charts as a big number, the bigger the sweeter, and inhibits low-density lipoprotein, or LDL, the "bad" cholesterol. High-density lipoprotein is not really cholesterol but a carrier of cholesterol, able to absorb cholesterol particles and other fats from the blood and donate them to tissues if needed, or to the liver for processing and excretion if not. The lipoprotein thus may serve as a fine source of energy transfer between mother and offspring during pregnancy and breastfeeding. Ever anticipating fecundity, estrogen tells the liver habitually to favor the production of HDL over that of low-density lipoprotein. (Intense exercise can have a similarly promotional effect on the liver's outlay of HDL; the rigors of chronic activity inspire the same anabolic spirit that reproduction does, the same need to scavenge available blood lipids for the sake of creating new cells.)

Estrogenesis, Part 17. Once again we've underestimated our steroid heroine. Estrogen, it turns out, doesn't need a receptor to make itself understood. Yes, it connects with alpha and beta. But that connection and the consequent shape-shifting of the receptors take time. Estrogen also can work almost instantaneously. It may, for example, rattle cell membranes just by touching them. As estrogen drifts through a cell membrane, it briefly opens tiny pores that allow ions to flow into and out of the cell. The membrane's charge changes — *zap!* — but then quickly reverts. For most tissues of the body, such transient fluctuations mean nothing. But for some organs, flux is the crux of strength. Think of the heart. The heart pumps blood to an electrochemical metronome, its pacemaker powered by ion flux. Estrogen just might help keep the transmembrane current of cardiac tissue flowing strongly and smoothly. Premenopausal women, whose bodies are bathed in estrogen, have hearts like bulls, and rarely suffer heart attacks. Undoubtedly some of the reason for the cardiopleasures of estrogen is indirect, for as we have seen, estrogen gives us high-density lipoprotein, which helps clear cholesterol from the blood before it can clog the arteries sclerotic. But here we see another possible reason that the heart loves estrogen: for the transient jolt. Estrogen as Edison. It gives the body a buzz.

And so we have at least two broad categories of responses to estrogen stimulation: one swift and transient, the other statelier, more thoughtful. Estrogen, we didn't know the half of you. Is there anything you can't do?

For one thing, sit still. Estrogen is a moving target. Even as it has, under scrutiny, revealed new talents, it has lost some that were previously ascribed to it. For years scientists thought that the hormone was essential to the raw beginnings of life. Studying embryonic development in such pliant "model animals" as the pig, researchers observed that right around the time when an embryo was about to implant in the uterus, *whoosh!* the cluster of cells released a burst of estrogen. The hormonal surge appeared to mark the transition between provisional pig — the blastocyst — and confirmed pig — the embryo. Nobody knew what that early-stage estrogen was doing, but obviously it was doing something big. When scientists experimentally blocked estrogen synthesis during embryo implantation, they killed the pig-in-progress.

There were other reasons for believing in the importance of estrogen to mammalian embryogenesis. A fetus can survive just fine without androgen or androgen receptors; Jane Carden and other women with androgen insensitivity syndrome are the unblemished adult evidence of that. But without estrogen? Nobody had ever found a person who lacked all traces of estrogen circuitry. Until the mid-1990s, a conceptus without estrogen was simply inconceivable.

The man was twenty-eight years old and six foot nine and sick of being asked if he played basketball. He didn't. He couldn't. His knees were too knocked, his feet were too splayed, and his gait was too awkward. What he could and did do was keep growing. He'd grown an inch since he was twenty-six. He wore a size 19 shoe, six sizes bigger than the biggest shoe you can find in an ordinary men's footwear department. And as the man grew, his gait worsened, which is why he finally consulted a doctor. The doctor referred him to an endocrinologist, who determined that the young man had bones that were both too young and too old for him. Too young, because the ends of them hadn't fused together, as they usually do in late adolescence; too old, because the bone shafts were full of holes. He had a serious case of osteoporosis. He had other problems as well, including insulin resistance like that seen in a diabetic. His blood estrogen levels were elevated, but he wasn't feminized, the way men are when they have a disease that results in excess estrogen production; he didn't have gynecomastia, and his voice wasn't high. He looked like a very tall, knock-kneed, but indisputably masculine fellow.

Eventually he ended up in the office of Dr. Eric P. Smith of the University of Cincinnati College of Medicine, who saw in the patient's symptoms evidence of what medicine had thought was impossible: the man was deaf to estrogen. Smith knew about experiments with mice at Rockefeller University. The researchers had created genetically engineered mice that lacked estrogen receptors. They were so-called ERKO mice — their Estrogen Receptor genes had been Knocked Out, or deactivated. The biologists had worried that such a manipulation would prove fatal — that without the ability to respond to estrogen, the ERKO mice would die in utero. But no, they lived, they were born, they seemed just about normal. Smith decided to check his patient's DNA to see whether his estrogen receptor genes were mutated as well. Had nature done to this man what the Rockefeller researchers had done to their mice? Nature had. Both copies of the tall man's estrogen receptor gene were defective. The genes couldn't direct the synthesis of estrogen receptor protein. The man had aromatase, so he made estrogen, plenty of it. But he couldn't make estrogen receptors. All that estrogen was going to waste, falling on cellular ears that could not hear.

From the first recorded case in history of an absence of estrogen receptors, Smith and his colleagues concluded several things, which they reported in the *New England Journal of Medicine:* that estrogen is essential to the maturation and preservation of bones not only in women, as had been known, but also in men; that estrogen metabolism affects glucose metabolism and therefore the risk of diabetes; and that, contrary to dogma, estrogen is not essential to fetal survival. Fetal mice don't need it, and fetal humans don't need it. Estrogen, we over-rated you.

"What the evidence now suggests," says Evan Simpson, of the University of Texas, "is that estrogen doesn't seem to be important to fetal development, but that it is more important than we thought to maintaining the body later in life."

I court caveats. Before we dismiss estrogen as an embryonic incidental, let's recall the latest finding: that genes have not one but at least two estrogen receptors. The man with no estrogen receptors and the mice who donated theirs to science turn out to lack only the alpha estrogen receptor. They still have their beta estrogen receptors, and so they may not be as unresponsive to estrogen as originally supposed. Nature loves redundancy. If something is critical enough, nature hires understudies. The understudies may not be perfect, but they'll do in a pinch. Estrogen receptor-beta is unquestionably a poor preserver of adult skeletal mass, and so the man with no alpha receptors has bones that look like kitchen sponges. But did he truly ignore estrogen when he was a desperate embryo, dangling between song and silence? Or did his beta receptors keep him alive, allow him to implant and to unfold, because they knew they were his last hope and that life cannot begin without estrogen?

Maybe, maybe not. This is the story of estrogen, the septuagenarian serial. Built of grease, estrogen darts from our grasp. We don't yet understand it. We can't quite control it. And when it comes to its impact on our behavior and sexuality, estrogen generously, slyly returns the courtesy. It doesn't control us, and its favorite phrase is *maybe*.

11

VENUS IN FURS

ESTROGEN AND DESIRE

A FEMALE RAT can't mate if she is not in estrus. I don't mean that she doesn't want to mate, or that she won't find a partner if she's not in heat and sending forth the appropriate spectrum of olfactory and auditory enticements. I mean that she is physically incapable of copulating. Unless she is in estrus, her ovaries do not secrete estrogen and progesterone, and without hormonal stimulation, the rat can't assume the mating position known as lordosis, in which she arches her back and flicks aside her tail. The lordosis posture changes the angle and aperture of the vagina, making it accessible to the male rat's penis once he has mounted her from behind. There is no rat's version of the *Kama Sutra*. An ovariectomized female won't assume lordosis, and hence she can't mate — unless, that is, she is given hormone shots to compensate for the loss of the natural ablutions of the ovarian follicle.

In a female guinea pig, a membrane normally covers the vaginal opening. It takes the release of sex hormones during ovulation to open up the membrane and allow the guinea pig to have sex.

For both the rat and the guinea pig, as well as for many other female animals, mechanics and motivation are intertwined. Only when she is in heat is the female driven to seek a mate, and only when she is in heat can her body oblige her. Estrogen controls her sexual appetite and sexual physics alike.

A female primate can copulate whenever she pleases, whether she is ovulating or not. There is no connection between the mechanics of her reproductive tract and the status of her hormones. Estrogen does not control the nerves and muscles that would impel her to hoist her rear end in the air, angle her genitals just so, and whip her tail out of the way, if she has one. A female primate does not have to be capable of becoming pregnant in order to partake of sex. She can have sex every day, and if she's a bonobo, she will have sex more than once a day, or once an hour. A female primate has been unshackled from the tyranny of hormones. In an almost literal sense, the key to her door has been taken away from her ovaries and placed in her hands.

Yet she still cycles. Her blood bears estrogen from place to place, including to the portions of the brain where desire and emotion and libido dwell, in the limbic system, the hypothalamus, the amygdala. The female primate has been freed from the rigidity of hormonal control. Now she can take the sex steroid and apply it subtly, to integrate, modulate, and interpret a wealth of sensory and psychological cues. For rats, hormones are thumpish, unmistakable, the world in black and white; for primates, they act like a box of crayons, the sixty-four pack, with a color for every occasion and at least three names for every color. Do you want it in pink, blush, or fuschia?

"In primates, all the effects of hormones on sexual behavior have become focused on psychological mechanisms, not physical ones," Kim Wallen, of Emory University, says to me. "The decoupling of physical from psychological allows primates to use sex in different contexts, for economic reasons or political reasons." Or emotional reasons, or to keep from getting bored. As Wallen speaks, we watch a group of five rhesus monkeys at the Yerkes Primate Research Center chase two other rhesus monkeys around and around in their enclosure, all seven swearing back and forth at each other in rhesusese, as you can tell because the more they scream, the faster everybody runs. In a primate, Wallen continues, hormone pulses may not make the female bow down in lordosis, but they clearly influence her sexual motivation. He points at the group of rhesus monkeys. The seven samurai are still screaming and running. Several other monkeys look on with rapt anxiety, like bettors at a racetrack. One large, scruffy male ignores everything and picks his teeth. None is doing anything remotely sexual. Rhesus monkeys are Calvinists, Wallen says, prudish and autocratic in matters of sex. When a female rhesus is alone with a familiar male and no other monkeys are there to spy on her, she will mate with the male regardless of where she is in her breeding cycle. But a female under the constraints of the social group does not have the luxury of freewheeling carnality. If she sidles up to a male and begins engaging in a bit of heavy petting, other group members strive to intervene, raucously and snappishly. A female rhesus doesn't often bother defying convention. What does she look like, a bonobo?

Hormones change everything. They tint her judgment and sweep her from Kansas to Oz. When she is ovulating and her estrogen levels soar, her craving overcomes her political instincts and she will mate madly and profligately, all the while outsnarling those who would dare to interfere.

When we think about motivation, desire, and behavior, we accord the neocortex and the thinking brain the greater share of credit. We believe in free will, and we must. Free will, of a sort, is a hallmark of human nature. This is not to say that we start each morning afresh, with an infinity of possible selves awaiting us — that is a figment, alas, and a durable one. Nevertheless, we have what Roy Baumeister, of Case Western Reserve University, calls an "executive function," the dimension of the self that exercises volition, choice, self-control. The human capacity for self-control must be counted among our species' great strengths, the source of our adaptability and suppleness. Very little of our conduct is genuinely automatic. Even when we think we're operating on automatic pilot, the executive function keeps an eye out, checks, edits, corrects the course. If you know how to touch-type, you know that the executive brain is never far removed from the drone brain. When all is well, you type along automatically, your fingers so familiar with the keys that it's as though each digit has a RAM chip embedded in its tip. But the moment you make a mistake, the automaton stops and the executive function kicks in, even before you're quite aware of what went wrong. With its guidance, your finger reaches for the backspace key to correct the error, and you see what happened and you fix things, and a moment later your hands have returned to robot mode. Athletes, surgeons, and musicians perform similar exchanges between intentional and programmatic behaviors hundreds of times a minute; such commerce is the soul of mastery. The human capacity for self-control is limited, and we get into trouble when we overestimate it and embrace the caustic ethos of perfectionism, but volition still deserves our gratitude.

At the same time, we know that there's a macaque darting about in the genomic background and that we feel like monkeys and can act like them too. The moment a young girl enters adolescence, she begins dwelling on sex, consciously, unconsciously, in her dreams, alone in the bath — however or wherever it happens, it happens. Her desire is aroused. The changes of puberty are largely hormonal changes. The shifting of the chemical setting stirs desire. Intellectually, we accept the idea that sexuality is a hormonally inflected experience, but we still resent the connection. If hormones count, we worry that they count too much and that therefore we have no free will, and so we deny that they count, all the while knowing that they count, because we see it in our teenage children and we remember, please goddess, our teenage greed.

Rather than denying the obvious, we should try to appreciate the ways in which estrogen and other hormones affect behavior. Granted, our knowledge of neurobiology is primitive, presimian. We don't understand how estrogen or any other substance works on the brain to elicit desire, or feed a fantasy, or muffle an impulse. But there are enough indirect strands of evidence to knit a serviceable thinking cap with which to mull over estrogen's meaning.

Desires and emotions can be fleeting, mayflies in the brain. They're born and they're gone. But they can also be persistent. They can change from whims to obsessions. If an emotion or drive is going to persist and resonate, a hormone is a useful object to turn to for the task. In the brain, steroid hormones generally work together with one or more of the neuropeptides. A neuropeptide is quick and transient. A steroid hormone is resilient and insistent. They work synergistically on neural circuits that subserve motive and behavior, integrating psyche with body. Take the sensation of thirst. When your body is low in water and salt, it reacts vigorously, because we all once dwelled in the sea and our cells still must be bathed in salty water to survive. Among the responses is the activation of the adrenal glands, which secrete steroid hormones such as aldosterone. Aldosterone is a practical hormone, and it seeks to conserve the supplies that exist — for instance, by reabsorbing salt from urine or gastric juice and returning it to the fluid between cells. Aldosterone also infiltrates the brain, where it galvanizes the activity of a neuropeptide, angiotensin. The neuropeptide in turn arouses the brain's circuitry of thirst. You feel thirsty. You have an urge to drink. The sensation can usually be satisfied with ease, with a glass of water, and the adrenals and the thirst locus settle down. But if your requirements for fluid and sodium are unusually large, as they are during breastfeeding, you will be awash in aldosterone and very efficient in your use of water and salt, but you will also feel chronically parched, and you will wonder if the Nile itself is large enough to slake you, and you will love salty foods as you never did before.

An emotion is a piece of information. It is a signal of need, of a temporary lapse in homeostasis. It is the body's way of encouraging or inhibiting behaviors, which the body hopes will fulfill the need and restore balance. We don't usually think of thirst as an emotion, but that's what it is, an emotion of the body's interstitial spaces. As an emotion, thirst can be disregarded or overruled by competing demands. If you are running a race in the heat and feel thirsty, you might ignore the desire rather than stop to drink and lose precious time and weigh your belly down with fluids. Panic can bring on enormous thirst, in part because the adrenal activity that comes with fear unleashes the flow of angiotensin in the brain; but panic can also clench the throat and stomach and make the thought of drink or food repulsive. Still, thirst gives you a comparatively short leash. You can only ignore it so long — a week without water, and you will die of dehydration. The synergistic impact of neuropeptide and steroid hormone on the circuitry overseeing the behavior of fluid acquisition is therefore quite extreme. The longer you refuse to engage in the requested behavior, drinking, the more exaggerated your adrenal output becomes and the more overwhelming the desire is. At some point, as you near death, you will drink anything — poisoned water, sea water that is too salty for your body to use. Even Jesus could not conquer thirst, and died with vinegar moistening his lips.

If, however, you don't reproduce during a particular cycle, it won't kill you. Humans are long-lived creatures who operate on the implicit assumption that they will have many opportunities to breed and can afford to override the whims and impulses of Eros for months, years, decades, and, oops, a lifetime if conditions of the moment are not quite optimal. Animals in whom reproductive drives are as relentless as thirst are short-lived species who may have only one or two breeding seasons in which to leave their Mendelian badge on the world. A corollary of longevity is a rich emotional life and a complex sexuality. We mistakenly equate emotionality with the primitive and rationality with the advanced, but in fact the more intelligent the animal, the deeper its passions. The greater the intelligence, the greater the demand on the emotions, the portmanteaus of information, to expand their capacity and multiply their zippers and compartments.

We impugn emotions, but we are lucky to be so thick with them. They give us something to think about and decode. We are brilliant because of them, not in spite of them. Hormones are part of the suitcase, and they are part of the contents. They relay information about themselves, and they carry information about others. They do not make us do anything, but they may make the doing of something easier or more pleasurable when all else conspires in favor of it.

Estrogen, puckish estrogen, works through many intermediaries in the brain, many neuropeptides and neurotransmitters. It works through nerve growth factor, and it works through serotonin, a neuropeptide best known for its role in depression. It works through natural opiates and it works through oxytocin. It may be thought of as a conjoiner or a facilitator, or as leavening, like yeast or baking soda. Estrogen has no particular emotion in mind, yet it permits emoting. For years researchers have sought to link estrogen levels to women's sexual behavior. The assumption is logical. Estrogen concentrations rise steadily as the egg follicle grows each month, peaking with the moment of ovulation, when the egg is released into the fallopian tube. If the egg has a need, a desire to be fertilized, in theory it could make the need known to the brain through estrogen, and estrogen would then stimulate a neuropeptide to encourage a particular behavior — to wit, seeking a sexual partner like a thirsty pedestrian seeks a water fountain.

The difficulties of correlating estrogen to human sexual behavior are considerable. What sort of behavior are you looking at? What are the relevant data points? Frequency of intercourse? Frequency of orgasm? Frequency of masturbation or sexual fantasy? The sudden urge to buy *Cosmopolitan*? Here is what we know. There is no association between rate of intercourse and where a woman is in her ovulatory cycle. Women do not have sex more often during ovulation than they do at any other time of the month, unless they're consciously on the fertility quest. But the completion of a behavior tells you little about the subliminal provocations of that behavior. If you plot the incidence of intercourse among couples, you'll see an amazing statistical high point, and it's called the weekend — not because people necessarily feel sexy each Sunday, but because people have sex when it's convenient, when they're not exhausted by work, and when they have the whole day to toy with. A hormone may lead you to water, but it can't make you drink.

There is also no correlation between estrogen levels and physical arousability — the tendency of the genitals to swell and lubricate in response to an overt sexual stimulus, such as a lovemaking scene in a movie. Women have been shown to be fairly invariate in their display of physiological arousal, regardless of their cycle. But physiological arousal says little about meaningful sexual motivation or hunger, for some women will lubricate during rape, and Ellen Laan, of the University of Amsterdam, has shown that women's genitals congest robustly when they watch pornography that the women later describe as stupid, trite, and distinctly unerotic.

We get a somewhat better kinship between hormones and sexuality when we look at desire rather than at genital performance. Some studies have taken female initiation of sex as the marker of desire. The results have varied considerably, depending on the type of birth control used, but they list in the predicted direction. Women on oral contraceptives, which interfere with normal hormonal oscillations, are no more likely to come on to their partners at the middle of the cycle than they are at other times. When the birth control method is reliable but nonhormonal — a vasectomized husband, for example — women show a tendency to be the initiators of sex at the peak of ovulation more than they are during other times of the month, suggesting that the estrogen high is beckoning to them. Add in the complicating factor of a less trustworthy barrier, such as a diaphragm or condom, and the likelihood of midpeak propositioning subsides. No great enigma there: if you don't want to get pregnant, you might not be eager to fool around when you think you're at your most fertile. In a study of lesbian couples, who have no fear of pregnancy, don't use birth control, and are free of supposedly confounding factors of male expectations and manipulations, psychologists found that women were about 25 percent more likely to initiate sex and had twice as many orgasms during the midpoint of their cycle than at other times of the month.

The strongest correlations between hormones and sexuality are seen when pure, disembodied desire is the object of scrutiny. In one large study, five hundred women were asked to take their basal temperatures every day for several months and to mark down the day of the month when they first noticed the stirrings of sexual desire. The pooled results show an extraordinary concordance between the onset of sexual hunger and the time that basal temperature readings suggest the women were at or nearing ovulation. Women may even express desire through unconscious body language. In a study of young women who spent a lot of time dancing in nightclubs, the scientists found that as the women approached the day of ovulation, their outfits became progressively skimpier, more flaunting of flesh: the hemlines rose with estrogen levels as if with a bull market. (Of course, it doesn't hurt that midcycle is also the best time to wear your tightest and most revealing clothing, as that is when you are free of premenstrual water retention and blemishes and any fear of leaking menstrual blood.)

A number of researchers lately have suggested that it is testosterone, not estrogen, that is the "true" hormone of libido, in men and women alike. They point out that the ovaries generate testosterone as well as estrogen and that androgen levels spike at midcycle just as estrogen levels do. How can we neglect testosterone when men have so much of it and men love sex so madly, don't they? Many textbooks on human sexuality declare flatly that testosterone is the source of all lust, and some women have added testosterone to their hormone replacement regimens in an effort to shore up their ebbing libido. But if testosterone is relevant to female lust, evidence suggests that it is as a handmaiden to estrogen rather than as Eros descended. As it happens, some proteins in the blood will cling to both testosterone and estrogen and in so clinging prevent the hormones from penetrating the barrier between blood and brain. Estrogen accelerates the production of these binding proteins, but the proteins have a slight preference for testosterone. Hence, as the levels of sex hormones and binding proteins climb with the menstrual cycle, the binding proteins seek out testosterone prejudicially, defusing it in the blood below before it can accomplish much of psychodynamic interest above. The testosterone proves useful indirectly, though: by occupying the binding proteins, it frees estrogen to reach the brain unimpeded. This power of distraction could explain why testosterone therapy works for some women with low libidos: it keeps the blood proteins busy and lets estrogen breaststroke straight to the brain.

But to view estrogen as the hormone of libido is to overstate it and underrate it. If estrogen is the messenger of the egg, we should expect the brain to pay attention, but not in any simple, linear fashion. Just as the mechanics of our genitals have been released from the hormonal chokehold, so have our motives and behaviors. We would not appreciate a hormonal signal that is a blind nymphomaniac, an egg groupie, telling us we're horny and must fornicate. We do not want to indulge an egg just because it is there. We live in the world, and we have constraints and desires of our own. What we might like, though, is a pair of well-appointed glasses, to read the fine print better. Estrogen's basic behavioral strategy is to hone the senses. It pinches us and says, Pay attention. A number of studies have suggested that a woman's vision and sense of smell are heightened at ovulation. So too do the senses shine at other times of high estrogenicity, such as right before menstruation, when your progesterone levels have dropped way down and left estrogen to act unopposed. During pregnancy, you can smell a dirty cat box from two flights away, and you can see dim stars and the pores on every face you meet. It must be emphasized that we don't *need* estrogen to pay attention or to smell a thing, but there it is, coursing from blood to brain and lending the brain a mild buzz, just as it does the bones and heart and breast and little gray basket.

If estrogen is to help at all, it should help us best when our minds must be wonderfully concentrated. Ovulation is a time of danger and of possibility. Estrogen is like hunting magic, the hallucinogenic drug that Amazonian Indians extract from the skin of the poison-dart frog to lend them the sensorial strength of heroes. The more we are of the world, the greater are our chances of meeting others who suit us, but the more incumbent it is on us to notice and assess those around us. If there is such a thing as feminine intuition, it may lie in the occasional gift of a really sweet estrogen high, the great emulsifier, bringing together disparate observations. But estrogen is also at the behest of history and current affairs. If you are in a sour, reclusive mood to begin with, the hump of estrogen at ovulation, or its unopposed premenstrual energy, may make you feel more rather than less reclusive. Estrogen is a promoter, not an initiator. We can understand this by considering how estrogen contributes to breast cancer. The hormone is not, strictly speaking, a carcinogen. It does not crack or destabilize the genetic material of breast cells, in the way radioactivity or toxins such as benzene can. Yet if an abnormal cell exists, estrogen may stoke and stimulate it, abetting its growth until a minor aberration that might otherwise regress or be cleaned up by the immune system survives and expands to malignant dimensions.

The strength of estrogen lies in its being context-dependent. It does not make us do anything, but it may make us notice certain things we might otherwise neglect. Estrogen may enhance sensory perception, giving us a slight and fluctuating advantage overlaid on the background of the self. If we are good, we may have our moments of being very, very good, and if we are mediocre, well, we can blame it on our hormones. They are there to be used.

As a lubricant for learning, estrogen is of greatest benefit in young women, who are sorting themselves out and gathering cues and experiences. Young women may reap advantages from intuition for lack of anything better to draw on as they assess the motives and character of another. But we can become too enamored of our intuitive prowess, our insight into others, and believe too unshakably in the correctness of our snap judgments. The older we get, the softer the peaks and valleys of our estrogen cycles are, and the less we need them and their psycho-togglings. Experience, after all, is a trustworthier friend than intuition. How many times do you have to encounter a man who reminds you of your cold, aloof, angry, hypercritical, and infinitely alluring father before you can recognize the phenotype in your sleep and know enough to keep your eyes and nose and hormones far, far away?

Each of us is a privately held chemistry lab, and we can play with ourselves if we want. You may find your ovarian cycle too boring to dwell on or you may try to explore its offerings, and you may be disappointed or you may not. It took me many years to realize that my orgasms were very strong at midcycle. I always knew that they were good right before menstruation, but I thought that had to do with mechanics, the congesting of the pelvis with premenstrual fluid, and I didn't attend to the other side of the equation, because I didn't believe in it. When I started to investigate the link between rising estradiol and the quality of climax, I found a wonderful connection. The midway orgasms are deep and resounding, accentuated, maybe by estrogen, maybe by decoy testosterone, maybe by autohypnosis. I could be experiencing a placebo aphrodisiac. It doesn't matter. As a chemist, I'm an amateur, and I can't do a controlled experiment with myself. Nevertheless, on matters that count I'm a quick study, and I've learned to find my way home to ecstasy whatever the moon, month, menses, may be doing.

We each of us have but one chemistry set and brain to explore, and the effects of estrogen will vary from head to head. Yet if there is a principle to be drawn from the general recognition that hormones can stimulate and emulsify the brain and sensitize it to experience and input, it is this: puberty counts. Under the influence of steroid hormones, the brain in early adolescence is a brain expanding, a Japanese flower dropped in water. It is also vulnerable to the deposition of dreck and pain, which can take a lifetime to dump back out again. The plasticity of the pubertal mind is grievously underestimated. We've obsessed over the brain of early childhood and the brain of the fetus, and though those brains matter deeply to the development of all-round intelligence, character, and skill, the adolescent brain counts in another way. As the brain stumbles toward maturity, and as it is buffeted by the output of the adrenal glands at age ten and of the gonads a year or two later, it seeks to define itself sexually and socially. The brain of a prepubertal girl is primed to absorb the definitions of womanness, of what counts and what doesn't, of what power is and how she can get it or how she will never get it. We've all heard about the crisis of self-confidence that supposedly strikes girls as they leave childhood and climb the Bunker Hill of junior high, but what has been less recognized is the correspondence between this period of frailty, this tendency for the personality to mutate beyond recognition, and the hormonal squall in the head. The pubertal brain is so aware of the world that it throbs, it aches, it wants to find the paths to calm it down and make sense of the world. It is an exposed brain, as tender as a molted crab, and it can be seared deeply. Who can forget adolescence? And who has ever recovered from it?

At the same time that hormones challenge the pubertal brain, they change the body. A girl's high estrogen content helps in the deposition of body fat on the breasts, hips, thighs, and buttocks, subcutaneously, everywhere. Because of estrogen and auxiliary hormones, women have more body fat than men. The body of the average woman is 27 percent fat, that of the average man 15 percent fat. The leanest elite female athletes may get their body fat down to 11 or 12 percent, but that is nearly double the percentage of body fat found on the elite male athlete, who is as spare as a pronghorn antelope. We can look at the deposition of body fat that comes with womanhood and say it's natural for girls to fatten up when they mature, but what *natural* means is subject to cultural definition, and our culture still hasn't figured out how to handle fat. On the one hand, we're getting fatter by the year, we westerners generally and North Americans particularly, and why should we expect otherwise? We are stapled to our desks; food is never far from our hands and mouths, and that food tends to be starchy and fatty and overrich; and we get exercise only if we exert willpower, not because sustained body movement is an integrated feature of work, social life, or travel. On the other hand, we are intolerant of fatness, we are repulsed by it, and we see it as a sign of weak character and sloth. Contradictory messages assail us from all sides: we must work all the time, the world is a competitive place, and technology requires that our work be sedentary, cerebral, but we must not get too fat, because fat is unhealthy and looks self-indulgent. So we must exercise and control our bodies, because our natural lives won't do it for us.

Girls, poor girls, are in the thick of our intolerance and vacillation. Girls put on body fat as they pass into adulthood. They put on fat more easily than boys do, thank you very much, Lady Estradiol. And then they are subject to the creed of total control, the idea that we can subdue and discipline our bodies if we work very very hard at it. The message of self-control is amplified by the pubescent brain, which is flailing about for the tools to control and soothe itself and to find what works, how to gather personal and sexual power. Dieting becomes a proxy for power, not simply because girls are exposed through the media to a smothering assemblage of slender, beautiful models, but because adolescent girls today are laying down a bit of fat in an era when fat is creeping up everywhere and is everywhere despised. How is a girl to know that her first blush of fatness will ever stop, when we're tearing our hair out over how the national fat index keeps on rising and we must wrestle it to the ground right *now?*

There are other, obvious reasons that a girl's brain might decide that a fixation on appearance is the swiftest route to power. There are too many of these *Beauty 'n' You, Beast* magazines around, far more than when I was a prepubescent girl circa 1970. (There were too many of them back then.) Supermarkets now offer no-candy checkout aisles for parents who don't want their children screaming for Mars bars as they wait in line. Where are the no-women's-magazine aisles? Where are the aisles to escape from the fascism of the Face? Any sane and observant girl is bound to conclude that her looks matter and that she can control her face as she controls her body, through makeup and the proper skin care regimen and parsing her facial features and staying on guard and paying attention and thinking about it, really thinking about it. No wonder a girl loses confidence. If she is smart, she knows that it is foolish to obsess over her appearance. It is depressing and disappointing; for this she learned to read, speak passable Spanish, and do calculus? But if she is smart, she has observed the ubiquitous Face and knows of its staggering power and wants that power. A girl wants to learn the possible powers. By all indications, a controlled body and a beautiful face practically guarantee a powerful womanhood.

I'm not saying anything new here, but I argue that people should see adolescence as an opportunity, a fresh coat of paint on the clapboards of the brain. Girls learn from women: fake women, amalgamated women, real women. The Face is inescapable, but it can be raspberried, sabotaged, emotionally exfoliated. Repetition helps. Reassuring a girl that she is great and strong and gorgeous helps. The exhilarating, indoctrinating rah-rah spirit of the new girl-power movement helps. Girls helping each other helps, because girls take cues from other girls as well as from women. Ritual helps, and anti-ritual helps. We can denude totemic objects and reinfuse them with arbitrary mania. Girls can use lipstick to draw scarification patterns on each other's backs or faces, or a line of supernumerary nipples from armpit to pelvis. Build a hammock with brassieres and fill it with doughnuts and Diet Coke. Combine the covers of women's magazines with cut-out parts from nature magazines to make human-animal chimerical masks: Ellephant

MacPherson, Naomi Camel. Glue rubber insects and Monopoly hotels onto the top of a bathroom scale. Girls can imagine futures for each other, with outrageous careers and a string of extraordinary lovers, because it is easier to be generous to another than to yourself, but imagining greatness for a friend makes it thinkable for yourself. Sports help. Karate helps. Sticking by your girlfriends helps. Writing atonal songs with meaningless lyrics helps more than you might think. Learn to play the drums. The world needs more girl drummers. The world needs your wild, pounding, dreaming heart.

12

MINDFUL MENOPAUSE

CAN WE LIVE WITHOUT ESTROGEN?

I RECENTLY HEARD Suzzy Roche, one of the three sisters who make up the clever-mellow folk group the Roches, perform a song in which she groans wryly about being over forty and listening to her friends talk about middle-aged things like wrinkles and estrogen. Not estrogen replacement therapy, mind you, just estrogen. When I wrote an article for the *New York Times* about estrogen receptor-beta and the complexity of the body's indigenous estrogen network, a number of readers thanked me for having clarified their thoughts on estrogen replacement therapy, although I'd barely mentioned the subject in my article. What we take seems stronger than what we have. Physiology is invisible and forgettable. Pills are tangible and melodramatic. They make grand promises and they raise grand hopes. And estrogen replacement tablets, being a nostrum for women, inevitably raise hackles as well.

What is it about women's "health" issues that turns people malign? Hysterectomies, cesarean sections, abortions, mammograms, hormone therapy: our bodies, our hells. Men are so serene by comparison, indifferent even to the brouhaha among doctors over the proper monitoring of the prostate gland. But here we are, saddled with another gynecrisis, another source of anguish over the cantankerous merchandise the female body, this crisis perhaps the biggest one ever. By the year 2000 there will be about 50 million women in the United States over the age of fifty, all of them potential candidates for hormone therapy. If every one of them were to take hormone pills for the next thirty years — to the age of eighty, which is close to the current female life expectancy — that amounts to 1.5 billion woman-years of drug consumption. What an absurdly huge number. Never before has a drug regimen been proposed on such a scale. Can we expect unity and revelation from the teeming ranks of womankind? Can we expect a simple yes-or-no answer to the question "Should I take hormone replacement therapy?"

Does the pope howl at the moon? Has your *hysteria* been wandering?

There is no simple answer. You already know that, but still you hope for a simple answer, if not now, then later, in the twenty-first century, when the results of bigger and better clinical studies come in. Unbate your breath. Whatever results emerge, from the massive Women's Health Initiative in the United States or similar trials in Europe, they almost surely will be complicated. Hormones have much to offer, but still they smirk ever so slightly. They're a little dangerous, a little threatening. They're not Flintstone Vitamins; they're hormones, strong messengers, and their shoes are cockily winged.

At menopause, the ovaries stop producing estradiol. Hormone therapy starts talking where the follicles fall silent. But does our body appreciate the perpetuation of noise? Or is midlife finally the time to throw the teenagers out of the house, blastocasters and all? Most gynecologists and internists today think that hormones are the right choice for most postmenopausal women. Yet they concur that the therapy is not without risks. The Women's Health Initiative will clarify the risks, but it won't make them disappear. Individual variation will not disappear. The so-called designer estrogens that pharmaceutical companies are racing to develop and perfect, which in theory will offer the benefits of tissue specificity, of protecting the parts that need protecting while ignoring the tissues, like the breast, that don't want the stimulus, are a grand hope. But designer estrogens such as tamoxifen and raloxifene are still hormones, and each one must be extensively tested, and hormones are never risk-free. Women must decide for themselves. Women do decide, but then, fie fie, they turn fickle, and run the other way. We love estrogen, we fear estrogen. Everybody wants to take it. Why do so few women take it?

We can't be blamed for our volatility. The scientific literature is volatile, and it is vast. We are chased and torn. We jump through all four carbon hoops of our exasperating steroid, and hop right back again. We live in the age of mindful menopause, forced to dwell on the change and its aftermath as our foremothers never did. My grandmother was proud of the fact that she hardly noticed her menopause — no insomnia or hot flashes to speak of, and good riddance to the monthlies. Undoubtedly she took disproportionate credit for the easy transition, attributing it to her stalwart will rather than her lucky phenotype, but still, the change came and went and that was that. If she were alive today, her doctor would raise the subject of hormone replacement therapy. There's no escaping the drone of menopause consciousness. I'm not advocating a return to the days when women were ashamed to talk about menopause and the discomforts they felt, just as they were ashamed of everything else having to do with the female body and with getting older. Yet in becoming a topic fit for public discussion, menopause has exposed itself to homily, reductionism, and medical sharecropping. You say middle-aged woman, they say HRT. "Counseling about hormone replacement therapy should be given to all postmenopausal women," a 1996 medical review from the University of Utah said. Over the past few years, the medical juggernaut in favor of hormone therapy has barreled ahead with spectacular determination. "Based on evidence that hormone replacement therapy is cardioprotective, enthusiasm for universal hormone replacement therapy in postmenopausal women has grown," wrote doctors from the University of Texas Southwestern Medical Center in Dallas.

What a vociferous, clanking tank the medical consensus can be. It has so much work to do, so many millions of women to persuade, that it becomes unyielding and intolerant of dissent. We're not allowed to have our fears and our irritations. We are scolded. The finger wags in our face. If we worry about the increased risk of breast cancer that hormone therapy can bring, we're told, Why are you worrying about breast cancer? Heart disease kills far more women than breast cancer does! You're swayed by sensational and inaccurate reporting in the popular press. Get your demography straight. Repeat it to yourself each night: heart disease is the number-one killer of women. Whenever a new study comes out suggesting an increased risk from hormone therapy of breast cancer, uterine cancer, or ovarian cancer, defenders of the universal solution storm in to put the results "in perspective," to remind us that heart disease, not cancer, is the biggest killer of women, and that the risk of osteoporosis is greater for a woman than her risk of breast, ovarian, and uterine cancer combined. When Susan Love, a renowned breast surgeon, wrote a book critical of hormone replacement therapy, and when she summarized her arguments on the op-ed page of the *New York Times,* many of her colleagues rallied with their blowtorches, attributing her exaggerated emphasis on breast cancer risk to her bias as a surgeon who sees a lot of breast cancer patients. Malcolm Gladwell parodied her in *The New Yorker* and accused Dr. Love of doing a disservice to womankind by scaring them away from one of the best proactive health measures yet devised. Dr. Love's statistics may be debatable and she may embrace some suspect alternative therapies such as homeopathy, but her basic message is valid. Hormone therapy is powerful, she says; it is meant as a prophylactic measure, to be taken in perpetuity by healthy women rather than as a medication to treat the sick. Shouldn't the bar of acceptable risk be higher for a preventive regimen, she asks, than for a therapeutic one? Absolutely, her critics respond, and hormone therapy clears the bar with an Olympian's might. Hormone therapy helps cut the risk of heart disease, osteoporosis, and possibly Alzheimer's, and the benefits of hormone therapy are large and incontrovertible and supported by scores of clinical studies. And they are. The benefits are real, but so are the risks. It's perfectly respectable to dither. The facts do it all the time. Here are a few of the more salient ones.

Considered broadly, hormone therapy "works" — that is, it reduces mortality by a fairly impressive margin. According to a 1997 report from the Nurses' Health Study, for example, the women on hormones had a 40 percent lower risk of dying during a given year than women who had never taken hormones, mostly as a result of a decline in heart disease. That's the big picture; the statistical miniatures are worth examining as well. In the nurses' study, hormone therapy helped best those who needed it most. For women who smoked, were overweight, had high blood pressure, high cholesterol levels, or other known risk factors for heart disease, hormones slashed their admittedly elevated risk of mortality by more than half. But for women who were in good shape and free of harbingers of heart disease, hormone use showed no statistical benefit in reducing mortality; it did *not* help those who helped themselves. Moreover, the survival benefits of hormone therapy for any subgroup declined with duration of use, as the rate of death from breast cancer began canceling out the reduction in coronary disease. The results jibe with other studies showing that long-term HRT use — ten years or more — is associated with a 50 percent hike in the risk of breast cancer.

Of course, there is more to life than dodging death. Hormone therapy can improve the tone of life. It inhibits the dissolution of bone, that gradual regression to the bog collective. Women who take hormones have a 50 percent lower risk of fracturing a hip than noncompliers, and the older you get, the less you want to crack a hip. Hip fractures are the primary reason that people over seventy end up in nursing homes. Hormone therapy maintains the pliancy of the bladder's sphincter and thus helps prevent incontinence, and it prevents the vaginal wall from getting thin and dry and prone to bleeding during intercourse. The performance of the urogenital tract is no small matter on the quality-of-life front. And then we have the brain, our beloved brain. Several studies have indicated that estrogen therapy may reduce the risk of Alzheimer's disease by about 50 percent. Many women who take estrogen replacement therapy like how they feel on the drug. They find that estrogen helps stabilize their mood and that it improves their memory. They had been growing forgetful in their middle years, and they hated that. They felt neuronally fragmented, as if there were too many skips, nicks, and blank spots on the hard drive. Estrogen tablets gave them back their fine minds, they said, and made them smart again. It's true that a number of studies have shown some improvement in memory in postmenopausal women when they are given estrogen replacement. Whereas before hormone supplementation they could remember only seven out of ten words in a list, for example, after estrogen they were able to recollect all ten. Experiments with brain cells and brain slices cultivated in laboratory dishes have demonstrated that applications of estrogen can nourish dendritic and synaptic complexity. If you look at pictures of rodent nerve cells before and after treatment with estrogen, it's like looking at images of a tree in winter versus in summer, or the mammary gland before or during lactation: how wild and weedy do the lines of life become! Yet it bears mentioning that estrogen is not a universal clever pill. It doesn't improve IQ scores. And in some studies of rodents, females who have had their ovaries, their biggest source of estradiol, surgically removed do *better* on certain maze tests than females with ordinary stores of estrogen.

Hormone therapy has much to recommend it, but then we are pulled back to the reality of the heightened risk of breast cancer that years — decades — of estrogen supplementation can bring. We may wonder, should we be on hormone therapy for our entire postmenopausal life, or should we be more circumspect in our use of it? We're waffling again, we women. Not just in this country, with its "inflammatory" press, but everywhere. Complain though American doctors will about the low compliance rate of their postmenopausal patients, American women lead the world in the use of hormone therapy, just as they do in the rate of hysterectomies. In the United States, 46 percent of postmenopausal women take or have taken hormone therapy. British, Australian, and Scandinavian women come next, with ever-used rates of around 30 percent. Continental Europeans are notably less enthusiastic about medication, the figures falling into the teens, while in Japan a mere 6 percent of postmenopausal women take hormone replacement therapy — perhaps because they import enough estrogen into their bodies through the foods they eat, notably that sink of phytoestrogens, soy.

In reporting on the relative rate of hormone use among their nation's womanpool, researchers wring their hands and ask, Why, why aren't we better missionaries than we are? The researchers look for defining characteristics of the hormone faithful. In America, hormone use is positively correlated with educational level: the more formal schooling a woman has received, the likelier she is to be a hormone enthusiast and to agree with the statement "the benefits outweigh the risks." But in the Netherlands, a country of bright, bookish women, educational level has no impact on hormone use, while in Norway, the more educated the woman is, the more likely she is to *reject* hormone therapy. The researchers of the various studies conclude by offering suggestions on ways to improve patient compliance, the most common being that doctors must learn to preach early and often. From a study in Rehovot, Israel: "We believe gynecologists should devote more effort to public education, in that those women who had discussed HRT with their physician were more likely to use it." From Copenhagen: "It is suggested that lack of knowledge of HRT may sometimes be the cause of rejecting it, or may influence the compliance regarding its use." From Scotland: "In conclusion, women around the menopause . . . are often anxious about HRT use. Better health education might improve HRT uptake."

Nobody will argue against patient enlightenment. Let's all talk ourselves hoarse. Yet a more interesting point emerges from the parade of studies on the psychological profile of the middle-aged woman. It turns out that one of the biggest reasons that many women reject hormone replacement therapy is that they have positive feelings about menopause. They don't think of it as an illness, so what's to treat? In two separate U.S. studies comparing black and white women, researchers found that "the African-American women had significantly more positive attitudes toward menopause" than white women did, and that though they had the same number of menopausal symptoms as whites did, the blacks "perceived them as not very bothersome." The African American women surveyed also had a fairly good understanding of the "proper" order of health risks an aging woman faces, placing heart disease at the top, yet still they were far less likely than whites to be on hormone therapy. After noting ruefully that among Dutch women, the "mean duration of HRT use is only seven months," investigators at Elkerliek Hospital in Helmond, the Netherlands, went on to say, "The positive attitude of most women towards the climacteric is an explanation for this very short duration of use." Comparing a group of forty-five-year-old women who expressed an intention to use hormone therapy after menopause with a group who planned not to, London researchers found that there were no significant differences in the women's health or socioeconomic status, but that "HRT intenders reported significantly lower self-esteem, higher levels of depressed mood, anxiety, and negative attitudes to the menopause. They also expressed stronger beliefs in their doctors' ability — as opposed to their own — to control their menopause experience."

Women who like the effects of estrogen therapy, who feel smarter and more energetic with it than without, need no persuasion. They will be proactive patients, and many will be proselytizers too, telling their friends at the menopause Maginot, Try it, you won't be sorry. But the women who are noncompliers — what of them? Are they necessarily ill-informed or misguided? Some may resist taking hormone therapy because they're afraid of breast cancer. Or they may try it but dislike the side effects, the breakthrough bleeding, the tender breasts, the moodiness, aqueousness, nausea, the pimples — symptoms so reminiscent of the premenstruum. Many women simply resent the implication that menopause is a disease, and they express their resistance by tossing their pills in a drawer and forgetting the whole business. Women in their fifties often feel quite fit. They remember when women were considered unsuitable for higher office because of their fluctuating hormones, and when women had to quit a job the moment they became pregnant. Enough is enough; enough queasiness over the female body. Must a woman go to her grave with a speculum chained to her thigh? Menopause is an event, just as menarche was, a female rite. Their mothers and grandmothers went through menopause, their friends go through menopause. It happens to everyone. Women can't help but feel that menopause is natural. They say as much to their doctors — menopause is natural. It's meant to be, it's what the body does, and why shouldn't I be pleased with, or at least tolerant of, what my body brings me?

Doctors have responded badly to this interpretation of menopause, this self-satisfied talk. They're faced with a challenge. If they're going to persuade large numbers of healthy women to take hormone replacement, they must dispel the notion of the good and natural menopause. They must raise the specter of infirmity, a weakening heart, a crumbling frame, an enfeebled mind. They contrast a woman's spectacular loss of ovarian estrogen with a man's far more gradual tapering of testosterone levels: he ages gracefully, you age overnight. They describe menopause as a state of "estrogen deficiency," comparing it to endocrine disorders such as hypothyroidism and diabetes. Just as a diabetic should be treated with insulin, so an estrogen-deficient woman should be treated with HRT, and any woman past fifty is almost by definition estrogen-deficient. Even women who are still menstruating may be estrogen-deficient, may be "perimenopausal," as the melodious little phrase has it, and candidates for hormone therapy. If a woman asks why it might be that all women lapse into this precarious state of hormone deficit in midlife and why nature has not better equipped them for their sovereign years, a doctor will reply, If it were up to nature, we wouldn't be having this conversation and I wouldn't be writing this prescription. A long life is good, it is desirable, it is a tribute to human ingenuity and modern medicine, but one thing it decidedly is not is natural. If it were up to nature, you, my postreproductive doyenne, would already be dead.

Or would you? Let's ask that old woman out there in the field, the one with the shovel in her hands. She's digging up something, and it sure doesn't look like her grave.

13

⚜

THERE'S NO PLACE LIKE NOTORIETY

MOTHERS, GRANDMOTHERS, AND OTHER GREAT DAMES

THE HADZA PEOPLE are a small group of hunter-gatherers who live in the dry and rugged hill country of the Eastern Rift Valley, in northern Tanzania. There are only about 750 of them, but they're not going anywhere. They speak a distinct language, Hadza, a percussive tongue of clicks and hisses reminiscent of but unrelated to the language of the !Kung. And the Hadza refuse to be domesticated. Time and again over the past sixty years, church and government agencies have tried to transmute them into farmers, but the efforts always fail and the Hadza return to the bush. They hate gardening! They hate milking cows! Instead, the Hadza subsist almost entirely on wild pickings — game, berries, honey, tubers. They're opportunists: see an impala, kill an impala. If the berries are ripening three miles away, they move three miles away. When the local bees slacken their honey production, the Hadza break camp to find busier ones. On occasion they'll steal a sheep from a neighboring herder, but usually they prefer barter, giraffe jerky for maize or tobacco.

The Hadza live a no-frills existence that supposedly retains some features of the Pliocene and Pleistocene conditions under which *Homo sapiens* evolved. They're Stone Age relics, more or less, which is why they attract the attention of Western anthropologists. What can they tell us about the essential us? For one thing, forget Hobbes. The Hadza's lives are not nasty or brutish, nor are they particularly short. As Kristen Hawkes, of the University of Utah, discovered when she and her colleagues descended on the Hadza and tracked their life histories, the women refuse to do what our forebears are said to have done routinely

— die by the time their eggs have run out. No, many Hadza women keep on going well past menopause, into their sixties, their seventies, sometimes their eighties, all without the purported life-extending benefits of the postindustrial age or even of the agricultural revolution. In the United States, demographers worry about the aging of the population and the potential drain of the elderly on the wealth and patience of the rest of us. The Hadza might worry about the opposite, what would happen if they didn't have their corps of old ladies. As the data from Hawkes and her colleagues reveal, postmenopausal Hadza women are the hardest-working members of the tribe. Every day they're out in the bush, digging, poking, reaching, clambering. They gather more food than any of their comrades. They share their food with young relatives who can't fend for themselves: grandchildren, great-grandchildren, great-nieces and -nephews, second cousins twice removed. When a young woman is breastfeeding a newborn and can't forage as effectively as usual for her older children, she turns for assistance not to her mate (where has that man got to now?) but to a senior female relative. Grandma, or her proxy, takes up the slack and keeps the kids in baobab and tubers. Hadza children are always thin, but without an elder's efforts they would become too thin, Karen Carpenter thin, whenever a new sibling arrives, and they might very well die early as a result. Hadza elders are truly great grandmas. They are not an option. They are not a Hallmark sentiment. In Hawkes's study, no nursing mother lacked a postmenopausal helper.

The Hadza are a small group. They have had extensive contact with bureaucrats, academics, cultural carpetbaggers, and exhortationists of all stripes, including some of their own members who received a Western-style education and came back preaching the gospel of agraria. The Hadza are not "pristine," and it's risky to draw too many conclusions about prelapsarian humans from them or any of the other hunter-gatherers remaining in the world. Nevertheless, if we're going to talk about the evolution of human menopause and squabble over whether it's natural or unnatural, meant to be or an unfortunate tag-along of our newfound longevity, we can't ignore all those Hadza matriarchs rooting around in the woods for the fruits of the future. To Grandmother's house we go.

·   ·   ·

The "grandmother hypothesis" of the origins of human menopause got its start in a paper that is nearly old enough to be a grandmother itself. In a classic 1957 essay about the charming inevitability of aging, the renowned evolutionary biologist George C. Williams addressed the strange case of the climacteric. He pointed out that most depredations of age, such as failing eyesight, arthritis, wrinkling, and the imperialism of flab, occur at varying rates and to varying degrees among individuals. Some aspects of aging can be forestalled for decades, through exercise or by wearing a hat in the sun. Not so menopause. Whatever a woman does, however rigorously she attends to her health, at the half-century mark, give or take a few years, she will go into what Williams called "premature reproductive senescence." Not every person ends up need- ing reading glasses, but all women who reach the age of menopause stop ovulating. By contrast, other female mammals, including our close relatives the apes, continue bearing young practically to the grave. Orangutans do not go into menopause. Chimpanzees do not need extract of mare pee. Men too can father children they may be too arthritic or cataracted to hold or behold. Only in human females, Wil- liams said, does the fertility program shut down years before death. How unlike nature, in designing women, to forget her beloved multipli- cation tables.

For the apparent conundrum Williams proposed a brilliant solution: blame it on the kids. Human children are so damned expensive. Each one requires years and years to rear to independence — thirteen or fourteen years at a minimum. They need to be fed, clothed, housed, schooled in whatever skills their environs require, protected from the wrath of the bored and the bullying. Assuming that mothers have always been the primary caretakers of their children and that in the past a child without a mother was a child without a prayer, Williams sug- gested that it behooved a woman to persist long enough to usher her children to puberty and autonomy. If a woman remained fecund to the bitter end, becoming pregnant even as her body was faltering, she risked dying in childbirth or its draining aftermath when she still had several dependent young. And all those kids could very well die in her wake, or at least fail to reach their potential. Better the woman should forgo the hazards of late-stage maternity and devote herself to mothering the children she already had. Better her ovaries should be programmed to senesce in advance of the rest of her. Better she should live to be a grandmother.

The Williams hypothesis was an instant success. Everybody loved it, especially women over fifty. It had the same clever, simplified appeal as Desmond Morris's proposal that a woman's breasts are bowsprit buttocks. Menopause is natural. It's built into the system, a registered trademark of humanity. We're smart, our kids are smart, and our ovaries show it: they cease production just in time to give us a fighting chance to see our last child out the door. Menopause is good, and it can feel good; Margaret Mead famously talked in the 1960s of the "zest" of the postmenopausal woman.

Others seized and expanded on the hypothesis. Jared Diamond, of the University of California at Los Angeles, has argued that older women have been crucial in human history not only for their mothering skills but as repositories of information, Alexandrian libraries for preliterate tribes. Elders keep track of where the edible plants are, and they can recall natural disasters of long ago that may have affected the distribution and safety of local resources. Writing of his experiences in New Guinea and the Pacific islands, Diamond has described how, whenever he would ask questions about the island's flora and fauna that stumped the young or middle-aged natives, he invariably would be led into a dark hut, where he would meet the Oldest Living Member of the Tribe — sometimes a man, but usually a woman — who knew the answer to his interrogations. It sounds like a trope of Rousseau's, or Hollywood's, but the wise elder had her synapses and priorities straight. Eat that plant, sir, and your body will shake and your eyes will bulge from their sockets and you will be dead by sunrise. Anything else I can help you with today? As Diamond sees it, young relatives profited from the memories and advice of old relatives, and so selection extended human longevity. Men can live for decades with spermatogenesis proceeding apace, but childbearing gets riskier over time. If women were to survive to the encyclopedia years, the mechanism of menopause had to be born.

Jocelyn Peccei, who decided to go back to graduate school at UCLA when she was close to menopause and then chose to study — why not? — the evolution of menopause, has calculated that menopause might have arisen quite early in the hominid lineage, perhaps 1.5 million years ago, when we were as yet *Homo erectus.* But evidence to prove her proposition is hard to come by. Soft tissues such as ovaries do not leave fossils behind.

The backlash against the organic grandmother began in the 1970s, coincident with attempts by the medical community to promote estrogen replacement therapy for middle-aged women. As doctors became convinced that estrogen is the primary reason that women don't usually have heart attacks until after menopause, they began to question the desirability and "naturalness" of programmed ovarian senility. The grandmother hypothesis posits that women stop ovulating so that they can live longer and tend to their existing young; why, then, would the cessation cut off the primary source of a wondrous hormone that can keep women alive? How silly and self-defeating. Surely the adaptationists must be wrong. Surely menopause was not selected by evolution but is, like gray hair, merely another sign of our decay. And just as gray hair can be dyed or highlighted into the verisimilitude of youth, so the worst side effects of menopause can, and should, be ameliorated with estrogen replacement therapy.

The backlashers brought out the scorpion whips and cat-o'-nine-tails. Paleontologists argued that middle age and old age are themselves quite new. Until a few thousand years ago, they said, almost nobody lived past their early forties. The bones that have been found of early hominids are overwhelmingly the bones of young people. There are few if any postmenopausal women, no merry crones, in the fossil record. It's ridiculous to argue that natural selection has favored the onset of menopause in humans when early humans rarely lived long enough to enjoy hot flashes or Meadian zest. Women, and men, died by the age of forty-five. A woman's eggs will last her until about forty-five. As paleodemographers see it, the fit is pretty snug: a woman has all the eggs she needs to live the life she did when selective forces carved out the rudiments of our fate tens of thousands of years ago. If women today breezily outlast their egg supply and write best-selling books about the experience, fine, bully for them, but we're all artifacts of fortified food, purified water, and Jonas Salk, and evolution has nothing to say about us or our geriatric athleticism.

Nor could anthropologists find support for the adaptive value of menopause among contemporary "primitives." In the 1980s, Kim Hill and Magdalena Hurtado, of the University of New Mexico, studied the Ache of the eastern Paraguayan forest, another group of hunter-gatherers who must shoulder the burden of prehistory's silence. The anthropologists amassed a large and exacting data set. They observed the help and succor that older Ache women gave to their children and grandchildren. They devised theoretical models comparing the indirect genetic benefits that the grandmothers reaped by devoting themselves to their existing children and grandchildren with the direct genetic benefits that the women would have accrued if they had been able to continue bearing babies past menopause. An adaptation supposedly enhances your reproductive fitness, the ability to throw your lovely and singular genetic garland into tomorrow. If the grandmother hypothesis were valid, then presumably the contributions that the elder Ache women made to the health and survival of their children's children should outweigh the genetic gains of having two or three more children of their own. Alas, the bonus babies won: the anthropologists concluded that the Ache grannies were making surprisingly little difference to the prospects of their grandchildren and that the seniors would be better off — from a strictly Darwinian standpoint — if they could be mothers past menopause.

Through mathematical simulations, Alan Rogers, of the University of Utah, reached a similar conclusion. In a 1991 paper, he estimated that a woman would have to be a comic-book heroine, Neutron Nana, to make menopause look like an adaptation. Her ministrations to her family would have to double the number of children that *all* her children bore and help keep *all* her grandchildren alive to give premature reproductive senescence an edge over maternity in haghood. Even Demeter, the great goddess of the harvest, couldn't prevent her daughter, Persephone, from going to hell for six months of the year.

I was reared at the knee of the grandmother hypothesis. Even as a girl whose menopause was decades away, I found comfort in the idea that when it happened, it was all part of an optimal design. The thought of it linked me to my mythical ancestors, those dusty, lanky, demimonde women striding across the veldt, their brains expanding with every step. Hence I despaired when, in the 1990s, the facts seemed stacked against it. Many of the scientists I talked to thought it was a charming notion, but probably wrong. "Adaptive menopause is an interesting idea, and I wish I could believe in it," Steven Austad, a zoologist at the University of Idaho, said to me in mid-1997. "But I just don't see the evidence to support it." And from Alison Galloway, an anthropologist at the University of California in Santa Cruz: "I don't buy the Grandmother Hypothesis. I don't think there's anything beneficial about menopause. I don't think it's been selected for. It's the result of recent expansions in our lifespan. We outlive our follicles." Margie Profet, architect of the menstruation-as-defense theory, told me that it didn't matter, in an evolutionary sense, if postmenopausal women lacked the protection menstruation afforded: women weren't supposed to live past fifty. Jane Brody, my colleague at the *New York Times* and a proponent of hormone replacement therapy, has written that women shouldn't worry about hormone therapy's being unnatural, because a "woman's current life expectancy, on average, of seventy-seven years is not natural either."

Menopause is rust. It's the system breaking down, a sign of the past catching up with you, not a well-wrought mechanism to help you shape your family's future. I loved the grandmother hypothesis, but it was time to put that pet theory out to pasture, right next to the naked ape with her rumped-up chest.

Then I learned about Kristen Hawkes and the Hadza and the Grandmothers of Invention, movers and shakers and humanity makers.

Let's start with the facts. Data nearly killed Grandma, and so it is by data that she must be revived. Hawkes and her colleagues were meticulous about collecting data on the Hadza. They spent months charting the hour-by-hour activities of ninety individuals, half male, half female, ranging in estimated age from three to more than seventy. They noted who shared food with whom and under what conditions. They weighed their subjects regularly to see who was gaining and who losing during any given season. Through such efforts, the anthropologists could measure the meat of the matter, to determine whether the foraging exertions of person A made a difference to the nutritional status of those with whom she or he shared the pickings. The researchers found beautiful linear correlations between effort and result. Hadza children start foraging in the bush at a remarkably early age — often as young as three — but they can't fend for themselves entirely. Until puberty, they depend on adults for about half their food. The mother is usually the one who gives them what they can't get. As the anthropologists saw, the efforts of the mother are reflected on the scale: the harder she forages, the more weight her children gain.

However, that correspondence disappears whenever the mother has a newborn to feed. A nursing woman continues to forage, but with much less to show for it. Not only does the infant slow her down, but lactation is costly, requiring about 600 calories a day to support, which means that the mother must eat most of what she reaps. She can't afford to share with a whimpering four-year-old. During breastfeeding, then, the association between a mother's foraging effort and the weight of her older children disappears. The two factors are uncoupled. Instead, the welfare of the weaned child shifts to another female — usually the mother's mother, but if she's not around, an older aunt, a great-aunt, or, once in a while, the mother of the children's father. Suddenly the exertions of Grandma, or her equivalent, are reflected in the children's weight gains or losses. The harder the grandmother gathers, the more pounds the children reap. The faster the children grow, the stronger and more resilient they become, and the more likely they are to reach adulthood and add greatness to Grandma in name as she has it in will.

And now a pivotal point: the older females are flexible. They're strategic. They don't restrict their assistance to children and grand-children. They help any young relatives who need their help. When Hill and Hurtado studied the Ache of Paraguay, they asked, How much do older women assist their grown children and grandchildren, and do their contributions make a significant difference to those children and grandchildren? (Answer: not enough to explain menopause.) Hawkes and her colleagues cast a wider net. They had to. The Hadza women were spending too much time to ignore outside the cozy nexus of the immediate family. If an older woman didn't have a daughter to help, she helped the daughter of a sister. If a nursing woman's mother was dead, she turned to an older cousin and threw her existing children on the cousin's mercy, and the cousin obliged if she could, if she was past the time when she had to worry about infants of her own.

"Senior females allocate effort with the biggest fitness bang," Hawkes told me. "If they don't have nursing daughters of their own to help, they find other relatives to help. With strategic critters like ourselves, you'd expect behavioral adjustments like that. You'd expect that natural selection would favor adjusting help to where it's needed most.

"If you looked at the Hadza and considered only the impact that a postmenopausal woman had on the reproductive success of her children," she added, "you'd underestimate the effects of senior help by a huge amount." But if you take into account the seniors' contributions to the nutritional status of all young relatives, suddenly the old ladies are worth it. They are enhancing their total genetic fitness to the point where they don't need late-stage maternity to make their Darwinian mark. Another baby or three would just get in the way of their foraging.

Where, you might ask, are the Hadza men in this picture? Why are they not providing for their wives and children, as men supposedly have always done, so giving rise to the nuclear family and division of labor by sex? The Hadza men work, all right. They hunt, and the meat they bring back serves as a meaningful source of calories for the whole group. But hunting is an irregular enterprise and often unsuccessful; you can't count on it for your daily bread. By rights, hunter-gatherers should be called gatherer-hunters. In addition, when Hadza men make a killing, they can't help themselves: they show off. They're big men, and big men share. They share with allies they're seeking to woo or enemies they want to appease. They share with girls they're trying to impress and children who throng to the carcass. In the end, very little of the meat finds its way to the mouths of the hunter's family. The Hadza pattern is not unique. Among many traditional societies, hunting is a political rather than a personal occupation. "Hunting supplies a collective good from which all benefit, regardless of their relationship with the hunter," Kristen Hawkes and her coworkers have written. "It is women's foraging, not men's hunting, that differentially affects their own families' nutritional welfare." Women's foraging keeps their families afloat, and older women can forage as effectively as their daughters — more effectively when the daughters have newborns.

The organic grandmother has come home, and not a minute too soon. We missed you. We felt sad and lonely and old without you, posthumous before our time. Besides, the kids are crying. They need to be fed. Here's your sack and shovel, Nana. Now will you please get back to work?

Taken at face value, the Hadza research is welcome enough, but

Hawkes does more than offer data to resuscitate the moribund Williams hypothesis or buff the reputation of menopause. She has grander plans than that. She has *ovarios*. In her ambitious, speculative, and perfectly plausible scheme, older women invented youth. They made human childhood what it is today: long, dependent, and grandiose. And in inventing childhood, they invented the human race. They created *Homo imperialis*, a species that can go anywhere and exploit everything. We think of childhood as having evolved for the good of the child, to give the child time to grow its fat, crenelated brain and acquire linguistic, motor, and social polish. Hawkes turns the arrow around and sees childhood as having evolved for the good of adults, as a period of enforced dependency that paradoxically gave parents enormous freedom. Adults wanted dependent kids. They wanted offspring who needed them enough to stick with them until these offspring were on the threshold of adulthood themselves. With dependent, totable children, early humans could pick up and migrate to lands beyond a pongid's wildest dreams. It's as though teenagers have it right after all: Mom may complain about all her sacrifices and burdens, but just try pulling away and the umbilicus will yank you right back. And helping the hand that reins in the cord and rocks the cradle and rules the world is Grandma. Before we could stay young, we had to learn to grow old.

Let's start by dispensing with menopause. From George Williams on down, the adaptationists have depicted menopause as a watershed event in human evolution, a trait that distinguishes us from other female primates. Their ovaries can keep working to the end, the adaptationists claim, while ours are wired to shut down prematurely, giving us time to raise our families. In Hawkes's view, menopause is beside the point. Women don't undergo "premature" reproductive senescence, she says. Our ovaries last as long as the ovaries of our closest primate kin, the chimpanzees, bonobos, and gorillas: about forty-five years. Presumably the mutual progenitor of humans and great apes also had ovaries that lasted about forty-five years. The forty-five-year ovary could represent the ancestral condition, the primordial seedpod of the anthropoid family, one that is not particularly amenable to adjustment or augmentation. There may be physiological constraints that prevent natural selection from adding much to a woman's reproductive lifespan. For example, we may be too small. The only female mammals that breed past the fifth decade of life are such giants as elephants and finback whales. If you want to carry a lot of eggs, you need a very big basket.

Whatever the constraints, there is nothing precocious about the senescence of our ovaries, Hawkes says. On that score, she agrees with the artifactualists: women go through menopause because women outlive their follicles. But she parts company with the artifactualists in their insistence that old age is a modern invention. To the contrary, old age is old news. Call us *Homo maturus*. Yes, people used to die young routinely, of infectious diseases, in the jaws of a leopard, or while giving birth to a fat-headed, rear-facing baby. But those who survived illness and accident very likely thrived to a respectable old age. The Bible puts our allotment at three score and ten, and that's not a bad figure, biologically speaking. We're built to last about seventy to eighty years. Add on the overengineering needed to push a sizable number of people toward that mark, and you get a century. Wherever you go, whatever industrialized, agrarian, or nomadic population you consider, you will find that one hundred years is pretty much the upper limit for the human lifespan. "This is the human pattern," Hawkes says, "and there's no reason to think that it wasn't true for our ancestors as well."

What distinguishes women from other primates, then, isn't menopause but the long, robust life that women can lead after menopause. A chimpanzee at age forty-five or fifty not only has fading ovaries, she is fading globally. All her organs are faltering, and she is close to death. No matter that she has spent her life under the pampering ministrations of an American zoo, with the best medical care and all the bananas she can peel, a female chimpanzee will still be, at fifty, a decrepit animal. She will be the equivalent not of a menopausal woman but of a centenarian, blowing out the birthday candles to the cheers of Willard Scott.

So while natural selection may have been hamstrung by ovarian physiology, unable to augment a woman's follicular capacity beyond the standard primate model, it has flexed its muscles rather floridly on a woman's lifespan. And now we must emphasize the her-ness of human longevity. Let us return to the role of grandmother, and let us gloat. Yes, any wizened elder can, as Jared Diamond suggests, serve as memoirist, botanist, and toxicologist to the clan. But is a good hippocampus worth enough to account for the ascent of the centenarian? Not likely. Life is lived by the day, and most days aren't Christmas. Just as hunting is an irregular occupation, so is playing sage. We need food every day. We need women every day, day after day after year after decade after menopause. Let's build them to last.

By the new and expanded edition of the grandmother hypothesis, the rudiments of human longevity, and of human global domination, can be found in a ritual we take for granted: the family meal. A chimpanzee mother nurses her infant for four or five years. That's a long time, but afterward, there are no more free lunches at Mother's Café. The weaned apeling is expected to fend almost entirely for itself — to find, pick, and eat its own food. On occasion its mother or another older chimpanzee will share foraged goods with the juvenile, particularly if the food is hard for young fingers to manage. But the offered item is a treat, a banana split if you will, and the young chimpanzee knows better than to expect routine handouts.

In food-sharing, though, lies a kernel of possibility. Chimpanzees and other social primates are restricted in their range. They must stay in an area where all members of the group can find enough to eat, and that includes the weaned young. The available resources must be accessible to even the fumbling hands and undeveloped strength of preadolescent animals. If the troop decided to migrate to an area where food was scarce and required adult skills to extract, the younger animals would soon die of malnourishment.

Unless, that is, the adults started sharing food with their weaned offspring on a regular basis. Adults means mothers. Among nearly all species of primates, fathers have little to do with their offspring and probably don't know quite who they are anyway. The males are busy with other things, like hunting. The mother must be the one to give to her children what they can no longer gather for themselves. And that's fine, and she will, but then comes a hitch. She gets pregnant again. She must breastfeed. Lactation is costly. She must eat more than ever. She can't provision the older children and nurse at the same time. Who's she going to call? We know the answer. Her mother. Her auntie. Her cousin Certain Age. Now the chance arises for the occasional robust older female to make a difference to her family's welfare. An aging chimpanzee has nothing to do in a society where the young are autonomous, so she might as well die — right, Mother Nature, you beloved, cavalier, monomaniacal bitch? By contrast, in a setting where provisioning weaned children is essential, Grandmother too becomes essential. The stalwart older female succeeds in keeping her kin alive. The moribund older female does not. Selection favors robustness after menopause, and the human lifespan begins exceeding the primate norm like a pair of outstretched arms, strong and sweet and there to hold you.

Now, with Grandma's help, early humans are free. They can go where other primates, and possibly competing hominids, cannot. They can invade adults-only habitats, where they must dig to unearth tubers and cook many food items to make them edible. (Tubers, incidentally, are fairly rich in protein and calories, and they compose a large part of the diet among many traditional human cultures but are only rarely eaten by great apes.) Mothers can provision their progeny much of the time, but when they give birth they know they'll have help. An elder relative can assume responsibility for weaned children. In fact, with a grandmother's help, a mother can get that new baby off her breast sooner than she might otherwise. Chimpanzees breastfeed for four to five years, the length of time required for the young to reach self-sufficiency. But if a child does not need to be autonomous before leaving the teat, why keep suckling? Even in traditional societies where Similac is unknown and breastfeeding expected, women nurse for an average of only 2.8 years, less time than for other higher primates. Shortened lactation means greater fecundity, and indeed women in traditional cultures have more offspring with their primate ovaries than chimpanzees or gorillas do. The intervals between children are comparatively briefer. More grandchildren enhance the genetic fitness of the senior female. Through food-sharing, then, an older woman becomes a genetic czarina, dynastic in her reach.

As Grandmother grows stronger, children get weaker. It is a developmental rule of thumb that the greater an animal's lifespan, the later the onset of its sexual maturation; if a body is to endure, it must be built with care. Hence the genetic changes that foster life past menopause end up keeping children small and prepubescent comparatively longer. On all fronts, then, children are being infantilized. They are dragged into habitats where meals are beyond a juvenile's means, and then their genes delay their coming of age. Not to despair; instead, gild the cage. The lengthening of childhood opens a window of opportunity for cerebral experimentation. The brain has time to ripen, its synapses to lace and interdigitate and loop back lazily to do it again. For the first two or three years of life, a human child is not that different from a chimpanzee. Both creatures are astonishingly clever and curious, passionate students of life. But within short order the chimpanzee must drop out of school and work for a living, whereas the child — let's be predictable and call her a girl — remains in most cultures in the luxury of the nanny state. The child has all those postmammary years when she is still getting fed and thus can devote her energies to her intellectual and social education. In fact, she is well advised to do so, because even as extended dependency offers opportunity, it poses risks. The young chimpanzee can feed itself. The child cannot. An adult, unlike a fig tree, is not particularly responsive to being shaken or plucked, but instead must be ever so subtly fleeced. That means the child must learn the trade of enchantment: the strategic smile, the well-timed whimper, the feckless eye-bat. She must become a symbiotic parasite, an organism that takes and takes and depletes, as a parasite does, but that conveys to its host a sense of reciprocity, of being pleasant, worthy, useful; and that's a hard behavioral feat to manage, requiring a flow chart of routines and subroutines. Another whetstone to a young wit is the nattering chorus known as her sisters and brothers. Mother is fertile. She's having many children. She's weaning them young, and they're loitering at home. All those children are dependent on their elders, and all must beguile and connive to be noticed. Adults may like you soft, but your siblings whittle you sharp. No wonder children are so desperate to grow up: Kinder Garten is infested with snakes.

To review our story: Early humans took a preexisting primate hobby, food-sharing, and professionalized it. By shouldering the burden of feeding children, adults freed themselves to infiltrate whole new lands. But they couldn't have moved without Grandmother's help. Young women needed older women. Robustness after menopause became the rule, as did its corollary, delayed puberty. With Grandma in stride and children in tow, no land was too bleak, no tuber too deep, to dampen humanity's imperial zeal. The more hostile the terrain, the greater the dependency of child on elder. Peter Pan set down roots. Childhood expanded. And with world enough and time, the conditions converged for another revolutionary expansion — of intelligence. Our minds hurtled outward in all directions. We became absurdly creative, *Homo artifactus,* intolerant of bare cave walls and naked clay pots. We built better tools, better spears, better mastodon traps. The earth that we were fast overrunning was no longer enough, and we laid claim to the heavens, peopling the terrible, silent dome above us with an exuberant divinarium of advisers, legislators, coaches, and entertainers. We lived so long and so self-consciously that we assumed we must live forever, and we buried our dead with enough talismans and spare change for eternity.

Think of it: the grandmother hypothesis inverts all the conventional sequences; it brays at the party line of human evolution. We usually assume that we got smart first and then had to have an extended childhood to cultivate the circuitry of that smartness, and then had to live long enough as adults to care for our smart, slow-growing kids. As Hawkes plays it out, the order of events is just the opposite. We got old, we got young, we got smart. She takes a thwack at the familiar figurine of Man the Hunter, questioning the role of the male in provisioning the young and allowing children to be children. The original division of labor, as she sees it, was between childbearing women and post-menopausal women. Mothers bred what grandmothers fed. Through that compact, human fecundity and human mobility knew no limits.

But what of men? They live a long time too. If longevity arose to benefit the female, what of the superannuated male? The answer to that can be explained mostly by the mechanisms of genetics. Women have no exclusive patent on any particular gene. Unlike genes located on the Y chromosome, which will be passed only from fathers to sons, mothers apportion all their genes to sons and daughters alike. Genes that en-hance robustness postmenopausally when a female inherits them will find their way into male zygotes as well. The male lifespan gets dragged along. Still, it is possible that somatic robustness operates at its peak against a female background. Men do not live as long as women do, after all, and the disparity in lifespan applies globally. Maybe they don't have to live as long. Or maybe they don't want to. Maybe they get tired of losing their hair, and of the political pomp of the hunt, and of making bad jokes about their mothers-in-law.

If we accept the grandmother as the bedrock of our past and life after menopause as an ancestral right rather than a modern gratuity, then we can examine with a certain tempered skepticism the concept of "estro-gen deficiency." Assuming that our bodies were built to senesce slowly, what should we make of the decline in estrogen that accompanies menopause? More to the point, should we treat it? Does the grand-mother hypothesis tell us anything about whether or not we should take exogenous hormones when our follicles cease to burst cyclically and bless us unasked? The answer is . . . complicated. On the one hand, nature is imperfect. She is a slapdash engineer whose motto is "It'll do." The body after menopause certainly looks like an example of "It'll do." Nasolabial canyons, liver spots, the occasional embarrassing sneeze-leak sequence. Hey, nature barks, you've got a pulse, haven't you? In other words, even if our somas persist in the absence of ovarian estradiol, that doesn't mean we can't do better and live stronger by taking estrogen tablets. There's a principle in evolutionary thinking called the naturalis-tic fallacy — making the mistake of assuming that what is, is for the best. Murder and infanticide are "natural," in our species as well as in most others, but they are not defensible human strategies. The same may be true for menopause. Living without ovarian estradiol may be natural but far from ideal. After all, if the senescence of our primate ovaries is not an adaptation per se but merely the result of evolutionary constraints on follicular supply, then the concomitant loss of ovarian estrogen may be an example of "Sorry, this was the best we could come up with. It'll have to do. You'll muddle through." Muddling unnecessar-ily is stupid. We're clever. We have organic chemistry. We have gynecol-ogy, cardiology, endocrinology. We have evidence that hormones help. Take your Premarin, darling — if we're clever by nature, it's the natural thing to do.

On the other hand . . . the old pink Cadillac still drives. Nature is slapdash, yet the engine turns over and sometimes purrs. The analogy that many doctors make between menopause and hormone deficiency disorders such as diabetes and hypothyroidism doesn't hold up. If I were to stop taking my thyroid supplements, I would begin falling apart within days or weeks. My thyroid has failed me; I have a disease, I admit it, and I have no choice but to seek outside assistance. Menopause is not so dire. A woman's bones don't crumble or her blood vessels shatter once she has run out of eggs. Most women do extraordinarily well for years or decades after menopause without taking hormones. We might expect that during the evolution of the hominid life extension program, the female body developed mechanisms specifically to compensate for ovarian "failure." Recall that aromatase activity picks up as we age. Aromatase can turn precursor products from our adrenal glands into estrogen, and our adrenal glands do not quiesce at menopause. Is the improved aromatase performance a coincidence, or an adaptation that helps keep us healthy in the postovulation years? The body's fat content increases with age, even if we stay the same weight as we were at twenty-five. Fat makes estrogen. Do not spit at fat! It too may have value. It too may be an adaptive feature of the centennial woman. Our brains are said to need estrogen. Can neurons make their own steroids, and does neuronal steroidogenesis become stronger with age, in the manner of aromatase activity? We don't know. What we do know is that most women stay remarkably smart as they age, even without the ostensible brain food from their ovaries.

We also know that hormone therapy has risks as well as benefits, and that there's no escaping the complexity of the body or the individuality of any one body and its history. We are back where we began, forced to decide case by case, and to decide for ourselves. A woman with a sparrow's frame might choose estrogen therapy to help prevent osteoporosis. A sedentary woman with a family history of cardiovascular disease might make the same choice for the sake of her heart. A woman who is fit and fine, who has a forager's soul and knows that the body evolved to gather vegetables, not to become them, and who resists being absorbed entirely by the creamy perilife that is the desk-computer dyad, may decide, Feh, I'll forgo the pills, I'll take a walk, I'll lift a weight, I'll visit my daughter and offer to babysit her kids *right now*.

If the evolutionary analysis of menopause suggests anything about the merits or risks of hormone therapy, it is a lesson in harmony with the results of epidemiology. As we've seen, a number of studies have shown that the risks of contracting breast cancer increase the longer a woman takes estrogen replacement therapy. It is as though the body were saying, I don't need as much as you're giving me; I'm not a total idiot; I can take care of myself better than you think. Some doctors have suggested that women consider a two-step approach to hormone therapy, using supplements for a short stint right at menopause if they need them to weather such transitory symptoms as hot flashes and

sleeplessness, and then postponing the use of maintenance supplements until the age of sixty or sixty-five, when the risks of heart disease
and osteoporosis become substantial and the threat of dementia looms
closer. This strategy seems reasonable to me. Even by the Gray Panther
standards of the grandmother hypothesis, you start scavenging your
reserve supplies once you're in your sixties. Aromatase and adipose
tissue may no longer be enough. You're trying nature's patience. She's
losing interest in you. You're *past* postmenopausal. If taking estrogen at
that point helps you defy her odds, take it. You're a wise elder. Wisdom
means realizing you've overstayed your welcome and not giving a damn.

Pharmacology is fine, but we want more from the organic matriarch,
and she has more to give. The elder female is somebody we have always
known. She is there in the corner of the female unconscious, quiet,
fierce, loving, obliterating. She explains some of the impulses that agi-
tate and confuse us. I've often noticed that daughters are hard on their
mothers, much harder than sons are. Women will romanticize their
fathers and forgive them many sins and failings, but toward their mothers they show no mercy. Whatever the mother did, she could do no
right. The mother was cold and negligent, the mother was overbearing
and smothering, the mother was timid, the mother was a shrew. Even
feminism did not cure us of our mother hatred, our mother flu. We
cling to our anger at our mothers. We don't want to give it up. It
protects us. Not long ago, an editor asked me to contribute to a book of
essays to be written by women about their mothers. My coauthors were
novelists, poets, critics, historians, many of them well known, all of
them intellectually formidable. I agreed, and I wrote a positive piece,
praising my mother for having taught me the value of earning a paycheck and for advising me on the best, though decidedly off-label, cure
for anorgasmia. The editor called to thank me. I added a tone that the
book needed, she told me. I was one of the few who said something nice
about their mothers.

This is not a boast. It could have been otherwise. I've gone through
long stretches of hating my mother mindlessly and obsessively, of crying bitterly when I think of her, of writing small fables in which she is
the Ogress, the Great Gaping Cardiophage with no heart of her own.
But then there are other times when I stop myself in the middle of a

mother fit and say, This isn't rational, it isn't fair, and it's a bad precedent. Think now how you might drag yourself out of the sewer of mother hatred, lest your daughter grow up and blast you with hate and blame of her own. I was in that deliberative, grudgingly generous, self-defensive frame of mind when I wrote my good-mother essay. Otherwise, oh how beautiful my bile can be. And, it seems, how typical. We daughters, like pit vipers, have nonretractable fangs.

At the same time, women often remain quite close to their mothers. They talk to their mothers much more often than sons do. On average, a woman calls her mother once a week, compared to the son's rate of once a month. Women need their mothers. They blame their mothers, they dream of killing their mothers, but they keep coming back for more mother time. They want something, even if they can't articulate the desire. They expect something. They expect their mothers to be there for them, for years and years after they have become adults. Sylvia Plath wrote poems of luxurious violence about her mother: "You steamed to me over the sea,/Fat and red, a placenta/Paralyzing the kicking lovers. . . . Off, off, eely tentacle!/There is nothing between us." She also, as an exchange student at Cambridge University, wrote long, earnest letters to her mother, describing every detail of her life — the men she met, the parties she attended, her dislike of English girls for being "fair-skinned, rather hysterical and breathless," her pitiable wish for "someone to bring me hot broth and tell me they love me." Her pitiable wish for her mother.

The emotional axon between mother and daughter often has been seen as a matter of their shared sex and the fact that the daughter identifies with the mother and does not need to individuate, as a son must, to assert identity. By this analysis, women remain like children with their mothers because they can. It's not threatening for them to cry "Mommy," as it might be for a man. Their selfhood and sexual identity don't demand rejection of the all-powerful female. Thus, any expectations a woman may have of her mother's help can be viewed as nothing more than a little girl's petulant demands, perpetually recycled.

The grandmother hypothesis suggests another interpretation, with less emphasis on the puerile. If young women have long needed older women, and if that need was an organizing principle in early human society, then our constitutional hunger for our mothers cannot, should not end at puberty. It is much stronger than that. It is like the river of our lives. It flows on, and we must navigate it, and it surges and howls and falls, but it doesn't end and we must ride it. If an older woman took care of your children, the older woman was like your children: profoundly loved and wanted, a part of yourself. At the same time, the older woman does not belong to you alone; she has other familial clients to attend to. She will disappoint you, and you'll be angry at her, but you won't stop needing her, and you won't stop asking for her help. She'll give it when she can, and when she does, you feel safe. And when she doesn't, maybe another senior female will.

The structure of Western lives doesn't easily accommodate long-term links between older and younger women. We marry, we migrate, we live in apartments or small houses where the last thing we'd want is to have our mothers move in. We have little or no connection to relatives other than the most immediate ones. Yet the yearnings and needs don't evaporate, they simply mutate. Every unmet desire in adulthood is laid at the maternal doorstep. If anything, the loss of the larger kinship matrix focuses the fury of our helplessness entirely on our mothers. We expect help from an older woman, and our mother is the only older woman we know. When women go to therapists, the majority of the time they choose to see a female therapist who is older than they are. They are seeking support from one who fits the template in their heads of the potential savior. They're not looking for their mother. To the contrary, they are probably furious at their mother, and that's part of the reason that they are in therapy. But in the senior female therapist, they are looking for the missing elder, the woman *in loco matris* who fills in when their own mother is dead or deficient or otherwise engaged.

The naturalistic fallacy warns us against elevating the presumed innate to the presumed optimum. We may not want to spend our lives surrounded by relatives. We find our families suffocating. We flee small towns because we get tired of having our neighbors know our business and gabble over our every social transgression. Still, we are all of us compendiums — of ancestral patterns, a thousand subsequent overlays, and the singularity of the self. It doesn't hurt to find strength wherever we can, in the precursor as well as in the present. For example, touch feels wonderful. It is also one of the most ancient transactions, a defiance of the plasma membrane and the loneliness it brought. Touch can heal. Even when a person is in a coma, the simple touch of a nurse will lower the patient's blood pressure. We need touch, and as a rule the appetite serves us well. In a similar vein, I would argue that a woman's mother-lust, her need for the older female and for other women generally, is also ancient, and also worth heeding. There's no evidence that humans have ever lived in a true matriarchy, where women ruled. But the phenomenon of matrilocality, in which daughters remain in their natal group while sons disperse as adults, is not uncommon among traditional societies and is the overwhelming rule among nonhuman primates. Females form a stable core, while males come and go, talking of Michelangelo or, more likely, the Knicks. "Any model of proto-human society that neglects a central role for relationships among females is probably wrong," says the primatologist Kim Wallen. Hadza culture is not matriarchal; in many ways, women remain subordinate to men. But because they have each other and are anchored in matrilocality, nobody goes hungry, and that tacit arrangement is powerful medicine for the mind.

In the 1970s, women talked about sisterhood, and they made a yeo-woman's stab at putting it into practice. But even the utopianists fell into the easy habit of apartheid by age. Young women bonded with young women. Older women split off and formed groups like OWL, for "older women's liberation," older at that point being anybody over thirty. It was a mistake to segregate then, and it's a mistake we still excel at. We codify barriers between generations with dreary names like baby boomers, Xers, and the latest edition, the millenniers, or the zeroasters ("Before us, all was negative"). We make friends among our chronological peers, rarely venturing more than a decade up or down. Thus we end up with girlfriends who are in the same precarious place as we are, anxious for all the same reasons, and we keep looking for our mothers, and those mythical creatures our female mentors, and a patch of earth where we can stop for one wretched little minute to breathe, safely breathe. A group of same-aged people is inherently unstable. Peers will compete just as siblings compete. The ancestral sorority was transgenerational, and if we want whatever strength and balm may come from sisterhood, it wouldn't hurt to recapitulate in some measure the time-worn model and brace our listing library of cohorts with bookends of the young and the seasoned.

That's my fantasy, anyway. I think I've always believed in the model of the diversified portfolio, the clan, the coven. For my college yearbook, I chose as my defining (if overly arch) quotation a line from *Ulysses:* "Youth led by experience visits notoriety." I loved the idea of being taken by the hand by a sharp older woman, her gray hair snazzily coiffed, and led toward the beckoning, threatening Elysium of notoriety. Notoriety was my gnosis, the spiritual truth, but firmer and darker, and my experienced one had to be a woman, for the idea of an experienced man smacked of the satyric. I had no idea how to find Experience; my female professors in college had to maintain a professorial distance, and they were worse than mothers and grandmothers in having so *many* dependents, pupils, to attend to. In any case, I was terrified of them and felt the weight of my weightlessness, of how little I had to offer in return. I still don't know how to make friends outside the age-concordant span, and I still yearn for the solace it would bring, though the mere image of that cover, and the hope of finding it, are comforts.

I have great, wild hopes of finding my daughter as she will be in adulthood, when she nominally stops needing me, when she is past the seizures and denunciations that I expect will come at adolescence because they came so brutally for me. I hope that I'm right in my interpretation of the organic grandmother, that mother hunger is a primal trait of womanness, and that my daughter's need for me may prove larger, more enduring, and more passionate than the child's need for meals, clothes, shelter, and applause. I hope that she needs me enough to show me who she is, to give regular dispatches, her intellectual progeny, and to trust me with their safekeeping. I hope that she likes to barter — Youth and Experience haggling over Notoriety. May she spit fire and leave me gladly, but sense in her very hemoglobin that she can find me and rest with me and breathe, safely breathe, if only for the fleeting intermission between cycles of anger and disappointment. For as long as they last, my bones, brain, and strength are her birthright, and they may not be much, but they're tenacious by decree, and they'll comply happily with the customs of dynasty. When Youth comes calling, Experience gets out her shovel and digs.

14

WOLF WHISTLES AND HYENA SMILES

TESTOSTERONE AND WOMEN

I DON'T KNOW WHY I still have a television set. By rights it should be broken, or at the very least have a nice, sneering crack snaking down the center of the screen. It doesn't, though. I don't keep a hammer or any other heavy object in the family TV room, so I haven't been able to satisfy the girlish rage that blackens my senses every time I hear a commercial for girls' toys. It's not that I hate dolls and dollhouses and training-wheel kitchenettes and Barbie wig-o-rama sets and Barbie minivans. I just hate the sound of the commercials, the caramelized music of them, the intimate, cooing voice of the pitch-mistress and the happy woos and ahs and giggles of the girls as they share the toy being hawked. The girls in these commercials are always great friends, and they are always gentle and generous, budding communitarians, fantasy kibbutzniks, although with consumerist flair. They love, love, love each other, almost as much as they love the object that has brought them together. Whatever else the producers of these commercials may have been, one thing is clear: they were never girls. Or if they were, they've grown up to have a serious sadistic streak to them. Giving a girl the impression that girlhood is an extended bounce on Barney's knee is like prepping a young gazelle for life on the Serengeti by dipping it in cream.

If you are or have ever been a girl, you know that the first job of being a girl is learning to survive in a group of girls. And girls in groups are not little Joni Mitchell tunes made particulate. Girls in groups are . . . how shall we say it, what's the word that we persist in thinking has a penchant for boys? Aggressive. Of course they're aggressive. They're alive, aren't they? They're primates. They're social animals. So yes, girls may like to play with Barbie, make the wrong move, sister, and ooh, ah, here's your own Dentist Barbie in the trash can, stripped, shorn, and with toothmarks on her boobs.

If you are or have ever been a girl, you know that girls are aggressive. This is news the way the Code of Hammurabi is news. Yet the girls in station break Candyland are never aggressive; in fact, they are getting gooier by the year. Nor are the girls who prance through the meadows of biological theory ever aggressive. No, they're *prosocial.* They're verbal, interactive, attentive, amiable. They're the friends you wish you could buy along with the Belchee Baby you saw on TV. Take, for example, a 1997 report that appeared in the journal *Nature.* Researchers from Britain described their studies of girls with Turner's syndrome, an unusual condition in which a girl has only one X chromosome rather than the two Xs found in most girls. The scientists began with the very intriguing observation that there are differences in social skills between Turner's girls depending on their chromosomal background. Normally a girl inherits one X chromosome from her mother, one from her father. A Turner's girl, who has but a single X chromosome, can receive it from either her mother or her father. What the scientists discovered, in their study of one hundred Turner's girls, was that those girls who had inherited their X chromosome from their fathers were more genial than those whose X had been bestowed by Mom. Daddy's girls tended to be friendly, socially adept, and well adjusted. The mother's lot were comparatively sullen, awkward, tongue-tied in company, prone to offensive or disruptive displays. All of which was fine and fascinating and offered a glimpse into the behavioral palette of Turner's syndrome, but the scientists went further. They extended their results to say something about the innateness of good behavior in girls — all girls. They proposed that the Turner's girls with the paternal X chromosome, the socially well-adjusted ones, were the girl-like girls, and those with the maternal X chromosome, the socially offensive or inept ones, carried a more boylike genotype. Their reasoning was serpentine and abstruse, but in the final analysis they spooned up a portrait of girls as genetically predisposed toward sociality, diplomacy, and affability. By their dubious hypothesis, the X chromosome carries a gene for social grace that is active in normal girls but is kept silent in normal boys, a sexually divergent pattern of expression with presumed evolutionary advantages to each. For males, an insensitivity to social niceties would in theory make it easier to be aggressive, to form dominance hierarchies, and to organize hunting parties and armies and bulldoze over any empathic fools standing in their way. For girls, having greater social skills could simplify the task of befriending other females, going along by getting along, and learning the craft of motherhood. "Little girls love to be little mothers," one of the researchers told me. "And women love to talk to other women. They have a flair for striking up social relationships with other women." *Flair* has an intrinsic sound to it, a touch of the chromosomal.

I have taken the liberty of designating this gene SSEN-1, SSEN referring to the ingredients in the ancient recipe for girlness and the 1 tacked on as a preemptive acknowledgment that the creation of social grace is surely a complex enough operation that many other girl-specific SSEN genes will be unearthed if we wave our spangled fairy wands with sufficient tenderness.

Forget for a moment that the study on which the florid and far-reaching speculations are based was limited to a population of one hundred children with a chromosomal anomaly, and that chromosomal anomalies are fraught with complexities and confounding factors of their own; and forget that the putative SSEN-1 gene is far from being identified or even proven to exist. What impresses me is the bleached and alien bearing of the generic girl who emerges from the report. The girl whose social aplomb and circle of friends are her birthrights. The motherette with the gift of gab. Where are the bossy girls, the morbid girls, the mean girls, the dreaming girls, the girls who are your best friend everlasting today and your Eve Harrington tomorrow? Where are the pyramid schemers, the social notaries who rank you A through Zed and you can't do a damned thing about it? Where are the hyena girls, the leopard girls, the coyote and the crow girls?

Where are the living, seething, aggressive girls who are the only girls I've ever known?

We don't talk much or hear much about aggression in girls and women, so we forget that it's there and has meaning. We associate aggressive behavior with males, and we get stuck on that note, and we can't talk or coo or screech our way past it. Scientists do it ritualistically.

We all do it reflexively, even when we think we're wise and enlightened and past that tired old stereotype. Once, while watching a group of seagulls battling over a pile of old crackers on the beach, I observed that the older seagulls, the ones with dirty white plumage and the red spot of maturity on the beak, spent all their time trying to assert their dominance by peevishly pecking at the younger, brown-feathered seagulls, while the younger seagulls ignored their betters and devoted their efforts to gulping down food. As I watched, I assumed that all the birds in the skirmish were male, had to be male, for they were so aggressive, and I had the whole story worked out in my mind, the older males obsessed with status, the younger males defiant and opportunistic. Only later did I recall that male and female seagulls look alike — brown in youth, white in age — and I realized, shamefacedly, that many of the birds in the free-for-all must have been female, because females have to eat and a scavenger's life is a bitch.

But let's not curse the knee for jerking. Our fixation on male aggression is not irrational. Among humans, male-type aggression can at times be as clear as a broken nose on your face. Men are overwhelmingly responsible for violent crime. They commit 90 percent of the murders, 80 percent of the muggings, nearly 100 percent of the rapes. Researchers who want to understand the basis of aggression must justify their curiosity on medical grounds; otherwise they'll have trouble getting grants. Male aggression is easily cast as a disease. Violence is a threat to public health. Men are more physically violent than women, and thus male aggression is of greater scientific concern than female aggression. Besides, we all know that women are much less aggressive than men and that girls are great friends, and if you, girl, beg to differ, we have ways to persuade you, starting with a mandatory bolus of kiddie TV.

The problem with ignoring female aggression is that we who are aggressive, we girls and women and obligate primates, feel confused, as though something is missing in the equation, the interpretation of self and impulse. We're left to wander through the thickets of our profound ferocity, our roaring hungers and drives, and we're tossed in the playground to thrash it out among ourselves, girl to girl, knowing that we must prove ourselves and negotiate and strut and calibrate but seeing scant evidence of the struggle onscreen or in books or on biology's docket. We are left feeling like "error variants," in the words of one female scientist, wondering why we aren't nicer than we are, and why we want so much, and why we can't sit still.

Yet even though we know something is missing from the biocultural, blond-wigged effigy of Woman, we're reluctant to explore the edges of our aggression. We don't want to be seen as aggressive or to think of ourselves as aggressive. Nobody likes aggressive people, of either sex. The people we call aggressive are the people we think of as pains in the ass, and we don't want them in our homes, our workplaces, or our heads. We have a monochromatic and wholly negative view of aggression, one that we've come to associate with wife batterers and crack addicts. It's fine to be assertive and determined; these are good, up-standing terms, and we like them, we busy global marketeers. But aggression is passé. Aggression is low. It's for losers, really. Aggression is what you resort to when you don't have genuine power.

It's like I was trying to tell you. Aggression is for girls.

Now is our chance. Aggression is unfashionable. It has been medical-ized and demonized and tossed on the landfill of public opinion, and it is no longer seen as a desirable trait or the mark of a real man. We are free to salvage aggression and do with it as we please. We can rehabili-tate it and recode it. We can share it. We can understand it in the context of our needs as girls and as women, and we can see when aggression is likely to appear and what form it will take. Aggressive behavior can be hostile and seek to wound, but it can also be creative and seek to engage. Psychologists routinely regard aggressive behavior as antisocial, but this is a disappointing, Panglossian view of life. Scratch the surface of many a seemingly innocent social behavior and you'll find aggression snicker-ing underneath. Friendliness can be deeply aggressive, as anybody who has gotten a soliciting phone call at dinnertime can attest: "How ya doing tonight? Give me money." Or take the following exchange, which routinely occurs when a person receives a visitor to her home. The hostess offers the guest something to eat or drink. The guest refuses. On the face of it, the behavior of each player is amicable, the antithesis of aggressive. The hostess is generous for offering, and the guest is thoughtful for declining and thus sparing the hostess her trouble. Sometimes the transaction is indeed simple and sweet and devoid of subtext; the guest may just have finished dinner and have no desire for more comestibles. But think of the aggressive potential of the ritual, the power dynamic resonant within it. By offering food, the hostess signals that she knows she is in charge. It's her home, and her resources surround them. She is the one with something to give, and she wants to profit from her position of bounty. She wants to establish the relationship on her terms, to be seen as trustworthy, generous, and well stocked. She wants to secure an alliance, however temporary, with the guest, who, in accepting the gift, would be mildly beholden to the giver.

By refusing the food, the visitor rejects the temporary position of confederate or subordinate, and in so doing sends the subtle message that *she* is in charge here; she is the one who can afford to forgo gifts and potential colluders. And the hostess may feel a touch of vexation at the refusal, may stiffen and decide, Okay, then, we won't be friends, state your business and let's get on with it. Not for nothing is a rejection of generosity sometimes likened to a slap in the face. Context sets the pitch for the aggressive kinetics of any social exchange, petting it into docility, fanning it into antagonism. To refuse food *is* generous if your hostess is an old friend who has kids and would just as soon not approach the event horizon of her kitchen. To refuse food if you are a boss who has dropped by your employee's home on the weekend is to give a despotic waggle of your red-dotted beak. You show up unexpectedly and shock the poor gal, and when she tries to equilibrate the relationship by offering you a beverage of your choice, you snub her. You're going to fire her, after all; it's she who will need the drink.

Context and reformation can make even frank aggression look appealing. Lady Macbeth is everybody's favorite she-abomination, a ruthlessly ambitious woman who begs the spirits, "Unsex me here, and fill me from the crown to the toe topful of direst cruelty," who connives and manipulates her husband into killing King Duncan and then dunks her hands in the bloody aftermath. "Hostile, aggressive bitch" doesn't begin to cover this dame. Given a little shakeup of our preconceptions, though, Lady Macbeth can take on an air of tragic nobility. What if we imagine Lady Macbeth as a Nordic matriarch, defender of her clan? Pekka Niemela, a philosopher at Uppsala University in Finland, has suggested that Lady Macbeth was a Viking, a character much like the powerful women who populate the classic Norse epic the Orkneyinga Saga. Niemela points out that *Macbeth* is set in Scotland about A.D.

1000, when Scotland was more pagan than Christian, dominated by Viking culture. Cast as a Viking, Lady Macbeth loses none of her brutality but gains much of our sympathy. Viking women were expected to curry ferocity, to be thick of blood and galled of milk. Viking men were away on raids for months or years. Viking women were in charge of the fiefdoms back home, and they had considerable power to make decisions about life and death, war and peace. But they had little time for pomp and mead parties. The plundering class is ever at risk of being plundered, and there were no laws, no local sheriffs, no Royal Canadian Mounties to protect a Viking's property or person. The only insurance against threats from the outside was kin and clan. A weak clan could not attract allies. A weak clan could be exterminated in a single spasm of slaughter. A Viking woman didn't have the luxury of indifference to status. Macbeth could always hop aboard a ship and take his middling thanely title and milk of human kindness overseas. For his lady, moored on the Scottish highlands, nothing short of a queen's crown looked strong enough to shield the clan, and there was no way to gain that crown but with the point of a knife.

Lady Macbeth is every actress's dream role, but we can be glad that we don't have to play the Norsewoman in everyday life. Our aggressions are more palatable, less indelible. Still, we have aggressions, *our* aggressions, and that we need them is what matters, and if we approach them without hostility or mental transvestism and search out their source and substrate, then we can forgive ourselves our woman's gall and blow a kiss to our friends.

Which brings me to testosterone, so formidable by reputation that you can practically hear its carbon rings clanking. There is no way to think about the source of aggression without looking testosterone in its cocky little eye. Testosterone the conquering concept has swaggered among us too long to ignore as a trifle. We have heard and heard again that testosterone mediates aggressive behavior — somehow, in some way, we're not sure of the details, but nevertheless the hormone is surely a contender. Testosterone is linked to all those traits covered by the umbrella term *aggression,* such as the urge to dominate or attack another, to show off, to bluster, to leave heaps of dirty laundry in the middle of the floor. It makes leaders and it makes crooks, and if it can be hard to tell the difference between the two, well, that's testosterone for you — as subtle as a sledgehammer. Testosterone is said to start its maneuvers young, pre-young, to shape the brain of a developing fetus and dispose the brain toward domineering, reckless, ham-handed behavior later in life. Testosterone is to aggression what breasts are to buttocks: think of one, and the other inevitably pops to mind.

Of course, lately we have all learned and been told that testosterone is not strictly a male hormone, that females have some too. But less of it, mind you, much, much less of it. The average levels of circulating testosterone among women fall between 20 and 70 nanograms per deciliter of blood. Half is made by the adrenal glands and half by the ovaries. Among men, 300 nanograms per deciliter is on the low side, and most men are in the 400-to-700-nanogram range — in other words, they have ten times the amount found in women, and nearly all of that plethora comes from the cells of the testes. So men have more testosterone. So we think men are more aggressive than women. And so we think that testosterone is partly if not largely to blame or to credit for the putative aggression asymmetry.

We have also come up with a new creature called the high-T woman, whose testosterone quotient is on the upper end of the normal female range and who is more aggressive than the average woman, more dedicated to her career, more sexually assertive, less interested in children — a *very* little mother. This high-T woman is a biologically tinted attempt to explain why some women behave like error variants, but there is in fact scant evidence to support the existence of the high-T gal, or, more precisely, the gal whose forceful, edgy, ambitious style is the result of elevated testosterone concentrations. Testosterone has been accorded vast powers, as the libido hormone, the aggression hormone, the dominance hormone. But if women had to rely on their testosterone to get anything done in life, to feel erotic or angry or noncomatose, they'd be a pathetic lot. There's so little there there. Even a high-T woman, with her 70 nanograms per deciliter, would not make a sub-passable man. It has been proposed that *because* women have low levels of testosterone, they are extremely sensitive to small variations and fluctuations of it. Can this be? Despite its reputation, testosterone is not a particularly active hormone; grain for grain, it is much less biologically potent than estradiol. Men appear to need great swells of it to subsist. Why should a woman be better equipped than a man to whip a feeble hormone into a source of behavioral power? The likely answer is, we aren't, and we don't need to be. We have paid a long and blind obeisance to testosterone the conquering concept, to the point where we assume it rules all rulers, male or female, present or wistful; but if we challenge the dominant paradigm and see how badly it fails us, we can begin to imagine a parallel universe, where the neural substrate of a Viking matriarch is not a booby prize but our birthright.

Testosterone is said to work in two stages on the brain, the organizational stage and the activational stage. Organization happens prenatally, when the testes of a male fetus begin releasing testosterone, which supposedly shapes the brain in male-specific ways. Much later, during adolescence, activation occurs; testosterone levels rise in a young man and switch on all the male-specific patterns that were set in the womb, and we are given the raw material for Fortune 500 executives (all but 10 percent of whom are male) or very large bruisers named Arnold (Schwarzenegger) or Norman (Schwarzkopf).

The female brain, by contrast, is the steady-state brain, the default brain, the plan we go with unless otherwise signaled. The female brain is not exposed to a burst of testosterone prenatally, because the female has no testes to release testosterone. The characteristic circuitry of the female brain is established by absence rather than presence. On reaching puberty and feeling the surge of estrogen and progesterone, that circuitry is activated in its female-specific conformation, forthwith to counsel behaviors like . . . well, it's hard to say, and naturally it differs from individual to individual, but in essence, all things muzzled — not quite as aggressive as the male, not quite as ambitious, not quite as obnoxious, not as obsessed with sex. That, at least, is the persistent presumption of the standard organizational/activational theory of the sexing of the brain — that the female brain is comparatively less primed to aggressive, dominant behavior and all accessories and permutations of such.

Now we can consider the blemishes and qualifications of the O/A hypothesis. First, testosterone as such may not be what matters during the prenatal imprinting. The thinking among many researchers is that much of the testosterone that reaches the fetal brain is promptly converted by the neurons to estrogen, and only as estrogen does it affect the sexual architecture of the brain. Yes, only as a "female" hormone can the male hormone masculinize the brain. Which means that estrogen is what counts for the sexing of the brain and the dispensation of aggressive, dominant, or satyric behavior. Females know from estrogen. In this hormone, we can't exactly be ranked as deprived. Still, one can preserve the O/A hypothesis by insisting that what counts is not estrogen versus testosterone but the quantity of steroid hormone to which the fetal brain is exposed. Supposedly, estrogen in a fetus's blood, whether from the mother or from the fetal ovaries, gets bound up by a fetal protein called alpha-fetoprotein and is unable to penetrate the brain. Supposedly, testosterone from a boy fetus's testes doesn't get bound up by this fetal protein, so it *can* reach the brain. If it is then converted to estrogen before influencing brain architecture, so what? It is nonetheless cortically present and accounted for, and a girl's estrogen is not. The great steroid surge remains the ken of the male fetus. The female brain keeps its hormonal virginity.

Except that it doesn't. Most of the experiments suggesting that it did were performed in rodents, where alpha-fetoprotein is adept at waylaying blood estrogen. In humans, the protein doesn't distract estrogen from reaching the brain. And so estrogen from the mother is free to affect a girl baby's brain, and estrogen from the girl's ovaries may do the same. A drizzle of estrogen plies the female brain throughout gestation, and who can say how much is flowing or what its impact on the neuronal conduits may be? Scientists assume that the dose is still relatively low compared to the hormonal swell that reaches a male fetus's brain from his testes, and that, to put it schematically, low estrogen feminizes a brain while high estrogen masculinizes a brain, and high estrogen comes from prenatal ejaculates of androgen which are converted to estrogen in the brain. Yet there is no proof for this assertion. Even in rodents, the tidy dichotamous model doesn't pan out. Take female mice that have been genetically altered so they lack estrogen receptor-alpha and therefore have one less way of responding to estrogen than a normal mouse does. If a brain that is spared the impact of estrogen during development is slated for femininity, these mice should be the murine equivalent of the goo-girls on television commercials, superfemmes. But they're not. On the contrary, they're unusually aggressive. Some are infanticidal. They see another female's pups, and they attack. The receptor-deficient females are more aggressive than the *male* mice that lack estrogen receptors. Those males appear somewhat feminized. They don't like to venture across open spaces, as male mice usually do. They mount females, but then they don't ejaculate. Their brains were also deprived of the developmental persuasions of estrogen; their testes made testosterone, but the testosterone couldn't exert its organizing influence on the brain because the hormone had to do its deed as estrogen, and the estrogen receptors weren't listening.

What, then, is the moral of our story? That if you're a chromosomal gal and you can't respond to estrogen in utero, you turn guyesque? But if you're a guy and you can't respond to estrogen, you turn gal? Or something like that, or something else altogether? Or is the moral that the old stories won't do, and that the female brain is made, not defaulted, and that if brain development in either sex is perturbed by a genetic anomaly, the resulting animal will defy expectations and laugh in all the wrong places?

Women have testosterone, but it's nothing to hang a helmet on. We can't count on testosterone, and there's a good chance we don't need to.

The studies that link testosterone to aggressive or dominant behavior in men are not pretty. They are a mess. Some studies have found that among male prisoners, the more violent the offense committed, the higher the man's testosterone level. Other studies have failed to find such a correlation. Among young adolescents, boys rated as "tough leaders" by their peers have been shown to have high levels of testosterone; yet one boy's "tough" is another boy's "tough luck," for the same study showed that those boys who had spent their childhoods getting into fights and trouble had fairly *depressed* levels of testosterone on reaching puberty. As a rule of thumb, a man's testosterone will rise right before a challenge, like a football game or a chess tournament, and if the man triumphs, his testosterone stays high for a time, but if he loses, it drops, and it has difficulty getting up again. Testosterone will rise when a man receives a medical degree or a professional honor. It will climb when he is awarded a cash prize for winning a tennis match, but not if he wins the same amount in a lottery and can't feel the peacock for it. The testosterone levels of male trial lawyers — who must get up in court and shake their verbal scimitars and slash at any who doubt them — are higher, on average, than the testosterone concentrations of tax lawyers, who do most of their work in the privacy of their office and may even keep an orchid plant on the desk.

But gearing up for a challenge does not always elicit a testosterone spike. Young men competing in a video game tournament show no detectable testosterone shift, neither beforehand nor in the wake of virtually exterminating their opponents. Before a male parachutist leaps from a plane, his testosterone *drops;* it sees what's coming, we can suppose, and swoons at the thought. A man's testosterone concentration also falls when he has fallen in love to the point where he is committed to the woman, and it falls when he is on the verge of fatherhood. Some scientists interpret these results to mean that men in a monogamous relationship don't need their testosterone. They don't want their testosterone. It does them no good if they're going to stay put and be a loyal lover and a devoted father. They don't need as much testosterone as they did when they were on the hunt and might be forced to rattle their chain mail at a rival en route. There are alternate storylines, though. Testosterone can fall when a man is under stress; that's presumably part of the reason why it dips with a drop in social status, or with the loss of a chess game. Is commitment not stressful? Is commitment not a match for the scream that precedes a parachute jump? And impending and new fatherhood — are they stressful? If you have to ask, you are inert, and need neither testosterone nor oxygen.

We don't know the meaning of testosterone fluctuations in men. They rise and fall every day, throughout the day, peaking in the morning, subsiding by late afternoon, and rising again before bed. If you cut off the major source of a man's testosterone, his testicles, he may or may not become less aggressive than he was before. Some men who have been chemically castrated for the treatment of prostate cancer report extreme mood changes, usually in a more passive and depressed direction; but they have cancer, for Thor's sake, and why expect them to be out there pretending they are jujitsu masters? Men who were castrated to guard a sultan's harem were not unaggressive. They could be pissy. That's why they were good watchdogs. In ancient China, court eunuchs could be notoriously bloodthirsty, arranging assassinations of emperors and enthroning chosen successors; some were military strategists, others fought as foot soldiers. In this country, surgical or chemical castration sometimes is used as a treatment for sex offenders, particularly child molesters. The therapy has its detractors, and rightfully so. Not only does the punishment smack of barbarism and anticonstitutionalism, but it can have tragic results. Some child molesters who were castrated have ended up killing their young victims rather than stopping at molestation. The loss of testicular androgen dampened their sex drive and made erections difficult, but their aggression was unslaked, and, furious with their failure to perform, they lashed out at the unfortunate objects of their pathological urges.

Men who are hypogonadal — whose testosterone levels have, for a variety of clinical reasons, dived into the subnormal range — say they feel more aggressive and angrier than they did before, not less, and when their androgen levels return to normal they feel calmer, happier, at ease with themselves once again. So it is with all our hormones — thyroid, sex steroids, cortisol. Too much or too little, it doesn't matter. We feel dis-eased, out of sorts, crotchety, aggressive.

If the link between testosterone and aggressive or dominant behavior in men is a mess, that for women is the floor under your refrigerator: you don't want to think about it. Female athletes don't have a testosterone spike before a competition, and they don't have a spike if they win a competition. Female trial lawyers are hardly more blessed with testosterone, on average, than female tax attorneys are. In one study, researchers sought to determine if the aggressiveness of a woman might track the rise and fall of her testosterone levels throughout the menstrual cycle, peaking at the phase when the egg is ripening and when androgen output is highest. Two dozen women were subjected to multiple rounds of a fast-paced game called the "Point Subtraction Aggression Paradigm," in which a person is given the option of either pressing a bar one hundred times to raise her score by one point, worth ten cents, or pressing another bar ten times to knock a point off the score of an unseen (and fictitious) opponent. The player is then provoked by the periodic subtraction of a point from her score, which is attributed to the hostility of her imaginary opponent. The researchers found no correlation between a woman's relative testosterone concentration and the chance that she would greet the provocation tit-for-tat, pouncing irately on her subtraction bar rather than staying focused on raising her own tally. What the researchers did find, however, is that women who reported suffering from premenstrual syndrome were generally more bellicose throughout the month, and more likely to press the "get that sucker" bar, than the women without PMS were — their testosterone levels notwithstanding.

Testosterone is lawless, unmanageable. In one study, the higher a female prisoner's testosterone level was, the more likely she was to have committed a violent crime like murder than a nonphysical offense like embezzlement. In another study, the correlation did not hold. Investigators have found that female inmates with high testosterone display more domineering and intimidating behavior than low-T prisoners do, and, conversely, that the low-Ts are "sneaky," "manipulative," and "conniving," acting like "snakes in the grass," according to the assessments of the prison staff. But let's bring some perspective to this study, a little aggressive extending of our cat's claws. The high-T women in the sample population were also younger, on average, than the lower-T women. Youth has its perquisites. When you're young, you have quite a bit of muscle tissue. You still think death is exciting and provisional. As a rule, people in prison have a history of bad habits — too much smoking, too much drinking, too many drugs in too many corrosive combinations — and so the older you are, the weaker, sadder, and more shopworn you are likely to be. Better to connive in the grass than to confront in the flesh.

Testosterone is oversold. We think too much of it. It is not what we need or want in attempting to understand the roots of a woman's aggressiveness. I don't know if testosterone is meaningful to a man's behavior, or if a man can feed off a testosterone high that comes in the wake of a personal victory and take the high and catapult from there to greater achievement. Men have a lot of testosterone, and they probably put some of it to behavioral use. The body does that: it takes what's available and plays with it, though the use will be deeply influenced, and often overruled, by experience, history, social constraints, and the placebo effect of a brain that wants to believe. But the fact that men have more testosterone than women and may use that hormone, unconsciously or even consciously, to exaggerate and prolong a response and sensation — just as some women can play the strings of their sexuality and orgasmic capacity when estrogen peaks at midcycle — doesn't much matter to the outcome. There are other ways to ascend to a throne of our specifications, or to grasp at liberation and transcendence. We must shake off the yoke of testosterone and the feeling that we can't keep up without it, that men have the monopoly on the designated hormone of libido and hormone of aggression and hormone of heroes. It is not that. There is nothing to fear from testosterone.

Let us think about some of our phylogenetic sisters and what they have to say about the roots of female aggressiveness. The spotted hyena is one of my favorite examples. The spotted hyena, *Crocuta crocuta*, is an African carnivore that some people say is ugly, but they are wrong. The spotted hyena doesn't look like any other mammal. Its rear legs are shorter than its front legs, the better to run long distances. Its neck is mammoth, a redwood trunk of muscle, which powers its jaw and allows it to pulverize every bit of its prey, meat, skin, bones. The spotted hyena mashes bone to powder; its scats look like chalk. The face of the spotted hyena is a blend of felid, canid, ursid, and pinniped. The hyena soul is pure fury. A lion cub is born helpless, blind and toothless. A hyena pup emerges with its eyes open and its canines fully erupted, and it strains toward the throats of its siblings. Often one newborn pup will kill another. After the initial bloodletting ceremony, the survivor settles down and, in the universal spirit of the young, turns playful.

What makes the spotted hyena truly unusual, though, is its sexual appearance and behavior. As I mentioned earlier, the external genitals of males and females look alike. Each seems to have a penis and scrotum. But where the male's genitals are indeed a penis and scrotum, the female's apparent phallus is a combination of her vagina and clitoris, while her faux scrotum is fused labia. The female does everything through her phallus — urinates, copulates, and gives birth. Her first birth, through that slender tunnel, is agonizing. She is ripped apart by the descending pup. Many female hyenas die during first parturition. For those who survive, subsequent births are much easier — a fact that even a human mother can understand. The first is the worst.

The spotted hyena's exceptional genitalia have misled naturalists from Aristotle through Ernest Hemingway, who thought the animals were hermaphrodites. Even after realizing that there were two sexes, per usual, scientists were stumped by the hyena's behavior and social organization. Males and females are roughly the same size, yet the females invariably rule. They are the dominant sex. An older, larger male will capitulate to a younger, smaller female. Where does female preeminence come from in this species? On first pass, the answer appears to be . . . testosterone. Male and female cubs are exposed in the uterus to extremely high doses of testosterone, which is why the females emerge from the womb with masculinized genitals. The source of the testosterone is the mother's unusual placenta. In most mammals the placenta is rich in aromatase, which converts maternal androgens to estrogens, and low in the enzymes that transform precursor molecules into testosterone. The ratio of conversion enzymes in the hyena placenta is just the opposite: high in the enzyme that turns precursor steroids into testosterone, low in the aromatase that would make testosterone into estrogen. Thus the bloodstream of a fetal hyena flows thickly with testosterone, and testosterone, more than estrogen, has access to the hyena brain, where it again may be converted to estrogen, but in any event it's there, so it could be what makes for hyena scald, and why a pup snaps its canines viciously the moment it rips its way free of its mother's phallic vagina. And as the testosterone levels in the pups' blood fall in the weeks after birth, the pups become more manageable and playful, all in keeping with the hormone's reputation.

Yet the ways and means of our dominant female elude us. The testosterone levels of hyena pups drop in both sexes postnatally, and still the juvenile female remains more aggressive than the male. In adolescence and adulthood, the testosterone levels of the male climb considerably above those of the female hyena, as happens with sexual maturity in a male mammal, and still the female hyena refuses to budge. If there is a zebra femur under dispute, she wins. She ladies it over him. It's become a habit. But wherefore this habit, this taste for preeminence? Testosterone is not the whole story. Scientists who study spotted hyenas have looked at hyena brains with an understandable expectation that the prenatal exposure of all hyena brains to high doses of testosterone would masculinize all brains and that they would find very few if any differences between the brains of male and female hyenas. In fact, the areas of the brain that are larger in males than they are in females of many mammalian species are also larger in male hyenas, including regions that control sexual behavior. Female hyenas have "feminine" brains, and still theirs is a jabberwockying, osteophagous matriarchy.

One interesting observation that has emerged from hyena studies is the importance of a steroid hormone called androstenedione (spoken in good, firm ladylike lilt, andro-steen-DIE-own). It is classified as an androgen — the same chemical category as testosterone — but it has never been viewed as an especially manly or exciting androgen. To the contrary. For years researchers dismissed androstenedione as a dull intermediary that signified nothing until its conversion into either testosterone or estrogen. It was assumed to be a product largely of the adrenal glands rather than of the gonads, and adrenal hormones have never seemed as sexy as ovarian or testicular hormones, because the adrenal glands of males and females just aren't different enough for those of us in thrall to sexual apartheid. Hyenas showed just what could be done with androstenedione. An adult female may not have as much testosterone as a male does, but she makes up for it with a profusion of androstenedione. The bulk of the hormone comes not from her adrenal glands but from her ovaries. For unknown reasons, a female hyena's gonads generate huge amounts of androstenedione. During pregnancy, the hormone is metamorphosed by the hyena's placenta into testosterone, which then infiltrates the bloodstream of the fetuses she bears. Yet even when the female isn't pregnant, her ovaries supply a steady current of androstenedione, and it could be this hormone that helps stoke her aggressive hauteur. Maybe, or maybe not. We don't know. What we can say is that androstenedione merits more attention than it has received heretofore. Feed, groom, and collar it, and you have a hormonal mascot of the furious female. In one study, aggressive teenage girls were found to have high levels of androstenedione in their blood. The researchers initially assumed that the findings were irrelevant, the result of the girls' being under stress and their adrenal glands' being hyperexcited, secreting excessive quantities of a number of adrenal steroids, including androstenedione. Now the researchers wonder if their subjects were really so stressed and adrenalized after all, or whether their ovaries were responsible for the androstenedione storm, with possible behavioral consequences or cadences — for instance, a brash, demonstrative, in-your-face style. Relative aggressiveness scores notwithstanding, women have much more androstenedione than testosterone in their blood plasma — four or five times the amount — and a greater percentage of that androstenedione is free — that is, unbound by blood proteins and so theoretically more accessible to the brain. A woman's androstenedione level equals that of a man. Here she is not muted. Here she has clay to play with.

I don't want to make too much of androstenedione, though. Testosterone isn't the only hormone that's overrated. All hormones are ultimately overrated, as well as poorly understood. But even though we know this mantra, we still get shackled by testosterone and need a new perspective to shake ourselves free. Hyenas have mighty jaws, ideal for cracking chains.

And don't forget our estrogen. That hormone too may catalyze a commanding, as opposed to a submissive or insular, spirit. In a study of female college students, Elizabeth Cashdan, of the University of Utah, found that women who had the highest blood titers of three hormones — estrogen, testosterone, and androstenedione — also had the most robust self-regard, tending to rate themselves as high on the peer pecking order. They also smiled infrequently, a rather unfortunate symptom of those who consider themselves important. Interestingly, the women with the most androstenedione were the likeliest to overstate their power, according themselves a much higher rank among their peers than their peers gave them when questioned. Androstenedione just may be the bitch's brew. But is it possible to have too much self-confidence? We think, oh, yes, certainly, and we think how pathetic are those who nurse delusions of grandeur; yet history has taught us that those who are wildly self-confident and repulsively self-promoting are the ones who end up not only obtaining power, out of sheer tenacity, but retaining it once seized. Can a woman have too much self-confidence? If an infusion of androstenedione could make a gal proud, I'd hold out my arm and help you find the vein.

And now I must reiterate the almighty fact that a hormone does not cause a behavior. We don't know what hormones do to the brain or the self, but we do know what they don't do, and they don't cause a behavior, the way turning a steering wheel will cause a car to veer left or right. Nor does the ability to behave in an aggressive or dominant fashion require a hormonal substrate. If hormones do anything, any little thing at all, they merely raise the likelihood that, other things being equal, a given behavior will occur. An estrogen peak at midcycle may make one's eros a shade brighter or tauter, nothing more. At the same time, it helps to remember the concept of biofeedback: behaviors and emotions can change the hormonal milieu and the connections between neurons. The brain is pliant. Synapses linking one brain cell to another arise and die and arise again.

For an example of neural and hormonal plasticity, few organisms can match *Haplochromis burtoni,* a cichlid fish found in Africa's Lake Tanganyika. Among this species, only one or a few males in a particular locus of the lake are dominant at any given time. The alpha males are brilliantly colored, nautical neon, while the females and the subordinate males are the shade of sand. Only alpha males have working gonads, and only alpha males can breed, and they are under constant threat — of predation, through the attractiveness of their scales, and of usurpation by other males. When a dominant male is forced from his position of power by another, stronger fish, his brain begins to change, quickly and dramatically. The neurons of his hypothalamic pulse generator, which control his gonads and his semen production, shrink down and disengage their synapses. Without the appropriate cues from the brain, his testes shrink as well, and along with the testes the fish loses his primary source of testosterone. He loses his bright coloration and turns dun. He stops devoting his energies to the aggressive patrolling of his territory and becomes low-key, remaining hidden as much as possible. He is not ashamed; he is sensible. He has no testes and no testosterone, so he can't make sperm and he can't mate; and if he can't mate, he might as well retreat until a new opportunity at dominance arises. If his usurper dies or is eaten, the dun fish will have a chance to compete once again for a colorful life, against other drab, agonadal aspirants, and if he wins the contest, his hypothalamus will inflate again, and so will his testes, his testosterone output, and his fecundity, and his scales will turn brilliant, iridescent, arrogant.

The cichlid fish exemplifies how a behavior, or, more precisely, an assessment of reality, can recondition the entire body, from brain to gonads. The behavior is the loss of a fight. The brain reacts first. Somehow the sense of loss induces neural retrenchment, the dwindling of the pulse generator of the hypothalamus. It is not a drop in testosterone that causes the cichlid's brain to change; his neural atrophy precedes any measurable drop in the hormone. Only subsequently, when his gonads have begun to shrivel, does the fish's hormonal content change significantly. Testosterone in this species is less an actor than a reactor. A drop in the hormone may facilitate or encourage cryptic behavior, but it doesn't *cause* it. In the wake of defeat, the intertwined systems of the brain, gonads, and hormones together effect the most sensible strategy for the cichlid to follow — wait and see and enjoy your vacation.

The moral of our small fish story is that the arrow does not point unidirectionally from hormone to behavior, or from neural circuitry A to outcome B. Instead the arrow is like a panel by M. C. Escher, the arrow turning to bird to human to interstitial space and back to arrow. The brain is never fixed. It is a moving target. Your hormones don't make you do anything. Habit and circumstance can have a more profound effect on behavior than anything hormonal. A person who is accustomed to deference will be obeyed into old age, whatever her or his estrogen or testosterone or androstenedione levels may be doing or failing to do. A tomcat that sprayed your house with territorial and reproductive resolve before being neutered may well continue spraying when his testicles are gone. He has learned how to do it, and though the impetus to start spraying may have come with a pubertal surge in testosterone, he no longer needs the hormone to know (as cats know, for they are infinitely wise) that a tomcat must leave a spackle of pong wherever he goes.

The brain is a moving target, and so too is our understanding of its circuitry of aggression. Aggression researchers categorize aggression. They speak of predatory offensive aggression, competitive aggression (also called intermale aggression), fear-induced aggression, irritable aggression, maternal-protective aggression, and sex-related aggression. But don't mistake the existence of categories for consensus. Researchers often disagree, irritably, on the definition of aggression, and on the validity of tests for aggression. A classic test is the intruder paradigm. If you put a mouse into a rat's cage and the rat attacks the mouse and kills it in, say, three minutes, and another rat takes thirty minutes before it kills the mouse, you could conclude that Rat the First is far more aggressive than Rat the Second. But many variables can affect a rat's propensity to strike, including its intelligence, degree of hunger, and mood, not to mention the craftiness and strength of the mouse with which it is presented. In any event, the assay is artificial: in nature, rats and mice almost never interact, and no mouse is stupid enough to enter a rat's quarters voluntarily.

Just as there is no single "hormone of aggression," so there is no one seat of aggression in the brain, no discrete place that controls or participates in aggressive feelings or actions. A recent text on neuropsychiatry by Jeffrey L. Saver and his colleagues links thirty-eight different parts of the brain to various behaviors that can be called aggressive. If the cortical tissue around a cat's hypothalamus is first stripped away and a rear portion of the hypothalamus is stimulated with an electric current, the cat will automatically assume the familiar posture of cat rage: hissing, raising its fur, extending its claws, and dilating its pupils. Thus the surrounding cortex is assumed to inhibit aggression, the hypothalamus to foster it, at least in the cat. If you excise a rhesus monkey's amygdala, usually the monkey will become tame and placid. But not always: monkeys that were submissive before the removal of their amygdala often become aggressive afterward. The amygdala is thought to play a role in learning and memory. So maybe what we are seeing in this experiment is that without it, the aggressive monkeys forget to be aggressive and the meek monkeys forget to be good.

Human patients suffering from a variety of head injuries and brain diseases have displayed aggressive, impulsive, violent behaviors, but never neatly, never in a sufficiently localized manner to allow scientists to say, Here is the primary pathway of irritable aggression, or maternal aggression. David Bear, a psychiatrist, tells the story of Rebecca, who as a ten-year-old girl lost consciousness after a head injury. Four years later, she began experiencing seizures, blackouts, and episodes of déjà vu. She turned irritable and hypergraphic, writing lengthy poems and philosophic musings. Electroencephalograms revealed abnormal spiking of her right temporal lobe. At age fifteen she started traveling long distances from home, speaking in a harsh, masculine voice, and becoming violent, often without being aware of her rages. On one occasion she woke up on a grassy knoll with a bloody stick in her hand, next to the unconscious body of a male stranger. Another time, during a therapy session, she abruptly attacked her doctor, holding a knife to her throat for three hours. Later, when Rebecca realized what she had done, she felt such profound remorse that she gave the psychiatrist a vial of her own blood in recompense. In the wake of her temporal-lobe injury, Rebecca turned aggressive, yes, but at the same time her emotional tone deepened; she felt driven to write, to wander, to find control, to lose control. She became a small, disorganized echo of Hildegarde von Bingen, the great twelfth-century nun, composer, poet, and visionary, who herself had migrainous auras and hallucinations.

When the brain becomes unfamiliar to itself, it often descends into a more primitive, less restrained posture, like a hissing, piloerecting cat. A woman who had her anterior commissure transected in an effort to control her epileptic seizures had difficulty afterward performing her daily ablutions or getting dressed, because her left and right arms would start physically abusing each other. The anterior commissure is a bundle of nerve fibers that allows the two hemispheres of the brain to communicate. Without the cord, each hemisphere was left adrift and fearful, seeing enemies everywhere, including in the arm controlled by the opposite, estranged side of the brain. But is this an expression of the aggressive brain or of the defensive brain? Or of involuted terror, the injured bird flapping its wings desperately, seeking to return to the homeostasis of flight?

The brain is said to be female by default and to be masculinized through exposure to androgens, and it is said that androgens stimulate or mediate or at least sympathize with aggressive behavior. Yet by some neural models, aggression itself is a kind of default humor, the 4/4 tempo to which the brain returns harmoniously; and so the human brain is wrapped with many layers of inhibitory duct tape to repress it and make it less aggressive. In 1848, Phineas Gage, a twenty-five-year-old foreman for a railroad company, suffered a spectacular injury. A metal tamping rod exploded from beneath his hands and shot up through his left eye and out through the top of his skull. His eye was destroyed, but otherwise he seemed surprisingly fine. He was able to talk. He was able to walk with the help of his men, who took him to a nearby tavern. Gage soon recovered from the accident, but he never recovered the Phineas that was expected of him. He became a different man — to others, if not to himself. Before, he had been intelligent, hardworking, abstemious, churchgoing. Afterward, he was intelligent, impulsive, and profane. He cursed at his superiors. He cursed people who tried to keep him from fulfilling his fleeting desires. He cursed himself for abandoning plans to live his fantasies. He couldn't keep a job or a promise. "He was no longer Gage," John Harlow, his doctor, wrote. Using brain imaging technology and computerized renderings of Gage's skull, scientists recently have reconstructed his brain injury, pinpointing the left orbitomedial frontal lobe as the site of greatest damage. They have suggested that herein lies a locus of impulse control — the brain's temperate zone, as it were, or its moral center, as the scientists have suggested. But there are other loci of restraint, in other lobes. Many mental illnesses manifest themselves as derangements of control, a de-domestication of the mind. Schizophrenia, manic-depression, posttraumatic stress disorder, phobias — in all cases, patients can lash out, bark, yodel, attack, catabolize. My ancestor Silas Angier fought in the Revolutionary War with a regiment from New Hampshire. Like his fellow New Englander Phineas Gage, he was hardworking, ambitious, and self-righteous, a prominent citizen in the obscure town of Fitzwilliam. Toward the end of the eighteenth century, though, Silas had a bloody encounter with a group of Indians and received a blow to the head. He was never the same again. He turned moody and surly. He stopped caring about his reputation. He stopped going to church. He became agoraphobic. Silas died in October of 1808, three days shy of turning seventy-one, in poverty.

We don't understand the endocrinology of aggression, or the anatomy of aggression, or the neurochemistry of aggression. Recently the neurotransmitter serotonin has risen to the fore of aggression research. You think of serotonin and you probably think of Prozac, Zoloft, and the other semihappy pills that have been among the most financially successful drugs of all time. The simple model posits that being "low" in serotonin puts you at risk of aggressive, impulsive, ugly behavior. Mihaly Arató, of McMaster University, has called serotonin the "civilizing" neurotransmitter. The same model also posits that being "low" in serotonin puts you at risk of depression. Depression is often considered a woman's disease, because women suffer from it at two to three times the rate of men (although men are catching up, according to recent international surveys). Aggression and depression sound like two different, even polarized phenomena, but they're not. Depression is aggression turned inward, directed against the self, or the imagined, threatening self. A seriously depressed person may look anesthetized to an observer, but the depressed person is never anesthetized to herself. She may wish to be, and she may seek to be with chemical aid, but she cannot truly placate her sneering, jabbering, nested aggressor. William Styron described the violence of depression, calling it the true "brainstorm" and a "gray drizzle of unrelenting horror," beneath which the sufferer becomes an old, mad, powerless King Lear. Thus, to compare aggression and depression is a logical step, and if serotonin is implicated in both, that too sounds logical.

But we are far from understanding what or how or where serotonin comes into the landscape of the aggressor or the ingressor. Like steroid hormones, serotonin is an ancient molecule. Lobsters have it, and they respond to it behaviorally, though not in the way we'd think if we simply equate "low" serotonin with aggression. An injection of serotonin will cause a lobster to assume a fighting stance, muscles extended, claws open. In mammals, serotonin's role is less stereotyped and more species-specific. Domesticated silver foxes that tolerate human contact have higher concentrations of serotonin in their midbrain and hypothalamus than silver foxes that bite and snarl at their keepers do. Rhesus monkeys with high serotonin blood counts tend to be socially dominant, while those with very low serotonin levels tend to be aggressive, socially deviant — the sort of monkeys you don't want in your barrel. For other species of monkey, though, those serotonin correlations don't hold.

In people, serotonin's influence is even more confusing. The brains of successful suicide victims are in some cases low in serotonin and in other cases not. Scientists have looked at the metabolites of serotonin in the cerebrospinal fluid of violent criminals with similarly inconsistent results. As a group, pyromaniacs and those who have committed impulsive manslaughter show reduced levels of serotonin metabolites, but rapists and wife beaters do not. Nor have studies of depressed patients been able to detect a decrement in serotonin metabolism, as much as we might want this as blood proof of depression's organic origins.

Whatever is going on with serotonin, it is polyphony. There are at least sixteen types of serotonin receptors, distinct proteins capable of responding in distinct ways to serotonin. To what end, though? We don't know. Do neurons like the taste of serotonin? Do they covet it? We don't know. The drugs called serotonin reuptake inhibitors, of which Prozac and Zoloft are examples, appear to work by discouraging the absorption of serotonin by neurons, thus keeping it in the synaptic cleft longer and allowing it to continue working. So a lot of ambient serotonin is "good." At the same time, recent genetic studies of people who score high on neuroticism ratings give us a different story of serotonin's "goodness." Neurotics supposedly have inefficient serotonin transporter genes, which means, in essence, that their transporters behave like the reuptake inhibitor drugs and keep serotonin in the synaptic cleft comparatively longer, making it available for neurons. These are neurotics, mind you — antsy, disgruntled, depressive characters who don't strike us as making particularly good use of their bioavailable serotonin. They're acting rather like lobsters on a serotonin high, striking defense poses and snapping their claws.

In short, we don't know how serotonin plays into aggression or depression or, for that matter, why drugs like Prozac often are accompanied by side effects such as a craving for carbohydrates and an indifference to sex. If serotonin is the "civilizing" neurotransmitter, maybe too much of it can be as suffocating as too little, making you feel as though you're sitting in a French drawing room, surrounded by Fragonard murals, a powdered wig on your head.

We don't understand the endocrinology, the neuroanatomy, or the biochemistry of aggression. We know it when we feel it, though, and sometimes it feels nasty, and sometimes it feels quite good.

15

SPIKING THE PUNCH
IN DEFENSE OF FEMALE AGGRESSION

THIS STUDY has been done many times. If you take a group of babies or young toddlers and dress them in nondescript, non-sex-specific clothes — yellow is always a good color! — and make sure that their haircuts don't give them away, and if you put them in a room with a lot of adults watching, the adults will not be able to sex the children accurately. The adults will try, based on the behaviors of each child, but they will be right no more often than they would be if they flipped a coin. This has been shown again and again, but still we don't believe it. We think we can tell a boy or a girl by the child's behavior, specifically by its level of aggressiveness. If you show a person a videotape of a crying baby and tell her the baby is a boy, the observer will describe the baby as looking angry; if you tell the person the baby is a girl, she will say the child is scared or miserable.

I am at a party with my daughter, who is sixteen months old. A boy who is almost eighteen months comes into the room and takes a toy away from my daughter. I say something humorous to her about how she's got to watch out for those older kids, they'll always try to push you around. And the boy's mother says, It's also because he's a boy. That's what happens at this age, she says. The boys become very boyish. A little while later, a girl who is almost eighteen months old takes my daughter's cup of milk away from her. The mother of the other girl doesn't say, It's because she's a girl, she's becoming girlish. Of course she doesn't say that; it would make no sense, would it? An older girl taking a cup away from a younger girl has nothing to do with the girlness of either party. But taking the toy away is viewed as inherent to the older boy's boyness.

I felt very aggressive about the whole thing; alas, not being a toddler,

I couldn't go and kick anybody in the kneecap. Which is the sort of thing that toddlers do, whatever their sex. They kick, they hit, they scream, they throw objects around, they act like pills past their expiration date. And we adults put up with it, and we subscribe to the myth of the helpless, innocent child, and it's a good thing we do and that children are cute, because otherwise we might well see the truth: that our children are born with astonishing powers, and with brains that seem by default to counsel aggression.

"Young children are like animals," says Kaj Björkqvist, of Turku Akademi University in Finland. "Before they have language, they have their bodies. And through their bodies they can be aggressive, and so that is what they do, that is how they are. They are physically aggressive — boys, girls, all of them." Björkqvist studies female aggression. He has done cross-cultural comparisons of children in Europe, North America, the Middle East, and Asia. Everywhere he has found that young children are physically aggressive, and that before the age of three, there are no significant differences between girl aggression and boy aggression.

We grow into our sex-specific aggressions. We own the code of aggression from birth, and we perfect its idiom through experience and experimentation. Now I must do something artificial and divide aggression into two basic categories, "bad" aggression and "good" aggression. Earlier I said that context determines whether we see a behavior as good aggression or bad aggression and that even Lady Macbeth looks swell in Nordic gear. But for the sake of examining how female aggression evolves and what its multitudinous sources and expressions may be, it helps to do as researchers do and distinguish between the malign and the resolute. Henri Parens, a child psychiatrist at the Medical College of Pennsylvania, calls the two phyla of aggression "hostile aggression," which is "generated by excessive unpleasure and motivates fantasies and acts of anger, hostility and hate," and "nondestructive aggression," which is "inborn and fuels assertive and goal achieving behaviors." In the infant and toddler, the two aggressions are one, and they are of the reactive nervous system — anger, hate, assertiveness, whatever it takes, or whatever can be done, to maintain momentum and attract the attention of the parent, the intermediary between self and no self.

With the awakening of the mind, the child learns to channel aggressive impulses and to calculate and compare actions and responses.

Children begin to learn the meaning of hurting another. A baby kicks you in the mouth and doesn't know she hurts you. By the age of two or three, a girl knows she can hurt other beings, and hurt them badly, and with that knowledge the distinctions between malign and resolute aggression become meaningful. The mainstream model posits that aggression is a public health crisis. Mainstream studies of female aggression focus on hostile aggression, the aggression aimed to hurt, with foreknowledge, with malice.

When the mind comes into its own and the child starts speaking fluently, purposefully, adults become less tolerant of physical aggression. Today, in most cultures, acceptance of physical aggression declines as the child gets older; by the time a person reaches puberty, the tendency to use physical force to wrest a desired object or behavior from another is considered frankly pathological. This is true for both sexes, but particularly for girls. Physical aggression is discouraged in girls in manifold and aggressive ways. Not only are they instructed against offensive fighting; they are rarely instructed in defensive fighting. Girls don't learn how to throw a punch. Humor is another form of aggression, and until recently humor has been used to squelch the very notion of a warrior female. Just the thought of a girl-fight, and people snicker and rub their hands with glee. Cat fight! Scratching, screeching, pulling hair, and falling on butt with skirt hiked in the air! Happily, the smirky parody of girl-fights has gotten a bit paunchy and dated of late, and instead we've been treated to images of GI Janes and bodiced Xenas wielding swords and Klingon women with brickbat fists, though whether the mass media's revisionist fighting female has been driven by attitudinal change or by the need to jolt a bored and distracted audience is unclear.

Whatever the media moment may be, girls still do not often engage in physical fights. The older children get, the less physically aggressive they become — though not always, and not everywhere — but the dropoff rate for the use of physical aggression in girls is much sharper than it is for boys. At least in the developed West, by the time girls and boys are in third grade, boys are about three times as likely as girls to kick or strike at somebody who makes them mad. What then do girls do with that aggressiveness, which in the bliss of preverbalism could speak through hands and feet? It does not go away. It finds a new voice. It finds words.

Girls learn to talk hornet talk. Mastering curse words and barbed insults is an essential task of childhood. Girls also learn to use their faces as weapons. Expressions like sticking out your tongue or rolling your eyes or curling your lip all seem funny to adults, but studies show that they aren't funny to children, and that they can be effective in conveying anger and dislike or in ostracizing an undesirable. Aggression researchers initially thought that girls had the edge over boys in verbal aggression and that they were more likely than boys to belittle their peers with words and facial flexions, but a series of Finnish studies of eight- and eleven-year-olds suggested otherwise. The researchers sought to determine how children responded when they were angry. They asked the children to describe themselves and their reactions to being roused to rage; they asked teachers and parents to describe how the children reacted in conflict; and they asked children to talk about each other, to rate each other's rileability and behaviors in a squall. The scientists found that boys and girls were equally likely to use verbal aggression against their cohorts, to call them nasty names to their faces, to yell, to mock, to try to make the despised ones look stupid. And so boys kick and fight more than girls do, and the sexes argue and chide in equal amounts. We might then conclude, So boys *are* more aggressive, for they shout with their mouths and on occasion with their bodies, while the girls keep their fists to themselves.

There are other ways in which rage emerges among girls, though, ways that are roughly girl-specific. A girl who is angry often responds by stalking off, turning away, snubbing the offender, pretending she doesn't exist. She withdraws, visibly so, aggressively so. You can almost hear the thwapping of her sulk. Among eleven-year-olds, girls are three times more likely than boys to express their anger in the form of a flamboyant snub. In addition, girls at this age, more than boys, engage in a style of aggression called indirect aggression.

I'll admit up front that I dislike this form of aggression, and that to mention it is to reinforce clichés about female treachery and female conniving. Yet it is an aggression that we gals know, because we grew up as girls and we saw it and struggled against it and hated it and did it ourselves. Indirect aggression is anonymous aggression. It is backbiting, gossiping, spreading vicious rumors. It is seeking to rally others against the despised but then denying the plot when confronted. The use of indirect aggression increases over time, not just because girls don't generally use their fists to make their point, but because the effectiveness of indirect aggression is tied to the fluency of a person's social intelligence; the more sophisticated the person, the cleverer her use of the dorsal blade. In this sense, then, a girl's supposed head start over boys in verbal fluency may give her an edge in applying an indirect form of aggression. But the advantage, such as it is, doesn't last, for males catch up, and by the time we reach adulthood we have all become political animals, and men and women are, according to a number of studies, equally likely to express their aggression covertly. Despite rumors to the contrary, systematic eavesdroppings have revealed that men and women gossip an equal amount about their friends, families, colleagues, and celebrities. Adults of both sexes go to great lengths to express their antipathy toward one another indirectly, in ways that mask their hostile intent while still getting the jab done. For example, a person might repeatedly interrupt an opponent during an office meeting, or criticize the antagonist's work, rather than attacking his or her character — even though the source of the aggressor's ire has nothing to do with the quality of the opponent's performance.

Indirect aggression is not pretty, nor is it much admired. To the contrary, it is universally condemned. When children and adults are asked to describe their feelings about the various methods of expressing anger, backstabbing behavior ranks at the bottom, below a good swift kick to the crotch. Yet there it is, with us, among us, not exclusively female by any means, but a recognizable hazard of girlhood. Part of the blame lies with the myth of the goo-girl, for the more girls are counseled against direct forms of aggression and the more geniality of temperament is prized, the greater is the likelihood that the tart girls will resort to hidden machinations to get what they want. In cultures where girls are allowed to be girls, to speak up and out, they are in fact more verbally, directly aggressive and less indirectly aggressive than in cultures where girls and women are expected to be demure. In Poland, for example, a good smart mouth is considered a female asset, and girls there rag each other and pull no punches and report feeling relatively little threat of intragroup skullduggery. Among female Zapotec Indians in Mexico, who are exceedingly subordinate to men, indirect aggression prevails. Among the Vanatinai of Papua New Guinea, one of the most egalitarian and least stratified societies known to anthropologists, women speak and move as freely as they please, and they sometimes use their fists and feet to demonstrate their wrath, and there is no evidence of a feminine edge in covert operations.

Another reason that girls may resort to indirect aggression is that they feel such extraordinary aggression toward their friends — lashing, tumbling, ever-replenishing aggression. Girl friendships are fierce and dangerous. The expression "I'll be your best friend" is not exclusively a girl phrase, but girls use it a lot. They know how powerful the words are, how significant the offer is. Girls who become good friends feel a compulsion to define the friendship, to stamp it and name it, and they are inclined to rank a close friend as a best friend, with the result that they often have many best friends. They think about their friends on a daily basis and try to figure out where a particular friend fits that day in their cosmology of friendships. Is the girl her best friend today, or a provisional best friend, pending the resolution of a minor technicality, a small bit of friction encountered the day before? The girl may want to view a particular girl as her best friend, but she worries how her previous best friend will take it — as a betrayal or as a potential benefit, a bringing in of a new source of strength to the pair. Girls fall in love with each other and feel an intimacy for each other that is hard for them to describe or understand.

When girls are in groups, they form coalitions of best friends, two against two, or two in edgy harmony with two. A girl in a group of girls who doesn't feel that she has a specific ally feels at risk, threatened, frightened. If a girl who is already incorporated into the group decides to take on a newcomer, to sponsor her, the resident girl takes on a weighty responsibility, for the newcomer will view her as (for the moment) her best friend, her only friend, the guardian of her oxygen mask.

When girls have a falling-out, they fall like Alice down the tunnel, convinced that it will never end, that they will never be friends again. The Finnish studies of aggression among girls found that girls hold grudges against each other much longer than boys do. "Girls tend to form dyadic relationships, with very deep psychological expectations from their best friends," Björkqvist said. "Because their expectations are high, they feel deeply betrayed when the friendship falls apart. They become as antagonistic afterwards as they had been bonded before." If a girl feels betrayed by a friend, she will try to think of ways to get revenge in kind, to truly hurt her friend, as she has been hurt. Fighting physically is an unsatisfactory form of punishing the terrible traitor. It is over too quickly. To express anger might work if the betrayer accepts the anger and responds to it with respect. But if she doesn't acknowledge her friend's anger or sense of betrayal, if she refuses to apologize or admit to any wrongdoing, or if she goes further, walking away or mocking or snubbing her friend, at that point a girl may aim to hurt with the most piercing and persistent tools for the job, the psychological tools of indirect, vengeful aggression, with the object of destroying the girl's position, her peace of mind, her right to be. Indirect aggression is akin to a voodoo hex, an anonymous but obsessive act in which the antagonist's soul, more than her body, must be got at, must be penetrated, must be nullified.

The intensities of childhood friendships, dyads, coalitions, and jihads subside with age, but sometimes just barely. Women remain, through much of their lives, unsettled about other women. We feel drawn and repelled, desirous of a connection and at the same time aggressive toward those who register on our radar screen. We want undying, infinite friendship, we want a Thelma, we want a Louise; but there can be no second act to *Thelma and Louise,* because to sustain that undying friendship required the women to die. When they proved themselves willing to forsake all else for the sake of each other, they were in a quandary. What could they do for each other, after all? There were just two of them, and there was a world arrayed against them, a world of men; and though they were stronger together in one sense, the sense of themselves, than they had been individually, they were also weakened in their unimpeachable dyad. They couldn't provide each other with everything — with money, home, security, physical gratification — but as great friends they were positioned, deliberately, heavy-handedly so, as a menace to the world of men, the workaday, home-a-day world. And because the world of men *is* the world, the women had nowhere to go but into the Grand Canyon, the grandest vagina on earth. Great female friendships often are presented as threats to the prevailing order, and to the females themselves. In the gorgeous movie *Heavenly Creatures,* Pauline and Juliet are great friends, inseparable fifteen-year-old girls, united in their mutual, isolating imaginative genius. They have to kill the mother of one of them to keep their friendship alive. Sisters united are tainted black and bloody. Goneril and Regan were united, and Machiavellian, and set in opposition to the patriarch Lear, and they were unnatural in their unity, with their pestilent and covert aggression. The stepsisters of Cinderella sought with unity of purpose to sabotage the most natural of dyads, Cinderella and the prince, and in their effort to prevail they were willing to shed blood and foot sections, to trim back their oversized feet to fit the glass slipper.

Women bond with other women, and yet our strongest aggressions and our most frightening hostilities may be directed against other women. We hear about the war between the sexes, but surprisingly few of our aggressive impulses are aimed against men, the putative adversaries in that war. We don't consider men our competitors, even now, in the market free-for-all, when they often are. It is so much easier to feel competitive with another woman, to feel our nerves twitch with anxiety and hyperattentiveness when another woman enters our visual field. We dress women in fairy white, we dress them in mafia black. We want them around us. We want to be alone among men.

Men say they envy women the depth of their friendships, their ability to emote with and engage each other. Men are also stunned when they see the ferocity of a failed friendship between women, the staggering thickness of the anger and bile. "Picking a fight can actually be a way for men to relate to one another, check each other out, and take a first step toward friendship," Frans de Waal wrote in *Good Natured*. "This bonding function is alien to most women, who see confrontation as causing rifts." It's not because we are nice and want to make nicer. Women know, from their experience and from their harrowing girlhood, that rifts often are hard to heal, and can last, and can consume them.

The fierceness of female friendships and the unease with which we regard other women are in my view related phenomena, and are the legacy of dissonance between our ancient primate and our neohominid selves and of our inherent strategic plasticity, the desire to keep all options open. Other females are a potential source of strength, and other females can destroy us. Or flip it around, as the English salonist Elizabeth Holland did, when she wrote at the turn of the nineteenth century, "As nobody can do more mischief to a woman than a woman, so perhaps one might reverse the maxim and say nobody can do more good."

In our primal primate brain, the world is gynocentric. The great majority of primate species live in social groups, and the core of those groups is female. The overwhelming rule of thumb is that females stay in their natal homes throughout their lives and males disperse at adolescence, so as to prevent inbreeding. This is true for macaques, howler monkeys, lemurs, patas monkeys, vervet monkeys, capuchins, squirrel monkeys, most baboons, and on and on. Outside males petition a group to gain entry, and the females permit them or forbid them citizenship. Females do not want a surplus of males around them, because males as a rule are underemployed, having little to do with care of the offspring, and they are easily bored and prone to picking fights with each other. Moreover, males often harass females. It's a common reproductive strategy. They want to mate with females and prevent them from consorting with other males, and so they harangue fertile females, roughing them up, pushing them around, trying in any way possible to circumscribe their activity. Females get tired of that perpetual harassment, and the best way to prevent the problem is to limit the number of resident males in the first place. Among rhesus macaques, for example, the group ratio of adult females to adult males is about six to one; among howler monkeys, there may be as many as ten females for every resident male. Bachelor monkeys prowl around the periphery, seeking vacancies, opportunities, and signs of local disarray.

Female primates are used to being surrounded by females, then, and they count on females to keep their world familiar and bearable. In species where females remain in their birth group, they depend on their close female kin to protect them from the aggressiveness of other females, who may be either unrelated or more distantly related. In a given group, the various members of the matrilines compete with one another and squabble over food, sexual behavior, or the excessive interest that females take in one another's young. The cohabiting females have their hierarchies, and when coalitions of female kin are rallied to a cause, the cause is generally to prove a point to the females of a vying matriline.

Even so, the disparate matrilineal strands will join in common cause to thwart the aggressiveness of males. "In species in which females normally remain in their natal groups, female-female coalitions typically involve close kin and are usually directed against females and juveniles from other matrilines," the primatologist Barbara Smuts has written. "In striking contrast, when the target is an adult male, females often form coalitions with females to whom they are not closely related. Such coalitions can mobilize very quickly in response to male aggression, since any females nearby can be recruited." In pigtailed macaques, patas monkeys, chacma baboons, olive baboons, blue monkeys, vervet monkeys, and again on and on, female alliances form with the dark speed of a thundercloud. Females gang up on males when they attack, herd, or frighten females. Females turn on a male who solicits sex from an obviously unwilling female. Swiftest of all are the unions that form when a male threatens or appears to threaten an infant.

The benefits of female solidarity are significant enough that in some cases when it is the young female who leaves her birthplace and must seek acceptance elsewhere, females aggressively, irrepressibly petition the friendship of the females in their newly adopted residence. This is true for cottontop tamarins, for example, among whom new female immigrants devote themselves tirelessly to the care of the resident females' young. And it is famously, brazenly true for bonobos, the Venusian apes. Females disperse at adolescence and must make their way in the world without the support of their mothers, sisters, and aunts. They must ingratiate themselves with a group of unrelated, mostly female apes. They ingratiate themselves with grooming and with sex. They pet the fur of resident females and pick out fleas. They rub their prominent genitals against the presiding genitals. If the local females reciprocate, the solicitor can stay. If they reject her, she must go elsewhere and find other pelts to pick and other pelvises to rub. In their sexually reinforced bondage, female bonobos gain an extraordinary degree of strength. They recapitulate the power of natality, of living within the matriline, and perhaps outdo it. The threat of infanticide by marauding males is a source of relentless anxiety to the females of many species — lions, langurs, rodents, seals, common chimpanzees. Nobody has ever seen a case of male infanticide among bonobos. The bonobo sisterhood is an artifice, constructed among nonrelatives without the mortar of genetic kinship and thus in need of perpetual behavioral reinforcement — the making nice, the making lewd, proving and proving again that we're all friends, we're all in this together. Vigilance becomes habit, and vigilance keeps the male fangs at bay.

Not all female primates are beholden to other females. Among common chimpanzees, females spend much of the day out on their own, scrounging for food, accompanied only by their dependent young. They don't forage with other adult females the way most monkeys do, and the way bonobos do. Chimpanzee dispersion patterns are variable. If a female is the daughter of a powerful female, she can stay in her natal group and derive the benefits of living near her kin. If she is the daughter of a low-status female, she generally must leave at puberty and find her way into another group, a band of strangers, and she must do so without the benefit of bonobo bonding rituals. When a female chimpanzee immigrates into a new group, she works hard to establish her reputation. She challenges resident females by grunting and hee-hawing at them, flapping her arms, making aggressive faces, or, on occasion, striking at them, pushing them, pinching. The period of settling in is brief, and after a few weeks the new female has her slot, her standing in the hierarchy, and it doesn't change much over time. Her relationship with other females is attenuated. They may come to her aid if she's attacked by a male, or they may not; female chimpanzees are under much greater threat of male coercion and harassment than many female primates are. But her nonkin female peers won't bother her either, and that's a comfort. And if she was able to prove herself a Viking maiden at the outset and was able to rise to a position of high status in her adopted gynocracy, her daughters will be allowed to stay in the troop, and she'll have launched a matriline, and that, at least, will keep her heritage strong.

We humans have within us a polychromatic phylogeny, a series of possible pasts. In the distant background are creatures like the Old World monkeys, for whom a gynocentric society of competitive but coexisting matrilines is the norm. Closer to the fore is the anthropoid past. Genetically, we are equidistant to bonobos and chimpanzees, and they are both our nearest living kin. We diverged from the bonobo-chimpanzee line about six million years ago, and we don't know if the common ancestor of the three of us great apes was more bonobo or more chimpanzee in its style and social structure. Among chimpanzees, males unequivocally dominate females. Among bonobos, the fabricated sisterhood gives females the edge over males. Among chimpanzees, males wage war against other troops of chimpanzees, sometimes to the point of committing genocide. Among bonobos, warfare is quite rare, although not unheard of. Chimpanzees have a keen appetite for monkey flesh; bonobos eat little meat. On the face of it, then, chimpanzees sound more hominid than bonobos do, yet the fossil evidence suggests that bonobos rather than chimpanzees are most like the primogenitor species from which the three of us sprang. In other words, bonobos may be a more ancestral species, while chimpanzees — and we — are the derived apes. Many evolutionary and anthropological reconstructions of protohuman societies have relied extensively on analogies between us and chimpanzees, as though we evolved from a chimpanzee-like ancestor. This assumption is open to question. In our restless lunges at metaphor, it is arbitrary to choose chimpanzees and ignore bonobos. The bonobo phylogeny is a legitimate sister archive, worth rifling through to collate and comprehend our own. "Our lineage," said Frans de Waal, who has written about bonobos, "is more flexible than we thought."

In the annals of our primate pasts, females are drawn to other females for strength. The females may be related or they may not be, and they may have to prove themselves or they may have been born to greatness, but the recurring theme is one of coalition and desire, of an aggressive need for female alliance. Here is the possible cradle of the fantasy best friend, and the reason that we care so much about girls and our position in the peerage, and that our female friendships feel like life and death as we steer our rickety little canoe through the breakers of childhood.

Female primates are not goo-girls, and they fight, and they're hierarchical and greedy, and they can be murderous toward each other. Nevertheless, the primate norm is a chronicle of female interdependence, of (dare I dip into archaisms?) female solidarity; and here is where we differ from most of our primate cousins. The question is, why? What does it mean, and does it matter? In the majority of human cultures today, and historically and presumably prehistorically as well, women do not live and have not lived in anything like a gynocracy. Nor do they inevitably rally to the cause of women's rights or think it is in their best interests to do so, with the result that, as the historian Gerda Lerner has noted, women are "ignorant of their history" and have had to "reinvent the wheel over and over again," the wheel being "the awareness of women that they belong to a subordinate group; that they have suffered wrongs as a group; that their condition of subordination is not natural, but is societally determined; that they must join with other women to remedy these wrongs; and finally, that they must and can provide an alternate vision of societal organization in which women as well as men will enjoy autonomy and self-determination." The subordination of women is not natural, not at all, and it is different in kind from anything seen in nature among other primates, who, as we've seen, join with other females on a habitual basis as well as spat with other females on a habitual basis, the predominant theme being barter and mutual, aggressively animated respect, gal to gal.

Evolutionary theorists such as Barbara Smuts and Patricia Adair Gowaty lately have emphasized the great efforts that the males of many species go to as they strive to control and monopolize female sexuality, to call it their own. The theorists have described the toll that the diverse forms of male coercion and male harassment take on females. Male chimpanzees slap, kick, and bite to force females to obey them, to follow them if they're going somewhere. If they see a female consort socializing with another male, they attack the female rather than the male. Male dolphins swim in violent synchronous patterns, slapping their flippers on the water and breaching the surface in unison, all to intimidate and corral fertile females for themselves. A female olive baboon can expect to be severely wounded by a male at least once a year — her flesh gouged, a piece of ear bitten off. Males and females of many species, particularly primates, may also get along, form friendships, and be affectionate and gentle with one another over a lifetime.

Aggression, placation, no matter: male efforts to manhandle female sexuality are at best limited. Whatever the female suffers at the hand of a male, or whatever she doesn't suffer, she is still, in a basic sense, an independent operator. That is, she feeds herself. She is not fed. She is not supported. She is on her own. A male may try to control her movements and her sexuality, but he can go only so far. Really, how much can he restrain her or manipulate her when she, in the end, will be out there foraging for her lunch, and will be the exclusive parent for her young, and will not need him for her daily survival? A male chimpanzee may be dominant over a female in certain one-on-one encounters, and he may be able to chase her away from the best cache of fruit if the two of them are within visual and olfactory range of each other. Nonetheless, the female can and does move on, to find another source of food. A male chimpanzee may punish a female with kicks and grunts when he finds her pulling ticks from a lesser male's coat. He may want to dictate the terms of her sexuality, and why not? It is in his reproductive interest to try to do so. He is not being mean for meanness's sake. He wants to procreate, and he's not a yeast cell — he can't just divide in two. He needs female chimpanzees if his genetic legacy is to survive, and if he has to beat them and squawk at them as he strives to get his way, he'll beat and squawk. Yet females are unfazed and unpersuaded. A recent DNA study of a group of chimpanzees in the Gombe, where Jane Goodall does her research, showed, to the astonishment of primatologists, that more than half the offspring in the clan had been fathered by males other than the males in residence. Primatologists did not expect to see such evidence of female restlessness. Female chimpanzees are hardly chaste, and when they are in estrus they are sexually quite active, but it was thought that they restricted their activities to the males within the group. They did not. Somehow, despite the vigilance of the local males and their regular use of intimidation, scowling, grunting, and slapping upside the head, the females had sauntered off and mated with outsiders. Who the outsiders were remains unknown. Presumably the females had their reasons for leaving home base and seeking foreign affairs. And when they returned, their lives were the same — the daily grind, the daily foraging, the nursing of the young.

Only among humans have males succeeded in stepping between a woman and a meal, in wresting control of the resources that she needs to feed herself and her children. Only among humans is the idea ever floated that a male *should* support a female, and that the female is in fact incapable of supporting herself and her offspring, and that it is a perfectly reasonable act of quid pro quo to expect a man to feed his family and a woman to be unerringly faithful, to give the man paternity assurance and to make his investment worthwhile. "I am convinced that male control over productive resources needed by women to reproduce lies at the heart of the transformation from male-dominated malephilopatric primate societies to full-fledged patriarchy," Sarah Blaffer Hrdy has written.

We don't know when this transformation took place, when women found themselves butting up against a male breastplate every time they tried to locate food or a place to curl up and slumber. By the standard model of human evolution, the long dependency of children necessitated increased paternal investment in a child's welfare, and women wanted, needed, demanded male help in rearing children; males could provide that help by hunting and bringing home meat, which is rich in calories and appeals to the hominid tongue so smartly. By this scenario, the origins of marriage, the human pair bond, and of female dependency on males are ancient, hundreds of thousands of years old, from an inchoate epoch that evolutionary theorists refer to as the "environment of evolutionary adaptation," when we supposedly became us, genetically and predispositionally. And by this scenario a woman began seeking in a man the signs of wealth and prowess and the wherewithal to support her and her children, while a man began seeking in a woman the signs of fecundity, a youthful capacity to breed a large brood, as well as the signs that such fecundity would be reserved for him, the provider: if he was to invest in her and her offspring, he did not want to be investing in offspring that were not his.

Now the conventional model of man the hunter is under persuasive attack, called into question by Kristen Hawkes and many others, whose recent analyses of traditional foraging societies suggest that male hunting counts for very little in the daily sustenance of their families and that a network of women gathers most of the calories to keep the kinfolk fed. The new work suggests that among ancestral humans, women still had a strong degree of autonomy, as chimpanzee females do, as the females of all other primate species do, and that "the patriarchy," the "nuclear family" — call it what you will, but it is the dependence of women on men for their bacon and bread — is, at least on a large and codified scale, a fairly recent event in human prehistory. The transformation may be one of the fruits of the agricultural revolution, as a number of historians and evolutionary scientists have proposed. "With the advent of intensive agriculture and animal husbandry, women, by and large, lost control over the fruits of their labors," Smuts has written. "Foraging and nomadic slash-and-burn horticulture require vast areas of land and mobile females, making it more difficult for men to control women's resource base and to restrict women's movements. However, when women's labor is restricted to a relatively small plot of land, as in intensive agriculture, or is restricted primarily to the household compound, as in animal husbandry, it is easier for men to control both the resource base upon which women depend for subsistence and women's daily movements."

The real innovation, if you want to call it that, in the evolution of patriarchy was the perfection of male alliances. Among most primates, females form alliances and males do not. Among chimpanzees, males form rudimentary alliances with each other, and they sometimes control females, but the alliances are usually unstable, and females resist — and they can resist, for they are self-supporting. Among humans, men are brilliant at allying themselves with other men, politically, religiously, intellectually, emotionally. Such alliances have served many purposes and have enriched and glorified and defiled our strut across this mortal stage, but not the least reason for male collaboration has been to extend and refine what chimpanzee males attempt in crude fashion, which is to control the means of reproduction, which of necessity involves the control of women. We think of male dominance as the corollary of male superiority in size and strength, but most male monkeys are larger and stronger than female monkeys and still they cannot subdue the females. Female alliances keep females free. When men learned the value of befriending other men, when they saw that their interests converged more often than they conflicted, whoops, there went female freedom.

The progression of patriarchy and its specific impact on women throughout prehistory and history is a long and involved tale, which has been explored beautifully by Gerda Lerner and others. It is a tale that will never be wholly understood. By the time written records first appeared, much of the social, economic, political, and emotional underpinnings of the fatherland already were in place and women had already accepted their secondary status. Three thousand years ago, for example, a Mesopotamian princess prayed not for her salvation but for the preservation of her lord, "that I for my part may prosper under his protection."

Women needed male protection because alliances among men were often military pacts, the combining of forces to capture what others have. And one of the earliest and most favored forms of booty to be seized was young women. When two tribes clashed, the victorious group killed the male prisoners and took the females back as slaves and breeders. The capture of females enhanced the reproductive potential of the triumphant males, and it enhanced their status as well. Wherever there are written records, the records describe the raping and taking of women in the aftermath of war. In Homer's *Iliad*, presumed to reflect social conditions in Greece circa 1200 B.C., the warriors haggle, sometimes petulantly, over the proper distribution of female spoils. Early in the narrative, King Agamemnon reluctantly agrees to give up his favorite concubine, Chryseis, a highborn war captive, when her priest father threatens to take his case to the gods. Agamemnon demands another woman in compensation for the loss, but his men point out that all the female captives already have been claimed. Being king, Agamemnon turns around and claims Achilles's concubine-slave Briseis for himself. That act very nearly leads to defeat for the Athenians, for Achilles spends much of the Trojan War sulking over the indignity in his tent and seeking the sexual sustenance of another of his concubines, "one he had taken from Lesbos, Phorbas's daughter, Diomede, of the fair coloring." Achilles shares the tent with another warrior, Patroklos, who has in his bed a gift from Achilles: Iphis, the "fair-girdled," whom Achilles captured when he conquered the city of Enyeus. Girls, girls, girls! We don't hear much from these captive women, of course, nor learn how they felt about being shuffled from man to man like baseball cards. Chances are they didn't raise a fuss. They were thankful to be alive. After all, there is no mention in the poem of enslaved men; the men of Enyeus, Lesbos, Troy, and other defeated poleis were slaughtered. Eventually, of course, men learned how to enslave other men as they did women, and to use men's muscle as they might use mules and oxen; but as a number of historians have argued and the evidence strongly suggests, the first human slaves were women, and the impetus behind slavery was the possession of nubile wombs.

The fact that female slaves were debauched by their abduction and that their humanity was peeled and shucked, as happens in slavery, and the fact that female slaves almost invariably served as concubines to their conquerors, helped to codify a distasteful mental association (which persists to this day) between the carnal female and the degraded female. A female slave was a sexual being; she had no choice, and very often she was dressed for the part. To distinguish herself from the race of slaves, a woman could do no better than to cherish her chastity and to flaunt it in flagrant modesty. There were many reasons that female virginity became an obsession in the world of bonded men. Alliances between kingdoms often were sealed through marriage, and the prince of one state wanted assurance that his bride did not conceal a bastard beneath her fair girdle. Even among families of the lower castes, the chastity of daughters could prove remunerative. In highly stratified societies such as those of feudal Europe, sometimes the only way for a lowborn family to better itself was through the marriage of a daughter to a nobleman. Thus, as the anthropologist Sherry Ortner has argued, the enforcement of female virginity became a family affair, guarded by the men — violently when necessary — and regarded mythopoetically among women. Females no longer banded together for the sake of resisting harassment or swatting back the infanticidal male; instead, the force of gynophilia, of love between mother and daughter, sister and sister, was turned to the task of protecting female chastity, a woman's greatest asset in the postforaging fen.

The abduction of women as war booty perforce resulted in taking the women from their natal homes and any protection their kin could give them. But on a larger scale, the elaboration of patriarchal social and economic structures resulted in, perhaps demanded, the extinguishing of matrilocality and the matriline in favor of patrilocality and the patriline. Almost without exception, women fare better in a matrilocal system, in which they stay where they were born, are surrounded by their friends and relations, and have their menfolk move in, than they do when they must leave home to join their husband's domain. The Iroquois, for example, were a strongly matrilocal culture, and the Iroquois had one of the most egalitarian cultures known to anthropology. But the more women came to be seen as resources to be bartered, the less sense it made to oblige them by moving to *their* pitched tents. Some biblical scholars have seen in Genesis a recapitulation of the struggle to replace matrilocality with patrilocality, a critical step in enabling the Hebrew tribe to exchange nomadism for statism, centered on the rule of the patriarch. Early in Genesis (2:24) is the passage "Therefore shall a man leave his father and his mother, and shall cleave unto his wife," a likely reference to a matrilocal system of wedlock. But later, Jacob, the son of Isaac, rejects the premise of matrilocality. He pledges to Isaac that he will return to his house, and after courting and marrying Laban's daughters, Rachel and Leah, he fulfills his vow. He takes his wives and their sons, camels, flocks of sheep, pottery, everything they can carry, back to the house of Isaac. To underscore the profound significance of her desertion, Rachel even steals her father's *teraphim,* his house gods, which represent the title to Laban's property. She accepts the overthrow of matrocentrism. She casts her lot with her husband and his primogeniture, and so pantomimes in her theft Jacob's right to claim her estate.

The plight of Briseis, the exaltation of the hymen, woman's loss of her natal infrastructure — all were hard enough on the cause of female autonomy. But when the goddess principle was expunged from the pantheon, women lost even their right to salute, however modestly, their fleshy fertility, the redemptive, regenerative power of the female body. Virtually all human cultures have had some sort of religion, some coherent creation narrative to consolidate and counterbalance human terrors, desires, limitations, and inclinations. Generally those religions are populated by a mix of animal and humanoid gods, some male, some female, some bisexual. Yet as Lerner convincingly shows, the ascendance of patriarchy is paralleled by a shift in the balance of power among the resident deities. "The development of strong kingships and of archaic states brings changes in religious beliefs and symbols," she writes in *The Creation of Patriarchy.* "The observable pattern is: first, the demotion of the Mother-Goddess figure and the ascendance and later dominance of her male consort/son; then his merging with a storm-god into a male Creator-God, who heads the pantheon of gods and goddesses. Wherever such changes occur, the power of creation and of fertility is transferred from the Goddess to the God."

With the advent of monotheism, even a metaphorically ovariectomized goddess is banished from the tabernacle, for she is a threat, with her fat thighs and her outlandish udders and her taint of the old, beloved fertility cults that held sway among so many for so long. In Genesis we see the ultimate pact between males, Yahweh and Adam, to expropriate female procreative power. Adam agrees to honor a monotheistic vision, stripped of the Goddess, and Adam in turn wins the right to name Eve and thus to give symbolic birth to her, and so to be the mother to the mother of us all, and so by rights to own the products of her womb. Eve shall be ruled by her husband and shall be exalted by him alone, and she will not be distracted by flattery and false hope. Eve shall see the serpent for what it is, her enemy, the embodiment of sin — the filth-eating worm, the detached phallus, the eternal umbilicus, the fugitive, the free. "In the historical context of the times of the writing of Genesis, the snake was clearly associated with the fertility goddess and symbolically represented her," Lerner writes. "We need not strain our interpretation to read this as the condemnation by Yahweh of female sexuality exercised freely and autonomously, even sacredly."

Under monotheism, patriarchy attained full grandeur. For women, the world had been bureaucratized, wrapped in red duct tape like a massive work by Christo. The old sources of strength were gone: the ballast of nearby blood relations, the deed to one's body, and the re-flection of the female self on larger stages — the mortal stage of the polis and the immortal stage of the gods. To gain what they needed to survive and to feed their young, women had to go through their inter-mediaries, their middle men. A man was no longer a mate. A man was air. You don't argue; you have to breathe. With this gradual, com-plex, and revolutionary transformation from foraging to the fatherland, the worth of women to one another also changed, for much the poorer. The strategic sorority was swept aside. If there are no tubers to be dug or forests to rummage through, and if vast tracts of resources are held by men, what can a woman do for you?

In the neohuman brain, a woman who is not your relative is a potential threat beyond anything seen elsewhere among primates. The woman may be your in-law, beholden to your husband by genotype or the affections cultivated by longstanding proximity. Or she may be a stranger and a potential competitor, in a new, ultimate, terrifying sense of the term. Another woman may take your man, and if your man is your air, that woman is a succubus, a true femme fatale, fatal to you and yours, to the sum of necessity, your food, your shelter, your young. What good can one woman do for another in the land of the middle man, of agraria and animus husbandry? Not much, practically speak-ing, not much at all. But the harm she can do is immeasurable. She can scratch your eyes out. She can rob you blind. Or so it can feel to the daughters of Eve, who are not shut out of the garden but locked within it. The costs of camaraderie begin to look exorbitant, and the risks of rebellion untenable.

Women are not and never have been innocents. Many have concurred with the process of being deprimatized. They have fed and accelerated their loss of autonomy. They have complied with customs that control female sexuality, such as infibulation, purdah, and claustration, and they have insisted that their daughters comply as well. They may even be the active agents of such customs.

They, we, are not fools, and we want our families. We want what is best for our children, and for thousands of years we have needed the help and love of men to keep our children safe. Many of us still do, and we still suffer in the absence of men. In this country, the vast majority of the people living in poverty are single women and their children. When a couple with children divorces, the woman usually gets poorer than she was during her marriage, while the man gets richer. It is still too costly to behave in a way that risks the investment and tolerance of a man, of the greater male coalition that is our post-tuber planet. And so at times we perform little clitoridectomy equivalents on ourselves. We reject the idea of sisterhood and of female solidarity. We make fun of it. We scorn the term *feminist*, roll our eyes at it. We say we're beyond it, we're all fine, we've fixed all the problems that feminism can fix, which were never problems to begin with anyway. We organize antifeminist groups and give them smart, snappy names with words like *freedom* and *independent* in them. We have so much aggression in us, we're so alive, we're wild, golden-eyed, and strong, and we take out our pistols and shoot at each other, or at the floor, at our glass-slippered feet.

What sort of nonsense do we swallow? What sort of slaphappy hee-hawing nonsense? Consider the movie *Jerry Maguire*, which is a silly movie and would be harmless but for a gratuitous and puzzling flourish of misogyny, stuck in there for the women in the audience, I guess, or for the men who accompanied the women who accompanied the men to a male-centered, sports-themed movie. The moviemakers inserted a "love interest" for Tom Cruise, who plays Jerry, in the fetching, bee-stung-lipped person of Renee Zellweger as Dorothy. Dorothy has an older sister, a graying divorcée, and the sister is part of a female support group, a cabal of abandonees who get together regularly to moan about the betrayals of men. This is annoying enough, for the women all look haggard, hardened, and unhappy, and they *never laugh,* although real women laugh constantly when they congregate to dish about men. At one point, for no discernible reason, Dorothy leaps to her feet and interrupts their gathering. "Maybe you're all correct," she says. "Men are the enemy. But I still love the enemy!" The women erupt in a chattering chorus of denials and confusion, as though they know they've been trounced and that Dorothy has a point (which is?). The women are trying to support each other, shore each other up, but Dorothy won't let them. She wants Tom/Jerry back. She needs him, not just emotionally but for her solvency. She is a single mother with a young son. In her need, Dorothy feels she must nullify these other women, dissociate herself from them and the grim future they represent. Their presence taints her. She wants a second act. There are no second acts for Thelma and Louise.

Okay, maybe we shouldn't read too much into fluffernutter entertainment. But if you think it's sweet and harmless and you keep eating it, one day you wake up and all your teeth have fallen out.

We are all women with many pasts. We are old primates and neo-hominids. We feel drawn toward other women, we feel a need to explain ourselves to them and to impress them, and we run away from women, we disavow them, or we keep them around only until the real thing comes along. We can do each other mischief, even violence, but we can do each other good as well. Both options are open to us, in the plastic, opportunistic flow chart of our strategies and choices. Chimpanzees and bonobos are equally related to us. Their genes are 99 percent identical to our own. To give you a sense of how close that is, the mouse genome is only 50 percent homologous to ours, and mice are mammals too, and thus very close to us taxonomically. But chimpanzees and bonobos, the two living members of the genus *Pan,* are our sister groups. Their milk would feed our infants beautifully. Chimpanzee females are attenuated allies. Bonobo females are a constructed matriarchy. We can go either way. We can draw upon both. What we women can't do is ignore each other. It is a man's world, but our aggressions are woman-centered, harsh and intimate.

16

CHEAP MEAT

LEARNING TO MAKE A MUSCLE

IN ALL THE YEARS that I have been working out in gyms and lifting weights and preaching to other gals, with admitted obnoxiousness, about the glories of strength training, the commonest and most irritating response I have heard goes something like this: "I wouldn't want to bulk up or look too muscular. I just want to get toned." The remark chafes at me for two reasons. To begin with, Holy Maria Lactans, I wish it were that easy to "bulk up" and build visible muscle. I wish that I could grow a bumper crop of fruits and moons and imitation buttocks on my shoulders, legs, chest, and back simply by working out on a regular basis. In fact, getting overtly muscular is extremely difficult for most women. People who watch me work out are always surprised to see how much weight I can lift, because I don't look particularly meaty. I don't conform to some sort of mythical image of Gunhilde du Brawn, slayer of golems and burster of spandex. I am perpetually disappointed by my biceps. They're strong, but they refuse to pop up when I flex my arms, the way I remember my father's biceps doing each time I begged him to "make a muscle."

For another, let us suppose that a woman does get more noticeably cut and hillocked than I can — and some women certainly can. What is wrong with looking muscular? Muscles are beautiful. Strength is beautiful. Muscle tissue is beautiful. It is metabolically, medically, and philosophically beautiful. Muscles retreat when they're not used, but they will always come back if you give them good reason. No matter how old you get, your muscles never lose hope. They are forward-looking. They are responsive to stimulation. Few cells of the body are as capable as muscle cells are of change and reformation, of achievement and transcendence. Your muscles can be sanctimonious, it's true, adhering to a materialist, puritanical, goal-oriented mentality, but at least they are reliable. You can spend every day on a therapist's couch and still wake up to your old frail spirit, but if you work out every day your muscles will grow strong.

Admittedly, the benefits of exercise can be, and are, oversold. People attribute vast magical powers to exercise, claiming that it will make you happy and optimistic and focused. Don't believe them. If you are a habitually unhappy person, exercise will not make you happy. You may feel a temporary sense of emotional expansiveness at the beginning of a new exercise regimen, as the improvement in blood flow transports comparatively more oxygen to your tissues and as you pat yourself on the back for your brave undertaking. But once your body grows accustomed to the more active pace and the gung-ho high of the novitiate dissipates, you will return to your biochemical and psychic baseline — to the problem, as D. H. Lawrence put it, of being yourself. We have heard that exercise can help cure depression, but most clinical studies have found no such therapeutic effect.

People also claim that exercise is the closest thing we have to an elixir of youth, and that if we could put it in a pill we'd all be taking it. They are right for many parts of the body, but for the face, your chronograph to the world, exercise will do nothing. The muscles of your face are not attached to the skull in as many spots as the other muscles are to the skeleton. The facial muscles have been liberated from the constraints of bone, the better to allow us to speak and grimace and smile and feign surprise or interest. But the downside to that freedom of expression is that we cannot lift up the facial muscles through strength training; there is nowhere to lift them to. It is too bad, really. No matter how much discipline and tenacity we may muster, the aesthetic benefits of exercise stop at the jaw.

If we don't ask of strength that it solve all our problems, though, we can start to make real use of it. We women need our muscles at least as much as men need theirs, and we should feel entitled to them. Yes, men are naturally more muscular, a result of their higher levels of testosterone. The hormone is anabolic — it builds muscle — and so having more of it allows for comparatively greater muscle bulk. Yet testosterone is not nearly as effective at enhancing strength as its reputation would suggest, and women should not lament their relatively low concentration of the hormone, nor think it means that they're not "supposed" to be strong. Ignoring official censure, athletes have long been injecting synthetic androgens on the conviction that steroids make them stronger and more muscular. In 1996, researchers finally substantiated the locker-room wisdom through a clinical trial and showed that super-high doses of testosterone did indeed increase muscle size and strength in normal, healthy young men. The results were not brilliant, though, and even the men whose blood was practically gelatinous with testosterone — five times the normal concentration — ended up no stronger, after ten weeks of steady exercise, than a lot of the men in the control group, who diligently worked out drug-free.

The results should not surprise us. After all, men's indigenous testosterone levels are ten times higher than women's, but men certainly are not ten times bigger and stronger than we. In fact, the size discrepancy between men and women — our so-called sexual dimorphism — is modest compared to that seen among males and females of many other species. The average man is only about 10 percent taller and 20 percent heavier than the average woman, while among orangutans and gorillas males are at least twice the size of females. Normally the sexual dimorphism of a particular species is attributed to evolutionary pressure on the males to grow large, the better to compete with other males for access to mates. As a rule, the more sexually dimorphic the species, the more polygamous it is, the theory being that the greater a male's opportunity to monopolize multiple females, the stiffer the competition among males and the more pronounced the pressure to be battle-ready. By contrast, among the more monogamous species males and females tend to be fairly similar in size and accouterments, for why should a male be outfitted for warfare when he is likely to find a mate and settle down and more or less mind his own business? Thus, a number of scientists have viewed the weak dimorphism in humans as evidence that we are a halfway, sexually opportunistic creature, semi-promiscuous, semi-monogamous, prone to pairing up and prone to philandering — fission, fusion, mass confusion. All of which may or may not be true; but the fact that men are not 400-pound gorillas doesn't on its own indicate a muting of competitiveness among males. The truth is that once humans started fashioning weapons, sheer brute strength became less important than inventiveness, and the arms race in body parts very likely gave way to the arms race in engineering skills. A good spear defeats a burly chest every time.

More to the point for our discussion, women and men may be closer in size than the males and females of some other great apes not because men have been freed of the selective pressure toward enlarged body size but because women have been under some pressure to become fairly large themselves. Assuming that women have been selected for enhanced longevity — a long life after menopause — it helps to have a respectable body mass to persist through the decades. Large animals generally live longer than small animals. Many factors besides lifespan influence the evolution of a female's body size, including habitat, method of locomotion, diet, and the demands of pregnancy and lactation, some factors serving to limit body size, others to augment it. But it is possible that in the triangulating, negotiating process of adaptive change, women's physiology has seen a modest thrust toward maximizing body size while still remaining within the developmental constraints of reproductive demands. After all, women are the second-largest female primates on the planet, bested only by female gorillas, who weigh an average of 185 pounds, compared to our nonobese norm of 125 to 130 pounds. Women are bigger than female orangutans, who weigh less than 100 pounds, and considerably bigger than female chimpanzees or bonobos. By comparison, men, with their standard weight of 160 pounds, are much smaller than male gorillas, and smaller too than male orangutans, who average 200 pounds.

I'm not saying this simply to have fun with numbers (although I am having fun with numbers, and as a fairly small woman it's heartening to think of myself as an impressively large female primate). What I am doing is offering grist for the argument that women need muscle mass more than men do, and that while nature has given us a nudge in a more monumental direction, we must take the hint and make the most of our long-lived vessel. We need muscle for practical reasons, and we need it for the mind's I, the uncertain self, and in both cases we need it now more than ever. We may not have large quantities of testosterone, and building muscle and strength does not come as easily to us as it does to men. But we have an extraordinary capacity for strength, the more impressive given our comparatively low levels of testosterone, as women throughout the world and history have always shown us. Women are workhorses in most of the developing world. !Kung women carry loads of a hundred pounds on their heads or backs for miles and miles. If the world's women went on strike, the world of work would effectively stop, and you cannot say that with certainty for the enterprises of men. For the vast majority of women, the injunction to be strong would ring silly. They are strong of necessity, by sweat and callus, and if they combined their strong ways with a better diet, clean water, and good medical care, they might prove a race of Jeanne Calments the longest-lived person the earth has yet seen.

In the West, however, women have experienced a kind of contrapuntalism, a clashing of lifelines. Longevity has increased while the need for physical strength has declined. We are living longer. We are women, after all, and how sturdy our systems are. At the same time, we are demyosinated, with ever less seduction of the muscle tissue, which yearns to be wooed. The more we persist, the more we need muscle. But our world gives us little opportunity to obtain it naturally, and so we must seek it through artifice, discipline, and homily. We must give ourselves reasons to be powerful, and the more reasons we conjure, the better. You don't want to look muscular? You just want to look toned? But you're not a Gregorian chant; you're a century-in-waiting. Pray to Artemis, goddess of the hunt, for her huntswoman's quadriceps and her archer's orbed arms. You'll be happy to have them when gravity, ruthless gravity, starts fingering your merchandise and toying with your heart.

To understand a woman's profound need of muscle, it helps to consider the constituents of a nonexistent yet utilitarian couple, the Reference Woman and the Reference Man. This couple is a medical and political construct, a post-Hiroshima Atom and Eve. In the 1950s, under the aegis of the Atomic Energy Commission, scientists set out to determine the potential impact of nuclear radiation on the human body. They wanted to know how much alpha, beta, and gamma radiation the body could tolerate, and because different tissues react divergently to radiation, they had to come up with estimates of what substrates the average man and average woman were made. In the portraits that emerged, the Reference Hominids are both twenty-five years old. This is the age at which the body's various organs are thought to be at their peak size and performance and its metabolic set point is well established. The weight that you are at age twenty-five is the weight at which your body is likely to feel most at home. It is the weight that your metabolism strives to attain, adjusting itself up or down if you gain or drop a few pounds, which is why dieters have such a vicious time of maintenance. The body is no rabble-rouser. It loves the status quo.

But Reference People never diet. Our Standard Woman weighs 132 pounds, the Standard Man 154. She is 27 percent fat, 63 percent lean body mass. He is 16 percent fat, 84 percent lean. When we think of lean we think muscle, but lean includes everything that is not fat — muscle, bones, organs, water. In the Atomic Woman, about half of the lean mass, or 34 percent of her body weight, is thought to be muscle tissue, which means that she is almost as fat as she is muscled. Fat is not a bad thing in itself. Adipose tissue is a great way to store energy for the famine times that we humans were supposed to withstand on occasion. A gram of fat holds more than twice as many calories as a gram of muscle tissue. The average person, male or female, has enough body fat to survive forty days without eating; the fact that Jesus Christ fasted in the desert for forty days suggests that the biblical authors, attentive ascetics that they were, had a good idea of the body's physiological limits.

Fat, though, can't do much for you on a day-to-day basis. It isn't a terribly ambitious tissue, and it weighs you down. It is the muscle tissue that colludes with the liver to generate and metabolize the proteins that keep the body alive and upright and operational, that repair the perpetual damage of living and of breathing oxygen — radical, skittish, inescapable oxygen. A woman who loses half or more of her body fat may stop menstruating, but she'll live. A woman who loses more than 40 percent of her lean body mass, as people did in the Nazi concentration camps, will die.

It is hard to exaggerate the utility of muscle. We have more than six hundred muscles in our body, some of them under voluntary control — our skeletal muscles — and some of them smooth muscles, the autonomic staff. Muscles allow us to move, of course. They stand between us and dissipation, apathy. But muscle tissue helps us even when we are immobilized by illness. In sickness, the body loses its power to tap the caloric reserves of fat. If you're fasting, intentionally or otherwise, but you are healthy, your insulin levels fall and your body begins to call on its fat reserves for energy. But when you're sick, with either an acute infection or a chronic illness, your insulin levels rise. Because insulin levels also rise when you eat, your body grows confused. It thinks it is fed, so it won't tap its stored fat for calories. Your body still needs energy, though, and if you're too sick to eat, it will begin breaking down its muscle for fuel. Muscle has fewer calories to offer: the average woman stores only about 20,000 calories in her muscle tissue, compared to the 180,000 or so in her fat. An acutely ill person who cannot eat will starve to death in ten days rather than forty. (Cachexia, the wasting of lean mass seen in people with cancer or AIDS, occurs more gradually than that, but it too is caused by a disruption of the body's ability to burn fat and its fallback tendency to cannibalize its muscle.) The more muscle you have, then, the better your chances are of withstanding illness. Young people survive an acute disease more readily than the old do in part because they have more muscle in escrow.

We women have less muscle than men to begin with, and we also have lighter bones. A man and a woman of equal height will differ in skeletal mass, the male's being about 10 percent denser than the female's. If muscle counters inertia, bones defy the swamp — the archaic spineless state we tetrapods gratefully scrambled away from. As women age, they lose bone more rapidly than men do — we're all aware of that, of course, in this era of the mindful menopause. Muscle cushions the bone as a rubber bumper cushions a fender, and the more muscle there is draped on the skeleton, the more protected the bones will be, even as they become more brittle and porous.

The body needs its muscle, especially as it ages. Yet the perverse reality is that in the absence of a concerted effort to remain strong, the aging body loses muscle and gains fat. A woman may stay the same weight throughout her adulthood, and still, if she is sedentary, the components of that body weight will change. The Reference Woman who at age twenty-five weighed 132 pounds and was 27 percent fat will by age fifty-five, without having gained a pound, be more than 40 percent fat. She will still have the same six-hundred-odd muscles, but many of them will have shrunk and become marbled through with lard and surrounded by a comparatively larger ring of fat. Because she has less muscle volume than when she was young, she will be weaker, of course, unable to lift her luggage, and she will be forced to purchase one of those odious, inexplicably popular wheeled suitcases with the retractable handles. She will grow breathless more readily when she climbs a flight of stairs, for muscle facilitates oxygen transport throughout the body and eases the strain on the heart. Men too exchange muscle for fat as they age, but because they start with more muscle, the transformation is less extreme.

Women need muscle, as much muscle as they can muster. They need muscle to shield their light bones, and they need muscle to weather illness. If they have less muscle naturally than men do, they must work that much harder to compensate. Young women must exercise and seek great strength. The more a young woman exerts herself before the age of twenty-five, while her skeleton is as yet a work in progress, the more robust her bones will be at their peak, and the longer her slide, as she ages, back to the mother lagoon. Vigorous, load-bearing activities such as running, gymnastics, and weightlifting can all augment a young woman's bone mass. And though some authorities have expressed concern that excessive sportiness in girlhood can interrupt the menstrual cycle, blocking estrogen production and therefore raising the risk of osteoporosis, in fact a wealth of research has demonstrated that active girls have denser bones than their unathletic peers. Young women who build a foundation of muscle will find it easier throughout life to recall that muscle from mothballs. They may lapse into years of physical torpor, but when they finally shake themselves awake and give themselves a princessly kiss, they will regain their strength and meat in surprisingly short order.

Muscle is gracious. It does not hold grudges. Even an elderly woman who never learned to do cartwheels or bothered to join a fitness club in early adulthood can, in her oxidized age, become a mighty virago. Her muscles will be there for her. Miriam Nelson, a physiologist at Tufts University, has taken women in their seventies, eighties, and nineties, women who couldn't leave their apartments or rise from their chairs, women in nursing homes, and she has trained them twice a week with weights the way weightlifters in gyms train with weights — not timidly, not holding back for fear of their frailty or fear that they might, heavens, "bulk up," but with intensity, using as high a weight as the women can manage. After only four months in the program, these women, these sedentary, often arthritic women with dowager's humps and hummingbird bones, grew astonishingly strong, were as though healed by a carnival preacher, tossing aside canes and walkers, getting down on their hands and knees to garden, canoeing, shoveling snow. The women did not become visibly larger. They gained about 10 percent in muscle mass — respectable, but not terribly detectable. Of far greater importance, they doubled or trebled their strength. They became stronger than they had been in middle age. Their muscles hadn't been chastened by time. They hadn't learned their lesson. They hadn't learned to submit. Instead, the muscles repaid use with their stalwart Protestant ways and became productive again. The coordination between muscle and nerve improved. The muscles became infiltrated with nerve twigs and with capillaries bearing blood and oxygen. They were like telltale hearts, still thumping under the floorboards, not dead yet.

A woman's need of muscle is practical. She is a long-lived specimen, one of the longest this planet knows. Time will try to steal muscle and bone, but time in this case is not invincible. Muscle can be retrieved and restored, and when the muscle swells, the bone rejoices. It's very difficult to add to your bone density after age thirty, but by owning muscle you can keep the bone you have from departing, for muscle yanks on bone, and the mechanical action goads the bone to turn over, to be replenished, rather than to stagnate and gradually dissolve. Muscle and bone, our wild quadruped scaffolding, on which a fine, long dramedy of a life can be draped. Even a bit of fat can be accommodated on a sturdy frame. The dangers of body fat are exaggerated. Fat ipso facto is not a bad thing. The problem for most overweight people is that the extra fat makes movement harder and more unpleasant, and so they tend not to exercise, and muscles must be moved to remain engaged. But if a chubby woman remains active, she may prove surprisingly strong. Overweight people not only have more fat than the slender, they often have comparatively more muscle. When you gain weight because you're overeating, you put on three quarters of that weight as fat but one quarter as muscle. Fat people are so cowed into self-loathing that they don't realize the potential they carry. If they choose to exercise their submerged muscle on a regular basis, they'll be able to beat the sprat out of any thin ones who call them pigs.

As a not-young mother of a very young daughter, I feel a new obligation to stay strong — to stay strong so that I can stay alive and vigorous and force her to go camping and hiking with her aging parents, and to stay healthy and independent and postpone the time when she'll have to worry about nursing homes. I feel, in other words, pragmatic about strength. When I visited Miriam Nelson, she made it clear to me that women like us — relatively small and slim women — must never stop seeking strength. We are not naturally blessed. We don't have enough mass, enough animal matter, to rest on our laurels. So now I'm practical. In the past I cared less about the nuts and bolts of muscle and more about its meaning, the mind of muscle. I haven't abandoned my cheap and wistful philosophy of muscle, though. Women need all the reasons we can gather to build the strength that comes with comparative ease to men. Here's another: physical strength is explicit. It is crude and clear and possible. A woman does not need to get as strong as she thinks before she can be a hobbyist Fury. It doesn't take much to become imposing, a figure to be reckoned with. If a woman can do a set of, say, fifteen to twenty-five straight-bodied pushups or a few pullups, if she can lift a dumbbell that's heavy enough to be on the dumbbell rack rather than tossed on the floor like a toy, then people will say, Oh, you're so strong, and they will admire her and think her brave. And being strong in a blunt way, a muscleheaded way, is easier than being skilled at a sport. It is a democratic option, open to the klutzes and the latecomers, and women should seize the chance to become cheaply, frowzily strong, because the chance exists, and let's be honest, we don't have many. Being strong won't make you happy or fulfilled, but it's better to be sullen and strong than sullen and weak.

Female strength is, even yet, seditious. It can make men squirm. They can get angry at a woman who is too strong, who may be stronger than they are. Part of me understands that reaction. I feel irritated and jealous when I see a woman who can lift more weight than I can. How dare she! I look for flaws, for evidence that her form is poor, that she is cheating. But once the initial irritation fades and I can see that she is good at what she is doing, I feel grateful toward her, and heartened by her power. She is a member of the sisterhood, the Vestal Subversions. Men seem to feel the need of absolutes, of an indomitable line between male and female strength. Physical strength hardly counts in this culture, and many men are lazy, and they don't necessarily mind if other men are stronger than they. Still, there must be abiding verities, and one of them is that in the arena of physical prowess, the categorical male will now and forever prevail over female. How else to explain the reaction I encountered while reporting the following story?

In 1992, Brian Whipp and Susan Ward, of the University of California at Los Angeles, presented their analysis of trends in competitive running over the past seventy years. As they saw it, female runners were improving their performance by such breathtaking leaps and sprints and heave-hos that if present trends continued, they would catch up to and possibly surpass male runners sometime in the next fifty years. The researchers pointed out that while men's times have been improving steadily since the 1920s, with no sign of slacking off, women's performance has been accelerating at two to three times the rate of the men's, also with no sign of slacking off. Project those divergent trends into the future, and the verity of male primacy begins to totter.

"Before I looked at the data, I would have thought the possibility of women catching up to men hovered somewhere between implausible and extremely unlikely," Whipp told me. "But then I looked at the data. I'm a scientist; that's what I do. And I saw that if current progressions continue, the consequence is that men and women might be running equivalent speeds in the next century." His voice took on a pleading tone. "This is not me talking, it's the data."

Take as an example the one-mile event. In 1954, when Roger Bannister broke the fabled four-minute-mile barrier, Diane Leather became the first woman to breach the five-minute mile. If they had been in the same race, she would have finished 320 meters behind Bannister. In 1993, when Whipp and Ward wrote their paper, the world champion female miler would have finished only 180 meters behind the top man, and that figure has since dropped to 178 meters. The data won't shut up.

Yet there was nothing so swift as the eruption of outrage and indignation from various jockhouses — male physiologists, male runners, male editors screening my copy — when I wrote this story. I asked Fred Lebow, then the high priest of marathons and the president of the New York Road Runners Club, what he thought of the findings. "Never!" he cried. "This may look good on paper, but women will never run as fast as men! Never, ever, ever!" Poor Lebow. He has since died of a brain

tumor, and I can still hear his incantatory iteration: Never, ever, ever . . .
Peter Snell, an exercise physiologist who won three Olympic gold med-
als for running in the 1960s, flicked the report aside like so much
dandruff on his collar. "I don't know why they bothered to do this," he
said. "It's a waste of time. It's not even worth discussing. To suggest that
women will approach men is ludicrous, just ridiculous." Absurd and Dr.
Seussious!

An editor looking over my story said, Let's move the skeptical stuff up
higher.

I already have skepticism in my *second paragraph*, I replied. Right
after the lead, I start in with the critics.

Yes, but there are other skeptical points later in the story that should
be moved up too, he said.

Why? I said. Why would I want to completely undermine the story
from the start?

Because it's sheer fantasy, the male editor said. It will never happen.

That's you talking, I replied. It's not the data.

Admittedly, the sneerers of Snell had a point. Elite female runners are
still far behind the men in all events. The best marathon time by a
woman is fifteen minutes slower than the world's record, a Grand
Canyon of a gap by championship standards. Many physiological factors give male athletes the edge, apart from their larger muscles. Female
runners, no matter how lean they are compared to most mortals, still
have more body fat than world-class male runners do, and that fat is
dead weight. Men have a greater ratio of red blood cells to plasma in
their blood and thus can deliver proportionally more oxygen to their
muscles. Their higher testosterone levels also help in muscle repair,
which means they can train more rabidly. And so on, trudging from
one page of *Gray's Anatomy* to the next. Just because the rate of improvement in female athletic performance has been spectacular, a linear
progression toward the ionosphere, doesn't mean it will stay linear
much longer. After all, if you carried that line out indefinitely, you'd
reach the point where female runners were running faster than the
speed of light, a feat beyond even the magic thighs of Jackie Joyner-
Kersee. Obviously, the trend will have to flatten out. The divisions
into male and female events at the Olympics are not going to disappear anytime soon, if ever. So wherefore the outrage, the indignation,

the thunderous guffaw at the proposal that they might? What is the fear here?

Never mind. We don't have to understand it. Let's just capitalize on it. Physical strength is a crude form of strength, and it won't solve much of the angst in life, but again, it's a flauntable property. Most women are much stronger than they realize, and they can be stronger still with a minimum of investment. I'm not talking about the buff-body ethos of egg-carton abdominals and striated quadriceps that now prevails in places like Los Angeles, New York, and Miami Beach, which is an aesthetic tyranny no less than the tyranny of thinness or of the Face. I'm talking about strong and earthy, a moosey strength, the strength that shrugs its shoulders and takes no bull. I've noticed in nearly every gym where I've worked out that women on the weight-training equipment use far too low a setting for their strength, particularly when they are exercising their upper body, where they are convinced they are weak. They'll stick with twenty or thirty pounds' worth of plates and then do many repetitions easily, and I can see that they could handle twice what they're pressing, but they're not doing it, and nobody's telling them to do it, and I want to go over and beg them to use a higher weight and tell them, Look, you're blowing it, here's your chance, your cheap and easy chance, to own a piece of your life and strut and be a comic-strip heroine, so please, stack it up, heave-ho, do it for yourself, your daughter, your mother, the International Maidenhood of Iron. I don't say anything. It's not my business. I'm not a personal trainer, and if somebody came over to give me unsolicited advice about my workout, I might be tempted to test the purported deficiency of my effort by dropping what I'm pumping on Gunhilde's great toe. Then she'd howl like a harpy and jump up and down and say, What the hell are you doing? That was meant as a compliment! And the next time I saw her in the gym, her foot in a cast, I'd invite her to join me in a workout, to see if there is more to me, and to her, than either of us knows.

Men grow up with the conviction that they are always stronger than somebody. Even men who as boys were always picked last for the softball team and who look like the packing material for stereo equipment nevertheless are convinced that they are stronger than women. They are taught that they should never hit a woman, never, ever, and that's a reasonable thing to be taught, because physical assault is almost always a bad idea; but if the presumed corollary of that doctrine is that women are profoundly and immutably vulnerable to male violence and that they must rely on the courtly behavior of men and the vigilance of the legal system to keep themselves in one piece, then the doctrine is not entirely benign and may even backfire. If men believe that they are always stronger than all women, and that here at least they have the upper hand, by rights, by testosterone, by bone and hemoglobin, and if our species' sexual dimorphism is overrated and the heft of women understated, then a man, an angry, idiotic, small-souled man, will view the cost of hitting a woman as depressingly low, and a woman will view the thought of protecting herself as ludicrous, ridiculous, because she can never, ever succeed. And sure enough, the prophecy will be fulfilled, the man will beat the woman at no physical risk to himself, because we all know that a woman can't stand up to a man and we all know that a woman should look toned, not bulky. I am not, absolutely not, blaming women who are assaulted by men for allowing themselves to be beaten, but I am questioning the mentality that effectively hypertrophies the size and strength dimorphism between men and women, and that makes men, even frumpy, lethargic, academic men, smug, and that makes women, even tall, substantial women, afraid. Think simian, subversive thoughts. Among patas monkeys, vervet monkeys, brown capuchins, stump-tailed macaques, and other species of monkeys, females often win in one-on-one agonistic encounters with males, even though the males are as proportionally bigger than the females as men are than women. Does this surprise you? A monkey tornado can pick you up and fling you to Oz and back. If a female macaque decides to fly in your face, her smallness, her fifteen pounds, will feel huger than any weather you have seen.

Women don't have to be as strong as men to be strong enough, to stomp around like maenads. It was a man who told me as much, back in college. He was a large, broad-shouldered man, a competitive swimmer who qualified for the Olympics. He was the largest and most athletic man I had ever dated, and I felt overwhelmed by the expanse of him.

You could snap me in two like a twig, I said to him.

Oh, no, I couldn't, he said. You're strong, and you've got a lot of muscle there, he said, poking at my midriff. It would be very difficult to break you in half.

Part of me wanted to yield to his power, to designate its authority, and to feel protected beneath it. But he knew his strength, and he had a measure of mine, and he had the strength to tell me that I was selling myself short. Men who respond with sputtering ire at the thought of female parity in athletic competition show that there is a faint, oaky note of doubt about male primogeniture. It can't hurt, and it may help, to question the absolutism of sexual asymmetry through any number of minor acts of smugness — a pushup here, a pullup there, a cueball bicep if you can get it. Bitch.

Of course, being swift and strong will not protect a woman from being raped or molested. Antifeminists argue the opposite, that women who labor under the illusion of strength and self-sufficiency are the ones who do foolish things, go places they shouldn't, and end up paying for it. In 1989, when a female jogger in Central Park was almost killed by a gang of wilding boys, many people blamed the jogger, an accomplished athlete, for being so reckless as to run in the park at night. But women get attacked in daylight, and in their homes, and when walking from their job to their cars. Obviously there are no guarantees. It's worth pointing out that although the Central Park jogger was grievously wounded, she didn't die. She refused to die. She amazed doctors by her recovery. Perhaps her strength kept her alive — the blunt strength of her body and the obstreperousness of her mind.

Men take strength for granted. Women have to fight for it. They have to trick themselves into their strength, or rather their strengths. Physical strength is but one allele of strength. There are all the other strengths: of self-conviction, of purpose, of being comfortable in your designated plasm. I don't know if physical strength can enhance those other, intangible strengths, if a better-braced body can give one *ovarios* of heart. It's a good gimmick, though, a place to start, or to return to when all else fails. The body will be there to do its bit, to take another crack at life, and to propel you forward, suitcase in hand, not on wheels. The trappings of physical strength are so persuasive that you can almost hear the spotted hyenas giggling in the dark.

17

LABOR OF LOVE

THE CHEMISTRY OF HUMAN BONDAGE

THE BRAIN IS an organ of aggression, and there are many roads to this Rome of imagined conquests — so many that mental disorders, regardless of their particulars, often result in a derangement of our aggressive drive. Schizophrenics stand on the streetcorner screaming obscenely at passersby; depressives lie in their beds screaming mutely at themselves. Our gentle aggressions, the drive to be, prods us out of bed in the morning and draws us toward each other. And in each other we find what our aggressive brain desires: love.

As we are wired for aggression, so we are wired to love. We are a lavishly loving species, aggressively sentimental. We are tireless in the pursuit of fresh targets for our love. We love our children so long that they come to despise us for it. We love friends, books, flags, nation-states, sports teams. We love answers. We love yesterday and next year. We love gods, for a god is there when all else fails, and God can keep all conduits of love alive — erotic, maternal, paternal, euphoric, infantile.

We are incorrigible romantics, who no more want to be relieved of our condition than an incurable optimist wants to have her rose-colored spectacles retinted. For a while it was the going wisdom among historians that romantic love was a relatively recent invention, arising from the mercantile and troubadour tradition of late medieval France. In premodern and non-Western societies, the historians argued, men and women do not marry "for love" — their marriages are usually arranged, or bought and sold; nor do people in most cultures dreamily conjure up images of the beloved. More recently, scholars have shown otherwise. They have uncovered a cross-cultural and cross-temporal trove of love ditties, love geysers, and eloquent swoons. In a survey of ethnographic data for 166 contemporary societies, Helen Fisher, of Rutgers University, found evidence of romantic love in 147; for the rest, the data were too incomplete to rule it in or out. Historically, the ancient Babylonians, Sumerians, Akkadians, Egyptians, Greeks, Romans, Chinese, Japanese, Indians, and Meso-Americans left behind paeans to romantic love. Lovers leap to an immortal heat in the Song of Songs, written in the ninth century B.C., she with teeth like a flock of shorn sheep, lips like a thread of scarlet, and breasts like twin roes, and he with eyes as the eyes of doves and cheeks like a bed of spices and legs as pillars of marble set upon sockets of fine gold: "Let him kiss me with the kisses of his mouth: for thy love is better than wine." Tutankhamen died before he was twenty, but he lived long enough to write love poems to his wife. If a Gothic cathedral is, as Rilke said, frozen music, then the Taj Mahal, which the Shah Jahan built for his beloved dead bride, is a frozen keen. "It's no use, Mother dear, I can't finish my weaving," Sappho wrote 2,600 years ago. "You may blame Aphrodite/soft as she is/she has almost killed me with love for that boy."

Love is universal, yet we can't help but want to clutch it to ourselves. We don't want it explained. We certainly don't want it anatomized and biologized. It seems at once too big and too private, too profound and too fleeting, for science to get its patch clamps and pipettes into. Relax! Your brain in love remains a sacred, suffocating swamp. We still need our poets and songwriters — the good ones, anyway. Science has not solved the love question. We know very little about what the biochemical and neural substrates of love may be. Love is a tremendously difficult problem to study. How do you define it? Which animals can you use? If scientists are going to do experiments on the deep biology of love, they need animals, and they need reliable assays. When cats are feeling hostile, they raise their fur, curl their lips back, and hiss in a stereotypical manner, and so cats are a favorite "model system" for studying aggression. But what are the dependable signs of animal love in the lab? What is the difference between two animals that huddle together to keep warm and two animals that huddle because they are "friends"? Is there a difference?

At the same time that the problem looms so unruly, the "biology of love" doesn't sound quite serious enough for many scientists. "What do you study?" "Love." "Oh. And they pay you to do that?" "Sometimes. If

I grovel, obfuscate, and use diversionary tactics. If I write my grants cleverly and talk about understanding the health risks of social isolation, say, or autism. If I never talk about love."

Yet through biology we can approach love and see parts of it that we may not see when we are acting as self-styled experts by falling in love. Love has its themes. Love is the child of outrage, arriving most readily in the wake of crisis. What we lose in great distress the body and brain strive to replenish in love, and ripe love that feels fattening *is* fattening, literally speaking, for it is designed to conserve our calories as well as our sanity. Love may feel impossible, but it is laughably easy, and once it has begun it is fed by every sense, every nerve fiber, every cell, and by the brain, our big remembering brains. With the brain, our proud throne of reason, we humans have become the best and longest lovers this world has known.

The circuitries of love and attachment are everywhere within us. They are as manifold as the reasons that we befriend and fall in love. Why *do* we bother with love? Let's count the categorical ways. We love, at bottom, because we must, for we are a sexually reproducing species. The reasons that sexual reproduction evolved in the first place are not entirely known. In theory, an asexual style of reproduction, an amoebalike splitting in twain, would be comparatively more efficient than sexual reproduction, the merging of sperm and egg. The study of the origins of sex is a vigorous discipline, with a plethora of proposed justifications and a dearth of proof for any one of them. Suffice it here to say that the regular shakeup and rearrangement of the chromosomes wrought by sexual reproduction must offer great advantages to the production of viable offspring, for the vast majority of earth's creatures have adopted sexual reproduction rather than asexual photocopying of self. Once the need for sex arose, so did the need for the rudiments of affection. Males and females needed the behavioral capacity to set aside any hostility that individuals might feel toward each other and instead take a chance on amity, at least long enough to exchange gametes.

We love because we are a species that nurtures its young. Sexual union can be perfunctory, and so can the dispersal of the fruit of that union. Many sexually reproducing species lay eggs and leave eggs, banking their posterity on chance, circumstance, and profligacy of output. But parental care for the young has its advantages. Parents can protect the young, feed them food they can't fetch for themselves, reserve territory in a world of tight real estate, and teach the young any number of skills, including how not to do things, for young animals learn by watching the fumblings of their elders as much as they do by observing their victories. Parental behavior has so many things to recommend it that it is found across the phylogenetic spectrum, among fish and insects as well as the more famously parental birds and mammals. "The evolution of parental behavior revolutionized reproduction," says Cort Pedersen, of the University of North Carolina. "Sustained parental protection and nurturing of offspring until they were able to fend for themselves allowed a much higher rate of survival and permitted a much longer period of brain development. Parental care was therefore a prerequisite for the evolution of higher intelligence. Species that care for their offspring have come to dominate every ecological niche in which they dwell." To care for your young means staying by your young, recognizing your young, and returning to your young again and again, even as your selfish, muttering self tells you, Hey, what about number one? A parent, a mother, must be drawn to her young, and the young must in turn be drawn to the mother, and the body and brain of a nurturing species must know how to love and be loved in turn.

That's personal. Then we have the political. There is strength in numbers, not just you and your immediate yours, but an army of yours. There is strength in being a social species and regarding the tribe as an extension of the self and engaging in civic behaviors. Social insects such as ants and honeybees, for example, spend a great deal of time in gestures of arthropod solidarity, exchanging chemical, tactile, and visual signals. They tell each other, Walk this way, dance like that, may I recommend the red flowers to your leeside, come fight with me, come fight come fight come fight. Through their continuous affirmation of community, social insects have become superorganisms, stampeding over any solitary species of insects in their path. "Wherever you go in the world, from rain forest to desert, social insects occupy the center — the stable, resource-rich parts of the environment," Edward O. Wilson has written. Solitary insects such as beetles and moths are driven to the fringes, to the ephemeral parts of the habitat not preempted by the social insects. As a result of their competitive edge, social insects propagate in huge numbers. They account for only 2 percent of all the earth's millions of insect species, but they make up 80 percent of the insect biomass.

Among mammals too the gregarians rule. Most feline species are solitary, with two exceptions: the lion, which lives in highly social prides, and the domesticated cat, which has focused its social exertions on its human keepers. Lions and housecats are thriving, while many of the other cat species are at risk of extinction. Elephants are elaborately social, while other pachyderms such as the rhinoceros and the hippopotamus are not. It may be no coincidence that elephants lately have managed to recover from human depredations and the lust for ivory, and in some parts of Africa their numbers are booming, while the rhinoceros, whose horn is among the most coveted body parts on the international black market, is unlikely to survive as a free-ranging species into the next century.

Sociality alone doesn't guarantee ecological dominance. African wild dogs, chimpanzees, bonobos, and gorillas are all social, and none is faring particularly well as a free-ranging species. Interestingly, though, the greatest threats to these social mammals come from other social mammals. Wild dogs, for example, have difficulty competing on the savannah against lions and spotted hyenas, themselves tribally minded carnivores. Chimpanzees and gorillas are up against us, their avaricious cousins, and even Nim Chimpsky, the language-trained ape, can't talk the talk that we can, the talk of everlasting love and the divine rights of man.

We humans also love because we think too much. We need to have our thoughts periodically shaken up and rearranged, like chromosomes, or like the immune molecules that fight disease. Allison Jolly, a primatologist, has compared the benefits of intelligence to the benefits of sexual reproduction. Both are systems for transferring information between individuals. Both allow information from different sources to be combined and used by one individual. If sex evolved so that your children are not condemned to be just like you, she said, then intelligence means that you are not condemned to remain just like yourself.

The greater the need for communication and for the transfer of intellectual gametes between individuals, the greater the need for affiliative gestures, behaviors, sensations. You can force a person with fist or sword to give you sex or food, but the more the currency of value is intelligence and ideas, the more we need to assuage and engage and befriend.

We love for posterity and protection, to preserve the self and to set the self aside. We love for the sake of fending off boredom and mental calcification. We have reasons to love, but what is the means, the biomedium of the art? It turns out that to understand love we must think again about aggression, for the pathways of love and aggression are linked, neurologically, hormonally, experientially. Sometimes the link is easy to see, for love can feel aggressive to the point of violence. We commit our most heinous acts of aggression in the name of love. The love of God drives crusades and jihads; the love of tribe drives genocide. When we are madly in love, we *are* mad. We are sleepless, anxious, panicky. At the thought of the loved one, our heart literally aches and our knees literally weaken. When we see the person, our pupils dilate, our palms sweat, our aching heart pounds. It's as though we were about to give a speech to an audience of thousands. The state of romantic passion is so overwhelming that we can be infatuated with only one person at a time.

What is going on here? Two things. A thousand things. In passionate love, the body's stress response, its fight-or-flight axis, is aroused, to heighten animation and possibility. The adrenal glands contract and flood the blood with adrenaline and cortisol, which prompt the heart to pound, eyes to widen, gut to wrench, sweat to leak. But there is more than anxiety and fidgetiness. Romantic passion is euphoric and obsessive too. On that analogy, Helen Fisher and others propose that romantic love taps into the same pleasure circuits of the brain through which such recreational drugs as cocaine and amphetamines ply their high. If you take cocaine, the concentration of stimulative neurotransmitters such as dopamine and norepinephrine in the brain rises, making you feel manic, hyperalert, sleepless, anorexic, expansive. These are also symptoms of passionate love. In the throes of romance, we want to take flight — from the loved one, to the loved one. We want to fight, with the lover for holding back, with ourselves for craving more. And we want to embrace the world for being uncommonly beautiful, and for giving us the flawless creature with lips like crimson threads and neck like the tower of David.

Needless to say, the brain's dopaminergic and norepinephrinergic circuits predate the use of speed and cocaine and certainly did not evolve to give us an appreciation for psychoactive drugs. Instead, the circuits of pleasure arose to reinforce behaviors and activities of possible use to the individual. If we assume that we are attracted to a particular person for good reason — that our instincts detect something worthwhile about the person, some reason to want to mate and spend time with the person — then a neural system designed to amplify our initial attraction, not to let us off the hook, might prove handy, for we are inclined toward laziness and sometimes need a kick in the pants. So romantic love could be the original addiction, and dopamine and norepinephrine and related catecholamines could be the neural stage on which Everywoman acts the part of Guinevere, Juliet, or Hildegarde von Bingen, who loved her God ecstatically and girlishly.

We love the heady swirl of romantic love. We also love the taste of our aggressions, often more than we care to admit. Yet enough is enough. As the Buddha said, life is pain, and this pain is caused by desire — the desire to seize and devour the beloved as you might seize and devour food. So in love we seek not just passion but a balm for passion, a cure for our aggression and its sidekicks, anxiety and fear. We seek to feel soothed, safe, and happy. We want, in love, our mothers, our idealized mothers, our soulful other halves, our children, our haven. We want a love of affiliation, or pair bonding, or, as many of us might call it, *true* love, as opposed to infatuation, dalliance, obsession. We even expect it. The extremities of passionate romantic love must be resolved, and dissolved, with true love, or we feel out of joint, cheated, surly. Who has not seen multiple productions of *Romeo and Juliet* without secretly, guiltily, wishing that just once Juliet would wake up in time to stop her lover from drinking the poison? Poor Charles Dickens was forced by public outcry to write a second ending to *Great Expectations*. His original ending had Pip and Estella meeting after a long hiatus and then going their separate ways, Pip glad to have seen in Estella's face and bearing the signs that "suffering . . . had given her a heart to understand what my heart used to be." The crowd-pleaser rewrite kept the pair together, walking hand in hand, the "tranquil light" of evening showing "no shadow of another parting" before them. William Dean Howells, editor of the *Atlantic Monthly*, tried to negotiate a bow to public sentiment while serializing Henry James's novel *The American*. Howells

urged James to allow the American hero and the French heroine to
be united in the final chapter. James refused, and the heroine stayed in
her convent. "I am a realist," he replied to Howells. "They would have
been an impossible couple." James wrote twenty novels, twenty works
of unsurpassed genius, but not one of them ends with a happy, ano-
dized pair bond. For him, all couples were impossible, and he himself
lived alone. If you spend too much time reading Henry James, you will
get sullen and tetchy, a state of literary angst best relieved by rereading
Jane Austen, the mistress of consummation.

We know that we expect a happy ending to follow from a story of
tribulation and upheaval, and that we crave consummation, the recip-
rocation of our love. What's interesting is that arousal, stress, and anxiety may be not merely antecedent to but instrumental in the creation of
deep love and attachment. The physiology of stress appears to set the
stage and prep the circuitry for a new set of cues: of openness, receptivity, and love. It tenderizes the brain. Many mammals that pair up or
form fast friendships are animals with an extremely vigorous stress
response axis. Their adrenal glands readily release stress hormones such
as cortisol and corticosterone. The animals fidget a lot, and they fall
in love. New World monkeys like cotton-top tamarins and marmosets
are rich in stress hormones and rich in social affections. Prairie voles,
a favored species for the study of attachment, are ridiculously pair
bonded. If they were humans you wouldn't want to invite them to your
party, because they'd bore you with their inseparability. Prairie voles —
mistakenly called field mice, although they're not mice — have five to
ten times the level of stress hormones of montane voles, which are the
same size but are nonmonogamous, loveless, and solitary. Guinea pigs
release rivers of adrenal hormones when under stress, and they too
develop close attachments to each other. In humans, stress can breed
unbreakable, uncanny bonds — between soldiers in a foxhole; between
kidnapper and kidnapped, as we see in the so-called Stockholm syndrome; between an abusive man and his doggedly loyal wife.

That aggression and stress can set the neurophysiological stage for
attachment makes sense. Aggression drives an animal outward and
toward another. Acts preceding the need for a bond between individuals
are rife with stress. For creatures that couple up to rear their young,
such as prairie voles, zebra finches, or cichlid fish, the act that cements

the bond between male and female is sex, and having sex, however consensual, is an act of aggression, anxiety, foolhardiness, and courage.

For mothers that will be expected to suckle and care for their young, the antecedent to the arrival of dependent newborns — that is, giving birth — is a feat of almost cataclysmic stress. This is true for mammals generally (think of the wretched hyena, giving birth through her clitoris!), yet the role of birth as crucible for bonding is nowhere better exemplified than it is among us. We extend the extreme agitation of parturition back in time. Even before her first uterine contraction, a woman who is approaching delivery is overcome by foreboding, panic, and a sense of vulnerability. She craves the support and companionship of others. The thought of giving birth alone terrifies her. In that sense, woman is matchless in her taxonomic class. When other female mammals are about to give birth, they seek solitude. They find a dark quiet spot away from troop or herd, and grunt and push alone.

Only among humans is birth almost universally a shared enterprise, the labor of a woman, her kin — usually females — and a midwife or two. For every culture documented, according to Wenda Trevathan, an anthropologist at New Mexico State University, women in labor routinely seek assistance or companionship rather than isolation. We have an image of the peasant woman who squats in the field, plops out an infant, straps it to her breast, and keeps working, but the image is a piece of apocrypha, or a rarity that's been inflated by rumor and repetition into the primitivist norm. Literally dropping a baby in the field is like giving birth in a cab or on the subway. It happens, but it is rare, and it is unintentional. What women intend to do when giving birth is to be attended to.

Midwifery, Trevathan proposes, is the oldest medical profession, dating back perhaps three to four million years, when we began walking upright. Our upright posture changed the mechanics of delivery, of the baby's odyssey down the infinite six inches of the birth canal. Because our pelvis had to be remodeled to accommodate bipedalism, and because a baby's head is unusually big and its shoulders unusually wide in proportion to its body, birth is comparatively painful and prolonged; and as the newborn starts to emerge from the vagina, it faces backward rather than toward the mother's front, as other primate newborns do. A chimpanzee mother can help pull her emerging young out and up toward her. If the umbilical cord is wrapped around the baby's neck, as cords often are, a chimpanzee mother can unwrap it herself. She can wipe the mucus from the baby's mouth and prevent it from aspirating the plasm of the uterus, the vestiges of its aqueous life.

Not so a human mother. The baby faces backward, and if the mother were to try pulling it forth with her own hands, she'd risk damage to its spine and neck. She can't negotiate the untwirling of the umbilicus if the cord is wrapped around the baby's neck. She can't clean its face and allow it to gasp its first breath. She needs help. She needs help so badly that she begins to panic shortly before the birth. She starts to anticipate pain and difficulty, and she feels lost and vulnerable, but the anxiety is not pathological, it is not the byproduct of the hormonal maelstrom of late-stage gestation, as some have said. It is rational anxiety, and as human as our opposable thumbs, our depilated breasts, and our Lamaze classes. The anxiety leads a female to pursue an audience for the birth rather than seclusion. Like the deep anxiety of romantic love, the anxiety of a woman in labor is tinged with fear, which spurs the autonomic urge to flee, but *toward* the other rather than away. The urges are inexorable and aggressive, which means they are rowdy. As a person in love can lash out at the loved one, a woman giving birth is a famous Wicked Bitch of the Nest, foaming and snapping at her beleaguered support staff.

When I was giving birth, I was surrounded by a loving and exhortative choir: my husband, my mother, two midwives, and a nurse. They urged me on and told me when to push. With each push they swore I was doing beautifully, I was so strong and so close, really, it wouldn't be long now, I was so close. And as I pushed, for an hour and fifty minutes, each minute a dog year of life, I looked out at my choir and I felt like Rosemary surrounded by Satan worshippers, and I thought, You are all liars, you are ridiculous, you are all full of shit, will you shut up please and leave me alone; but if they had left me alone, I would have gone into shock, unable to push or to breathe, reptilian to the core. After the birth, I was in love with all my tormentors — my daughter and husband, yes, yes, and also the women who were there, chanting the truth, absorbing my despair, and unwrapping the umbilical cord coiled around my baby's neck. O wondrous women! "I have compared thee, O love, to a company of horses in Pharaoh's chariots."

In the extraordinary mechanics of human birth, then, we see still another reason that humans must have others around them, and that humans are the most social of primates. We also see another thread of evidence that the gynocracy, the unified front that females can assume in times of need, is not alien to the human race but is rooted in our distant past and in the loneliness of standing on our own two feet.

The chemistry of stress bears the seeds of its own relief. When you get past lust and obsession, or when the expulsive frenzy of birth is through, you may reach a state of attachment, a neurochemical antidote to the spattering profligacy of aggression and desire. Anxiety is catabolic and energy intensive. Attachment is anabolic and energy conservative. We are born to aggress. We are born to coalesce. We know something about the former. We know much, much less about the latter, its counterweight. We suspect (and *suspect* is the word we must use) that the state of attachment has something to do with the peptide hormone oxytocin and its close molecular cousin, vasopressin.

Oxytocin has been called the love hormone. It's a dopy, wishful phrase, so patently reductionist that, like the terms *the gay gene* and *the intelligence gene*, it hardly deserves being gainsaid. Still, oxytocin may be a player in the sensation of love. Our feelings must be felt somehow, through a physical medium, and oxytocin has the lipstick traces of an emotional emulsifier. Oxytocin shows up in circumstances where affiliative behaviors are called for. During childbirth, it is released from the brain into the bloodstream. It has a practical and mechanical job to do. It triggers uterine contractions. Pitocin, the drug given to pregnant women to jumpstart recalcitrant labor, is a synthetic version of oxytocin. Oxytocin also stimulates the letdown reflex, the pulsing of milk from the breast cells through the ducts and out the nipple. Oxytocin stimulates maternal muscle contractions above and below the belt. It gets the baby born. It gets the baby fed. It might as well help get the baby loved, for without love the mother may look at the small and squawling creature before her and ask, Well, how did I get here? And how can I escape?

Vasopressin also is a good candidate for a bonding hormone. It is molecularly similar to oxytocin, and it has a practical function that, like oxytocin, is essential to lactation. It helps the body retain water, and if you can't retain fluids, you can't make milk. Vasopressin enhances memory, and it's a good idea to remember those who are significant to you — your children, for example, or a lover worth loving. Oxytocin and vasopressin are quite swift in their actions, which is what you want of hormones expected to help referee behavioral revolutions in a brief period of time. One minute you're a pregnant dam, still antsy, still free; the next you're a nursing mother, expected to sit and to give and to love and to sit.

"Nature is conservative," says Carol Sue Carter, of the University of Maryland, the grande dame of oxytocin research. "She rarely comes up with something she uses only once. The functions of oxytocin evolved from something primitive and basic to something far more elaborate."

Oxytocin and vasopressin sound good, sound lovely, but the data on their ramifications for human affairs remain slender, because you can't do good experiments with the hormones. Oxytocin is a peptide hormone, as opposed to a greasy steroid hormone like estrogen or testosterone. The greasiness of a steroid allows it to slip back and forth from brain to peripheral bloodstream and back to brain. For a peptide hormone, traffic is unidirectional, from brain to blood. The hypothalamus generates oxytocin for the body as needed, and keeps some for itself, for local behavioral or cerebral purposes; but whatever oxytocin is released into the bloodstream cannot penetrate the blood-brain barrier and go home again. When a pregnant woman is given an intravenous drip of Pitocin, it doesn't reach her brain. It reaches her uterus, and makes her think her midriff is being winched by Josef Mengele himself, but that's it. Thus, you can't do an experiment where you give a person an oxytocin tablet and ask, Are you feeling maternal yet? How about affiliated, cuddly, or at one with your oppressors? The exogenous oxytocin won't get to where it needs to go to sway behavior, if it is to sway.

Most of what we know about oxytocin and vasopressin we know from experiments on animals such as prairie voles, hamsters, and rats, whose brains are considered fair game for hands-on manipulations. When oxytocin is delivered directly into the central nervous system of a rat, the rat will start sidling up to another rat, seeking physical contact, a soft place to lay its snout. Female prairie voles form pair bonds after they have sex, and they also release oxytocin upon having sex. A female vole, given a shot to the brain of either oxytocin or vasopressin and then presented with a male, will act as though she has copulated with him and want to be around him and never leave his side. The same for a male vole: deliver a bolus of oxytocin or vasopressin to his central nervous system, and he will bond faithfully with the next female he meets. Conversely, a female vole treated with an oxytocin antagonist, which blocks the activity of the peptide, will have trouble settling down with a partner or caring for one wheat-furred fellow over another.

Oxytocin can make virgin females motherly. When female voles are given oxytocin through their cerebrospinal fluid, within thirty minutes they're snuffling pups presented to them, picking them up and retrieving them if they stray. A ewe usually is a good mother, but she will turn bad if for some reason she is separated from her lamb shortly after birth. Then she is likely to reject the lamb, refusing to nurse it. Sheep farmers have a way of persuading her otherwise. They stimulate her vagina with a kind of sheep dildo. The tickling releases a stream of oxytocin in her brain, and she then takes the lamb to udder. An oxytocin pump in her spinal cord will have the same maternogenic impact.

Vasopressin is somewhat statelier than oxytocin. It can instigate maternal behaviors in female rodents, but it takes an hour or so longer than oxytocin. By the reigning theory, vasopressin is of comparatively greater importance to the induction of loving and parental behavior in males than in females. Among prairie voles, who form the close-knit monogamous pair bonds so heartwarming to humans, vasopressin levels soar in males after mating, but not in females; it is after mating that a male will cleave to his partner. Among laboratory rats, males show varying degrees of paternal involvement, depending on the strain. The least fatherly of rat varietals is the Brattleboro rat. He is a dirty rat. He is also notably deficient in vasopressin.

What is sweet for a rodent is suggestive for a simian. In one of the few oxytocin experiments performed on primates, virgin female rhesus monkeys received injections of the hormone to the central nervous system. A few minutes later, an infant monkey was placed in their enclosure. The females walked over to it. They ogled it. They poked it gently and smacked their lips at it in a kind of kissing gesture. The monkeys also became friendlier toward their human observers, refraining from yawning and grimacing and otherwise displaying typical signs of rhesus resentment. By contrast, virgin females given control shots of saline showed no maternal leanings, did not smack their lips at a presented infant, and yawned peevishly at their captors.

Scanty though they are, the data from human studies conform to the model of oxytocin and vasopressin as emotional ligaments. Kerstin Uvnas-Möberg, of the Karolinska Institute in Sweden, has done much of the human work. She studies nursing mothers, in whom oxytocin levels are particularly high. Think of a breastfeeding woman, she says. Think of her singular physiology. Oxytocin is stimulating her milk letdown — that much is familiar. But milk ejection is only part of the story. Oxytocin, in concert with other peptides, also expands blood flow to the breast. The engorgement turns the breast warm, warmer than it's ever been. Heat radiates from the nursing woman as though she were feverish, as though she were a flagstone in the sun. She feeds the baby fluids and bathes the baby in warmth.

"There's a whole transfer of warmth, and that's very important, isn't it?" Uvnas-Möberg says. "Isn't that the substrate for love? To transmit warmth? When we talk about a loving person, we call her a warm person. A person who refuses to love is called a cold person. In this case, psychology has borrowed from very deep aspects of physiology." Uvnas-Möberg speaks in a warm voice, a hushed and intimate voice, as though we were sitting in a room and breastfeeding together rather than sitting in an office at the Karolinska Institute fully buttoned up, no infants in sight. She wears a suit the color of grasshopper pie, and her cheeks are round, and her face is rosy and shiny, like polished fruit.

"To mother a child is a matter of giving out energy and warmth, which both require calories," she says. "Which is a very dangerous thing, an expensive thing. Which means that oxytocin has another side, a saving side. Because if there is going to be an equation that comes out right, you have to take in somewhere what you're losing in warmth and milk."

Oxytocin is a giving hormone, and it is a conservative hormone, she says. It acts on the gut to slow digestion and allow every possible ingested calorie to be captured by the body. It increases insulin concentrations, so that as much sugar in the blood as possible is pulled into cells rather than peed away. A nursing mother should save energy in her behavior too. She should feel calm, be able to sit and sit. Fidgeting wastes calories. Feeling anxious wastes calories. Feeling calm conserves them, helps balance the equation, giving warmth, radiating warmth, but gaining anabolic strength, for the more you give, the more oxytocin is produced, and the greater the gut's conservation capacities are, and the more serene you feel. It's like one of those white sales in a department store: the more you spend, the more you save.

Uvnas-Möberg and her colleagues have studied women as they nurse and hold their infants. They watch the behavior of the mothers and have the mothers take personality tests. They ask the mothers how long they generally breastfeed during each session. The scientists measure oxytocin and other hormone levels in the blood, taking samples every thirty seconds for ten minutes of breastfeeding. They have found that oxytocin secretion patterns differ among women. In some there are peaks and valleys: the oxytocin is secreted in bursts. In other women, the pattern of secretion is fairly flat, basin and range rather than mountains. "It turns out that the more peaks you have, the higher your total oxytocin concentration, and the longer a woman tends to breastfeed," she says. "It's also correlational to personality changes. Women with the most peaks report feeling the greatest calm. They say they feel more emotionally accessible than they did before. They say they feel attached to their children. Which is very reasonable. The higher the oxytocin, the longer they breastfeed. The longer they breastfeed, the more time they spend in contact with the baby, and the closer they feel, physically, emotionally, and, I might add, neurochemically."

A mother does more than nurse and warm the baby. As she holds the baby, she touches it. She strokes the infant to soothe it. "You know the right way to stroke somebody," Uvnas-Möberg says. "You know what works and what doesn't. If you do it like this, too fast, that's irritating." She rubs her hand up and down rapidly on her arm to demonstrate. "If you do it too slowly, that doesn't work either." She gives her arm a dull, slow stroke. "But now, if you do this, if you stroke steadily and calmly, you know, this is right, this is good and true." She strokes her arm rhythmically, and I watch, and as I watch I feel vicariously stroked and vicariously soothed. "This rate is about forty strokes per minute," Uvnas-Möberg says. "This is the same rate at which we stroke our pets." Oxytocin again enters the picture. When the scientists take blood samples of women as they stroke their infants, they see the same activation

of oxytocin systems seen with breastfeeding. The mother secretes oxytocin as she caresses her child, for her hand is feeling the soothing sensation of stroking, just as her child feels the balm of being stroked. The
mother describes a sense of calm, and if you pinch her, she will hardly
feel it. "We know that you can induce pain reflexes from anywhere with
a pinch," says Uvnas-Möberg. "But we can induce sedation and pain
relief by touching and stroking any part too. Somehow we know that,
don't we? It's an innate knowledge, though we forget it sometimes, or
feel embarrassed that we know it."

Touch conveys warmth. To stroke is to underscore that we are touching, and giving, and there. Perhaps we were depilated for the sake of
touch and the ease with which it coaxes love. We stroke our babies, and
we rock them back and forth. Shopping for a nursing rocker is one of
the pleasures of impending motherhood, and just the thought of rock-
ing the baby back and forth fills you with warmth and joy. Women in
China take a warm shower during labor, and they almost never need
Pitocin, for the warm, pulsing water liberates their natural stores of
oxytocin; and women in the West are learning as much, for some
natural birthing centers now offer Jacuzzis. Other mammals lick themselves during labor, lick lick lick. And afterward they lick their pups or
kittens, and the babies nuzzle into it; this is as lovely as life will be. A
steady caress inveigles oxytocin secretion. The gentle rhythmic stroking
is like the pulsing of a milk duct, like the rate at which the infant
reflexively, rhythmically suckles at the breast. This is the rhythm of love:
forty beats a minute.

The rhythm of love. Orgasm is another rhythmic sensation, and it too
clocks in at about forty to fifty throbs a minute, and the uterus contracts
during orgasm as it does in giving birth. Oxytocin's frequency; oxytocin's handiwork. In one study women were asked to masturbate to
climax, and their blood levels of oxytocin were measured before and
after orgasm. The concentration of oxytocin climbed slightly but meas-
urably with climax, and the greater the increase, the more pleasurable
the women reported their climax to be. Some nursing women say they
feel not so much sedated while they breastfeed as exhilarated, almost
orgasmic, their uterus pulsing along with their milk ducts, along with
the baby's suckling mouth. Exhilaration is not really different from

tranquillity. Both states are characterized by a dampening of the sympathetic nervous system, a lowering of blood pressure, a declination of stress. Nirvana is defined as an ideal condition of rest, harmony, stability, and joy. A meditative state can be attained through measured, rhythmic breathing. Love and joy are at once animating and restorative. They are built on harmonics, a vivid wave form that can be maintained with a minimal investment of energy at the point of origin — as close as we'll come to the impossible dream, a perpetual motion machine.

"Patterns are beginning to emerge," says Uvnas-Möberg. "I think we're going to find subgroups of people who have high levels of oxytocin and low levels of anxiety and low blood pressure. Well, should that surprise us? You wouldn't be surprised if I told you that people with high cortisol or adrenaline levels were more stressed. The opposite is probably true as well. We just haven't looked for that systematically. But anecdotally, everything fits. Women with high anxiety levels also have low oxytocin levels. Children with recurrent abdominal pain who come to the hospital often have extremely low oxytocin levels. Recurrent abdominal pain is a classic symptom of anxiety in children."

The gut knows more than we realize, and it keeps the brain apprised of what it has learned. It speaks in the language of hormones, among them cholecystokinin, a metabolic hormone known to foster a feeling of satiety. "A lamb becomes bonded to its mother by the act of suckling," says Uvnas-Möberg. "That suckling motion does a number of things. It releases oxytocin in the lamb's brain, and it releases cholecystokinin in the lamb's gut. If you block oxytocin release, you prevent the lamb from attaching to its mother. The same for cholecystokinin. Block its release, and you interfere with the lamb's ability to bond.

"The brain and gut are linked," she says. "Psychologists know the importance of the gut to learning. Babies take something into the mouth to know it, to understand it. We say we know something in our gut. We say the way to a man's heart is through his stomach. We become pleasant and generous once we've eaten. It's hard to be pleasant and generous when we're feeling hungry." And now we see another reason that a person who refuses an offer of food is a person we are wary of. The person doesn't want to be calmed. The person wants to stay alert, high-strung. The person is a threat. No wonder we dislike eating in the company of somebody who forgoes food. We can't afford to be unilaterally lulled. Hold the cholecystokinin, please. There will be no oxytocin klatches tonight.

The body attaches us with the strength of every sense and substance at its disposal. Extreme stress plays the midwife to deep devotion. A woman gives birth yowling and screaming, begging that this creature, this Willy the Whale, be freed, goddamn it, be removed by enema if necessary. For the baby the passage is no smoother, and during birth its stress hormone output shoots up to impossible heights, a hundred times the level seen in a normal human being. And not long afterward, there the two of them are, fastened to each other, warmed and beaming, Buddha and her bodhisattva.

Smell too is a subcognitive minister, preaching bonds that we are at a loss to describe or understand. A human newborn is helpless, pathetically uncoordinated, but if you place the infant on the mother's stomach after birth it will inch its way up to her breast, driven almost entirely by olfactory cues; and if one breast is washed and the other left unwashed, the infant will seek out the unbathed nipple. The fontanel of a baby's head, where the plates of the skull have not yet fused together, is rich in sweat glands that exude odors, and a mother smells the fontanel often, lowers her head without thinking and takes a sniff. Parent and child may become bonded to each other prenatally, through an exchange of odors or odorlike molecules. The fetus secretes its signature scent into the urine that makes up the amniotic fluid of the womb. The fluid is turned over and excreted into the mother's urine, and thus she gets to know her baby's smell before birth, and the father may become familiar with his gestating infant's smell as well, by being in close proximity to the mother. Fathers love their newborns as profoundly as mothers do, even without the physical and hormonal changes that come with pregnancy. Ambient fetal odor types may serve to indoctrinate the circuits toward a receptive and compliant condition. John Money, a caliph of sexology research, has said that a person who is anosmic — who has no sense of smell — can feel lust but cannot form attachments. When one spouse dislikes the other spouse's smell, the marriage is doomed to fail. "'Don't marry Hermengard,' Pope Stephen III wrote to Charlemagne. 'She stinks like all the Longobards.' Charlemagne married her anyway, and ended up repudiating her," Guido Ceronetti writes in *The Silence of the Body*. "He couldn't stand her stench."

Touch, taste, smell: in the solicitation of love, no sense is left unseized. And because we are above all a visual species, babies play on this by pleasing the eye — by being almost too cute, literally, to bear. During the very last weeks of pregnancy, a human infant lays down a layer of subcutaneous fat. The difference between a slightly premature and a full-term baby is largely a matter of two pounds of fat tissue, and the extra bulk makes the birth harder for the mother. A gorilla baby is born with almost no fat on it and instead starts gaining fat and weight postpartum. Why a human baby arrives prefattened isn't clear; there's no obvious physiological justification for the adipose stores. Some have proposed that the fat is there for the sake of the brain, but if great doses of lipids were needed to stoke the infant's fast-growing brain after birth, we would expect to see a high fat content in human milk. Instead the opposite is true, and human milk is comparatively low in fat. Sarah Blaffer Hrdy suggests that babies are fat to make them look adorable. Fat is an aesthetic epoxy. We are drawn to the sight of a chubby, soft, rounded baby, with its round cheeks, round buttocks, fleshy arms and thighs. The visual seductions of a baby, its cuteness quotient, may magnify its power to win the warmth, the nose, the touch, the low-fat holy water of its mother. What comes round stays around.

Rounded too is the sound of love, the rising and falling voice with which we coo at babies and at a mate. Babies respond most strongly to a voice modulated in clear highs and lows. They must learn language. They must wrap their brains around language, and they learn through well-defined pitches and ups and downs and each word spoken clearly and spoken to them. If baby talk sounds warm, it is a transfer of another sort of warmth, for through baby talk a parent gives a baby mind food, gives the founder units of language, the surest source of human strength. As adults, we coopt the warmth of baby talk to win a lover's affections. We step ontogenically backward, offering through burbles, coos, swoops, and fey nicknames of our own invention.

We know when we are in a groove, and it feels good, and it feels as though we can go on with it forever. A loved one sedates us when we are frazzled and elates us when we have lapsed into inertia. A well-bonded pair of old marrieds are synchronized watches. Their faces have become

alike, because their facial muscles have taken to mimicking, unconsciously, the motions of the other. Their speech rhythms are similar.
They walk at the same pace. When a husband or wife dies within a few
days or weeks of his or her long-term spouse, we infer that the second
person dies of grief or shock. But often there is no sign of shock or
despair, for after all, the couple has lived long lives and known that
death is there. Instead, one death may follow the other coincidentally.
Over the years, the cells of the spouses had assumed a similar rhythm,
were beating apace, and so ran out of molecular time in tandem.

There are the stimuli of attachment that we know of, and those that
slip in unsung and unknowable. Years and years after a woman has
delivered a child, she continues to carry vestiges of that child in her
body. I'm talking about tangible vestiges now, not memories. Stray cells
from a growing fetus circulate through a woman's body during pregnancy, possibly as a way for the fetus to communicate with the mother's
immune system and forestall its ejection from the body as the foreign
object it is. The fetal-maternal cell dialogue was thought to be a short-
lived one, lasting only as long as the pregnancy. Recently, though, scientists have found fetal cells surviving in the maternal bloodstream decades after the women have given birth to their children. The cells didn't
die; they didn't get washed away. They persisted, and may have divided
a few times in the interim. They're fetal cells, which means they've got a
lot of life built into them. A mother, then, is forever a cellular chimera,
a blend of the body she was born with and of all the bodies she has
borne. Which may mean nothing, or it may mean that there is always
something there to remind her, a few biochemical bars of a song capable
of playing upon her neural systems of attachment, particularly if those
attachments were nourished through a multiplicity of stimuli, of sensorial input — the hormonal pageantry of gestation, the odors of fetal
urine, the great upheaval of delivery, and the sight and touch of the
newborn baby.

For all the reasons that I remain a staunch supporter of abortion
rights, for all the reasons that a woman is entitled to her full sexuality
regardless of the unreliability of birth control and of the human heart,
here is another one. It is vicious to force a woman to bear a baby she
doesn't want, to prod her vengefully through the compound priming of
pregnancy and force her to be imprinted through every physiological

contrivance at evolution's disposal with an infant she can't keep, an infant that will remain forever stuck in her blood, an antigen to the attachment response, try as she will to shed her sad past. The "adoption option" is fine if a young woman chooses it and is at peace with it. But option it must remain, for the body is a creature of habit, and the longer it has been exposed to the chemistry of bondage, the more prone it becomes to emotional flashbacks, to recurrent neuroendocrine nightmares, the sort of nightmares where you keep returning to your childhood neighborhood and you're not sure why, and you know you don't belong there anymore, yet still you return, step up to your old door, and ring the bell. Nobody answers. It's the wrong house. Your house is gone.

All is fair in love, and love knows that, and love conquers all with anything it can get its tender talons into, at forty strokes per minute. There are multiple, interlacing neural systems of attachment, and the gut jumps in, and the heart plays too, through the graces of stress. But love is more than a gut feeling or a raw emotion. It has its cognitive side as well. Too often we ignore the thoughtfulness of love. We may even deride the intellect when we talk of love, accusing somebody of being too "cerebral" or "analytical" about love, as though cognition were the antithesis of emotion. It is not. Thought can strengthen love as readily as it can allow the passive-aggressive rationalist poseur to weasel out of love. A thought alone can arouse the entire sensorial panel of love. When a lactating mother is away from her baby and imagines nursing it, her chest grows warm and she may start secreting milk. Susan Love described a colleague of hers, a surgeon, who said that once she started thinking about her baby in the middle of performing an operation, and within moments breast milk had leaked through her clothes and onto her unconscious patient.

Cort Pedersen has pointed out that we humans can maintain with our mind's eye the neuronal state of attachment, which other animals need their real eyes, noses, and ears to keep alive. We rarely can sever all components of an intimate bond, he says. We have photographs. We have friends who mention the loved one. We walk the same streets and eat in the same restaurants where once we strolled and dined and released cholecystokinin with the loved one. We have Sam playing that song, you *must* remember this. We have too many senses and systems eager to reenact the past, and we have too much memory. Again and again the pathways of old love are reignited. Our analytical minds feed and protect the circuits of attachment. The human capacity for thought and memory keeps love alive long after the lower brain, the *Rattus* brain, would have thrown love away. Eternal love is a myth, but we make our myths, and we love them to death.

18

OF HOGGAMUS AND HOGWASH

PUTTING EVOLUTIONARY PSYCHOLOGY ON THE COUCH

WE CAN LOVE, and there are many reasons to love, but whom do we love, and why do we love them? We understand the genetic logic behind loving our children and our parents, although there are limits to these loves. Conflict between parent and offspring is an abiding fact of life, as much as we wish it otherwise, as much as we think we can talk our way out of it. The conflict is built into the system. Children want more than their parents are willing to give, and they'll try to manipulate things to procure their share and then some; but parents usually have more than one child, and they may plan on having even more children down the road, so they resist devoting too much to any single child and having their resources and strength sucked dry. As children — real or inner — we privately nurse a little myth of the perfect mother, the all-giving, all-loving mother. Mothers know they can be no such thing, that they cannot and will not give their all for one. Mothers must keep some for themselves, for the others, and for the eggs they have yet to hatch.

Mother-offspring conflict begins before birth, in a clandestine skirmish between the fetus, which tries to build a very big placenta and to absorb as many maternal calories as it can, and the mother, whose body responds by inhibiting the explosive growth of the placenta and protecting the mother from the precipitous depletion of her energy stores. The conflict continues throughout childhood. Babies cry, toddlers throw tantrums, children wheedle. And then, when the children reach puberty, the nature of the conflict shifts dramatically. The offspring want independence and a garden of their own; they might even hope that the parents soon will die and leave their resources to them. For their part, the parents may try to keep their grown children around a bit longer, enlisting them in the care of younger siblings and thereby enhancing the parents' personal reproductive success. Oh, it goes on. Children need love and nurturing to thrive, and parents are inclined to give it, are strung like fine violins to give it. But then the sweetness and filial light turns taut and sharp, snaps back to our old beetle-browed friend: aggression. Love and aggression are conjoined like Chang and Eng, the most famous sideshow act of all time: where you find one, the other must be.

Yet parent-offspring conflict pales in comparison to the war of love we all know best, the war we know so well that we've given it a morose, flaccid tag line, the Battle of the Sexes. To talk of the physiology of love and the evolution of love raises the question of what we want from love, what we look for when we search for love. We don't choose our children or our parents, and so the love we feel for them is leavened by a sense of fatalism; only a few New Agey types have the gall to blame a person for choosing his or her parents badly. But for our choice of mates and the expectations we hold for our mates, we must accept at least a modicum of responsibility. So what do we want from a mate, which for most women means a man, and what do men want from us? What is the taproot of romantic love? Why do we bother getting married? Is it nature? Is it habit? Are we the marrying kind — *we* meaning humans in general, and then, parsed a notch or two closer, women in particular? Certainly we see marriage everywhere around us. In most cultures today, and historically, people have gotten married through some sort of ritualized ceremony, a public declaration that this man and this woman are an item on the tribe's register. Still, commonness doesn't necessarily indicate innateness. Just because we do get married doesn't mean we really want to get married, down to our Darwinized stem cells. Marriage could be like the written word, a tool so useful that it has become almost universal. But really, does anybody enjoy writing? And none would argue that writing is natural, even as natural as speech.

Let me confess right here and now that I don't know when, where, or how marriage was invented. I don't know if we're naturally inclined toward marriage or if it's like your mother's wedding gown — you'll need a brilliant tailor to make it fit you. Prairie voles *are* the marrying kind, or rather, the pair-bonding kind. They're born to affiliate, Noahfashion, male by female. So are a lot of birds. They couple up and raise their fledglings as a nuclear family unit. Nonhuman primates are *not* the marrying kind. Chimpanzees, bonobos, orangutans, monkeys — almost none of them are inclined to pair bond. They are polygamous. Males mate with many females. Females mate with many males.

Do you feel like a vole? A macaque? A canary, perhaps? Were you born to bond? Do you know? I don't. I surely don't. Sometimes I think that marriage suits us as well as or better than any alternative, and that children recognize the inherent rightness in having a daddy and a mommy on hand to rear them. Sometimes the words of Samuel Johnson sound like Newton's *Principia*. "Sir," he said to a dinner companion, General Paoli, "it is so far from being natural for a man and a woman to live in a state of marriage, that we find all the motives which they have for remaining in that connection, and the restraints which civilized society imposes to prevent separation, are hardly sufficient to keep them together."

I don't know the depths of our desire to marry. I don't know why we choose the partners we do, or what women really want from men and what men want from women. What I do know is that nobody else knows either. I know that the deep psychology of human love and human bondage is as yet a great mystery, though there are a few glittering sequins scattered here and there that tempt some to think, Oh yes, we see the light.

Love and marriage are considered womanly arts. They are ostensibly our property. We are said to want them. Men cadge, men scramble, men sweat, but finally men capitulate, sighing like stallions being led to the stable, while we, as women, need no persuasion. They bridle; we are brides! We are the marrying sex.

This, of course, is the party line, and has been for many years. It has earned a little ditty — written by William James, no less — which R. V. Short quoted, coyly, at the conclusion of his recent book, *The Differences Between the Sexes:*

> Hoggamus, higgamus
> Men are polygamous
> Higgamus, hoggamus
> Women monogamous.

And lately that idea has found new fodder and new fans, through the explosive growth of a field known as evolutionary psychology. Evolutionary psychology professes to have discovered the fundamental modules of human nature, most notably the essential nature of man and of woman. Now, it makes sense to be curious about the evolutionary roots of human behavior. It's reasonable to attempt to understand our impulses and actions by applying Darwinian logic to the problem. We're animals. We're not above the rude little prods and jests of natural selection. But evolutionary psychology as it has been disseminated across mainstream consciousness is a cranky and despotic Cyclops, its single eye glaring through an overwhelmingly masculinist lens. I say masculinist rather than male because the view of male behavior promulgated by hardcore evolutionary psychologists is as narrow and inflexible as their view of womanhood is.

Evolutionary psychology likes to think of itself as new and thrilling, but it is really just a subset of sociobiology, a discipline that is more than thirty years old. The grand patriarch of sociobiology, E. O. Wilson, defined his field as "the systematic study of the biological basis of all social behavior," though by biological he really meant evolutionary, for he was less interested in the proximate end of things — the "how" behind a behavior — than he was in the ultimate cause, the why of it. Many sociobiologists long have applied their reasoning to the study of human behavior; evolutionary psychologists simply formalized the application through the use of the anthropic term *psychology*. Evolutionary psychologists have been enormously successful at promulgating their views, I give them credit for that. Writing in *The New Yorker* in 1997, the movie critic David Denby talked about how fashionable evolutionary psychology is and how it has replaced Freudianism as the preferred method at cocktail parties for ad hoc dissections of a lover's despicable conduct. In my view the evo-psycho rendering of human nature has been granted far more homage than it deserves, perhaps because so much of it endorses our old prejudices and conforms to our mental Dewey decimal system. I don't like jabbering in perpetuity about the differences between men and women and who is better at mentally rotating a geometric figure in three-dimensional space or why it might be that different parts of the brain light up on a magnetic resonance scan when men and women think about the same things. As I said in the beginning, I have chosen to write a fantasia of the female body and mind rather than hashing and thrashing over what we do and don't know about X versus Y. I'm not going to explain to men what they really want or how they should behave. If a fellow chooses to tell himself that his yen for the fetching young intern in his office and his concomitant disgruntlement with his aging wife's housekeeping lacunae make perfect Darwinian sense, who am I to argue with him? I'm only going to propose here — in good humor, honest — that the hardcore evolutionary psychologists have got a whole lot of us gals all wrong, and that we want more and deserve better than the cartoon Olive Oyl handed down for popular consumption.

The cardinal premises of evolutionary psychology of interest to our discussion are as follows:

1. Men are more promiscuous and less sexually reserved than women are.
2. Women are inherently more interested in a stable relationship than men are.
3. Women are naturally attracted to high-status men with resources.
4. Men are naturally attracted to youth and beauty.
5. Our core preferences and desires were hammered out long, long ago, a hundred thousand years ago or more, in the legendary environment of evolutionary adaptation, or EEA, also known as the ancestral environment, also known as the Stone Age, and they have not changed appreciably since then, nor are they likely to change in the future.

In sum: higgamus, hoggamus, Pygmalionus, *Playboy* magazine, eternitas. Amen.

Hardcore evolutionary psychology types go to extremes to promote their theses, and to argue in favor of the yawning chasm that separates the innate desires of women and men. They declare ringing confirmation for their theories even in the face of feeble data. They suffer amusing internal contradictions of their data. They pick and choose, one from column A, one from column B, and good food, good meat, holy Darwin, let's eat!

For example: Among the cardinal principles of the evo-psycho set is that men are innately more promiscuous than women are, and that men are much more accepting of casual, even anonymous sex than women are. Men can't help themselves, they say. They are drawn to covet a multiplicity of partners. They are led by the blunt little nose at the end of their pricks, and women can't understand that, they say. When a female friend of mine questioned Robert Wright, the author of *The Moral Animal* and one of the prime popularizers of this position, about some of his unshakeable convictions in the male-female contrariety, he opened his eyes wide, stared at her, and said manfully, "You don't know what it's *like*." And she replied, "You don't know what it's like for us either." David Buss, of the University of Texas, another evolutionary psychologist of the unerring Nicene Creed, has said that asking a man not to lust after a pretty young woman is like telling a carnivore not to like meat.

At the same time, the biobehaviorists recognize that the overwhelming majority of men and women get married, and they have much to say about the differences between innate mate preferences among men and women. Men look for the hallmarks of youth, like smooth skin, full lips, and perky breasts; they want a mate who has a long childbearing career ahead of her. Men also want women who are virginal and who seem as though they'll be faithful and not make cuckolds of them. The sexy vampy types are fine for a Saturday romp, but when it comes to choosing a marital partner, men want the earmarks of modesty and fidelity. They want a little Lassie.

Women want a provider. They want a man who seems rich, stable, and ambitious. They want to know that they and their children will be cared for. They want a man who can take charge, maybe dominate them just a little, enough to reassure them that the man is genotypically, phenotypically, eternally a king. Women's innate preference for a well-to-do man continues to this day, the evolutionary psychologists insist, even among financially independent and professionally successful women who don't need the man as a provider. It was adaptive in the past to look for the most resourceful man, they say, and adaptations can't be willed away in a generation or two of putative cultural change.

And what of the evidence for these male-female verities? For the difference in promiscuity quotas, the hardcores love to raise the example of the differences between gay men and lesbians. Homosexuals are seen as a revealing population because they supposedly can behave according to the innermost impulses of their sex, untempered by the need to adjust to the demands and wishes of the opposite sex, as heterosexuals theoretically are. What do we see in our ideal study group? Just look at how gay men carry on! They are perfectly happy to have hundreds, thousands of sexual partners, to have sex in bathhouses, in bathrooms, in the Rambles of Central Park. By contrast, lesbians are sexually sedate. They don't cruise sex clubs. They couple up and stay coupled, and they like cuddling and hugging more than they do serious, genitally based sex. There's a phenomenon called "lesbian bed death," in which some lesbian couples, after an initial flurry of heated passion, settle into a near sexless relationship, measuring their encounters by the month rather than the day or week. Here is a joke the evo psychos like: Q. What does a lesbian bring on a second date? A. A U-Haul. Q. What does a gay man bring on a second date? A. What second date?

In the hardcore rendering of inherent male-female discrepancies in promiscuity, gay men are offered up as true men, real men, deep men, men unfettered, men set free to be men, while lesbians are real women, ultra-women, acting out every woman's fantasy of love and commitment without the fuss and slop of sex. Interestingly, though, in other theoretical instances, gay men and lesbians are not considered real men and real women, but the opposite: gay men are feminine men, halfway between men and women, while lesbians are posited as mannish women. Thus, in brain studies that purport to find the origins of sexual orientation, gay men are said to have hypothalamic nuclei that are smaller than a straight man's and closer in size to a woman's, and thus they are attracted to men. Their brains are posited as being so incompletely masculinized that they are said to be comparatively poor at math, girlish rather than boyish in their native talents. Lesbians are said to have relatively good visuospatial abilities, more like a man's than a woman's. One report in 1998 even implicated the lesbian inner ear as a source of her sexual orientation, finding it to be partly "masculinized," possibly, the researchers suggested, as a result of exposure to prenatal androgens. Young boys who like to play with dolls and tea sets are thought to be at risk for growing up into homosexual men; young girls who take tomboyishness to extremes are said to have a higher-than-average likelihood of ending up as lesbians. And so gay men are sissy boys in some contexts and Stone Age manly men in others, while lesbians are battering rams one day and flower into the softest and most sexually divested of feminine gals the next.

On the question of mate preferences, evo psychos rely on surveys, most of them compiled by David Buss. His surveys are celebrated by some, derided by others, but in any event they are ambitious — performed in thirty-seven countries, he says, on various continents and among a reasonable sampling of cultures and subcultures. His surveys, and others aspiring to them, consistently find that men rate youth and beauty as important traits in a mate, while women give comparatively greater weight to ambitiousness and financial success. In New Zealand, in China, in France, in Bangladesh — everywhere we speak in species-specific-speak. Men want a young, pretty wife, women want a mature, resourceful man. When a man is thinking about whether or not a woman is worth a significant investment of his time, surveys again come to the rescue, demonstrating that yes, men like their women to be good — madonnas, hold the latte, please. When shown pictures of women who are portrayed as either kohl-eyed temptresses or squeaky blond cheerleaders, men will choose Type A for a good time but Type B as a potential long-term partner. Surveys show that surveys never lie. Lest you think that women's mate preferences change with their mounting economic clout, surveys assure us not. Surveys of female medical students, according to John Marshall Townsend, of Syracuse University, indicate that they hope to marry men with an earning power and social status at least equal to and preferably greater than their own. This is obviously an immutable, everlasting female longing. Secretary or CEO, Cinderella wants her Rockefella.

But what happens if we go back to our favorite pure population group, homosexuals, and ask, Well, what do *they* choose when they choose their loved ones? Jokes about no second dates notwithstanding, gay men do couple up, in great numbers, even if they are not necessarily monogamous within their pair bond. So gay men and lesbians look for partners — but are they sex concordant or sex discordant in their mate criteria? Six of one, zilch of the other. Gay men like young, attractive gay men, while lesbians place comparatively little emphasis on their partner's beauty — yep, fits the stereotype. But do gay men have their infidelity monitors turned up high, as real men should? For real men don't want to be taken for a ride; real men have the adaptive anticuckold module firmly in place. No, sorry, no evidence for that premise. Gay men do not express any need for their chosen partner to be loyal. And a lucky thing too, for they are natural men, aren't they, and incapable of being faithful, so a gay man who demanded as much from his mate would remain forever single. As for the ingrained female desire that her partner be a provider, a dominant, resourceful go-getter, lesbians fail completely to toe the adaptive lady line. They don't require the promise that they and theirs will be provided for. To the contrary, they are suspiciously egalitarian in their style. They don't consider a woman's income or power to be particularly aphrodisiacal, as Henry Kissinger claimed a man's power was. In their study of three different permutations of American couples — heterosexual, gay male, and lesbian — Pepper Schwartz and Philip Blumstein found that only lesbians were able to avoid the squabbles over money that characterize so many failed relationships. Only among lesbian couples was the power balance in the relationship decoupled from each partner's income.

What does it mean if surveys show that women want a man who earns a living wage? It means that men can earn a living wage better, even now, than women can. Men still own and operate most of what can be claimed and controlled. They make up about half of the world's population, but they own somewhere between 75 and 95 percent of the world's wealth — the currency, the minerals, the timber, the gold, the stocks, the amber fields of grain. In her superb book *Why So Slow?*, Virginia Valian, a professor of psychology at Hunter College, lays out the extent of lingering economic discrepancies between men and women in the United States. In 1978, there were two women heading Fortune 1000 companies; in 1994, there were still two; in 1996, the number had jumped all the way to four. In 1985, 2 percent of the Fortune 1000's senior-level executives were women; by 1992, that number had hardly budged, to 3 percent. A 1990 salary and compensation survey of 799 major companies showed that of the highest-paid officers and directors, less than one half of one percent were women. Ask, and he shall receive. In the United States the possession of a bachelor's degree adds $28,000 to a man's salary but only $9,000 to a woman's. A degree from a high-prestige school contributes $11,500 to a man's income but subtracts $2,400 from a woman's — yes, subtracts, though no one knows why. The same disparity applies for overseas experience. A

man who spends time abroad can expect to enhance his salary by
$9,200. A woman who lives abroad can come back to a $7,700 decrement in her compensation. The most successful women in the world are
more precariously positioned than comparable men. In Hollywood, the
careers and asking price of actresses and female directors are easily
derailed by the occasional flop, even when the women are superstars
such as Sharon Stone and Barbra Streisand, while actors such as Kevin
Costner and Sylvester Stallone can appear in dog after dog and still
command the salary of plutocrats. If women continue to worry that
they need a man's money to persist because the playing field remains
about as level as the surface of Mars — or Venus, if you prefer — then
we can't conclude anything about innate preferences. If women continue to suffer from bag-lady syndrome even as they become prosperous, if they see their wealth as still provisional, still capsizable, and if
they still hope to find a man with a dependable income to supplement
their own, then we can credit women with intelligence and acumen, for
inequities abound and find new and startling permutations even in the
most economically advanced countries and among the most highly
skilled populations of women.

There's another reason that smart, professional women might respond on surveys that they'd like a mate of their socioeconomic status
or better. Smart, professional women are smart enough to know that
men can be tender of ego — is it genetic? — and that it hurts a man to
earn less money than his wife, and that resentment is a noxious chemical in a marriage and best avoided at any price. "A woman who is more
successful than her mate threatens his position in the male hierarchy,"
Elizabeth Cashdan, of the University of Utah, has written. If women
could be persuaded that men didn't mind their being high achievers,
were in fact pleased and proud to be affiliated with them, we might
predict that the women would stop caring about the particulars of their
mates' income. Sarah Blaffer Hrdy writes that "when female status and
access to resources do not depend on her mate's status, women will
likely use a range of criteria, not primarily or even necessarily prestige
and wealth, for mate selection." She describes a *New York Times* story
written by Donatella Lorch in 1996, called "Bride Wore White, Groom
Hopes for Parole." The story is about women from a wide range of
professions — bankers, judges, teachers, journalists — who marry male

prisoners. The allure of the men is not their income, for you can't earn much when you make license plates for a living. Instead, it is the men's gratitude that proves irresistible. The men are happy to have the love of these women, these smart, free women, and they focus all their thoughts, attention, and energy on their wives. The women also like the fact that their husbands' fidelity is guaranteed; the longer the inmates' sentences are, the more attractive the men become. "Peculiar as it is," Hrdy writes, "this vignette of sex-reversed claustration makes a serious point about just how little we know about female choice in breeding systems where male interests are not paramount and patrilines are not making the rules."

Do women love older men? Do women find gray hair and wrinkles attractive on men — as attractive, that is, as a fine, full head of pigmented hair and a vigorous, firm complexion? The evolutionary psychologists suggest yes. They believe that women look for the signs of maturity in men because a mature man is likely to be a comparatively wealthy and resourceful man. Of course, the thesis can't be taken too far. Desmond Morris once expressed his surprise that baldness wasn't considered a particularly attractive state. One might predict, he said, that since baldness comes with age and a man's status generally rises with age, the bald head, gleaming in the midday sun of the veldt or the fishbelly glow of a fluorescent office light, would lure the attention of every woman on the prowl for her alpha mate. But no, he admitted, there was no evidence that baldness was adaptive, nor that women admired rather than merely accepted a thinning hairline. Nevertheless, the legend of the sexy older man persists, particularly among older men. The older male moguls in Hollywood can't stop casting older male actors in roles that have them flinging about on the wide screen like elephants in musth, and the age gap between the men and their female costars gapes ever wider, leaving nothing to the female imagination but things we'd rather not imagine. Jack Nicholson, Clint Eastwood, Robert DeNiro, Al Pacino, Woody Allen: no matter how much their faces come to resemble a bassett hound's, no matter to what extenuated proportions their cartilaginous features grow, the men are portrayed as sexy, comely, frisky, desirable, to women twenty-five, thirty years their junior, to women who are themselves considered "mature" for being older than, oh, thirty.

Do women find older men innately attractive? Is it the men's alpha status? Or could it be something less complimentary to the male, something like the following — that an older man is appealing not because he is powerful but because in his maturity he has lost some of his power, has become less marketable and desirable and potentially more grateful and gracious, more likely to make a younger woman feel that there is a balance of power in the relationship? The rude little calculation is simple: He is male, I am female — advantage, man. He is older, I am younger — advantage, woman. By the same token, a woman may place little value on a man's appearance because she values something else far more: room to breathe. Who can breathe in the presence of a handsome young man, whose ego, if expressed as a vapor, would fill Biosphere II? Not even, I'm afraid, a beautiful young woman.

In the end, it matters not the reason why older men have access to younger women. As long as they do, some of them will partake. If they need Viagra to partake, they will petition their urologists forthwith. And women will feel cheated and pissy about the disparity in options of the middle-aged. What is important to question, and to hold to the fire of alternative interpretation, is the immutability and adaptive logic of the discrepancy, its basis in our genome rather than in the ecological circumstances in which a genome manages to express itself. Evolutionary psychologists insist on the innate discordance between the strength of the male and the female sex drive. They admit that many nonhuman female primates gallivant about rather more than we might have predicted before primatologists began observing their behavior in the field — more, far more, than is necessary for the sake of reproduction. Nonetheless, the credo of the coy female persists. It is garlanded with qualifications and is admitted to be an imperfect portrayal of female mating strategies, but then, that little matter of etiquette attended to, the credo is stated once again.

"Amid the great variety of social structure in [ape] species, the basic theme . . . stands out, at least in minimal form: males seem very eager for sex and work hard to find it; females work less hard," Robert Wright says in The Moral Animal. "This isn't to say the females don't like sex. They love it, and may initiate it. And, intriguingly, the females of the species most closely related to humans — chimpanzees and bonobos — seem particularly amenable to a wild sex life, including a variety of partners. Still, female apes don't do what male apes do: search high and low, risking life and limb, to find sex, and to find as much of it, with as many different partners, as possible; it has a way of finding them." In fact, female chimpanzees do search high and low and risk life and limb to find sex with partners other than the partners who have a way of finding them. As we have seen, DNA studies of chimpanzees in the Gombe show that half the offspring in a group of closely scrutinized chimpanzees turned out not to be the offspring of the resident males. The females of the group didn't rely on sex "finding" its way to them; they proactively left the local environs, under such conditions of secrecy that not even their vigilant human observers knew they had gone, and became impregnated by outside males. They did so even at the risk of life and limb — their own, and those of their offspring. Male chimpanzees try to control the movements of fertile females. They'll scream at them and hit them if they think the females aren't listening. They may even kill an infant they think is not their own. We don't know why the females take such risks to philander, but they do, and to say that female chimpanzees "work less hard" than males do at finding sex is not supported by the data.

Evo psychos pull us back and forth until we might want to sue for whiplash. On the one hand we are told that women have a lower sex drive than men do. On the other hand we are told that the madonna-whore dichotomy is a universal stereotype. In every culture, there is a tendency among both men and women to adjudge women as either chaste or trampy. The chaste ones are accorded esteem. The trampy ones are consigned to the basement, a notch or two below goats in social status. A woman can't sleep around without risking terrible retribution, to her reputation, to her prospects, to her life. "Can anyone find a single culture in which women with unrestrained sexual appetites aren't viewed as more aberrant than comparably libidinous men?" Wright asks rhetorically. Women are said to have lower sex drives than men, yet they are universally punished if they display evidence to the contrary — if they disobey their "natural" inclination toward a stifled libido. The diagnosis of "nymphomaniac" is never made on a man. Women supposedly have a lower sex drive than men do, yet it is not low enough. No, there is still just enough of a lingering female infidelity impulse that cultures everywhere have had to gird against it by articulating a rigid dichotomy with menacing implications for those who fall on the wrong side of it. There is still enough lingering female infidelity to justify infibulation, purdah, claustration. Men have the naturally higher sex drive, yet all the laws, customs, punishments, shame, strictures, mystiques, and antimystiques are aimed with full hominid fury at that tepid, sleepy, hypoactive creature the female libido. How can we know what is "natural" for us when we are treated as unnatural for wanting our lust, our freedom, the music of our bodies?

"It seems premature to attribute the relative lack of female interest in sexual variety to women's biological nature alone in the face of overwhelming evidence that women are consistently beaten for promiscuity and adultery," Barbara Smuts has written. "If female sexuality is muted compared to that of men, then why must men the world over go to extreme lengths to control and contain it?"

Why, indeed. We must keep asking why, why, why, and asking why the answers that the hardcores offer sound so tinny, one-sided, and self-exculpating. Consider a brief evolutionary apologia for President Clinton's adulteries that appeared in *The New Yorker,* written by the cognitive psychologist Steven Pinker, of the Massachusetts Institute of Technology. "Most human drives have ancient Darwinian rationales," Pinker wrote. "A prehistoric man who slept with fifty women could have sired fifty children, and would have been more likely to have descendants who inherited his tastes. A woman who slept with fifty men would have no more descendants than a woman who slept with one. Thus, men should seek quantity in sexual partners; women, quality." And isn't it so, he says, everywhere and always so? "In our society, most young men tell researchers that they would like eight sexual partners in the next two years; most women say that they would like one. On several college campuses, researchers have hired attractive assistants to approach students of the opposite sex and proposition them out of the blue. What proportion says yes? Of the women, zero percent; of the men, seventy-five percent. (Many of the remaining twenty-five percent ask for a rain check.)"

Let us hold a kaffeeklatsch about some of these statements, starting with the last. Women don't want to take a man up on his off-the-quad overture. Fancy that. Women don't want to take a strange and obviously aggressive man back to their dorm room or apartment for a quickie.

Could it be that they are in fear of their life rather than uninterested in the pleasure a handsome man might bring them? And could it be that young women just don't scare men physically the way young men do women? If there were no legitimate fear among the women, surely at least a couple of them would have turned out to be of the "whore" phenotype that supposedly characterizes some women and said yes. Moreover, I wonder how many of the men who said "Count me in!" to their solicitor would have followed through to a bona fide act of intercourse, would not have been a little nervous when push came to shove, if you will, about this forward, lascivious, inappropriately behaving dame, and perhaps started wondering if they were setting themselves up for a private screening of *Fatal Attraction*? In other words, were the men for real, or was it bluster? And do men truly like sex with women when the women are in charge? What if the man fails to perform, if he proves impotent or ejaculates prematurely, and what if the woman who propositioned him expresses her disappointment or disgust rather than acting as women do in these circumstances and reassuring him, it's fine, she doesn't mind, it happens to the best of them? Will he be so eager to jump into bed with the next stranger, or will he feel shame — a powerful deterrant to sexual behavior that women know quite well indeed?

Men say they want eight partners in two years. Women want but one. Yet would a man find the prospect of a string of partners so appealing if the following rules were applied: that no matter how much he may like a particular woman and be pleased by her performance and want to sleep with her again, he will have no say in the matter, will be dependent on her mood and good graces for all future contact; that each act of casual sex will cheapen his status and make him increasingly less attractive to other women; and that society will not wink at his randiness but rather sneer at him and think him pathetic, sullied, smaller than life? Until men are subjected to the same severe standards and threat of censure as women are, and until they are given the lower hand in a so-called casual encounter from the start, it is hard to insist with such self-satisfaction that, hey, it's natural, men like a lot of sex with a lot of people and women don't.

Consider Pinker's philandering caveman who slept with fifty women. Just how good a reproductive strategy is this chronic, random shooting of the gun? A woman is fertile only two or three days a month. Her ovulation is concealed. The man doesn't know when she's fertile. She might be in the early stages of pregnancy when he gets to her; she might still be lactating and thus not ovulating. Moreover, even if our hypothetical Don Juan hits a day on which a woman is ovulating, his sperm has only a 20 percent chance of fertilizing her egg; human reproduction is complicated, and most eggs and sperm are not up to the demands of proper fusion. Even if conception occurs, the resulting embryo has a 25 to 30 percent chance of miscarrying at some point in gestation. In sum, each episode of fleeting sex has a remarkably small probability of yielding a baby. Specifically, if we assume that the woman makes no effort at birth control — and this is a concession to the philanderer's point of view, for there is archaeological evidence that the use of rudimentary forms of contraception is quite ancient — the probability is less than one percent. ("In a chimpanzee," says Sarah Blaffer Hrdy, "maybe one in 130 copulations results in a conception, and that's copulations around the time of ovulation.") And because the man is beating and running, he isn't able to prevent any of his one-night stands from turning around and mating with other men. The poor fellow. He has to mate with so many scores of women for his wham-bam strategy to pay off. And where are all these women to be found, anyway? Sure, today there are interstate highways connecting one city and its singles bars to the next, and there are six billion people in the world, half of them egg-bearers. But population densities during that purportedly all-powerful psyche-shaper the "ancestral environment" were quite low, and long-distance travel was dangerous and difficult.

There are alternatives to wantonness, as a number of theorists have emphasized. If, for example, a man were to spend a bit more time with one woman rather than dashing breathlessly from sheet to sheet, if he were to feel compelled to engage in what animal behaviorists call mate-guarding, he might be better off, reproductively speaking, than the wild Lothario, both because the odds of his getting the woman during her fertile time would increase and because he'd be monopolizing her energy and keeping her from the advances of other sperm-bearers. It takes the average couple about four months, or 120 days, of regular sexual intercourse to become pregnant. That number of days is approximately equal to the number of partners our hypothetical libertine needs to sleep with to have one of them result in a "fertility unit," that is, a baby.

The two strategies, then, shake out about the same. A man can sleep with a lot of women — the quantitative approach — or he can sleep with one woman for months at a time, and be madly in love with her — the qualitative tactic. Forget about whether or not Romantic Joe will invest in any babies that come forth. He may just want to do what it takes to impregnate a woman whose ovulatory status he cannot be sure of, and to be her exclusive partner for the requisite "insemination episode," all factors operating under the chromosomal constraints that make human conception less assured than that of, say, a hamster or goat.

The problem with the two strategies is that they require rather contradictory emotional backdrops in order to operate at peak efficiency. The quantitative approach demands emotional detachment. The qualitative approach requires the capacity to fall in love rather quickly, to be smitten, and to seek out the woman's company all the time, day after day, month after month. Now it's possible that these two reproductive strategies are distributed in discrete packets among the male population, with the result that some men are born philanderers and can never attach while others are born romantics and perpetually in love with love; but it's also possible that men teeter back and forth from one impulse to the other, suffering an internal struggle between the desire to bond and the desire to retreat, with the circuits of attachment ever there to be toyed with, and their needs and desires difficult to understand, paradoxical, fickle, treacherous, and glorious. It is possible, then, and for perfectly good Darwinian reason, that casual sex for men is rarely as casual as it is billed.

Do men become infatuated with women, even women they have no intention of marrying? Of course they do. Men who see prostitutes often return to the same prostitute. Is the qualitative mating strategy the reason that men are hardly immune to romantic obsessions? Maybe, maybe not. I raise it in lawyerly style, as an objection to the glib assertion that men have a zest for noncommittal sex and women don't, and isn't it obvious why it is so? I'm disturbed by the ease with which inert and inadequate interpretations of human sexual behavior become engraved in the communal consciousness, to the point where nobody questions the stereotypes any longer, nor offers alternative explanations, nor dares to suggest that change is possible, nor dares to suggest that love and lust are not the characterological property of either sex.

There is so much left to be understood. Why do women have concealed ovulation, anyway? Why don't their buttocks turn bright red when they're fertile, as they do on a rhesus monkey? A standard proposal is that by keeping her ovulatory status a secret, a woman invites the long-term investment of a man and lures him to stay around day after day; and as I've said above, a man might be compelled to do so, in the hope of finally hitting a bull's-eye, a viable egg. But if the woman needs the man's extended investment, and if she can extract that investment only by disguising the current status of her fecundity, we might be surprised at the extreme visibility of the human *pregnancy*, which is more visible than that of any other female primate, particularly given the hair loss that has exposed the belly to public scrutiny. Even if a man stayed around for a few months until conception occurred, her pregnancy could be his cue that it was time to move on, which means that the woman would lose his help just when she needed him most, if need him she did. Men appear to be very tuned in to the state of a woman's waistline. Several cross-cultural studies have shown that men have a preference for women with a waist that is at least 30 percent smaller than her hips. The ratio is what matters, not the absolute body size. The woman may have hips as wide as a hippo's, but if her waist is 30 percent narrower by comparison, she still rates as comely. A cinched-in waist is a feature unique to women. Men have waists and hips of similar circumference. So too do other female primates, which is part of the reason that their pregnancies are not terribly obvious. In women, the surest disruption to an alluring waist-to-hip ratio is not getting fat, for many women deposit their fat on their hips and thighs rather than on their bellies, but being with child. What is the good of having cryptic ovulation for the purpose of attracting the sustained attentions of a man if a woman then goes ahead and gives him a laughably easy visual clue that his job is done, he's impregnated her and can move on to narrower pastures?

Perhaps a woman's body isn't designed to attract the long-term investment of a mate. A number of theorists have suggested that cryptic ovulation lends a woman a certain amount of control over her mating strategies, by making it more difficult for a man to monopolize her fecundity than it would be if she advertised her status during the few days when the egg is willing. A man attempting to claim exclusive rights to her must now attempt to guard the woman over an interval of weeks or months rather than days, and since the attention of even a vigilant male is likely to lapse now and again as the weeks pass, the woman can be freed to wander, thereby gaining whatever benefits philandering might bring. She can be freed to mate with several local males, thus confusing the issue of paternity and lessening the chance that one of them will commit infanticide, or increasing the total intake of male help for her offspring.

Who knows the reason for cryptic ovulation, or any other salient feature of human sexuality? I don't — but neither do the evolutionary psychologists. They just sound as though they do, and disagreeing with them is like trying to tell a carnivore you're taking away its meat. Men want sex with many partners more than women do, and women want love more than men do. These are the truths that we hold to be self-evi-dent. But they are not self-evident when you run them through the meat grinder of analysis. Why in the name of Demeter should a woman be prone to fall in love and hitch her future to the commitment of one man and forsake the possible contributions of other prospects if men are by nature so prone to abandon her? The answer is, they're probably not. They're probably prone to be opportunistic by nature, which is the nature of most intelligent, highly gregarious creatures. Human nature, in other words.

If men today appear to be more interested in all manner of sexual stimuli than women are, if they are the major consumers of pornogra-phy and prostitution, and if they say in surveys they'd like to dabble around with as many gals as will approach them on the street with a clipboard in hand, we gals can only reply, It's a man's world, designed for the pleasures of men; and on those rare occasions when a female-friendly sexual nerve is tapped, females respond with crows and roars of hunger and delight. "Why are women so seldom whipped up into an onanistic frenzy by pictures of men?" Robert Wright asks. Except when they are. For example, Raul Julia, may he not be resting in peace, was in the mid-1970s one of the great sex symbols for New York's womankind. A poster of his face, with his dark, knowing, heavy-lidded eyes and his full, beestung lips, was plastered everywhere, advertising the Broadway production of *The Threepenny Opera,* in which he played Mack the Knife. I was a teenager, and I remember stopping and staring at the poster frequently, feeling lust in my parts, and I remember talking about the poster to my friends, and I guess everybody must have been talking about that poster, because one of the alternative newspapers ran a story with the headline "Why Every Woman in New York Wants to Fuck Raul Julia." More recently, the actor Jimmy Smits has played a similar sex-puppy role, and the producers of *NYPD Blue* must have realized as much, for they gave us not one but several episodes in which his naked butt was displayed.

Oh, opportunity. Bill Clinton has affairs; Hillary Clinton does not (or so we're told). The funny thing is, it looks like Bill didn't always have to work that hard for his sex; sex had a way of finding him. (He's become a female chimpanzee!) Were handsome young interns hurling themselves at the first lady? Or were they intimidated rather than aroused by her power? Former congresswoman Patricia Schroeder has observed rue-fully that powerful middle-aged women are not exactly a turn-on for men. We can't deny that young people are as a rule prettier than older people, and if an older man can attract a younger woman, we can see why he might be tempted to indulge. But if the older woman is unable to manage likewise, her innate desire and temptation have nothing to do with it. Assuming that our sexual drive is adapted to maximize our fitness at the time when such fitness counts — for women, during the years of their peak fertility, between the ages of sixteen and twenty-eight — then the basic machinery of that drive would be our gift or burden for our entire adult life. In other words, even though a woman of forty-five is considerably less fertile than a woman of twenty-two, she still feels, in some cloaked part of her soul, like a greedy young woman. One of the commonest symptoms of neurodegenerative disease and stroke in older women is the release of sexual inhibitions. The women lose their "dignity." They become dirty old ladies. Lynn Johnston gave a rare voice to an old lady's lewdness in her comic strip *For Better or for Worse* when she showed an elderly woman, her health failing, being lifted from her bed into a stretcher by two strapping young ambulance workers. "My, you two boys are strong — and handsome, too!" the woman says with a grin, at which her middle-aged daughter exclaims,

"Mom!" In the next panel, the old woman's thought balloon is "I've always wanted to make passes at handsome young men — and now I'm finally free to do so." Freed by dint of grave illness; the character died soon afterward.

We don't have to argue that men and women are exactly the same, or that humans are meta-evolutionary beings, removed from nature and slaves to culture, to reject the perpetually regurgitated model of the coy female and the ardent male. Conflicts of interest are always among us, and the outcomes of those conflicts are interesting, more interesting by far than what the ultra–evolutionary psychology line has handed us. Patricia Gowaty, of the University of Georgia, sees conflict between males and females as inevitable and pervasive. She calls it sexual dialectics. "Human mating systems are characterized by conflict from start to finish," she says. Karl Marx saw workers and managers as locked in an eternal struggle over who controls the means of production. The thesis of sexual dialectics is that females and males vie for control over the means of *re*production. Those means are the female body, for there is as yet no such beast as the parthenogenetic man. Women are under selective pressure to maintain control over their reproduction, to choose with whom they will mate and with whom they will not — to exercise female choice. If they make bad mating decisions, they will have less viable offspring than if they are clever in their choices. Men are under selective pressure to make sure they're chosen or, barring that, to subvert female choice and coerce the female to mate against her will. "But once you have this basic dialectic set in motion, it's going to be a constant push-me, pull-you," Gowaty says. "That dynamism cannot possibly result in a unitary response, the caricatured coy woman and ardent man. Instead there are going to be some coy, reluctantly mating males and some ardent females, and any number of variations in between.

"All of these strategies and counterstrategies are going on in real time, so that we have responses associated with learning and experience rather than as a result of coded genetic modules," Gowaty says. "The ecological problems that one sex has to solve are produced by the other sex. Nothing is fixed. Until we incorporate that notion, of the dynamic and dialectic pressures underlying human mating systems, we'll never get to the real meat of human behavior, and we'll continue repeating the extreme, and extremely boring, parodies.

"I think that female choice has to give some viability benefits — that is, a female will choose to mate with a male whom she believes, consciously or otherwise, will confer some advantage on her and her offspring. If that's the case, then her decision is contingent on what *she* brings to the equation. For example, some theorists talk about the 'good genes' model of mate selection, the idea that a female looks for a male who exhibits signs of having a superior genotype. The 'good genes' model leads to oversimplified notions that there is a 'best male' out there, a top-of-the-line hunk whom all females would prefer to mate with if they had the wherewithal. But in the viability model, a female brings her own genetic complement to the equation, with the result that what looks good genetically to one woman might be a clash of colors for another."

Maybe the man's immune system doesn't complement her own, for example, Gowaty proposes. There's evidence that the search for immune variation is one of the subtle factors driving mate selection, which may be why we care about how our lovers smell; immune molecules may be volatilized and released in sweat, hair, the oil on our skin. We are each of us a chemistry set, and each of us has a distinctive mix of reagents. "What pleases me might not please somebody else," Gowaty says. "There is no one-brand great male out there. We're not all programmed to look for the alpha male and only willing to mate with the little guy or the less aggressive guy because we can't do any better. Some women might find it exciting to be with the little guy. He might be a fabulous lover. She might like him for all the subliminal reasons of chemistry that we find hard to articulate. But the propaganda gives us a picture of the right man and the ideal woman, and the effect of the propaganda is insidious. It becomes self-reinforcing. People who don't fit the model think, 'I'm weird, I'll have to change my behavior.'"

It is this danger, that the ostensible "discoveries" of evolutionary psychology will be used as propaganda, that makes the enterprise so disturbing. And evolutionary psychologists sometimes do dispense advice. Robert Wright is persuaded that the madonna-whore dichotomy is "rooted firmly in the male mind." Not just his mind, or the minds of his like-minded friends, but *the* male mind. Thus he gently and generously advises women who want to get married to abide by the old verities and resist the sexual overtures of a suitor, lest their easy capitulation "stifle any budding feelings of love" the man may have had for them. Consciously or unconsciously, he says, men put women to the test. They try to get women into bed, and if the women agree too readily, that's it, the women are tramps and can't be trusted. "Women who would like a husband and children have been known to try the Emma Wedgwood plan for landing a man," he writes, referring to Mrs. Charles Darwin. "In its most extreme form, the plan runs as follows: if you want to hear vows of eternal devotion right up to your wedding day — and if you want to make sure there *is* a wedding day — don't sleep with your man until the honeymoon." But where is the evidence that women who "give in too easily" do not get married, while those who remain chaste do? There is no such evidence, and Wright admits as much. Nevertheless, the principle of delayed gratification is a sound one, he insists. "Some women have found that a move of *some distance* toward austerity may make sense" (emphasis in original). But how long is this "some distance toward austerity" supposed to be? What will it take to calm a man's cuckold-control monitor? No sex until the third date? The third month of dating? A year? Oh dear. Every man has one, it seems, but the sizes are all different. What is a millennial gal to do? Maybe she should just ask the fellow. How long is it, sir? How long, oh lord, how long?

In fact, women who start trudging down the path of austerity for the sake of proving to men their "goodness," chastity, and marriageability may find their Cinderella slippers splattered with all sorts of unpleasant effluvia. A full concordance with the familiar portrait of female modesty may demand other behavioral concessions beyond keeping our legs tightly crossed — for example, not seeming overtly clever. Smart girls have always been told that they should try to hide their intelligence, that men don't find bright, outspoken women terribly appealing. Could the man's fear of female intelligence be linked to his ostensibly innate fidelity surveillance equipment, reflecting his worry that a shrewd woman will figure out how to cheat on him the moment his back is turned? I have no data to support this proposition. But it makes sense, doesn't it? So if you're going to start advising a woman to act virtuously, even when she doesn't feel particularly virtuous, why not go the distance and advise her to seem docile and insipid as well? Ladies, if you want your Mrs. degree, you'll have to forgo the Ph.D.

I might also point out that by the very principles to which hardcore evolutionary psychologists subscribe, it's a waste of time to listen to any man's advice on how to catch a man, for Wright himself says that men are selected to be extraordinarily "treacherous," more treacherous than males in most species are, and to lie to women constantly, and to be so good at their lies that they themselves believe them to be the truth. Why then should a woman believe a man who tells her that she should be good to win a man's heart, and that she shouldn't believe a man who swears to her as he tries to yank off her clothes that yes, he'll still love her in the morning?

As Gowaty sees it, biologists have yet to develop good theoretical models to explain variations in female strategies. "It's been an uphill battle in behavioral ecology to get people to the point where they don't think of female animals as all coming from the same cookie cutter and having the same needs," she says. "For bluebirds, we might talk about variations in metabolic rate, foraging skills, or the local abundance of insects. For humans, it might be a variation in the ability to remember where the tubers are that you need to eat. Evolutionary psychologists like to talk about the environment of evolutionary adaptation. Well, we don't have time machines, so to say what this ancestral environment may have been is a real puzzle. But if we look around us at the phenotypes we see among modern humans, it's safe to say that whatever the EEA was, it surely selected for an enormous amount of variation. We're not all virgins, we're not all whores."

While the strategies and means may differ from one woman to the next, the basic ecological problems that we must solve have always been fairly straightforward: gaining access to the resources we need to survive and reproduce. As Gowaty puts it, "We're still foragers at heart, though today we may forage at Kroger's rather than in the bush. We're still concerned with retaining control over mate choice. Society constrains our choices dramatically. If we don't get equal pay for equal work, that deficiency affects our ability to forage at Kroger's, which in turn influences our choice of mate. What has feminism been about but equity issues and reproductive issues? That's what we've been talking to each other about for the last thirty years."

These are the issues at the heart of feminism. They are also the obsessions of any female transient at the Gaia Arms Hotel, whether feathered, furred, or depilated. Who says that feminism and evolutionary biology must inevitably spit on each other's slippers? The hardcore evolutionary psychologists see feminism as a myopic and possibly doomed enterprise, a utopian prayerbook that denies ancient human drives and the fundamental discordance between male and female opportunities and limitations. If their depictions of men and women sound stereotyped, that is because they are, and for a reason. In the Darwin-o-gram reckoning of human nature, a stereotype is not an intellectual pitfall to guard against; it's an opportunity! What is a stereotype if not an expression of a potentially universal truth, which means it could be the signpost of an adaptation, a trait that might have conferred selective advantage on those who bore it? All of which merits further exploration by the distribution of a questionnaire to a couple of hundred willing college students to see whether or not they believe the stereotype to be true.

But there are many scientists and scholars who denounce the unilateral version of neo-Darwinism that has trampled across the campus of public opinion like a pack of fraternity brothers on a panty raid, feeling no humbleness for want of evidence or for the many exceptions to their book of rules. There are plenty of evolutionary biologists who know that their effort to understand human nature is far, far from over, is a neonate who has yet to find its way to its mother's teat. There are female primatologists who have spent too many years watching female primates carry on like . . . well, like stereotypical gay men to accept the prefabricated image of the coy female, however airbrushed with concessions and caveats the image has lately been. There are ornithologists who have observed birds living in family arrangements that remind them of human families, with the father there and contributing and the grandparents and cousins and uncles nearby; and they have seen female birds refusing to act like gentle bluebirds of happiness, and they have cried out for better models to account for the extraordinary variation flapping its wings before them.

Variation and flexibility are the key themes that get set aside in the breathless dissemination of evolutionary psychology. "The variation is tremendous, and is rooted in biology," Barbara Smuts said to me.

"Flexibility itself is the adaptation." Females vary. So too do males. Smuts has studied olive baboons, and she has seen males pursuing all sorts of mating strategies. "There are some whose primary strategy is dominating other males, and being able to gain access to more females because of their fighting ability," she says. "Then there is the type of male who avoids competition and cultivates long-term relationships with females and their infants. These are the nice, affiliative guys. There's a third type, who focuses on sexual relationships. He's the consorter. He's not around females when they're pregnant or lactating, but when they're in estrus, he knows how to relate to them in a way that decreases the females' motivation to go after other guys. The strategy that a male pursues is not related to status or age. A high-status male can be an affiliative male, while a male who's low in the hierarchy may stake his future on his fighting power. Instead, the differences in mating strategy seem to be born largely of temperament, of innate differences in personality and physiology. And as far as we can tell, no one reproductive strategy has advantages over the others."

Men are at least as complicated as baboons — aren't they? Their temperaments vary, and their life circumstances vary, and so too must their reproductive tactics. "Some men have resources to offer, and they may tend toward promiscuity," says Smuts. "Some men can offer help with child care. One strategy is not necessarily a better route to reproductive fitness than the other. The man who is helping a woman take care of the children won't necessarily benefit if he suddenly decides to try the promiscuous strategy." The cost of his adultery may be greater than the small odds that he will sire an extra child through his philandering. Not only will his disloyalty distract him from his paternal duties, possibly leading to a poorer outcome for his existing offspring, but his wife may herself become less devoted to the relationship and start dallying around.

Men have tried to circumvent this problem with the creation of the double standard, the notion that it's acceptable for a man to commit adultery but iniquitous for his wife to do so. The double standard is the ultimate attempt by males to have it all, to have the guaranteed, true-blue reproducer at home and the slot machines that you play on the side. And evolutionary psychologists have argued that women are willing to accept the double standard provided the man keeps providing.

They claim that surveys show that men and women feel differently about threats to the primary relationship: men, they say, are most outraged at the thought of sexual infidelity in a mate, while women are less disturbed at the idea of a sexual infraction and more distressed at the thought of emotional infidelity in a husband. Their interpretation of the discrepancy is that a man's reproductive success is compromised by the possibility of being unwittingly saddled with another man's offspring, while a woman's success is most jeopardized if her husband leaves her for another love. Thus, the theory goes, it is adaptive for men to feel insane sexual jealousy and women to dread emotional betrayal. But for the life of me I can't see how a woman can "know," in that Stone Age way they supposedly know, the difference between a husband's harmless dalliance and a serious threat to her marriage, or how she can trust a man who has cheated on her sexually to be emotionally reliable and to stick around long enough to pay for college tuition. I *can* imagine how a woman might put up with bad behavior because she has no choice, because she is too poor to leave a rotten marriage and make it on her own.

It's hard to know what we really want to do beneath the multiple sheaths of compromise and constraint. Let's turn again to olive baboons. Female baboons, as they start heading toward estrus, become outrageously promiscuous. "I have seen them literally hop from one guy to the next," says Smuts. "They'll mate with ten different males in the space of an hour." But as the female's day of ovulation proper approaches, the males around her become ever less tolerant of her dabblings and begin to constrain her behavior. "You see a dramatic shift at peak estrus, from radical promiscuity to the female being with one male," says Smuts. The male she is with might be a rugged fighter type, an affiliator, or a lubricator; the point is, a male has claimed her, and males can make their position felt, for they are much bigger than the females and have a wicked set of slashing canines. Rebecca Dowhan, a student of Smuts's, wanted to know how a female would behave during peak estrus, the moment of truth, if not constrained by a single male. Working with a population of captive baboons, she took a female who had already formed an exclusive estrus consortship with one male, and she put the female in an area with that male and two other familiar males. The males were in separate cages, so the female could interact with each one, but they could not restrict her movements. How did the female respond to this unprecedented degree of freedom, a sexual sovereignty that would not exist for natural-born female baboons? She reverted to her Lotharia ways, fraternizing first with one male, then jumping to the next for a quick groom. She showed no preference for her consort — the male who had chosen *her*. The thing she seemed to crave was diversity.

We don't know why a female baboon bothers with being promiscuous, what she gets from all the effort. What we do know is that she must get something, for she works at it wildly unless strong-armed into good behavior. Most female animals are promiscuous. They go to great lengths to be promiscuous and to avoid being coopted by a mate-guarding male. Scientists often are flummoxed by the female sex drive. They can't always find good Darwinian justification for all the erotic energy. Male ejaculations are so genomically well endowed; why does a female get rapacious and take the time and expose herself to the risk of predation and disease to gather more than her spermic share? Every so often, though, the scientists find irrefutable, quantitative proof that promiscuity pays. A seven-year study of Gunnison's prairie dogs, for example, showed that females who mated with three or more males in a breeding season had a 100 percent conception rate and gave birth to an average of 4.5 pups, while females that mated with only one male had a 92 percent conception rate and an average litter of 3.5 pups. We can't say why the extra matings made for surer and bigger broods, but they did, and consequently female prairie dogs do everything in their power to resist males intent on keeping them down in the burrow and monopolizing their favors.

Humans don't have litters, yet still women philander, and sometimes it does a body, and the fruits of that body, demonstrable good. The hardcore evo-psycho brigade insists that males never invest in babies of whom they have the slightest doubt of paternity. But is the premise uniformly true, and has it always been true, even when humans lived in small bands of foragers who had yet to start worrying about property rights and the siring of undisputed heirs? The evidence brays otherwise. Among a number of traditional societies of lowland South America, people believe in "partible paternity" — the idea that a child can have more than one biological father. They believe that a child is a sort of spermic quilt, and that the multiple ejaculates of different men make for better and sturdier children than the discharge of one fellow alone can. In such cultures, married women often take a lover or three during pregnancy, and all of those lovers are considered fathers to the baby, with concordant responsibilities to show up with at least the occasional speared fish. Among the Ache foragers in eastern Paraguay, for example, the majority of women count on their consorts to help protect and provide meat for their offspring. In interviews with 17 Ache women, anthropologists Kim Hill and Hillard Kaplan found that each of their 66 children was attributed to an average of 2.1 possible progenitors. The Ache go so far as to recognize three different categories of fatherhood: one refers to the man to whom a woman is married when her child is born; the second, to the man or men she had extramarital relations with just before or during her pregnancy; and the third, to the man whom the woman believes actually inseminated her.

A similar state of affairs holds for the Barí people of Venezuela and Colombia, foragers and simple horticulturists who plant manioc and supplement their starchy diet with fish and game. More than two thirds of Barí women engage in extramarital sex during pregnancy, and their children benefit significantly from the practice. None of this is done clandestinely. When a woman is giving birth, she tells the midwife who her lovers were, and the midwife goes out afterward to announce to each of the men, "Congratulations. You have a child." The men are expected to help their partible offspring in hard times, and usually they do. Barí children with two or more fathers to their name have an 80 percent chance of surviving past the age of fifteen. For those with just a primary father, the survival rate is 64 percent.

What is in it for the Barí husbands? Why do they tolerate their wives' peccadilloes? For one thing, they have their affairs as well, usually with other married women. For another, their wives are not supposed to be promiscuous unless they are already pregnant, so presumably the husbands are the biological fathers of most, if not all, of their wives' offspring.

"We can hypothesize about the origins of partible paternity," says Stephen Beckerman, an anthropologist at Pennsylvania State University who has studied the Barí. "It's possible that females took control of the etiology, that it's working mainly to their benefit, and that men have no choice. But the truth is, the men don't seem to mind. They don't object. They're not demonstrably jealous. So you can speculate that partible paternity works for men as a kind of life insurance, a series of bets against the odds. A man allows other men to have sex with his wife. He bets that he will be the father of most if not all of his children. But if he should die, some other man will have a residual obligation to care for some of those children. If you look at it that way, you can see how partible paternity might be adaptive for both the women and the men."

There's so much gorgeous material left to be mined. Women are said to need an investing male (or more than one, if they can get it). We think we know the reason why. Human babies are difficult and time-consuming to raise. Chimpanzee females may be able to provision their offspring on their own, but women cannot. Stone Age mothers needed husbands to bring home the bison. Yet as we've already seen in the discussion of the organic grandmother, the age-old assumption that male parental investment lies at the heart of human evolution is now open to serious question. Men in traditional foraging cultures do not necessarily invest resources in their offspring. Hadza men hunt, but they share the bounty of that hunting widely, politically, strategically. They don't deliver it straight to the mouths of their progeny. Women rely on their senior female kin to help get their children fed. The men are often away hunting, in quest of big game. The women gather. There is a division of labor by sex. But in hunting, the men are not engaging in the most calorically productive enterprise. In many cases, they would be better off gathering, or combining an occasional hunt with the trapping of small prey. The big hunt, though, is a big opportunity, to win status and allies. The women and their children in a gathering-hunting society clearly benefit from the meat that hunters bring back to the group. But they benefit as a group, not as a collection of nuclear family units, each beholden to the father's personal pound of wildeburger.

This is a startling revelation, which upends many of our presumptions about the origins of marriage and what women want from men and what men want from women. If the environment of evolutionary adaptation was not defined primarily by male parental investment, the bedrock of so much of evolutionary psychology's theorizing, then we can throw the door wide open and breathe again, and ask new questions, rather than endlessly repeating ditties and calling the female coy long after she has run her petticoats through the presidential paper shredder.

For example: Nicholas Blurton Jones, of the University of California at Los Angeles, and others have proposed that marriage developed as an extension of men's efforts at mate-guarding. Just as male baboons demand exclusivity during peak estrus, so a man might attempt to claim access to a woman and keep other men away from her. The invention of lethal weapons of war very likely upped the ante for male-male competition relatively early in human evolution. When armed men fight, they can kill with far greater ease than the males of other species can. If fighting for access to females resulted in too high a cost too often, then the average archaic male wouldn't have wanted to get into such contests terribly often. In other words, the bedhopper, who tried to spread his seed quantitatively, might not have survived long enough to have many successful hits, for each effort at wooing a fertile female would have pushed him smack up against a thicket of other suitors' spear tips. The cost of philandering becomes ludicrously high. The man might be better off trying to claim rights to one woman at a time. Regular sex with a fertile woman is at least likely to yield offspring at comparatively little risk to his life, particularly if sexual access to the woman is formalized through a public ceremony — a wedding. Looked at from this perspective, we must wonder why an ancestral woman bothered to get married, particularly if she and her female relatives did most of the work of keeping the family fed from year to year. Perhaps, Blurton Jones suggests, to limit the degree to which she was harassed. Chronic male harassment can be a terrible problem for a female, he said, and if a woman has to forage to feed herself and her dependent young, the cost of harassment to her efficiency may be too high to bear. Better to agree to a ritualized bond with a male, and to benefit from whatever hands-off policy that marriage may bring, than to spend all of her time locked in one sexual dialectic or another.

Thus marriage may have arisen as a multifaceted social pact: between man and woman, between male and male, and between the couple and the tribe. It is a reasonable solution to a series of cultural challenges that arose in concert with the expansion of the human neocortex. But its roots may not be what we think they are, nor may our contemporary mating behaviors stem from the pressures of an ancestral environment as it is commonly portrayed, in which a woman needed a mate to help feed and clothe her young. Instead, our "deep" feelings about marriage may be more pragmatic, more contextual, and, dare I say it, more egalitarian than we give them credit for being. If marriage is a social compact, a mutual bid between man and woman to contrive a reasonably stable and agreeable microhabitat in a community of shrewd and well-armed cohorts, then we can understand why, despite rhetoric to the contrary, men are as eager to marry as women are — sometimes, it seems, even more so. Are not men the ones who gain most in health and happiness from being married? A raft of epidemiological studies have shown that marriage adds more years to the life of a man than it does to that of a woman. Why should that be, if men are so "naturally" ill-suited to matrimony?

Many critics have pointed out that the international mate preference surveys on which David Buss and other hardcores base their presumptions of the nativist male and female differences show striking similarities between the sexes. When asked what qualities are most important in a prospective mate, men and women alike rate love, dependability, emotional stability, and a pleasant personality as the top four traits, whatever the country, whatever the creed. Only when we descend to the fifth tier do we find the familiar dialectic, men requesting physical attractiveness, women financial endowment. If we see as the archaic cradle of marriage a social compact between independent agents rather than a plea by a needy female for a male provider, then the consanguinity of responses becomes easy to comprehend. Whom do we want to love and live with? A lovable person. A kind person. A trustworthy person who doesn't skitter all over the place and pull a Houdini on you. A person who doesn't stand on the streetcorner shouting obscenities. And though evolutionary psychologists like to toss up stock footage of the wealthy older man with the radiant young model draped on his arm as evidence of some sort of subliminal truth in motion, the more prevalent truth is that most men and most women marry people with whom they have a great deal in common. They marry people who are close to them in looks, education, wealth, religious belief, politics, age. They marry people they like and feel comfortable with. Marriages often fail, of course, and where divorce is an option, divorce is common. Traditional foraging people like the Hadza and the !Kung get divorced at rates similar to those seen in Western countries. When asked the reason for the divorce, the commonest answer is, We didn't get along.

What do women want? None of us can speak for all women, or for more than one woman, really, but we can hazard a mad guess that a desire for emotional parity is widespread and profound. It doesn't go away, although it often hibernates under duress, and it may be perverted by the restrictions of habitat or culture into something that looks like its opposite. The impulse for liberty is congenital. It is the ultimate manifestation of selfishness, which is why we can count on its endurance.

When intelligent and articulate women have created the men of their dreams, as the great female novelists of history have done, the men read like the men of many women's dreams, for they are men who love women of strength and intelligence, who do not want their women emotionally and intellectually spayed and chastened. Charlotte Brontë gave us Jane Eyre and Edward Rochester, two well-matched blades of fire, tit for tat down the checklist of debits and credits. She is plain, thin, and pale. He is ugly, "a Vulcan — a real blacksmith, brown, broad-shouldered." He is rich, self-possessed, and worldly but bordering on middle-aged. She is poor, provincial, and alone but has youth in her favor and, more to the point, a rich inner life. Rochester's love for her is stirred when he sees her watercolors of fabulous Blakean landscapes. "And who taught you to paint wind?" he demands. "Where did you see Latmos? For this is Latmos." Each lover is scorchingly bright, and glad of the other's depth and quickness. Charlotte Brontë wants her heroine to come to her mate in full strength, in the purity of desire and self-invention. She even throws in an inheritance for Jane three quarters of the way through the novel, to liberate her from any need of Rochester beyond the man of him. Oh, they are equals all right, for though Rochester towers over Jane physically, he is perpetually getting himself injured and calling on her small, pale frame to help prop him up.

Jane Eyre is fiction, Mack the Knife the archetypal smoldering poster puff. The throngs of us who have loved her and lusted onanistically after him, though, are flesh-and-bloody phenotypes. We and our fantasies are the fruit of evolution, and we are waiting to be known. It all begins with the first small, sly bite. You will come back for more.

19

A SKEPTIC IN PARADISE

A CALL FOR REVOLUTIONARY PSYCHOLOGY

WHEN FRANS DE WAAL talks about love, he tells a tale of two monkeys: rhesus monkeys and stump-tailed macaques. The species are in the same genus, *Macaca,* and they look fairly similar, but they are dramatically different in disposition. Rhesus monkeys are nasty and edgy, quick to fight and slow to reunite. Stump-tails are much less inflammatory, and when they do quarrel, they seek to make amends within ten minutes, through grooming and unmistakable gestures of rapprochement like holding on to one another's hips. "Rhesus monkeys are despotic species, while stumpies are egalitarian," de Waal says. "Presumably a cohesive group life is comparatively more important for stumpies, and so they have become experts at compromise and apology. But is it genetic? Are the stumpies simply nicer by nature? I would argue otherwise. I would argue that reconciliation behavior is a learned social skill."

De Waal believes this because some years ago he and his colleagues did the following experiment at the Wisconsin Primate Research Center. They reared several young rhesus monkeys together with a group of stump-tailed macaques for five months, a long stretch in the life of a rhesus. Under the influence of the prosocial stumpies, the rhesus monkeys grew into diplomats. They learned reconciliation behaviors. They became great groomers and hip-huggers, every bit the stumpies' equals in pacifism. They became so good at reconciliation that when they were returned to their own kind — a group of despotic rhesus monkeys — they continued to use their civic skills to calm tempers after a rhesus quarrel. "The encouraging lesson is this," says de Waal. "If we can make peacemakers out of rhesus monkeys, we can surely do it with human children."

Certain habits come more easily than others. It is easier to add a good habit to your life than to eradicate a bad one. It is easier to say yes than to say no. That's why people who try to lose weight succeed better by adding exercise to their lives than by struggling to cut calories. You may still want that occasional bar of Toblerone, and to go against the urge may feel too unnatural, too grim; but if the indulgence is tempered by counterindulgence, then the sin is effectively detoxified. I have a short, snarly temper. Of the four dispositional humors the ancients described — choler (mostly hot), phlegm (mostly cold), black bile (mostly dry), and blood (mostly moist) — I'll claim three parts choler, one part bile. I need my anger. It is my Toblerone, my dope. I can't give it up entirely. So I have adjusted by learning to do the next best thing. I have tapped my inner stump-tail, and I have learned to reconcile, quickly, quickly. Ten minutes or less! Pick a flea, hang my head, beg for mercy, make an offering of chocolate. Call it rhesus peaces.

The additive strategy reflects the way nature works. She rarely subtracts or clears the deck. Instead she appends and expands. She thumbtacks on and spackles over. We are all little Romes, an amalgam of biocivilizations. Our cells are still yeasty in their basic design. We have perfectly functional genes that have evolved hardly at all in the 600 million years between us and fungus. We are old-fashioned monkeys and futuristic apes. We are sympathetic, canny, crude, and dazzling. We are profoundly aggressive, and we have many loci of control over that aggression. We feel our way to the narthex of love and think our way down its nave. We are like nothing else that has ever appeared on this thrashing blue planet, and we will become, in the next few centuries, like nothing we can fathom now. And we will do it all wearing our same old Stone Age genes.

Ernst Mayr, one of the grand figures of twentieth-century biology, is now in his nineties, and his eyes have become "a pale boiled blue," as the novelist Penelope Fitzgerald once described a character's eyes; but Mayr is still working, still writing, and still thinking too quickly for comfort. He told me recently that he believes human beings have stopped evolving genetically. We are stuck with ourselves, he insisted. We yam what we yam.

"There is absolutely no chance of the human species evolving," he said. "We cover every niche, we cover every spot on the earth. There's no system of isolation, and so we can never speciate. You need a system of isolation for the mechanism of natural selection to operate. There's no basis for a real change in our genes, for a physical change. Granted, there have been people like Francis Galton, Darwin's cousin, who introduced eugenics and the concept that we can 'improve' the species through controlled breeding. But eugenics is impossible for various reasons, and we don't want to try it. We don't want another Nazi horror on our hands. We don't want to try to evolve a race of supermen. Whatever evolution we see from this point on will have to be cultural evolution rather than genetic evolution. That's unfortunate, because cultural things can be lost so easily. But that's where we are. That's what we have to work with."

I published Mayr's opinions in an article that appeared in *Natural History* magazine, and a lot of readers were outraged. They waxed incredulous at Mayr's conviction that humans have stopped evolving genetically. They thought he was shortsighted, behind the times, naive. They talked about biotechnology and advances in gene therapy and the ability to manipulate the human genome. They talked of populations of humans colonizing other planets, being freed from the mother ship, thenceforth isolated well enough to mutate off on a parallel lifeline.

I'm with Mayr, and happily so. Sure, cultural evolution is shakier than genetic evolution, and more prone to backsliding and amnesia. But the engine of natural selection does not give us better, nobler, or more righteous individuals. Natural selection gives us whimsy and excess. Natural selection advises, Go forth and multiply. Conquer and divide. We've conquered and divided quite enough, thank you very much. We need a little culture here, a little education and deliberation. Cultural evolution works pretty well. Culture has a way of becoming a habit, and habits have a way of getting physical, of feeding back on the loop and transforming the substrate. Think of a simple good habit, such as wearing a seat belt. You get in the car and you automatically reach for the seat belt. If something upsets the routine — say, you're toting a large package into the seat with you — and you fail to fasten the seat belt as soon as you sit down, you'll probably feel a vague sense of discomfiture, as though your body were trying to tell you something, as though a little red light were blinking on your internal dashboard. Warning! Warning! Do not relax! The seat-belt routine is now operating on a subconscious, physicalized plane. You have become habituated. Neurobiologists have shown that habituation occurs through structural changes in brain cells. The cultural practice, the wearing of the seat belt, shapes your synapses as surely as a mutant gene might do. You can't bestow the behavior on your children passively, through cracking open an egg. It is not specified in your genome, of course, and so every generation must learn it anew. But no matter; if you start 'em on the seat-belt habit young enough, they won't be able to escape. Where heredity ends, stump-tailing begins.

Women are proof that it is easier to add than to overhaul. In recent decades, women have assumed new roles while scarcely abandoning the old. We have become breadwinners, and we still do most of the child care. We have learned to like the taste of acclaim, whether it comes in large drafts of professional eminence or in the extraordinary ordinary appearance of a regular paycheck. At the same time, we have not given up our taste for the old, socially approved female drug, the laudanum of personal intimacy. Power and warmth: they both taste wonderful. And though women are warned that they can't have it all, that they can't be accomplished whatevers and still be loving mothers (and wives!), women can say, Brazzz! We can, we're doing it, we're paddling our little canoes to that fine autarchic shore as fast as we can, and there's no turning back, no matter how many tridents you wag and thunderbolts you throw. Feminism can't take all the credit for opening up economic and educational opportunities for women, as feminism's many foes have been at pains to point out. Feminism has mattered laughably little, they say. The mass entry of women into the workplace over the past thirty to forty years was driven by economic necessity and the shrinking of the economy. The model of the father as the sole support of a family was a socioeconomic aberration, a twentieth-century straw man slapped together by postwar economic expansion. That expansion could not be sustained, so of course women must work. Feminism has nothing to do with it. Women worked before, and they're working now. Women have always worked. Nothing new there.

True enough. Except that there are some new features in the world of near-tomorrow. Women are doing more than working, as they always have. They are gaining ground, albeit slowly, in the acquisition of genuine wealth. In the postindustrial nations, women account for better than half of all the owners of new small businesses. In America, businesses owned by women employ more people than all the Fortune 500 companies combined. The percentage of women purchasing a home in the United States has risen sharply over the past twenty years, and the claim to territory remains a deep source of hominid might. Of equal importance, women are being educated now as never before. As recently as the early 1960s, only 4 percent of the students in law school and 3 percent of the students in medical school were women; today, the figures are about 50 percent for both. American high school girls are slightly more likely to attend and complete a four-year college than high school boys are. Higher education is becoming a habit, and educated people are scandalously prone to ambitiousness, and to making demands, and to expecting parity and fairness. Whenever and wherever women are educated, they rediscover their core female desires — to gain direct access to resources and to control the means of personal reproduction. As a rule, educated women have smaller families than uneducated women do, not only because getting that education takes time, but because educated women want a good education for their children, and they know that they can't afford to feed, clothe, and credential more than a handful of progeny. Educated women are surprisingly apelike in their family planning practices, for female apes generally have small families; one of the most prolific and successful chimpanzee matriarchs on record, named Fifi, has given birth to only seven young in her long life, two thirds the number of offspring spawned by Darwin's wife. Educated African women, says Rogaia Mustafa Abusharaf, a Sudanese anthropologist, are more likely than uneducated women to reject the practice of pudendal desecration. They want their clitoris intact. They want to keep learning, with every brain in their bodies.

We'll take help wherever we can get it, and there are tides in our favor that have nothing to do with feminism or the quest for parity. We have the cataract of the global market, with its demands that all hands be on deck and its call for an educated (at least technically educated) workforce. Moreover, the planetary distribution of infomerchandise may work modestly to women's advantage, because the image of the liberated Western woman in her pumps and smart skirt, toting a laptop en route to the airport, however fabricated and delusive the image may be, has a certain marketing appeal, speaks to the female thirst for freedom, and can be, may be, a source of subversion, a reminder that we are bipedal foragers, unstoppable nomads.

Nonetheless, cultural evolution demands permanent revolution, which means never giving up, never coasting or falling prey to complacency, never saying, Okay, we don't want to push or offend and we don't want our canines to show. Virginia Valian cites the example of Monica Seles, the tennis player who in 1991 argued that men and women should compete for equal prize money in tournaments. "Two other female players responded publicly," Valian writes. "Steffi Graf was quoted as saying, 'We make enough, we don't need more,' and Mary Joe Fernandez reportedly said, 'I'm happy with what we have; I don't think we should be greedy.' A lack of entitlement thus interprets equality as greed." Women have to keep asking, that much is clear. We have to be on sentry duty, for if our attention lapses, wham, there's the local Taliban, kicking us to the ground and throwing a black chador over our heads. The Icelandic singer Björk recently complained about feminists. They really bugged her, she said. They whine about things not being equal and that men get all the breaks. She could understand that feeling for people of her mother's generation, or her grandmother's, but not now. Today the prison door is open, she insisted. All you have to do is walk out of it.

Part of me was happy to hear her say that, to know that she sees the door as open and herself as a free and fiery primate. More of me thinks, Get thee to an optometrist, Lady Magoo, for thy pale eyes are boiled blind. Sure, the door may be open — for now — but it's kept open by the strength of a lot of blistered female fingers and female feet and the wedging in of a rounded female haunch or two. Björk is a successful avant-garde rocker and has little personal cause to doubt the splendor of the system; nevertheless, the world of rock and roll remains overwhelmingly male, and women musicians still are tarred with assessments like that of Juliana Hatfield, the slacker pop singer, who has spluttered publicly that "female guitarists suck."

Women have done much by pushing and whining and getting habituated to sovereignty, but we are not there yet; we're still gripped with self-doubt, gynophobia, and cramps of spiritual autism. We are so hard on one another. We dismiss women for not being serious enough about their work. Chrissie Hynde, of the Pretenders, is a legend among female rockers for her rasping, crafty, lyrical style. But Chrissie Hynde, now in her forties, doesn't want to be an icon for the growling grrlhood. "I never said I'm a feminist, and I don't have any answers," she told the critic Guy Garcia. "As long as we're getting paid and can vote, what's the problem?" She, for one, prefers playing with the boys. "I work with men," she said. "They're single-minded, straightforward, and they can rock. Most women can't."

We're not dedicated. We're not quite up to the task. But the woman who wants to be up to the task, to flog away at work year after year even when she has young children, is subjected to another sort of animadversion, the guilt sling. She is warned of the damage she will do her baby by not affixing it to her bosom for the first three crucial years of brain development. She is told repeatedly that nothing beats parental care when it comes to maximizing her child's potential. All of biomedicine now weighs down on the side of full-time parenthood and the ineluctable demands of the baby's growing brain. Always it is assumed that the mother will be the primary brain sentry, by nature and personal predilection. Every magazine you flip through, there it is, the mommy dreck, the disquisition on the guilt that working mothers feel and how it persists despite decades of feminist change, to the point where if an employed mother doesn't feel guilty about working, she feels guilty about her lack of guilt. Some fathers feel the guilt, we are told, but not many of them, and not as severely. That's not their job, even now. They haven't added the guilt habit to their repertory. Why should they feel guilty? They're not supposed to feel guilty. During the 1997 trial of the British nanny accused of killing a nine-month-old boy in her charge, the mother of the boy, a physician, received a flurry of angry letters, mostly from women, placing the child's death on *her* shoulders for having gone back to work (a mere three days a week) rather than staying home with her children full-time. Needless to say, the boy's father, also a doctor, escaped public outrage for daring to be a dedicated professional.

It's a sad business when women indict other women for their take on life, for their choice of reproductive and emotional strategy. It may be understandable, given the role of female-female competition in recent human history, but I argue that it is maladaptive for women to continue on this course of she said/she said, the yowling and mud wrestling. We need each other now. The next phase of the permanent revolution needs an infusion of Old World monkey sorority. We're not supposed to talk about women's rights anymore, for to do so is to commit the sin of "victimology," to act the weak whiner, the neurasthenic corseted Victorian lady. The charge of victimology, like that of political correctness, instantly squelches all effort at precise protest, neutering a complaint before it has been uttered, for complain is what victimologists do. But if you don't ask for a raise, you won't get one, and if you don't snarl about an injustice, it won't go away. If women are prejudged as women to be lesser this or that, if a female guitarist is assumed to "suck" before she has taken out her instrument and played a single note, if women are still blamed for being bad mothers because they work outside the home, and if women are told there is an evolutionary reason that they don't really want sex, or if they do they should hide it, then we are not done with our women's moil yet.

Women care about their children, of course. Yet just as mate choice is contingent on what you bring to the bargain — the particulars of your needs, upbringing, temperament, immune system, metabolism, and so forth — so the ways in which women choose to invest in their children will differ from woman to woman. Mothering strategies are as diverse as mating strategies, and no one strategy is the one, the twenty-four-carat, the alpha and omega of maternity. Some mothers may feel that the best thing for their children is their attention, love, touch, comfort on command, and they will do everything in their power to be there for their children, getting by on less money, part-time jobs, piecework, patchwork. Some mothers may feel that their children need a show of strength, a facsimile of adult autonomy — grindstone evidence that women deserve their work, income, and authority and that you, daughter mine, will deserve yours as well in time. These mothers will not stop working, even if they can afford to. They want to work, and that appetite is part of their game plan, their customized investment in their children. But if a horrible accident befalls the child in day care, leading to the child's death or disability, how disgusting to blame the mother and only the mother for working; how reprehensible, when children die in their mothers' care all the time. They drown in bathtubs, they fall down stairs, they drink contaminated apple juice. Every mother learns this lesson, of life's porosity and her impotence against it. She can't shield her child against all hurt.

Whatever mothers do, by choice, chance, or necessity, we mothers need help. We need emotional support, not the slam from one side, dunk from the other: You're a feckless worker! You're a narcissistic mother! Enough already. We're guilty. It's the X chromosome's fault — it has too much DNA on it. It's Eve's fault — when she wasn't busy stuffing her face with fruit and tubers, she was leaving Africa and bringing us here. It's Lilith's fault — she abandoned us to the merciless docility of Eve. It's our mothers' fault (goes without saying). It's our eggs, our cunning, our blood, our bustiers, our hip-to-waist ratio, our fat depots, our salmony smell, our solar flair. We've confessed. Now where is our mamal indulgence, our feminine, heathen writ of absolution? Where is our vim and forgiveness, the Dallas Cowgirls for woman-kind?

Mothers need practical help as well. They always have. It takes 13 million calories to raise a child, and these days nearly as many dollars. Businesses have been arthritically slow about helping parents. We beat our leaky breasts over child care. We grouse and grouse and get a few stale animal crackers tossed our way. After decades of feminist change, the slogan of the business world is still "Your babies? Your business." National child care must be an ongoing goal, a system like the public schools, available free to all. We can't afford it? Says which voting bloc? Women vary widely in their sexual and maternal strategies, and as Patricia Gowaty has pointed out, correctly, the feminists of the 1970s erred in their assumption that all women share the same goals; but if there's any objective that comes close to being of universal benefit to women, it's fine, free day care. Even women who don't have children will gain from universal day care, for anything that keeps women in the world, visible and unrelenting, that neutralizes the acidic effect of mother guilt and its corollary presumption that women are not up to the task of professional tenacity, buoys all women, raises all our madly paddling canoes.

And then there are the men, the fathers. Every time I read an article about the guilt of working mothers and the comparative lack of said guilt among working fathers, I want to know, why don't they feel guilty?

And why don't we talk about their feelings and their responsibilities more than we do? Why are paid paternity leave and the full-time home-making father still the stuff of cultural sideshows? While it is true that in some segments of postindustrial society fathers now are more involved with the dailiness of child care than men have ever been, men still have not habituated themselves to babies as readily as women have to paychecks.

In explaining the asymmetry of newly acquired burdens and male lassitude and exculpation, we lazily grope toward biology. Women are said to be naturally inclined to motherhood, to bonding with their babies, to nurturance, patience, and generosity. Real mothers know that mothering is not a reflexive behavior but an acquired art. "We learn, often through painful self-discipline and self-cauterization, those qualities which are supposed to be 'innate' in us: patience, self-sacrifice, the willingness to repeat endlessly the small, routine chores of socializing a human being," Adrienne Rich has written. We indoctrinate ourselves to motherhood, through nursing, through touch, through the willingness to sit and stroke and capitulate. We give our bodies the chance to wrap around the infant and devour it with all our senses, and to present it to our bodies as our immune cells present the antigenic mark of selfhood to each other and thus declare, I am of you, and I belong. And our bodies give us back a whole-body blast. "We are . . . to our amazement, flooded with feelings both of love and violence intenser and fiercer than any we had ever known," Rich writes.

The habit of loving and nurturing an infant is not restricted to women. It is a habit that women fall into out of habit, because they spend so much more time around infants than men do. But sex be damned. The body is threaded through and through with the cilia of affiliation, which can be tapped and adapted and taught to beat in unison, provided we give them the chance. Look at the male rat. A male rat does not normally care for newborn pups. Fatherly devotion is not in the standard contract. Yet he has the raw goods of affection. If you put a young male rat into an enclosure with a litter of newborns and give him a chance to grow accustomed to their smells and hear their squeaks, he will eventually start nuzzling them. He'll huddle over them and lick them. If one should stray from the nest, he'll retrieve it. He has fallen in love with a pile of squirming pink pencil erasers. An essential factor in the experiment: the mother rat must be removed from the scene, for if she were there, she would sooner kill the male than allow him near her young.

Men can love babies madly, and the more they sit and smell and clutch their babies against them, the more sensorily embellished the love becomes. How often, though, does the average father sit and rock his baby against his naked breast? Not often enough, and not nearly as often as the average mother does. Mothers tend to monopolize their babies. Of necessity they must hold their infants to breastfeed, and so they get into the habit of holding, and they are reluctant to let go. Too often a father's contact with his baby is restricted to those times when the mother is tired and wants a break, and so it becomes a chore and a duty to him rather than a rite. He keeps his shirt on. He's buttoned up. The nerve endings of his flesh detect the baby's frequency only faintly. And the mother watches the father to make sure he is doing everything properly. She is the baby expert, after all, and he is forever callow, a babe in the woods. Women chortle about men's clumsiness in holding babies, their fumblings, their bafflement. The nursery is still the mother's domain. There, she is poobah. Yet if we want men to do their share and to shine at it, it's unfair to give them the handicap of our doubt, to practice a reverse form of discrimination: "We suckle; you suck." If women expect men to dive into the warm, rich waters of body love and to feel the tug of baby bondage, we must give over the infant again and again. Between feedings, between breasts, play touch football, baby as pigskin — pass it along.

Not all men may want to throw themselves bodily into compleat parenthood, or spend their nights with their nose buried in a baby's fontanel, or take paternity leave if offered. But I'll bet that many more of them would than currently do if such behavior became possible, acceptable, and fashionable. Which it might, as the economy goosesteps onward and women must work harder than ever before to stay abreast of life, and as they negotiate for reciprocity and fairness. I don't buy the arguments that men are inevitably less invested in their children than women are, that because there is always a chance to do better reproductively, to conquer new wombs, their feet are always shod and halfway out the door. In this murderously competitive habitat of ours, this teeming global agora, men's reproductive success may well hinge on their capacity to do just the opposite, to pay attention to every offspring, to shower each child with every possible advantage. Men need women and children now, just as women and children are always thought to need their men.

Human bonds are deep, as feral as civets, and for that, paradoxically, we have our brains to thank and rebuke. We love long and hard because we know too much. We know that we will die, and that awareness has shaped us profoundly. It has given us the world's religions. It has taken all our ancient hungers — for power, esteem, love, connection — and buffed them till they gleam like chrome, bouncing our reflections back at us. Stop for a moment, please, and talk. Stride away in full strength, but remember that time and space are curved and you will come back to talk again to me, your friend, your daughter, your mother, your love.

I am a utopian pessimist by nature, a mechanistic phantasmagorist. I believe in permanent revolution of the mind and will. In 1987 I sat over dinner with my grandmother, who was then in her late seventies, my mother, and my eighteen-year-old cousin, Julie. We talked about whether we would choose to be men if we could. Yes, we all said, even, to my surprise, my grandmother. "Men have more freedom," she said.

Recently I reminded my mother of that conversation. We agreed that we no longer felt the same. We no longer wanted to be men. It isn't merely a function of getting older and more accepting of ourselves. My grandmother was older than either of us when she said, I would if I could. Nor is it because I think women have made so much progress in the past decade, or that the prison door has melted and the merry inmates are now in charge. Instead, for me, and I think for my mother, the change of heart is the result of revelation, the realization that our strength and our anima stem in good part from our womanness, and from thinking about what it means to be a woman, here, now, in this culture, and in our imagined future. Our tribe is the tribe of woman. It is our tribe to define, and we're still doing it, and we will never give up. We live in a state of permanent revolution. The *frisson* of it! We will not abandon the tribe or the battle. We will not define the tribe as a default zone or a consolation prize. The wish to be a man is a capitulation to limits and strictures we never set for ourselves. It is lazy. It does not belong to us.

I have a daughter now. She's still too young to know that she has any limits at all, that she is not queen of the Milky Way, and that someday she will die. She knows she's a girl but she doesn't yet care about it, or realize what it means. Maybe it should mean nothing. Maybe that's what I want for her: that she will not think about being a girl, or a woman, in any categorical way. That it will not interest her, for she is too consumed with a glamorous calling, like calculating comet paths, playing the harpsichord, or pandering to her generation's nostalgia for purple pedophilic dinosaurs and the Internet. Maybe she'll pull a Björk on me, rolling her eyes and miming a patted yawn whenever I mention the political trilobite called feminism.

Or maybe she will trade up her mother's tatty bark canoe for a mighty ship of gold and joy, with a mutinous crew of mad-haired Valkyries, cloven mermaids, and chafing nymphs. My daughter will sing herself hoarse as she rows firmly forward through squalls and calm waters, now in tune with her mates, now roaring against them. She hasn't yet found the fabled free shore, but no matter. She is always at home in the sea.

Abusharaf, Rogaia Mustafa. 1998. "Unmasking Tradition." *The Sciences,* Mar.–Apr.

Alberts, Bruce, et al. 1989. *Molecular Biology of the Cell.* New York: Garland.

Anderson, Peter B., and Ronelle Aymami. 1993. "Reports of Female Initiation of Sexual Contact: Male and Female Differences." *Archives of Sexual Behavior* 22: 335–43.

Arn, Pamela, et al. 1994. "SRVX, a Sex Reversing Locus in XP21.2–p22.11." *Human Genetics* 93: 389–93.

Austad, Steven N. 1994. "Menopause: An Evolutionary Perspective." *Experimental Gerontology* 29: 255–63.

_____. 1997. *Why We Age.* New York: John Wiley & Sons.

Ayalah, Daphna, and Isaac J. Weinstock. 1979. *Breasts: Women Speak About Their Breasts and Their Lives.* New York: Summit.

Bachmann, Gloria A. 1990. "Hysterectomy: A Critical Review." *Journal of Reproductive Medicine* 35: 839–62.

Bailey, J. M., et al. 1994. "Effects of Gender and Sexual Orientation on Evolutionarily Relevant Aspects of Human Mating Psychology." *Journal of Personality and Social Psychology* 66: 1081–93.

Baker, Robin, and Mark A. Bellis. 1996. *Human Sperm Competition: Copulation, Masturbation and Infidelity.* New York: Chapman & Hall.

Bardoni, B., et al. 1994. "Dosage Sensitive Locus at Chromosome Xp21 Is Involved in Male to Female Sex Reversal." *Nature Genetics* 7: 497–501.

Barentsen, R. 1996. "The Climacteric in the Netherlands: A Review of Dutch Studies on Epidemiology, Attitudes and Use of Hormone Replacement Therapy." *European Journal of Obstetrics, Gynecology and Reproductive Biology* 64: S7–11.

Barker, Tara. 1998. *The Woman's Book of Orgasm.* Secaucus, N.J.: Citadel.

Barnard, Mary. 1958. *Sappho: A New Translation.* Berkeley: University of California Press.

Bass, Thomas A. 1993 *Reinventing the Future: Conversations with the World's Leading Scientists.* Reading, Mass.: Addison-Wesley.

Bear, David. 1991. "Neurological Perspectives on Aggressive Behavior." *Journal of Neuropsychiatry* 3: 53–58.

_____. 1997. "The Neuropsychiatry of Aggression." In *Neuropsychiatry: A Comprehensive Textbook.* Edited by B. S. Fogel, B. Schiffer, and R. B. Schiffer. Baltimore: Williams and Wilkins.

Beauchamp, Gary K., et al. 1995. "Evidence Suggesting that the Odortypes of Pregnant Women Are a Compound of Maternal and Fetal Odortypes." *Proceedings of the National Academy of Sciences* 92: 2617–21.

Beauvoir, Simone de. 1952. *The Second Sex.* New York: Random House.

Beckerman, Stephen, et al. 1998. "The Barí Partible Paternity Project Preliminary Results." *Current Anthropology* 39: 164–67.

Benderly, Beryl Lieff. 1994. "The Testosterone Excuse." *Glamour,* Mar.

Benton, Robin, et al. 1993. "'Breaking the Law,' a Metaphor for Female Empowerment Through Aggression." *Journal of the American Academy of Psychoanalysis* 21: 133–47.

Bhasin, Shalender, et al. 1996. "The Effects of Supraphysiologic Doses of Testosterone on Muscle Size and Strength in Normal Men." *New England Journal of Medicine* 335: 1–7.

Bianchi, Diana W., et al. 1996. "Male Fetal Progenitor Cells Persist in Maternal Blood for as Long as 27 Years Postpartum." *Proceedings of the National Academy of Sciences* 93: 705–8.

Binkley, Sue A. 1995. *Endocrinology.* New York: HarperCollins.

Bjork, J. M., et al. 1997. "A Positive Correlation Between Self-Ratings of Depression and Laboratory-Measured Aggression." *Psychiatry Research* 69: 33–8.

Björkqvist, Kaj. 1994. "Sex Differences in Physical, Verbal, and Indirect Aggression: A Review of Recent Research." *Sex Roles* 30: 177–88.

Björkqvist, Kaj, and Pekka Niemela, eds. 1992. *Of Mice and Women: Aspects of Female Aggression.* New York: Academic Press.

Bjorkqvist, Kaj, et al. 1992. "Do Girls Manipulate and Boys Fight?" *Aggressive Behavior* 18: 117–27.

_____. 1994. "Aggression among University Employees." *Aggressive Behavior* 20: 173–84.

_____. 1994. "Sex Differences in Covert Aggression among Adults." *Aggressive Behavior* 20: 27–33.

_____. 1994. "Testosterone Intake and Aggressiveness." *Aggressive Behavior* 20: 17–26.

Blum, Deborah. 1997. *Sex on the Brain.* New York: Viking.

Blumberg, G., et al. 1996. "Women's Attitudes Toward Menopause and Hormone Replacement Therapy." *International Journal of Gynaecology and Obstetrics* 54: 271–77.

Blumberg, M., et al. 1992. "Facultative Sex Ratio Adjustment in Norway Rats: Litters Born Asynchronously Are Female Biased." *Behavioral Ecology and Sociobiology* 31: 401–8.

Blumstein, Philip, and Pepper Schwartz. 1985. *American Couples: Money, Work, Sex.* New York: William Morrow.

Blurton Jones, Nicholas. Forthcoming. "Hunter-Gatherer Divorce Rates and the Paternal Investment Theory of Human Pair-Bonding." In *Adaptation and Human Behavior.* Edited by L. Cronk et al. Hawthorne, N.Y.: Aldine de Gruyter.

Boston Women's Health Collective. 1992. *The New Our Bodies, Ourselves.* New York: Simon & Schuster.

Brody, Jane. 1997. "Personal Health: First of Two Columns on Hormone Replacement." *New York Times,* Aug. 20.

Brotherton, Peter N. M., and Martha B. Manser. "Female Dispersion and the Evolution of Monogamy in the Dik-dik." *Animal Behaviour* 54: 1413–24.

Burleson, M. H., et al. 1995. "Heterosexual Activity: Relationship with Ovarian Function." *Psychoneuroendocrinology* 20: 405–21.

Buss, David. 1989. "Sex Differences in Human Mate Preferences." *Behavioral and Brain Sciences* 12: 1–49.

_____. 1994. *The Evolution of Desire.* New York: Basic Books.

_____. 1995. "Psychological Sex Differences." *American Psychologist,* Mar.: 164–68.

Cadden, Joan. 1993. *Meanings and Differences.* Cambridge, England: Cambridge University Press.

Carani, Cesare. 1997. "Effect of Testosterone and Estradiol in a Man with Aromatase Deficiency." *New England Journal of Medicine* 337: 91–95.

Carlson, Karen J., et al. 1993. "Indications for Hysterectomy." *New England Journal of Medicine* 328: 856–60.

Carter, C. Sue. Forthcoming. "Neuroendocrine Perspectives on Social Attachment and Love." *Psychoneuroendocrinology.*

Carter, C. Sue, et al., eds. 1997. *The Integrative Neurobiology of Affiliation.* New York: New York Academy of Sciences.

Cashdan, Elizabeth. 1995. "Hormones, Sex, and Status in Women." *Hormones and Behavior* 29: 354–66.

_____. 1997. "Women's Mating Strategies." *Evolutionary Anthropology* 5: 134–42.

Ceronetti, Guido. 1993. *The Silence of the Body.* New York: Farrar, Straus, & Giroux.

Chard, T., and J. G. Grudzinskas. 1994. *The Uterus.* Cambridge, England: Cambridge University Press.

Chehab, F. F., et al. 1997. "Early Onset of Reproductive Function in Normal Female Mice Treated with Leptin." *Science* 275: 88–90.

Clutton-Brock, T. H., and G. A. Parker. 1995. "Sexual Coercion in Animal Societies." *Animal Behaviour* 49: 1345–65.

Constantino, J. N., et al. 1993. "Testosterone and Aggression in Children." *Journal of the American Academy of Child and Adolescent Psychiatry* 32: 1217–22.

Crews, David. 1993. "The Organizational Concept and Vertebrates Without Sex Chromosomes." *Brain Behavior and Evolution* 42: 202–14.

Dabbs, James M., Jr., and Marian F. Hargrove. 1997. "Age, Testosterone, and Behavior among Female Prison Inmates." *Psychosomatic Medicine* 59: 477–80.

Dabbs, James M., et al. 1998. "Trial Lawyers and Testosterone: Blue-Collar Talent in a White-Collar World." *Journal of Applied Social Psychology* 28: 84–94.

Denby, David. 1997. "In Darwin's Wake." *The New Yorker,* July 21.

DeVries, Courtney A., et al. 1996. "The Effects of Stress on Social Preferences Are Sexually Dimorphic in Prairie Voles." *Proceedings of the National Academy of Sciences* 93: 11980–84.

de Waal, Frans. 1989. *Peacemaking among Primates.* Cambridge, Mass.: Harvard University Press.

_____. 1995. "Bonobo Sex and Society." *Scientific American,* Mar.: 82–88.

_____. 1996. *Good Natured.* Cambridge, Mass.: Harvard University Press.

de Waal, Frans, and Frans Lanting. 1997. *Bonobo: The Forgotten Ape.* Berkeley: University of California Press.

Diamond, Jared. 1996. "Why Women Change." *Discover,* July.

Dumas, Janifer. 1997. "Tales of a Lingerie Saleswoman." *New York Times Magazine,* Sept. 21.

Eagly, Alice H. 1995. "The Science and Politics of Comparing Women and Men." *American Psychologist,* Mar.: 145–58.

Eagly, Alice H., and Valerie J. Steffen. 1986. "Gender and Aggressive Behavior: A Meta-analytic Review of the Social Psychological Literature." *Psychological Bulletin* 100: 309–30.

Eschenbach, David A. 1993. "History and Review of Bacterial Vaginosis." *American Journal of Obstetrics and Gynecology* 169: 441–45.

Fausto-Sterling, Anne. 1992. *Myths of Gender.* New York: Basic Books.

Fieser, Louis F., and Mary Fieser. 1959. *Steroids.* New York: Reinhold.

Fildes, Valerie. 1986. *Breasts, Bottles, and Babies: A History of Infant Feeding.* Edinburgh: Edinburgh Press.

Fink, G., et al. 1996. "Estrogen Control of Central Neurotransmission: Effect on Mood, Mental State, and Memory." *Cellular and Molecular Neurobiology* 6: 325–44.

Finkelstein, Jordan W., et al. 1994. "The Relationship Between Aggressive Behavior and Puberty in Normal Adolescents: A Longitudinal Study." *Journal of Adolescent Health* 15: 319–26.

Fisher, Helen E. 1982. *The Sex Contract: The Evolution of Human Behavior.* New York: William Morrow.

_____. 1992. *Anatomy of Love.* New York: W. W. Norton.

_____. 1998. "Lust, Attraction, and Attachment in Mammalian Reproduction." *Human Nature* 9: 23–52.

Frank, L. G., et al. 1994. "Giving Birth Through a Penile Clitoris: Parturition and Dystocia in the Spotted Hyena." *Journal of Zoology* 234: 659–90.

Frisch, Rose E. 1994. "The Right Weight: Body Fat, Menarche and Fertility." *Proceedings of the Nutrition Society* 53: 113–29.

Fuller, Roy W. 1995. "Neural Functions of Serotonin." *Scientific American Science & Medicine,* July–Aug.: 48–57.

Gagneux, Pascal, et al. 1997. "Furtive Mating in Female Chimpanzees." *Nature* 387: 358–59.

Gale, Catharine R., and Christopher N. Martyn. 1996. "Breastfeeding, Dummy Use, and Adult Intelligence." *The Lancet* 347: 1072–75.

Garcia, Guy. 1994. "Chrissie Hynde Still Rocks; She's Just Mellower." *New York Times,* June 12.

Gladwell, Malcolm. 1997. "The Estrogen Question." *The New Yorker,* June 9.

Goto, Hiromi. 1996. "Tales from the Breast." *Ms.,* Sept.–Oct. Readers' responses, *Ms.,* Jan.–Feb. 1997.

Gougeon, Alain. 1996. "Regulation of Ovarian Follicular Development in Primates: Facts and Hypotheses." *Endocrine Reviews* 17: 121–55.

Gould, James L., and Carol Grant Gould. 1997. *Sexual Selection.* New York: Scientific American Library.

Gould, Stephen Jay, ed. 1993. *The Book of Life.* New York: W. W. Norton.

Gould, S. J., and R. C. Lewontin. 1979. "The Spandrels of San Marco and the Panglossian Paradigm: A Critique of the Adaptationist Programme." *Proceedings of the Royal Society of London* 205: 581–98.

Gowaty, Patricia Adair. 1996. "Battles of the Sexes and the Origins of Monogamy." *Partnerships in Birds.* Oxford, England: Oxford University Press.

_____. 1996. "Field Studies of Parental Care in Birds." *Advances in the Study of Behavior* 25: 477–531.

_____. 1996. "Multiple Mating by Females Selects for Males That Stay." *Animal Behavior* 51: 482–84.

_____, ed. 1997. *Feminism and Evolutionary Biology.* New York: Chapman & Hall.

_____. 1997. "Principles of Females' Perspectives in Avian Behavioral Ecology." *Journal of Avian Biology* 28: 95–102.

_____. 1998. "Ultimate Causation of Aggressive and Forced Copulation in Birds: Female Resistance, the CODE Hypothesis, and Social Monogamy." *American Zoologist* 38: 207–25.

Gravanis, A., et al. 1994. "Interaction Between Steroid Hormones and Endometrial Opioids." *Annals of the New York Academy of Sciences* 734: 245–56.

Grodstein, F., et al. 1997. "Postmenopausal Hormone Therapy and Mortality." *New England Journal of Medicine* 336: 1769–75.

Gustafsson, Jan-Åke. 1997. "Estrogen Receptor β — Getting In on the Action?" *Nature Medicine* 3: 493.

Haas, Adelaide, and Susan L. Puretz. 1995. *The Woman's Guide to Hysterectomy.* Berkeley: Celestial Arts.

Hager, Lori D., ed. 1997. *Women in Human Evolution.* London: Routledge.

Hamer, Dean, and Peter Copeland. 1998. *Living with Our Genes.* New York: Doubleday.

Hawkes, K., et al. Forthcoming. "The Grandmother Hypothesis and Human Evolution." In *Adaptation and Evolutionary Biology.* Edited by L. Cronk et al. Hawthorne, N.Y.: Aldine de Gruyter.

_____. "Hadza Women's Time Allocation, Offspring Provisioning, and the Evolution of Long Postmenopausal Life Spans." *Current Anthropology* 38: 551–77.

_____. 1998. "Grandmothering, Menopause, and the Evolution of Human Life Histories." *Proceedings of the National Academy of Sciences* 95: 1–4.

Hillier, Sharon L. 1993. "Diagnostic Microbiology of Bacterial Vaginosis." *American Journal of Obstetrics and Gynecology* 169: 455–59.

Hollander, Anne. 1994. *Sex and Suits.* New York: Knopf.

Hoogland, John L. "Why Do Female Gunnison's Prairie Dogs Copulate with More than One Male?" *Animal Behaviour* 55: 351–59.

Horgan, John. 1995. "The New Social Darwinists." *Scientific American,* Oct.

Hrdy, Sarah Blaffer. 1981. "'Nepotists' and 'Altruists': The Behavior of Old Females among Macaques and Langur Monkeys." In *Other Ways of Growing Old.* Edited by P. Amoss and S. Harrell. Stanford, Calif.: Stanford University Press.

_____. 1981. *The Woman That Never Evolved.* Cambridge, Mass.: Harvard University Press.

_____. 1995. "Natural-Born Mothers." *Natural History,* Dec.

_____. 1997. "Raising Darwin's Consciousness: Female Sexuality and the Prehominid Origins of Patriarchy." *Human Nature* 8: 1–50.

Hrdy, Sarah Blaffer, and Daniel B. Hrdy. 1976. "Hierarchical Relations among Female Hanuman Langurs." *Science* 193: 913–15.

Hubbard, Ruth, et al., eds. 1982. *Biological Woman: The Convenient Myth.* Rochester, Vt.: Schenkman.

Hunter, M. S., and K. L. Liao. 1994. "Intentions to Use Hormone Replacement Therapy in a Community Sample of 45-Year-Old Women." *Maturitas* 20: 13–23.

Hyde, Janet Shibley, and Elizabeth Ashby Plant. 1995. "Magnitude of Psychological Gender Differences." *American Psychologist*, Mar.: 159–61.

Institute of Medicine Committee on Nutritional Status During Pregnancy and Lactation. 1990. "Milk Composition." In *Nutrition During Lactation*. Washington, D.C.: National Academy Press.

Jafrati, Mark D., et al. 1997. "Estrogen Inhibits the Vascular Injury Response in Estrogen Receptor α-Deficient Mice." *Nature Medicine* 3: 545–48.

Kalloo, N. B., et al. 1993. "Sexually Dimorphic Expression of Estrogen Receptors, But Not of Androgen Receptors, in Human Female External Genitalia." *Journal of Clinical Endocrinology and Metabolism* 77: 692–98.

Kandel, Eric R., et al. 1995. *Essentials of Neural Science and Behavior*. Norwalk, Conn.: Appleton & Lange.

Katzenellenbogen, Benita S., and Kenneth S. Korach. 1997. "Editorial: A New Actor in the Estrogen Receptor Drama — enter ER-β." *Endocrinology* 138: 861–62.

Kauppila, Olavi, et al. 1985. "Prolapse of the Vagina after Hysterectomy." *Surgery, Gynecology & Obstetrics* 161: 9–11.

Kevles, Bettyann. 1986. *Female of the Species*. Cambridge, Mass.: Harvard University Press.

Koldovsky, Otakar. 1994. "Hormones in Milk." In *Vitamins and Hormones*. New York: Academic Press.

Kuhnle, U., et al. 1993. "Partnership and Sexuality in Adult Female Patients with Congenital Adrenal Hyperplasia." *Journal of Steroid Biochemistry and Molecular Biology* 45: 123–26.

Kuiper, George G. J. M., et al. 1996. "Cloning of a Novel Estrogen Receptor Expressed in Rat Prostate and Ovary." *Proceedings of the National Academy of Sciences* 93: 5925–30.

_____. 1997. "Comparison of the Ligand Binding Specificity and Transcript Tissue Distribution of Estrogen Receptors α and β." *Endocrinology* 138: 863–70.

Laan, Ellen. 1994. *Determinants of Sexual Arousal in Women*. Amsterdam: University of Amsterdam Monographs.

Laan, Ellen, et al. 1994. "Women's Sexual and Emotional Responses to Male- and Female-Produced Erotica." *Archives of Sexual Behavior* 23: 153–69.

Landau, Carol, et al. 1994. *The Complete Book of Menopause*. Berkeley: Perigee.

Laqueur, Thomas. 1990. *Making Sex: Body and Gender from the Greeks to Freud*. Cambridge, Mass.: Harvard University Press.

Lavoisier, Pierre, et al. 1995. "Clitoral Blood Flow Increases Following Vaginal Pressure Stimulation." *Archives of Sexual Behavior* 24: 37–45.

Lerner, Gerda. 1986. *The Creation of Patriarchy*. New York: Oxford University Press.

_____. 1993. *The Creation of Feminist Consciousness*. New York: Oxford University Press.

Levin, R. J. 1991. "VIP, Vagina, Clitoral and Periurethral Glans — An Update on Human Female Genital Arousal." *Experiments in Clinical Endocrinology* 98: 61–69.

Levin, R. J., and G. Wagner. 1985. "Orgasm in Women in the Laboratory — Quantitative Studies on Duration, Intensity, Latency, and Vaginal Blood Flow." *Archives of Sexual Behavior* 14: 439–49.

Lorch, Donatella. 1996. "Bride Wore White, Groom Hopes for Parole." *New York Times,* Sept. 5.

Love, Susan M. 1997. "Sometimes Mother Nature Knows Best." *New York Times,* Mar. 20.

Love, Susan M., and Karen Lindsey. 1995. *Dr. Susan Love's Breast Book*. New York: Perseus.

_____. 1997. *Dr. Susan Love's Hormone Book*. New York: Random House.

Lowry, Thomas P. 1978. *The Classic Clitoris*. Chicago: Nelson-Hall.

Lowry, Thomas P., and T. S. Lowry, eds. 1976. *The Clitoris*. St. Louis: Warren H. Green.

Manson, Joseph H., et al. 1997. "Nonconceptive Sexual Behavior in Bonobos and Capuchins." *International Journal of Primatology* 18: 767–86.

Martin, Emily. 1992. *The Woman in the Body*. Boston: Beacon Press.

Masters, William H., and Virginia E. Johnson. 1966. *Human Sexual Response*. Boston: Little, Brown.

Matteo, Sherri, and Emilie F. Rissman. 1984. "Increased Sexual Activity During the Midcycle Portion of the Human Menstrual Cycle." *Hormones and Behavior* 18: 249–55.

Mazur, Allan. 1998. "Testosterone and Dominance in Men." *Behavioral and Brain Sciences* 21: 353–97.

McClintock, Martha K. 1971. "Menstrual Synchrony and Suppression." *Nature* 291: 244–45.

_____. 1981. "Social Control of the Ovarian Cycle and the Function of Estrous Synchrony." *American Zoologist* 21: 243–56.

McEwen, B. S. 1997. "Meeting Report — Is There a Neurobiology of Love?" *Molecular Psychiatry* 2: 15–16.

Michael, Robert T., et al. 1994. *Sex in America*. Boston: Little, Brown.

Michel, George F., and Celia L. Moore. 1995. *Developmental Psychobiology*. Cambridge, Mass.: MIT Press.

Miles, Margaret R. 1986. "The Virgin's One Bare Breast: Female Nudity and Religious Meaning in Tuscan Early Renaissance Cultures." In *The Female Body in*

Western Culture. Edited by Susan Rubin Sulerman. Cambridge, Mass.: Harvard University Press.

Mitchell, George W., Jr., and Lawrence W. Bassett, eds. 1990. *The Female Breast and Its Disorders.* Baltimore: Williams and Wilkins.

Modney, B. K., and G. I. Hatton. 1994. "Maternal Behaviors: Evidence That They Feed Back to Alter Brain Morphology and Function." *Acta Pediatrica Supplement* 397: 29–32.

Money, John. 1997. *Principles of Developmental Sexology.* New York: Continuum.

Morbeck, Mary Ellen, et al., eds. 1997. *The Evolving Female.* Princeton, N.J.: Princeton University Press.

Morgan, Elaine. 1982. *The Aquatic Ape.* New York: Stein and Day.

_____. 1994. *The Scars of Evolution.* New York: Oxford University Press.

_____. 1995. *The Descent of the Child.* New York: Oxford University Press.

Morishima, A., et al. 1995. "Aromatase Deficiency in Male and Female Siblings Caused by a Novel Mutation and the Physiological Role of Estrogens." *Journal of Clinical Endocrinology and Metabolism* 80: 3689–98.

Morris, Desmond. 1967. *The Naked Ape.* New York: McGraw-Hill.

_____. 1985. *Bodywatching.* New York: Crown.

_____. 1994. *The Human Animal.* New York: Crown.

Myers, L. S., et al. "Effects of Estrogen, Androgen, and Progestin on Sexual Psychophysiology and Behavior in Postmenopausal Women." *Journal of Clinical Endocrinology and Metabolism* 70: 1124–31.

Nelson, Miriam E. 1997. *Strong Women Stay Young.* New York: Bantam.

Nelson, Randy J. 1995. *An Introduction to Behavioral Endocrinology.* Sunderland, Mass.: Sinauer Assoc.

Neville, Margaret C. 1987. *The Mammary Gland: Development, Regulation and Function.* New York: Plenum Press.

Newman, Jack. 1995. "How Breast Milk Protects Newborns." *Scientific American,* Dec.: 76–79.

Nicolson, Paula. 1995. "The Menstrual Cycle, Science and Femininity." *Social Science and Medicine* 41: 779–84.

Niemala, Pekka. 1992. "Lady Macbeth as a Problem for Shakespeare." In *Of Mice and Women.* Edited by K. Bjorkqvist and P. Niemala. San Diego: Academic Press.

Nilsson, Lennart, and Lars Hamberger. 1990. *A Child Is Born.* New York: Doubleday.

Nishimori, Katsuhiko, et al. 1996. "Oxytocin Is Required for Nursing But Is Not Essential for Parturition or Reproductive Behavior." *Proceedings of the National Academy of Sciences* 93: 11699–704.

Nissen, E., et al. 1998. "Oxytocin, Prolactin, Milk Production and Their Relationship with Personality Traits in Women after Vaginal Delivery or Cesarean Section." *Journal of Psychosomatic Obstetrics and Gynaecology* 19: 49–58.

Nuland, Sherwin B. 1997. *The Wisdom of the Body.* New York: Knopf.

Ogawa, Sonoko, et al. 1997. "Behavioral Effects of Estrogen Receptor Gene Disruption in Male Mice." *Proceedings of the National Academy of Sciences* 94: 1476–81.

_____. 1997. "Reversal of Sex Roles in Genetic Female Mice by Disruption of Estrogen Receptor Gene." *Neuroendocrinology* 64: 467–70.

Oliver, Mary Beth, and Janet Shibley Hyde. 1993. "Gender Differences in Sexuality: A Meta-analysis." *Psychological Bulletin* 114: 29–51.

Osterman, Karin, et al. 1994. "Peer and Self-Estimated Aggression and Victimization in 8-Year-Old Children from Five Ethnic Groups." *Aggressive Behavior* 20: 411–28.

Packer, Craig, et al. 1998. "Reproductive Cessation in Female Mammals." *Nature* 329: 807–11.

Palmon, Aaron, et al. 1994. "The Gene for the Neuropeptide Gonadotropin-releasing Hormone Is Expressed in the Mammary Gland of Lactating Rats." *Proceedings of the National Academy of Sciences* 91: 4994–96.

Peccei, J. S. 1995. "A Hypothesis for the Origin and Evolution of Menopause." *Maturitas* 21: 83–89.

Pedersen, Cort A., et al., eds. 1992. *Oxytocin in Maternal, Sexual, and Social Behaviors.* New York: New York Academy of Sciences.

Perry, Ruth. 1992. "Colonizing the Breast." In *Forbidden History.* Edited by John C. Font. Chicago: University of Chicago Press.

Pham, K. T., et al. 1997. "Ovarian Aging and Hormone Replacement Therapy. Hormonal Levels, Symptoms, and Attitudes of African-American and White Women." *Journal of General Internal Medicine* 12: 230–36.

Pinker, Steven. 1997. *How the Mind Works.* New York: W. W. Norton.

_____. 1998. "Boys Will Be Boys." *The New Yorker,* Feb. 9.

Plath, Sylvia. 1966. *Ariel.* New York: Harper and Row.

_____. 1992. *Letters Home: Correspondence 1950–1963.* New York: HarperPerennial.

Population Council Research. 1997. "Female Genital Mutilation: Common, Controversial, and Bad for Women's Health." *Population Briefs* 3, no. 2.

Profet, Margie. 1993. "Menstruation as a Defense Against Pathogens Transported by Sperm." *Quarterly Review of Biology* 68: 335–86.

Pusey, Anne, et al. 1997. "The Influence of Dominance Rank on the Reproductive Success of Female Chimpanzees." *Nature* 277: 827–31.

Quakenbush, Debra M., et al. 1995. "Gender Effects of Romantic Themes in Erotica." *Archives of Sexual Behavior* 24: 21–35.

Redmond, Geoffrey. 1995. *The Good News about Women's Hormones.* New York: Warner.

Rhode, Deborah L. 1990. *Theoretical Perspectives on Sexual Difference.* New Haven: Yale University Press.

Rich, Adrienne. 1986. *Of Woman Born.* New York: W. W. Norton.

Rink, J. D., et al. 1996. "Cellular Characterization of Adipose Tissue from Various Body Sites of Women." *Journal of Clinical Endocrinology and Metabolism* 81: 2443–47.

Rissman, Emilie F., et al. 1997. "Estrogen Receptors Are Essential for Female Sexual Receptivity." *Endocrinology* 138: 507–10.

Rosenberg, Karen, and Wenda Trevathan. 1996. "Bipedalism and Human Birth: The Obstetrical Dilemma Revisited." *Evolutionary Anthropology* 4: 161–68.

Rosenthal, Elisabeth. 1991. "The Forgotten Female." *Discover,* Dec. 22–27.

Roth, Philip. 1995. *Sabbath's Theater.* Boston: Houghton Mifflin.

Roueche, Berton. 1996. *The Man Who Grew Two Breasts.* New York: Plume.

Ryan, K. J., et al., eds. 1995. *Kistner's Gynecology: Principles and Practice.* 6th ed. St. Louis: Mosby.

Sane, Kumud, and Ora Hirsch Pescovitz. 1992. "The Clitoral Index: A Determination of Clitoral Size in Normal Girls and in Girls with Abnormal Sexual Development." *Journal of Pediatrics* 120: 264–66.

Sapolsky, Robert. 1997. "Testosterone Rules." *Discover,* Mar.: 45–50.

Schaal, B., et al. 1996. "Male Testosterone Linked to High Social Dominance But Low Physical Aggression in Early Adolescence." *Journal of the American Academy of Child and Adolescent Psychiatry* 35: 1322–30.

Schiebinger, Londa. 1993. *Nature's Body.* Boston: Beacon Press.

_____. 1993. "Why Mammals Are Called Mammals: Gender Politics in Eighteenth-Century Natural History." *American Historical Review* 98: 382–411.

Schlinger, Barney A. 1994. "Estrogens and Song: Products of the Songbird Brain." *BioScience* 44: 605–12.

Schmid, Patricia C., et al. 1997. "Changes in Anandamide Levels in Mouse Uterus Are Associated with Uterine Receptivity for Embryo Implantation." *Proceedings of the National Academy of Sciences* 94: 4188–92.

Schwartz, Charles E. 1993. "X-linked Mental Retardation." *American Journal of Human Genetics* 52: 1025–31.

Schwartz, Lynne Sharon. 1987. *The Melting Pot and Other Subversive Stories.* New York: Harper and Row.

Shaw, Evelyn, and Joan Darling. 1985. *Female Strategies.* New York: Touchstone.

Short, R. V., and E. Balaban, eds. 1994. *The Differences Between the Sexes.* Cambridge, England: Cambridge University Press.

Shulkin, Jay, ed. 1993. *Hormonally Induced Changes in Mind and Brain.* San Diego: Academic Press.

Silber, Marta. 1994. "Menstrual Cycle and Work Schedule: Effects on Women's Sexuality." *Archives of Sexual Behavior* 23: 397–404.

Simons, Anna. 1997. "In War, Let Men Be Men." *New York Times,* Apr. 23.

Singh, D. 1993. "Body Shape and Women's Attractiveness — The Critical Role of Waist-to-Hip Ratio." *Human Nature* 4: 297–322.

Singh, D., et al. 1998. "Frequency and Timing of Coital Orgasm in Women Desirous of Becoming Pregnant." *Archives of Sexual Behavior* 27: 15–29.

Skuse, D. H., et al. 1997. "Evidence from Turner's Syndrome of an Imprinted X-linked Locus Affecting Cognitive Function." *Nature* 387: 705–8.

Sloane, Ethel. 1993. *Biology of Women.* New York: Delmar.

Small, Meredith F. 1993. *Female Choices.* Ithaca, N.Y.: Cornell University Press.

_____. 1995. *What's Love Got to Do with It?* New York: Anchor Books.

_____. 1998. *Our Babies, Ourselves.* New York: Anchor Books.

Smith, Eric P., et al. 1994. "Estrogen Resistance Caused by a Mutation in the Estrogen-Receptor Gene in a Man." *New England Journal of Medicine* 331: 1056–61.

Smuts, Barbara. 1992. "Male Aggression Against Women: An Evolutionary Perspective." *Human Nature* 3: 1–44.

_____. 1995. "Apes of Wrath." *Discover,* Aug. 35–37.

_____. 1995. "The Evolutionary Origins of Patriarchy." *Human Nature* 6: 1–32.

Smuts, Barbara, and Robert W. Smuts. 1993. "Male Aggression and Sexual Coercion of Females in Nonhuman Primates and Other Mammals." *Advances in the Study of Behavior* 22: 1–63.

Stern, Kathleen, and Martha McClintock. 1998. "Regulation of Ovulation by Human Pheromones." *Nature* 392: 177–79.

Stevens, Jane E. 1995. "Hyenas Yield Clues to Human Infertility, Aggression." *Technology Review,* Feb.–Mar.

Strassmann, Beverly I. 1992. "The Function of Menstrual Taboos among the Dogon: Defense Against Cuckoldry?" *Human Nature* 3: 89–131.

_____. 1996. "The Evolution of Endometrial Cycles and Menstruation." *Quarterly Review of Biology* 71: 181–220.

Strausz, Ivan. 1993. *You Don't Need a Hysterectomy.* Reading, Mass.: Addison-Wesley.

Suplee, Curt. 1996. "Animal Researchers Transplant Sperm-producing Cells from Species to Species." *Washington Post,* May 30.

Symons, Donald. 1979. *The Evolution of Human Sexuality.* New York: Oxford University Press.

Taylor, Timothy. 1996. *The Prehistory of Sex.* New York: Bantam.

Tilly, Jonathan L., and Valerie S. Ratts. 1996. "Biological and Clinical Importance of Ovarian Cell Death." *Contemporary Ob/Gyn,* Mar.

Tingley, Deborah. 1996. "Evolutions: Steroid-Hormone Receptor Signaling." *Journal of NIH Research* 8: 81–87.

Toesca, Amelia, et al. 1996. "Immunohistochemical Study of the Corpora Cavernosa of the Human Clitoris." *Journal of Anatomy* 188: 513–20.

Toubia, Nahid. 1994. "Female Circumcision as a Public Health Issue." *New England Journal of Medicine* 331: 712–16.

Townsend, John Marshall. 1995. "Sex Without Emotional Involvement: An Evolutionary Interpretation of Sex Differences." *Archives of Sexual Behavior* 24: 173–205.

_____. 1998. *What Women Want, What Men Want*. New York: Oxford University Press.

Travis, John. 1997. "Brave New Egg." *Discover*, Apr.

Trevathan, Wenda. 1987. *Human Birth: An Evolutionary Perspective*. New York: de Gruyter.

Ussher, Jane. 1989. *The Psychology of the Female Body*. London: Routledge.

Uvnäs-Moberg, Kerstin. 1994. "Role of Efferent and Afferent Vagal Nerve Activity During Reproduction: Integrating Function of Oxytocin on Metabolism and Behavior." *Psychoneuroendocrinology* 19: 687–95.

_____. Forthcoming. "Neuroendocrinology of the Mother-Child Interaction." *Trends in Endocrinology and Metabolism*.

Valian, Virginia. 1998. "Running in Place." *The Sciences*, Jan.–Feb.

_____. 1998. *Why So Slow?* Cambridge, Mass.: MIT Press.

Verkauf, Barry S., et al. 1992. "Clitoral Size in Normal Women." *Obstetrics & Gynecology* 80: 41–44.

Voda, Ann M. 1992. "Menopause: A Normal View." *Clinical Obstetrics and Gynecology* 35: 923–33.

Wallen, Kim. 1990. "Desire and Ability: Hormones and the Regulation of Female Sexual Behavior." *Neuroscience & Biobehavioral Reviews* 14: 233–41.

_____. 1995. "The Evolution of Female Sexual Desire." In *Sexual Nature/Sexual Culture*. Edited by P. R. Abramson and S. D. Pinkerton. Chicago: University of Chicago Press.

_____. 1996. "Nature Needs Nurture: The Interaction of Hormonal and Social Influences on the Development of Behavioral Sex Differences in Rhesus Monkeys." *Hormones and Behavior* 30: 364–78.

Wederkind, Claus, et al. 1995. "MHC-dependent Mate Preferences in Humans." *Proceedings of the Royal Society of London* 260: 245–49.

Weller, A., and L. Weller. 1993. "Human Menstrual Synchrony: A Critical Assessment." *Neuroscience and Biobehavioral Reviews* 17: 427–39.

Wilcox, Allen J., et al. 1995. "Timing of Sexual Intercourse in Relation to Ovulation." *New England Journal of Medicine* 333: 1517–21.

Wilson, Edward O. 1975. *Sociobiology*. Cambridge, Mass.: Harvard University Press.

_____. 1996. *In Search of Nature.* Washington, D.C.: Island Press.

Wilson, J. D., and D. W. Foster, eds. 1992. *Williams Textbook of Endocrinology.* Philadelphia: Saunders.

Wilson, Robert Anton. 1974. *The Book of the Breast.* Chicago: Playboy Press.

Witt, Diane M. 1995. "Oxytocin and Rodent Sociosexual Responses: From Behavior to Gene Expression." *Neuroscience and Biobehavioral Reviews* 19: 315–24.

World Health Organization. 1994. "Female Genital Mutilation." A Committee Report.

Wright, Robert. 1994. *The Moral Animal.* New York: Vintage.

Yalom, Marilyn. 1997. *A History of the Breast.* New York: Knopf.

Zorrilla, Eric P., et al. 1995. "High Self-Esteem, Hardiness and Affective Stability Are Associated with Higher Basal Pituitary-Adrenal Hormone Levels." *Psychoneuroendocrinology* 20: 591–601.

Zussman, Leon, et al. 1981. "Sexual Response after Hysterectomy-Oophorectomy: Recent Studies and Reconsideration of Psychogenesis." *American Journal of Obstetrics and Gynecology* 140: 725–29.

ACKNOWLEDGMENTS

In the course of doing research for this book, I have spoken with hundreds of thoughtful, eloquent, and generous people, many of them scientists and doctors who qualify as authorities, others who are simply authorities on the subject of their own bodies. I can't possibly cite by name everyone who should be thanked, but I want to express here my appreciation to all who took the time to talk with me, and speculate wildly with me, about why women's bodies are the way they are.

I am particularly beholden to the following researchers: Sarah Blaffer Hrdy, Patricia Adair Gowaty, Barbara Smuts, Nancy Burley, Kristen Hawkes, Kim Wallen, Sue Carter, Kerstin Uvnas-Möberg, Susan Love, Wenda Trevathan, Kaj Björkqvist, Frans de Waal, Ellen Laan, Sharon Hillier, Maria Bustillo, Jerrold Meinwald, Thomas Eisner, Benita and John Katzenellenbogen, Thomas Insel, Roger Gorski, Florence Haseltine, Martha McClintock, Geert de Vries, Dominique Toran-Allerand, Margie Profet, Londa Schiebinger, Barney Schlinger, Miriam Nelson, Ronenn Roubenoff, Pentii Siiteri, Nicolette Horbach, Jay Schulkin, Michael Toaff, Diane Witt, Luis Figuera, and Virginia Valian.

I am also deeply indebted to the following individuals, who shared their personal histories and in some cases allowed me to observe medical procedures of an admittedly intimate nature: Hope Phillips, Beth Derochea, Antonia Alba, Sandra Gandsman, Jane Carden, Cheryl Chase, Martha Coventry, and the members of the Intersex Society of North America.

My heartfelt thanks to the editors at Houghton Mifflin for mingling compassion, precision, and patience with the occasional act of lifesaving ruthlessness. I am grateful as well to my research assistant, Laura Beitman, for her energy and resourcefulness.

Finally, my profound love and gratitude to my husband, who kept me going through the perpetual squalls of doubt and gloom, and who answered each of my proposed excuses for quitting with a reminder of why I must not.